NO O]
The Journey ᴅᴇɢɪɴᴜ

Chapter xxxxxx00 of a Never-ending Series

As told by
Stephanie Patel
steppatel@gmail.com
nooffbuttons.com

ISBN: **ISBN-13: 978-1536800081**

All artwork by Stephanie Patel c. 2016

Coverart: watercolor portrait by S. Patel. The Fool in Tarot is associated with new beginnings, as well as endings, the spiritual quest, the journey of spirit through materiality, innocence, infinite potential, belief in self, trust in the universe. It is usually assigned the number "0", although it is considered unnumbered.

ACKNOWLEDGEMENTS

When I mentioned that I should not take full credit for writing this book, Mr. Jobs described it as a "collage". I would like to thank the following who contributed to the collage that is this book:

My father, Ralph William Slone; my mother, Dorothy Katherine Schulte Slone Brown; my brother, Edgar Francis Slone; my son, Sanjai Jitendra Rambhai Patel; my daughter Valerie Boston-Patel; and many other relatives and friends who have passed through my life and now lend their support from the Otherside. Although they may not be mentioned in this book, or only rarely, they consistently were there with their encouragement, and to help smooth the path.

I wish also to thank my delightful soul-partners in this adventure:
Steve Jobs
Robin Williams
Erik Medhus
Thomas Jefferson
Nikola Tesla
Johnny Cash
June Carter-Cash
Karen Carpenter
Alan Watts

On the Earthside, I wish to thank Cathy Oslie Waters, my amazingly connected friend since childhood; Susie Grimmett, one of the most extraordinary women and psychic mediums I have ever met; Dean McMurray, who "talks to dead people", who listened to my story and brought me the peace of acceptance; Tony Leggett, who took the time to do a very detailed hand reading that was simply awesome; Elisa Medhus, who opened her own story and her heart to all those who cared to share; and my family members who gave me space to allow this story to develop.

I share this thought: the power of LOVE is not thwarted by the flimsy veil between the dream of Earth and the reality of Heaven.

Note: some names of family members or others still on this side have been changed to protect privacy.

Song List:

The following songs formed a large part of the communications and ambiance of the story. Although it was always intended that the lyrics would be provided, and copyright permission has been requested, I have been urged to get the book out for those who might benefit. Therefore, for those who wish to explore the fullness of this tale, it is suggested that you locate the lyrics online as they become relevant to the story. You might also wish to download the songs and listen to them as they arise in the story, although that is not necessary. [1]

The Highwayman, performed by the Highwaymen
I Can't Fight this Feeling Anymore, REO Speedwagon
Man in Black, Johnny Cash
Making Love Out of Nothing at All, Air Supply
Forever in Your Love, Kris Kristofferson
Spirit in the Sky, Norman Greenbaum
Home, Phillip Phillips
Fight Song, Rachel Platten
Evening Falls, Enya
I Have a Dream, ABBA
Top of the World, The Carpenters
Let it Be, The Beatles
If I Were a Carpenter, Bobby Darin
No One, Alicia Keyes
I Am a Rock, Simon and Garfunkle
Have You Ever Seen the Rain, Creedence Clearwater Revival
Wake Up!, the Vamps
I've Had the Time of My Life, Bill Medley & Jennifer Warnes
How Can I Tell You, Cat Stevens
That's Life, Frank Sinatra
I Did it My Way, Frank Sinatra

---

[1] This edition is somewhat cheaper because it does not include the anticipated cost of copyright permissions, although I understand the omissions are annoying.

Table of Contents

Note: Please go to website, www.nooffbuttons.com to download audio or order CD; proof of purchase of book from Amazon or other retailer is required. No additional cost for download, shipping and handling charge for CD. Audio consists of 90 minute compilation of excerpts from the "Susie Sessions", conversations with Steve Jobs, Thomas Jefferson and others. Much of this is transcribed in Part V above, but there is limited additional material in the audio.

Part I
Introduction

I thought of it as but a whim, the day I sat down at the computer to try my hand at communicating with the spirits of those who have passed to the Other Side. The following words are burned into my memory, for they began a conversation that has not stopped to date:

-Hello. This is Steve Jobs. Thanks for hosting me.

The wizard had come knocking at my door, calling me out of my little hobbit-hole. And he made it clear from the beginning that I was to record our conversations, as well as accounts of our many travels into what you might call the astral realm, as I obligingly did. Had my discussions with Mr. Jobs contained only his messages to the world, or to his own family and friends, this would have been an easier story to write. But as you shall see, our connection took a personal turn very early on and continued down that path.

Mr. Jobs made it clear that he was not opposed to his name being used—in fact he clearly envisioned a book from our first contact. It was my own resistance that had to be overcome. I am a very private person, and he was a well-known one; I recoiled at the thought of stepping out of my secluded little world, of making this connection publicly known. However, I also learned that I had a soul contract to write this book (and at least one to follow) long before this lifetime. The purpose was to provide information, guidance and confidence to others as they pursued their own journeys.

I was given great assistance from higher energies to

overcome my misgivings, and much validation was provided to satisfy my skeptical mind. Yet it took me many months, much inner work and encouragement, before I could capitulate and face the consequences of openly joining my name—not only with Mr. Jobs, but with others across the veil.

This is not a book for everyone. Not all are at the same place on the journey, and that means many will be skeptical or disinterested. There remain many in this world who still believe that life begins in a messy gush of blood, and ends in a coffin, although the time is coming when even the most stubborn will find it difficult to hold onto that belief system. Life—that is, the experience of human life here on Earth—has always pushed the boundaries that define it. The first microscope would have been a bust if there had not existed anything new to see through it. What use of a telescope if there is not a cosmos unseen by the naked eye? We are easily blinded by the limits of our vision. Time and space look very different from a position on the Earth's crust to a location beyond its gravitational pull.

It might be helpful for some to view this account as a fantasy, although with so much validation in all its parts that it must slurp over at some point into reality. It can be seen as a pattern, an archetype. For, as with all archetypes, the heroic story does exist. It is *there*, waiting for each of us to answer the call, to step out of our box into that much larger world of adventure and wonder, challenging us to become bigger and better than we ever thought we could be. Like the home-loving hobbit that I was, I was to be astounded that a whole world existed beyond my ken—a world of sunsets and heart-felt touches, of light and sound, smiles and fury. A world where the beyond-imagination came alive, where one can fly over rooftops and pilot spaceships. I might have read about it, heard about it, but I was about to enter into it—to step into the page of the book. To become part of the narrative.

It can be said my story began that October day when the door opened and Mr. Jobs stepped through, but to fully understand it, you must understand what went before. There is always a backstory (as we know from all the prequels to *Star Wars*). While I can truly say that I was not anticipating this adventure, that I was, like Luke and Bilbo, just minding my own business in my remote corner of the universe, it cannot be said that I was unprepared. In fact, my entire lifetime—unbeknownst to me—was about preparation, readiness. As with Luke, my true identity was hidden from me, yet it peculiarly fitted me for the part I was to play when I felt the call. While you are on the path, you may not know where it is going—how the dots will connect in retrospect. It is nothing short of fantastic when you can look back and see how they do, that it was always written that way. Coherence, indeed.

But, from my early years, I *had* seen the clues that something was up. A story was brewing in the pattern of my unfurling life: symbols, archetypes, and omens appearing along the pathway as in every good hero's journey. And so I set about to recount my history long ago. I wrote many chapters and humorous essays drawn from my lifetime, shared them with my writing group, and they remain still to be read. But then these stories sat in my filing cabinet: how could I finish the book when I did not know the ending?

Now I do—and as it turns out, the ending is but a beginning.

I have set forth a simple summary of my personal history (Part III) because it is relevant to the present chronicle, there is much synchronicity, and it will be discussed at great length in both this book and the one to follow. You may want to read through this narrative in its entirety before commencing the story of my connection with Mr. Jobs, or you may wish to simply refer back to it as it becomes relevant.

Part IV of this book is based upon my journals, contemporaneous emails, accounts and recordings from the amazing third-party psychic medium, Susie Grimmett, who provided extraordinary independent validation of all that I was experiencing. Additional excerpts from the hours and hours of recordings of the "Susie Sessions" are provided on the accompanying CD (or downloadable audio for those purchasing off Amazon). Selected portions of transcripts of the "Susie Sessions" are also included in Part V.

Part VI consists of supporting materials which contribute to the validation of my relationship with Mr. Jobs.

Because of the immense amount of material that has been

received, both by myself and through Susie, it would have been impossible to include everything in one book. Therefore, this first book will focus upon the initial forty days from contact, and how I came to be awakened from the deep slumber in which, like Snow White,[2] I lay. The next book will take up our personal story—that is, mine and Steve's—but more so, it will focus on the purpose for which I was called out of that deep sleep.

This is a story that never ends; it begins wherever you are. It is interactive. Read on and you will enter into and become a part of that story. If you do read on, it was because you were chosen to be part of it: in some way, great or small, to make a difference. You cannot walk through life and not leave a footprint.

This is reality.

---

[2] I know, I know. Many metaphors. But we mustn't overlook the interplay of the hero and the heroine's journey. And Snow White *was* tempted and poisoned with that biblical-style bite out of an apple. Something to think about.

PART II
THE STORY OF THE TWINS

This is the story of two complementary souls that were both bent upon simplification, reduction, finding the common denominators. It is a remarkable story. A beautiful story. But you might find it difficult to believe in the beginning, if you did not first understand what I did not—that it is only one example of the many archetypal accounts of the Divine Marriage, or the reunion of twin flames, that are being enacted right this moment all over the Earth. At this moment, I am aware of at least four other personal narratives that involve a connection of twin souls across dimensions—and I am sure there are very many others. And that there are many more to come, for the fruit is ripe on the tree.

I did not set out to find my twin soul, twin flame, or divine complement as it is sometimes called. Nothing could have been further from my mind. Yes, I was on the spiritual path, seeking reunification with God. I had dedicated myself, after my retirement from a legal career, to that goal. But if you had asked me, I would have said the idea of twin souls was nonsense, the fantasy stuff of Harlequin romances. The goal, for me, was completion within myself—not hooking up with some super-duper love relationship. In fact, I had been single and celibate for twenty-five years; when I was forty I had come to terms with the realization that it was highly improbable that I would ever find what I desired and required in a relationship, so why bother? I would no longer settle for anything less—I could not. And so I gave up. I would make the final journey alone.

I was always intuitive and empathic. It was not, however, psychic phenomena that truly drew me forward. It was the desire to know peace. To come to rest, which I perceived as the process of returning to the place where it had all begun—with the Godhead from which we were all cast, as sparks off the anvil. To shed my ego, my sense of specialness, and to return to the totality. Words easily spoken—but, as you must suspect, not so easily realized.

When my present adventure began, I had none of the

information that I provide in this section. I was being led along, step-by-step, through the dark. Hugely skeptical, I questioned everything, threw hurdles in the path, and clung to my prior worldview. But, fortunately, my mentor was at least as stubborn as I was, and with a steely determination to break through my thick head and the fortress around my heart.

I have chosen not to draw you along the path entirely as I was. This story will make more sense if you know up front what I was to learn only gradually, in stages, as I was able to digest and absorb it. I will take you along that route, and there will be many reveals upon it. But I see no purpose in not divulging the critical piece, the hinge pin of it all. Therefore, I am providing below the description of the archetype of the twin flame, so that you may see for yourself as we go how closely this adventure matched the pattern:

The twin soul phenomena cannot be understood without an underlying conception of soul creation and soul evolution. It is said (and I once so saw) that the souls are like sparks from the Light Source, or God. Some say that there are numerous divisions of the light before the final level of the individual soul; in any case, the final division is the individuation of one soul into two segments, a feminine component and a masculine component. The universal energy between male and female, that which draws them together, could be said to be both the product of this division and the plan to keep them from straying too far apart and ultimately bring them back together. Twin souls are said to be identical in their resonance, but also complementary in their centers; e.g. certain traits may be primarily associated with the male or the female, but when the two are joined, it becomes a cohesive whole where both sides benefit.

Twin souls may have many lifetimes together, prior to re-merger, and those lifetimes may be in the same or different gender, and in any configuration.[3] Souls "evolve" through experience, and that experience may include lifetimes as male

---

[3] I am not aware of whether at the time of final merging both incarnations can be of the same gender or not, so cannot speak to that. However, the merger happens on a soul level, so I suspect it is not be affected by the particular physical manifestation.

and female. All souls are equal, but can attain different vibratory levels dependent upon their engagement and understanding in all the lessons provided through life. In utilizing the term "life," I do not limit it to experience as a human on Earth. Life is that which flows through everything, and might even be synonymous with light, energy or love.

The human body is designed to permit the feminine and masculine energies to experience the result of that final split. It is not the bodies that are attracted to each other. Dead bodies do not move toward each other. It is the energy that inhabits them, animates them, experiences *through* them that calls out to each other. This energy is not limited by "death." There is no death. It is impossible. That part of the energy that was put into service to create the human body is gradually broken down, dissipated and recycled after the soul energy departs the body. You might say some of the energy, or as I like to call it, the "information" of the universe, is utilized to create the hardware, and some is the software, and some remains as the user. In Earth terms, the physical reality is the hardware, the soul is the software, and the user is that part which remains "inchoate." Thus, one might think of the body as the computer, the soul as the program, and the higher self/soul as the operator. The "ego" would be the part of the program which thinks it is operating itself. There is not a complete one-on-one correspondence in this comparison, but it will do for the purposes of this discussion.

When one is playing a video game, one's attention is on the game—that is, the program—even though the greater part of oneself remains in the room where the computer is located. When the game is over, the experience gained through play remains with the player, although his attention now shifts back to his "greater" reality. As more and more experience is gained, through many games, the player becomes more adept at basic manoeuvers and may have more mental capacity remaining for planning, understanding, analyzing. The player may make the same stupid mistake over and over, but between games may have time to reflect upon what was learned, and finally overcome it. Some players will grasp the lessons faster than others, but all players are entitled to derive the same enjoyment and experience from playing the game. Being the best doesn't mean having the most fun. "Fun" is the name of the game, and in multi-player games there are many lessons to be learned about that one factor.

The trip of the twin flames from split to reunion is about "fun," about enjoying the trip, about gaining experience. It is not necessarily "fun" in the sense of "ha-ha," but "fun" in the sense of challenge and achievement. Maybe some falls. Maybe some early losses. But up and ready to get back in the game the next day.

It has been said that the original split of the twins was painful—it was rending asunder what was complete. However, as nearly every birth mother knows, pain is only pain in the moment; it disappears in the smile (or grimace if you like) of the newborn. Of course, the ache of one twin for the other remains—or, to flip the coin—the desire of one for the other continues. You might even call it a magnet instead of a coin.

The distinction between a twin soul and a soulmate is an important one. I like to use the terms "twin flames" or "divine complements" to distinguish the former. Since a twin flame is one half of what was originally a single soul, each of us has only one twin; however, throughout our experience—through many lifetimes—we will have a great many soulmates. Our soulmates give us the experience of many different types of relationships. All of this experience is what we bring back for the reunion with our twin.

The twin soul reunion is also described as the divine marriage—sort of like when Mr. and Mrs. Pacman meet, for those who remember that game.

When it is time for the twins to reunite, when they have each attained a certain level of experience and synthesis and are ready (or gobbled up enough of those dots), they will find each other. It is said that this generally occurs during their last incarnation (or Earth game) as part of the ascension process—that is, a movement back to the Source, or toward God. During this lifetime, the incarnated soul may become acutely aware of an unfulfilled need for the other, who remains unrecognized. They may attempt to fill that need with others, although always with a sense of incompletion, or they may attempt to satisfy it in other ways—through work, travel, study, etc.

The reunion of the twins has a big impact upon the game—not just for themselves, but for everyone playing. It is said that a great deal of energy is released through this connection, available to raise the level of the play. The twins united have more power, in their completeness, to work toward spiritual purpose. That, ultimately, is the name of the real game: being the richest man in the cemetery is just the "ego's" version. Finding the love, the joy, is the soul's.

The twin-soul concept is not new. There have been guidebooks around for eons. Plato described it 2,500 years ago. Here is an excerpt:

> ...and when one of them meets the other half, the actual half of himself, the pair are lost in an amazement of love and friendship and intimacy and one will not be out of the other's sight even for a moment...
>
> If Hephaestus, son of Zeus, were to ask the pair; 'do you desire to be wholly one, always day and night to be in one another's company? For if this is what you desire, I am ready to melt you into one and let you grow together, so that being two you shall become one, and after your death in the world beyond you will still be one departed soul instead of two - I ask whether this is what you lovingly desire?' - and there is not a man or woman of them who, when they heard the proposal, would not acknowledge that this melting into one another, this becoming one instead of two, was the very expression of their ancient need. And the reason is that human nature was originally one and we were a whole, and the desire and pursuit of the whole is called love." [4]

And from Sufi spiritual writings 800 years ago:

---

[4] Taken from *Twin Soul Relationships,*
http://www.fromthestars.com/page123.html

Out of the original unity of being there is a fragmentation and dispersal of beings, the last stage being the splitting of one soul into two. And consequently, love is the search by each half for the other half on earth or in heaven...[5]

The following description is from *A Dweller on Two Planets*, written and published by Frederick S. Oliver in 1886:

Each man we see, except those who have been transfigured, is but a semi-ego, and each woman the same - two of these having one spirit. When the perfection time cometh, all the halves shall unite, each with its own - and lo! this is the marriage made in heaven. But first comes the Trial - the Crisis of Transfiguration.[6]

The following discussion is from the book *Messages from Heaven*[7]:

People feel that finding their twin flame - their divine counterpart who was conceived out of the same white-fire of God - is the answer. But really, finding your true self and resolving your psychology is the greatest gift you can give to your twin flame.

Ascended twin flames cannot interfere with the free will of their counterparts who are still in embodiment... The twin flame longs for the return and the victory of the divine compliment, but not in any human sense... The one in embodiment may feel a profound loneliness, a sense that something cannot be found on this earth. This one can be married and still sense that something intangible is missing. The solution is to become the Christ, to fulfill your dharma.

---

[5] *Id.*

[6] *A Dweller on Two Planets,* Frederick S. Oliver, P. 350, Poseid Publishing. Co., Los Angeles, Calif., 1920

[7] *Messages from Heaven, Patricia Kirmond, c. 1999, Summit Publications, Inc., Gardiner MT,* www.SummitUniversityPress.com

For every act of good and love you render others, you serve your twin flame as well.

Everyone seems to search for a twin flame in embodiment. It is important to remember that many twin flames are ascended, waiting for their divine counterparts to join them. The best favor you can offer your twin flame is your willingness to face and conquer your human self.

If your twin flame is ascended, you are never alone.

The twin flame is far more apt to find you or appear to you if you place the (spiritual) path before all else.

As twin souls are so alike to begin with, it seems necessary for them to go their separate ways before they can complete each other. Identity and complementarity are the two driving forces and axes of love... For the complete being there must be a blending of the two.

Once recognition occurs, they will tear apart the heavens to be together.[8]

Every relationship between a twin and various soulmates through every lifetime, including the last incarnation—every marriage, romance, relationship of parent/child, siblings, friend—rests on its own merits. Like all relationships, it is founded in love—the only way it can be founded. The love between twin flames can never diminish the power of other relationships—in fact, it only enhances them, glorifies them, for all the love that resides in each heart of the pair is reflected and magnified throughout eternity. Each of those soulmates is, likewise, in practice with the twin for ultimate reunion with its own divine complement. Therefore, the greater the growth in each relationship, the sharper the lessons, the more benefit to all concerned. Each soulmate gave something to the twin, and is forever valued for that contribution to the path. *No one* can presume to know the path of another, and therefore no value

---

[8] *Id.* at 231-232

scale is appropriate in viewing the relationships of others. Oftentimes the ultimate benefits are not appreciated by the participants until they themselves look back down the mountainside. Therefore, trust in the ultimate value of every connection. None of them are accidental.

In sum, the hallmark symptoms of a twin-flame reunion, also referred to as the divine marriage, are:

a) Telepathy

b) Probably last Earth lifetime

c) Probably, but not always, one of the set is not incarnate

d) Individual spiritual evolution, desire to overcome limiting issues

e) High compatibility of intelligence, humor, perceptions, etc.

f) Complementary characteristics of primary organizing principles, the yin and yang: e.g. strength, vision, drive in one and compassion, trust, humility in other. (Although both must have achieved some balance, as they must with the individual feminine and masculine energy, the union creates a powerful third "entity" drawing strengths of both.)

i) Intense masculine/feminine energy connection, magnettism, desire to merge

h) Accelerated spiritual growth, resolution of issues and lessons

i) Unconditional love, first one for the other, secondly the union for all of creation

The union may be marked by incredible synchronicity in the lives of the twins and the circumstances of their meeting, as well as a sense of destiny.[9]

---

[9] Some websites from which information about twin souls can be obtained: http://www.beautyandtruth.org/twin-flame-relationship.html (Michael, Twin flame Relationship); ; http://www.the-open-mind.com/the-phases-of-the-twin-flame-relationship/ (Dec. 26, 2014);, http://lightascension.com/arts/TwinFlames.htm (S.Stevens, *Twin Flames and Soul Mates*); http://thespiritscience.net/2016/01/07/the-difference-between-soul-mates-and-twin-flame-unions/; Outside material provided herein comports with my own experiences and understanding, but I cannot speak to other parts of the source material.

Please remember that I knew nothing about the descriptions given herein as I embarked upon my own journey of reunion; it would be many weeks after my "adventure" began before I came upon the research I have provided above.

♋♋♋

Stephanie (ca. 1952) in her alter identity as little Dotty Margaret, ready to embark upon the journey of life with a stolen bike, still blissfully ignorant of all the trials and tribulations, gullies and mountains and fallen trees upon the path. And yes, it was not my tricycle; this rare vehicle belonged to a more fortunate neighbor child (with many fewer sibs) in the CAA compound in McGrath, Alaska, where we lived. One of my earliest memories is of coveting that neighbor's trike. I was off to a rollicking start in life, already breaking the Ten Commandments before I even heard of them.

PART III
A Summary Account of the Life of Stephanie
(The Trials of Job?)

I was born on June 24, 1950—the feast of St. John the Baptist—in McGrath, a little village in the interior of Alaska. I was born at home, the ninth of my parents' children, amid concern that I was lost, for I was not breathing—what my father called a blue baby; however, after some effort on the part of him and the midwife, I returned to life. It was the first of my youthful brushes with death, of which there would be several. I was named Dorothy Margaret Slone, the first name after my mother.

At the age of three I wandered away during the winter and was lost for so long that it was feared I was dead; however I was finally found, once again blue, this time with cold, stuffed inside the coat of my rescuer, next to his heart, and somehow revived with no lasting damage.

When I was four years old, after thirteen years in the interior of Alaska, my parents moved to a sleepy fishing village on the Kenai Peninsula, south of Anchorage, called Homer. It was there that I put together my first coherent picture of the world. I have strong recollections of standing on the bluff near our home, looking down upon the long tail of land—the Homer Spit—that stretched out into the bay, surrounded by snow-drenched mountains. It was one of the most beautiful scenes in the world, although I did not know it at the time. It was there, among my brothers and sisters, soon numbering twelve, that I spent what were the most treasured days of my life. It was a wild existence, playing in the woods, on the beach and the lake. Thus we grew, strong and self-reliant, but marginally equipped for life in the conventional social world of 20th Century America. It would be a feat of adaptation when the time came.

My oldest five siblings were all girls. The next set of children included my four brothers and me; as the boys were the closest in age, they were my playmates at home. The youngest children were a mix of boys and girls. There was a high school in Homer, unlike in McGrath, where there had been only a one-room schoolhouse for grades one through eight; thus, my older sisters, who had been sent to far flung places to attend school as they reached adolescence, were now able to remain at home. When I was seven years old, there was a Slone child in every grade 1 through 8, a couple in high school, and several at home.

I was a very bright child, and although I did not read before starting school at age six, I learned quickly and became a voracious reader. I soon had outpaced my classmates, and by third grade was allowed to read all day in the back of the classroom, except when a new concept was introduced in any of the lessons; as soon as I could demonstrate that I understood it, which usually only took a few minutes, I was allowed to return to my book. Thus I traveled far in time and space from that remote corner of the universe where my body remained, as if anchored in the mud of the bay.

I was very attached to my father. My father was one of those men who seemed to be able to do anything: he was an engineer with the CAA (now FAA), a published author, a carpenter, hunter and commercial fisherman. There was a special rapport between us, and I felt like a little princess in a magical kingdom. In 1959, when I was nine years old, my father was drowned, along with my eleven-year-old brother, during a month-long fishing absence. My last words to my brother, with whom I had a contentious relationship, were: *I wish you were dead.*

And with those words, now come true, all was lost: the king and the kingdom. My mother, having no means of supporting her remaining brood, moved with us to North Dakota, where she had grown up. It was so hot on the day we arrived in Dickenson that the candy bars we were offered as a welcoming gift had melted. I thought we had landed in Hell. And as it turned out, I was not so far wrong. I was now disinherited, the lost princess. I had been stripped of nearly everything of value to me: my father, my friends, my beautiful wild world. I (along with my siblings) had been thrown out of Heaven. All that remained to me was my love of learning, my desire to understand life, and my unquenchable yearning to find my way back—if not to that place, for I knew it could never be the same—then to that sense of beauty, love and freedom. It would be a lifelong quest, searching for something so elusive—a memory of the heart more than the mind.

My siblings and I were introduced to street lights and pavement, television and nuns. My three years spent at St. John's Academy in Jamestown, North Dakota were like a prison sentence. It's a wonder I held on to that love of learning, for there were no exceptions in the lockstep world of St. John's for the bright or the not-so-bright. I sat through excruciatingly boring classes, forbidden to read, drawing mazes and creating puzzles behind my open text book to soothe my restless mind. Eventually I would learn to tuck a paperback book inside the text, or write stories when I was supposed to be doing in-class work, so I did adapt.

I do not complain of my education at St. John's. It was of good quality, if at a slow pace for me, and I was learning about the modern world in ways that I might never have back in Homer. I was shocked, however, to discover that I would be required to wear a dress for the remainder of my school years—in Alaska I had dressed like my brothers, in boxer-waisted pants and long-sleeved pullovers. While, as an adult, I am not opposed to dresses, and was never uncomfortable with my femininity, as a child I was a tomboy and understood how the skirt is designed to handicap one in the midst of male peers. If my father had left me with only one last legacy, it would have been that I could do and be anything I wanted—gender be damned.

During this period of time, things did not go well for me at home. My mother, although able to provide for our basic needs moderately well due to my father's life insurance and a small pension, was nevertheless burdened by her large family and had no time to give attention to individual children. She and I were, in addition, cut from very different cloth. What we shared was a love of home, of being the homemaker; but where we differed was in intellectual capacity, in curiosity about the world, in adherence to social mores. I never understood my mother, and she never understood me.

I fell between the cracks in that family, almost as if I were invisible. If I was noticed at all, it seemed to be always with emphasis upon my inadequacy as a human being. From my mother's point-of-view, I was stubborn, high-strung, "too smart for my pants." Without my father's protection, my brothers teased me mercilessly, calling me "Ugly" even at the supper table, as if it were my given name. My older sisters were all pretty and popular, with an instinctive sense of style. I was a scuzzy scow in their wake. Even my younger sisters had a sense of social acuity that I lacked. Nor did I fit in with the other girls my age, who had grown up in a world apart from my own. For my high school-aged sisters, their remote Alaskan background made them more interesting; for me, in fourth grade, it only made me different.

My ability to survive might have been lost completely were it not for my great fortune—a year after our move—in making a good friend. Cathy, who lived on the next block, became a lifelong ally and, with her family, was an important resource and a stabilizing force.

A year or two after my father's death, my mother married an electrician who came to help remodel the basement in our house. He was a childless widower. They would have two children together. We moved to a very small town, Kathryn, where I spent my junior high years in a combined classroom of 7th and 8th graders—numbering about twenty total. Despite the small size of the school, I had an excellent teacher for those two years, a man with a hands-on approach to learning, who took us on many field trips. At that point I was testing out at equivalent to the end of high school, and he did show appreciation for my abilities—or at least kindness—although I was still bound to the lockstep advancement of the educational system. I made some friends in Kathryn and was happier.

My mother, however, was *not* happy there, with little opportunity for shopping and social activity, or options for her children. After those two years, my family moved to Valley City, located between Kathryn and Jamestown—a sort of compromise with my stepfather—where we were again placed in a Catholic school. My unhappiness grew there until, when I was a sophomore, I refused to attend school and locked myself in my room for many weeks. At that point, terribly insecure, I believed that I was so ugly that I was a blight upon the eyes of all who beheld me.   Eventually I ran away from home, ended up in Montana where I got a job at the hospital by lying about my age.   However, my location was revealed to my mother through a third party and she felt impelled to require me to return to Valley City.   I refused, spent several nights in jail, went through some other travels and adventures, and ended up at my oldest sister's house in Cincinnati. My sister was in her mid-twenties, but already had several children and could use some household help; her husband was almost twice her age.

I was quite naive for my years, even in that more conservative era. In spite of my adventures, I was more Oliver Twist than the Artful Dodger. I still didn't swear, smoke, drink, or steal. I had never had a boyfriend. Therefore, when I awakened one night to find my nightgown around my neck and my brother-in-law on top of me, I was so shocked that I couldn't even comprehend what was happening. I knew that I could not tell my sister or my mother; in order to protect the family, they would surely call me a liar, and I knew that my mental state was so fragile that it could not withstand any further damage. I considered running away again, but decided that a) either I was fatally flawed and such misfortune would find me wherever I went or b) everybody had similar things happen to them, but they didn't talk about it, they just toughed it out in silence. I realized that I had to finish high school if I was going to have any chance at all of making it on my own, so I stayed put, mouth shut. There was occasional continued sexual use while I remained there, until I returned to Valley City for my final year of high school.

By then I was older and wiser; I worked two jobs and between that and school, was hardly ever home.   I made arrangements on my own to go to college, benefitting from the generous financial aid packets than available, and in the fall of 1969 traveled to Columbia, Missouri, where I intended to study interior design.

I met my first boyfriend during that first year of college. I also was to experience a fair amount of trauma during that same period. It was too far for me to return to North Dakota for spring break, and the house in which I lived (similar to a sorority, but not) would close for the vacation. A roommate begged me to come home with her to her farm, but I decided to hitchhike to Cincinnati to visit old high school friends. I did so, avoiding a potentially disastrous ride with a truck driver through some quick thinking. When I returned to Columbia, I learned that the roommate had killed herself with a shotgun during the vacation.

I was devastated. I blamed myself for being insensitive to another. I wandered around the campus for hours, tears mingling with the rain. I ended the relationship with my boyfriend, as if he were to blame—or maybe just because he reminded me of the whole sad affair. That summer I was brutally raped by someone with whom I worked, left miles out in the country to find my way back. At the advice of my housemother, I kept mum. In the fall of my second year of college I learned that my financial aid had been reduced due to some administrative cut-backs. I decided it was time to call it quits, to end this miserable existence, to spare the world my presence, and I took all the pills I could find.

I ended up in the hospital. I was not aware of being taken there or of anything until the next morning, but was eventually released with no ill effects. However, ever after that I had the odd thought that I had died—and that this was what happened when you died, you just ended up back where you had left off, possibly in some parallel experience, until you got it right. In other words, there was no escape. I could not tell this to anyone else, for it was just too odd of a concept—this was before the phenomenon of near-death experience was well-documented and generally known—but it *did* stop me from trying to kill myself again. What was the use? I might as well keep plugging along and try to get it right sooner than later.

After I got out of the hospital, I decided to change my name. I told everyone that I wanted to be called Stephanie thereafter. I had no explanation for choosing that name, other than I liked it, and I didn't want to be Dorothy anymore. I was required to drop a number of classes because of the loss of financial aid, and a few months later I left Columbia and returned to North Dakota.

I enrolled immediately at Moorhead State College (now Minnesota State University Moorhead), just across the river from Fargo, where I met my husband, handsome and dark-haired. He was a native of Kenya, Africa, but of Indian descent, who had spent a couple of years in England after his high school graduation and then come to MSC on a student visa. We each noticed the other independently, and were immediately smitten—it was clearly meant to be. He was a bright young man, who was convinced he would be a millionaire (when that meant something), although I cared little about wealth. Two months after we met, in April, 1971, we were married. I was twenty years old. I had legally changed my first name by then, and so I became Stephanie Patel, which I have remained to this day.

After I graduated from college, I applied for law school at his urging; although I had never been interested in the legal field, I saw few career possibilities with my teaching degree at a time when the baby boomers were flooding out of colleges. One could go to law school with any kind of bachelor's degree, so it had the allure of not requiring any educational "back-tracking" to change career paths. I was accepted at the University of North Dakota School of Law, the only school to which I applied, and in 1975 we moved to Grand Forks. At that time we had a one-year-old boy, and a year later—during the break between first and second year law school—our second son was born. My 7-year-old niece also came to live with us, so it was a busy time between studies and raising children. I had to drop out one semester when my baby suffered from recurring illness. In December, 1978 I graduated from the University of North Dakota with a Juris Doctor. However, our marriage had foundered and we divorced.

Approximately a year before my graduation, I had become involved in the study of karate, which I had begun because I needed a break from classes and babies. Although the whole concept of martial arts was novel to me, I immediately fell in love with the practice. I had the strange sense that I had "come home." One of the things I most loved was that once you were in your white *gi* (with the exception of the upper levels who wore colored belts), you were all the same—it didn't matter what your profession, level of education, family influence. Everything fell away except individual character. Doctors could mingle with dishwashers, and the quality of the performance was a reflection of the inner being. There was an intriguing humbleness about it. And I soon found that somehow the training activated some latent ability, almost as a by-product, causing me to experience numerous "psychic" phenomena: a sense of knowing, as well as a new interaction with physical reality—almost instant manifestation. However, these experiences were so far out of my normal world concept and social structure that—although they seemed inherently natural—they were disconcerting, and through the future years I would find myself both welcoming and avoiding the practice of karate for that very reason.

At about the time I graduated from law school—in fact, the day after I took my last exam—I had a peak experience that I can only describe as "revelation." There was a "real time" physical component that is beyond the scope of this section to describe; the important factor is that I experienced a "download" of information that turned my view of the world on end.

I would describe this experience thus: imagine living in a world that is always covered by clouds. One day you happen to be standing in just the right spot as the clouds momentarily part and you see the sun. Suddenly you understand what brings the light and warmth to the Earth, what makes the grass grow and the birds sing. However, this rare experience is not one you can share with others—how to describe what one must see for himself? It seems impossible to deliberately replicate—just the happy circumstance of being in the right spot at the right time. And unfortunately, in the Midwest world of the 1970s, who would believe it? It would be a sign of dementia, insanity, egotism. And so, after one failed effort, resulting in the loss of a friendship, I did not speak of this incident again for more than ten years, until the social mentality had shifted enough to allow a select few enough curiosity to listen.

However, from that moment, I understood there was no death. It was like a joke: that which doesn't exist cannot die. I saw that everything was love, in which I was temporarily flooded, and that all things flow to the good, like the rivers to the sea. I was allowed to know much, much more during the ten or fifteen minutes of the "cloud parting," but of course it came to me in those ineffable terms with which such information arrives; nevertheless, knowing that I would not be able to remember it if I didn't quickly commit it to words, I spent weeks writing descriptions and images as a way to try to capture this truly wondrous experience. Those writings have now been lost, but the essence of what I was allowed to recall remained forever with me, and from that day forward became the standard by which I judged all information and knowledge.

I had turned away from my Catholic upbringing in my teens, and at the time of this experience had no belief or interest in spiritual matters. But now I had been introduced to what I could not at that time call God, for—as I was wont to say, due to my rebellion against the religious indoctrination of my youth, I only used that word in vain; I called it the puppet-master,[10] something so powerful and good and loving, the existence of which I could not deny, but which could not be known except by knowing it. I suddenly understood that all major religions are based upon similar insights, that their visionaries had all drank at the same well.

For the first time I became interested in reading the types of metaphysical or spiritual matters that I had previously ignored: Hesse's *Siddhartha*, Gibran's *The Prophet*, Yogananda's *Autobiography of a Yogi,* S. Suzuki's, *Zen Mind, Beginner's Mind*, and a lovely little book called *Moving Zen* by C.W. Nicol. I read more, of course, anything I could get my hands on, but in those days the pickings in this area were slim. As time passed, as the "New Age" movement took root, there would be many channeled books, NDE books, works exploring science and philosophy in new ways, and my hunger for Knowledge would cause me to read extensively.

After my divorce, I decided to move back to Alaska with my children; my ex-husband did not object. I found a job in Kenai, not far from where I had lived as a child, and remained

---

[10] The experiential component of this episode included the splitting of what I thought of as "me" into three distinct facets, the Puppet Master, the Puppet (the body), and the Observer (with which I personally identified). This experience might be similar to what some individuals experience as "channeling", although I had no experience to think of it in those terms.

there for several years. I was astonished to learn that there was a karate group in that area of a similar style to which I was accustomed; I studied with this group, but found it less conducive to the inner growth that had marked my earlier study. Nevertheless, I stuck with it as I was able, and continued to have some extraordinary experiences. During this time I became pregnant, but did not desire to marry or live with the father; I gave birth to a girl, who I subsequently raised. About this time my second oldest sister, back in North Dakota, who was suffering from great depression, took her own life.

I then met the man that would be my second husband, and we actually lived together for a time, becoming engaged, but I put off marriage; after one such experience I was leery of a repeat performance. It was only after I had spent a winter back in North Dakota with my children, staying with my mother in Valley City, that I decided I might as well be conventional and get married (just like women were supposed to do—certainly Midwestern women). My soon-to-be second husband and I reconnected, drove together up the Al-can Highway to Fairbanks with five of our six combined children, married and lived there for a couple of years (where we both worked). I had already lost one pregnancy when we had lived together previously, and now found myself pregnant again. The baby, a girl, was born dead due to a knot in the umbilical cord that pulled tight in the final stages. The marriage did not survive this trauma, and I again found myself divorced.

At this time, at the age of 40, I decided that I was not marriage material—it was unlikely or impossible that I would ever find what I craved, and why put any additional men through the misery of hooking up with me? However, before embarking upon my self-enforced period of celibacy, I wished to have one more "fling" during which I would not be concerned about children, permanency or social mores. This was just for me, finally. Just for the fun of it, and to satisfy a few experiences I wished to have. I got involved shortly thereafter with a man for this temporary purpose. He advised me that he could not have any more children—he had a boy aged fifteen—and I took him at his word, happy not to have to worry about birth control, but ended up pregnant. Although not opposed to abortion on principle, I was not inclined in that direction myself, so I elected to have the child. My youngest son was born, deemed "full term" by his physician, after eight months of pregnancy, at 2 a.m. on Christmas morning.

At that time we had moved from Fairbanks, where I had been working for a law firm, to Anchorage. My baby's father had wanted to marry, but I knew that would be a mistake, and the change in location was good for me and my children. The baby's father had no interest in a continuing relationship with his child without a relationship with me (a pattern that my first husband had already established). I myself was devoted to all my children and would move hell and high water to care for them, as best I was able—which was not always that well, given financial issues and personal limits. On several occasions throughout the years, in fact, we were homeless and forced to sleep in our car or with friends or family. But always, somehow, I managed to find a way to muster through, to get back on my feet, and to provide a home for them.

Shortly after arriving in Anchorage, when I was still pregnant, I attended a fire-walk with my sister and her husband. That was an eye-opening experience as I watched dozens of ordinary people walk across twenty feet of red-hot coals. I was a little hesitant because of my advanced state of pregnancy, but finally made the walk myself, unscathed. For the first time, I had a concrete example of how "normal" limitations can be dropped by the willingness of a group of people to experience a different reality.

We remained in Anchorage for more than twenty years. I had been practicing law since I arrived in Alaska after my first divorce, but at the time of moving to Anchorage was impelled from some inner desire to start a school. I was never attached to the practice of law—I considered myself an accidental attorney, having sort of fallen into the profession. I yearned to turn my hand to something more "real," more in keeping with my inner dreams, but my ability to do so was limited by my need to support a family. So for years I worked part-time, raised my baby and older children, and learned everything I could about education and methods of reaching disaffected young people. I was particularly motivated by the problems my oldest son was having—a very bright child, he was nevertheless troubled by a problem that went undiagnosed: dyslexia, which I did not discover until I began my own studies in education. He also did not fit well in the traditional school paradigm.

I finally started a very small private school for grades 7-12, with a strong emphasis upon the Socratic method and Adventure Education—a mostly outdoor experiential program that I contracted with the University of Alaska. By then my son was too old to benefit, although my daughter did attend. I found the methods very effective, but funding was a problem. Eventually I was able to gather a group of interested community members and design a charter school, which began operation in about 1997, the first year charter schools were authorized in Alaska, with me as the head. Because I was very careful with the bottom line, we had more than sufficient funding that first year. The program was popular and had a waiting list. However, I soon ran into problems with the school district, in particular the assistant superintendent, who collaborated with some disgruntled teachers to undermine the program and get me removed. It was not personal, apparently, as she had set out to undermine all the new charter schools and bring them under the control of the school district. Obviously, the *status quo* was threatened by these upstart schools and the district could not afford to let them be successful. I was truly shocked by the unethical methods utilized to attack the heads of each school—one poor woman was driven out of town—and it would take me many years before I could learn to forgive the assistant superintendent behind this assault, or release frustration over this corruption at the core of the educational system. Of course, once the district got control, funds were wasted, there was no one to understand or maintain the vision, and the school fell apart after one more year.

As I was going through these difficulties with the school district, my oldest son, Sanjai, took his life on Good Friday at the age of twenty-three. On the same day his twenty-seven-year-old cousin, who had been the golden boy until developing schizophrenia at about age eighteen or nineteen, took his life, also in Alaska. Several years later, I met a man online who had had a near-death experience sometime before, and consequently was able to communicate with the spirits of those who had passed. It appears that NDEs often open up the psychic abilities. This man, with no knowledge of my history or family, was able to describe my son and provide many details over a number of personal online sessions; he advised that "it was agreed" or "written" before this lifetime that my son and his cousin would leave on the same day.

Through these communications, complete with many validations, I derived some comfort about my son's soul experience since his passing.

After recovering from the school fiasco, I returned to the practice of law. My second son, meanwhile, struggling with addiction issues, had gone to North Dakota temporarily and decided to remain there. My daughter graduated from high school, married, and had two children. My youngest son, who was half-Black, had a comparatively even-keeled life, growing up in Anchorage; he was a gifted athlete, a well-liked boy, with many friends; but about the age of thirteen he started having emotional difficulties and he gradually lost everything he had enjoyed. At age eighteen, after many traumatic years filled with counseling and attempts at various other interventions, he was diagnosed with bipolar disorder.

When he was seventeen years old, he was accosted one morning, a few blocks from our house, by several policemen and severely beaten, then left on the street to find his way home. I was shocked when I saw the distinct thumb and fingerprint marks around his neck where he had been choked and his arm cut up from wrist to elbow. He was not charged with anything, and there was no evidence of any crime (on his part)—just a black boy riding his bike in a white neighborhood and some policemen with a little bit too much testosterone in their systems. To my thinking, what happened to him was the equivalent of being raped by those in authority—to whom do you turn when the police are the aggressors? What does this do to the tender sensibilities of a young person, especially one who is already having difficulty coping with an illness that affects his understanding of the way the world works?

My efforts to obtain some kind of redress were useless. After that, my son started having trouble with the legal system, and eventually I realized that he was doomed in that city. It was a very difficult time as I watched the system trying its best to destroy him and him struggling to conquer the effect of his biology, which he had clearly inherited from his father (his brother on the father's side suffered from the same issues, as did his nephew).

It was particularly difficult because I was an attorney and this was hitting very close to home. One day, in one of his manic rages, my son broke a window in his bedroom. A passerby called the police, and when I politely refused to let them into my home (knowing they would try to arrest him for "domestic violence" or otherwise escalate the situation), I was put in handcuffs and paraded around my neighborhood while they searched my home (my son had fortunately run off into the woods until they left, where he was able to cool down). It was a shocking humiliation, to have my home and my person invaded like this, constitutional protections disregarded, as if I lived in a third-world country. I knew that something terrible had happened to the Alaska that had once been my childhood paradise.

At one point, I was so overwhelmed by these difficulties that I lay on the couch and thought I just couldn't go on. I wanted to die. The world seemed so strange to me. It always had, but I just could not understand how there could be so much corruption and hatred toward others, so much ignorance and selfishness among those in power. I thought about all the books I had been reading—Dolores Cannon in particular, but many others as well—about the wonderful teachers in the Afterlife, that anyone could study with: Socrates or Einstein or whoever. How I wanted the benefit of such teachers! I was so lonely for those with whom I could communicate, who would be able to help me navigate this strange world, in which I felt like such an alien. Why couldn't I seem to find the teachers in the world? Did I have to wait until I died?

It was then that I formulated what was perhaps the greatest desire of my latter years: to not have to wait until I died to get the benefit of the wisest teachers, the ones that could help me understand why the world operated the way it did, not only in purely physical terms, or metaphysical terms, but in human interaction. I began to look for those teachers, and my search led me online, and I found many there with much to say. Among them all, my favorites became Byron Katie, creator of The Work, Bashar, an entity channeled by Darryl Anka, and Alan Watts. I listened to many many *youtube* videos related to each, bought some books and tapes.

In the fall of 2011 the unexpected thought of leaving Alaska first entered my mind. I had loved Alaska all my life. I had thought I would die there, but something was stirring inside me. I did some research and found that North Dakota was actually one of the better places for someone like my son, where the chances of ending up in jail (rather than treatment) because of similar mental illness problems were only about 50% as compared to percentages ranging in the 90 percentiles in most states, including Alaska. In February of 2012 I traveled to Fargo, North Dakota to look for a house, returning again in March to continue the search. On the last day, not having found what I was looking for, I was shown a couple of properties, one of which had just come back on the market after having been taken off the year before. I was working out the details for an offer with my realtor while walking through the airport in Minneapolis. Two months later we closed on that house.

I subsequently traveled back and forth from Anchorage to Fargo four or five times a year while various family members resided in the house. Gradually I wound down my law practice and in June of 2014 I drove my old heavily-laden Caravan down the Al-can Highway, sleeping in the car and taking showers at public facilities along the way.

In Fargo I settled into retirement, but family problems continued. Each of my children (all then living in Fargo) seemed to be going through their own crises—my divorced daughter with her career and financial issues; my older son with a divorce and child custody issues; my youngest son with continued issues related to his bipolar condition. I felt worn down, as if life refused to give me rest. I had intended, upon retirement, along with my writing—I had several novels in progress—to take up film-making, perhaps attending classes at a local college. I could never bear not to have *some* challenging project(s). I liked to be physically active as well to be stimulated mentally: e.g. I had taken up soccer at the age of 56, regularly did remodeling projects on my homes, and had indulged a passion for creating one-sixth scale dioramas and photo-stories. But now, with the constant stress of dealing with "everyone else's" problems, I found myself losing the will to throw myself into any new projects. Yet, even with new financial concerns as I attempted to help family, I was grateful for my release from the practice of law, which I always felt was counter-productive to my real inclinations. Finally, I found myself free to pursue my deepest calling—my interest in spiritual matters.

I had been a student of *A Course in Miracles*, and I still picked it up from time to time, with its essential message: *there is nothing in this world worth holding onto.* I had long thought that this might be my last life—or maybe that was only wishful thinking. As someone who always felt like a stranger in a strange land, I was not eager to have to come back. In any case, I didn't want to take any chances; I desperately wanted to tie up all the ends, to resolve all the issues I had taken on, to find forgiveness for myself and others. To clean the slate.

At this point, I saw no purpose in life, nothing that I wanted out of it, nothing to work for beyond this effort to get back to zero. Back when I was 28, in that moment of grace when the clouds parted, I had understood that all of humanity are sparks from the God Source, that the spark of divinity remains in every chest—albeit hidden beneath layers of soot—and that one day it must return to where it originated. And inasmuch as I had a goal, it was a straight forward one: reunion with God. My main manual for this project was *A Course in Miracles*. By October of 2015, I found myself at the point of wondering: if, as *ACIM* suggests, there is nothing worth keeping in the world, then what happens when nothing is left?

My world, once again, was about to be turned on end. It is not called *A Course in Miracles* for nothing.

Stephanie practicing her pout: little girl front and center with eleven of what would eventually be fourteen siblings, ca. 1955. Edgar, who drowned with his father at age eleven, is the tallest boy in white (tallest but second oldest). Note: chopped heads a photographer problem.

Stephanie 1969-1970,
Columbia, MO

Right:
Stephanie wedding April 1971

Stephanie husband,
Wedding April 1971

Stephanie with Sanjai (first year law school, 1975)

Sanjai with his father, 1975

Stephanie with daughter, California
vacation ca. 1986

Stephanie dance recital ca. 1986

Below: middle two kids Europe 1991

Stephanie Christmas 1991 hours
before birth of youngest child

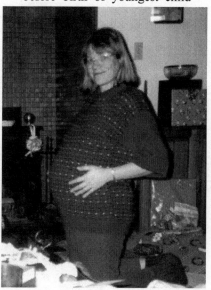

34 The Journey Begins

Stephanie's little melting pot family, all of whom trace their American lineage back to a father-son duo who arrived in Jamestown, Virginia from England in 1624.

Stephanie, August 2016, at the computer where so many conversations took place. Yes, she does wear glasses (since age 10) like the cartoon character throughout this book—just had her contacts in this day.

PART IV
Forty Days and Forty Nights

CHAPTER 1
Say What? Say Who?

For months I had been hanging around the *Channeling Erik* blog. Erik was a young man who shot himself when he was twenty years old. He suffered from bipolar disorder and the Earth experience was very painful for him. You will notice that I did not refer to the Earth experience as life; that is because I do not see it as "life." As Pierre Teilhard de Chardin said, "We are not human beings having a spiritual experience. We are spiritual beings having a human experience." Life exists beyond the bookends of physical "birth" and "death"—nevertheless, I may use the terms "life" and "death" throughout this book as they are commonly understood: *i.e.* when we enter this world and when we leave it.

Erik's mother became determined to discover if there was evidence that any remnant of her son continued after his death, and she consulted with various "spirit communicators" or psychic mediums until she found the very talented Jamie Butler.[11] For several years, Elisa and Jamie collaborated to bring the words of the very "alive and (figuratively) kicking" Erik from the "afterlife," another term that I dislike for obvious

---

[11] *Channeling Erik, http://channelingerik.com/;* see also *My Son and The Afterlife,* Elisa Medhus, MD, c. 2013, ATRIA paperback, A Division of Simon & Schuster, Inc., N.Y.; Beyond Words, Ore.

reasons. I prefer "afterworld," although that is not as accurate as I would like, either. I enjoy a term gleaned off the internet: "post-corporeal world." I may use any of these terms interchangeably, as well as others, to express that "invisible" realm beyond our senses where disincarnate spirits are reputed to congregate.

The Channeling Erik blog is a compilation of interviews with Erik, but also with many other disincarnate personalities. The Erik energy is apparently very helpful in these communications with third-parties. I found these interviews to be fascinating; they seemed to match the interests and personalities of the interviewees, as far as I could discern. I was not aware of any other medium doing these types of communications with the amazing clarity of Ms. Butler. And I soon fell in love with Erik and grew to admire Elisa's resolute determination to both remain in contact with her son and to bring this information to the public's attention.

I also came to appreciate the opportunity, kindly provided by Elisa, to post comments upon this site. It was there, as I thought about the material coming through from the "non-corporeal realm," that I was inspired to expose many of my own dilemmas and analysis as I worked out my private life issues. Not so private anymore, as I was publicly exposing them (although anonymously). I had a theory that when we communicate—share our thoughts, especially those most tightly bound up inside ourselves—we open up space for new information, new ideas, new conclusions. As I was wont to say, if we want God to write in our books, we have to leave him some blank pages. Another way I look at is that you have to unclog the pipe if you want the inspiration to flow.

The factor that I most appreciated about the CE blog was that I could say just about anything—and did—even if it conflicted with the prevailing mindset (there as elsewhere) and nobody revoked my library card or showed up at my door to confiscate my keyboard. I think I stepped on a few toes, and there were a few yelps, but other than that, everyone was tolerant. And through these exercises—through the necessity of careful analysis as I so publicly displayed my failings—I began to see my issues more clearly. I came to better understand the concept of forgiveness through regurgitating my own painful experiences in life, I came to see more clearly how someone like Byron Katie, who I consider one of the most enlightened teachers on the planet, could "love all her thoughts." Indeed. As I came to see, my own thoughts represented only one of two modes: either I was extending love, or I was grasping for it. Usually the latter, but either way, it was clear that I was in touch with the presence or absence of the only thing worth worrying about in this world. As are we all, if we only take the time to consider.

And so, after a few months of vomiting up the secrets of my soul, I began to find some serenity. In fact, I had the distinct image of myself as a butterfly finally emerging from the chrysalis. That said, it seemed I had gotten what I needed from my connection to the site, and it was time for me to give them a break from my constant verbal rumination, and avoid stepping on any more toes. But before I exited, I got into an argument with Erik, which was very funny, because I didn't communicate with spirits. Not like that. In fact, a week or two before, when Elisa was looking for new spirit communicators to work with, I found Erik jumping up and down in my head, saying "You, you, you!" I of course discounted this little display, since I didn't— as I said—communicate with spirits, and I certainly wasn't going to pretend just to please him. But after advising Elisa that I had enjoyed the blog, but wouldn't be around much, Erik protested to me. I told him I was sorry, but it was just the way it was, I felt the need to leave. I couldn't help him.

There is one other matter—actually two—that I need to mention at this time. During the summer of 2015, as previously discussed, I was barely hobbling along emotionally and psychologically. I had lost my zest for life. I seemed to have no desires left in life, no goals to work toward, no purpose. I still had my hobbies, and my interests, so I was not bored. But I *was* depressed as I looked at the years stretching ahead of me until that day when I might roll up my bedroll, so to speak, and say good-bye to this world. What happens once you realize, as *A Course in Miracles* espouses, that there's nothing left in this world that you want or that is worth keeping? What happens then? What's left when there's nothing left? Does something new pop out of the vacuum or what?

I decided, on a whim (well, I thought it was a whim, but my whole thinking on whimsy was soon to change) that I should consult with a psychic medium or intuitive. Perhaps I could get some guidance about what to do with those years stretching ahead of me, like a lonely country road across the endless prairie. I actually consulted with two. The first one was a local man who, over the course of an hour on August 1, 2015, told me a great variety of things that seemed to have absolutely no bearing on me or my life. I therefore decided that it was a waste of time and failed to remember anything except two major points: that in mid-October I was going to become important to many people and that maybe I should try channeling. I pooh-poohed these ideas as absurd, and maybe that's why I remembered them—the sheer absurdity of it all. The second was someone distant with whom I communicated over Skype, and again there seemed to be no relevancy to my life, and thus I forgot everything I was told, with the exception that something important would happen in October.

The second phenomenon was somewhat intriguing to me. For a period of several days during late August and early September, every time I got in the car and the radio would come on, the same lyrics would play from the song *See You Again,* [12] about reconnecting with an old friend. It was so consistent and so odd that I mentioned it to my daughter and we laughed about the fact that some spirit was trying to communicate with me.

Of course, it never even occurred to me that there was any significance to the fact that since I had purchased my house three-and-a-half years prior, with its highly productive apple tree in the back yard—spewing apples all over the yard, that I seemed to have developed some kind of apple fetish in the kitchen. I had apple decorated mixing bowls, apple coffee cups, a complete 12 setting collection of apple dishes, apple plaques hanging on the wall, apple salt shaker, apple pot holders, apple hot plates, apple cookie jar—even an apple adorned key holder and a switch plate I'd found with apples strewn all over it. It

---

[12] *See You Again*, Wiz Kalifa, Charlie Puth, Songwriters: Andrew Cedar, Cameron Jibril Thomaz, Charlie Otto Puth, Jr., Justin Scott Franks: Published by: Lyrics © Universal Music Publishing Group

was again that whim thing; I had no explanation for why I had suddenly developed a penchant for apples in the kitchen—I never had been attracted to them before—or why I got such a warm "homey" feeling whenever I used any of them. I adored my matching mixing bowls and coffee cups, particularly.

The above described "clues" became of significance to me only in retrospect. I had no reason to think any of it meant anything, other than the rather persistent message off the radio, and even that was far too ambiguous to point in any particular direction. It would be, in fact, quite a while, and with some prompting, before I even started putting two and two together.

October 14, 2015 is an important date on my calendar because it is the day when I was effectively launched on this amazing journey that I relate herein. It was the day after I had bid my farewell to the Channeling Erik blog. Normally I have little "free" time, for the temporal space allotted to me in this world—such as has not been taken up by such dreary matters as job, dishes, and laundry—is quickly filled with my many hobbies and activities. I have a low boredom threshold, as mentioned, but I can hardly recall a time (outside of work, cocktail parties, and Continuing Legal Education seminars) when I have been bored, for I find so much of interest in the world around me. If I were to state the premise succinctly and rather bluntly: people often bore me—life does not. I adore learning new things, like to be physically active, and have always had a variety of projects going: writing, sewing, artwork, carpentry projects, soccer, etc.

That particular day, coming off the CE blog as I was, where I had been spending a lot of time, I found a temporary lull in the afternoon. I decided, on one of those whims, that maybe I *should* try to channel some disincarnate entity. I wasn't expecting much. But what was there to lose? I had the computer fired up, my word processing program was always open, I might as well give it a go while I sipped my coffee.

It didn't take me long to decide who to try to contact. I (like a large part of the connected world) was intrigued by those last words some guy, apparently well-known in his sphere, had uttered a few years prior. I didn't normally pay much attention to the news—same old thing, recycled year after year with a few name changes—but I had happened to catch a reference to these famous last words on some news report, and it had stuck with me. I even remembered the name of the guy—Steve Jobs—although I knew nothing else about him other than a vague impression that he had something to do with technology. I couldn't have picked him out of a police line-up or even remembered what company he was associated with. But like many others, I suspect, I was really curious if those words, "oh, wow. oh, wow. oh, wow," indicated some view of the afterworld. What had he seen?

It spoke to my one point of real interest during that segment of my life: what was left when you left the world behind? Were there any clues to my own dilemma in the end-of-life and NDE experiences of others? What happened when nothing in life mattered anymore, when you realized that you couldn't keep any of the "stuff," and you shouldn't want to anyway?

Here was someone who might know. So I chose Steve Jobs as the lucky recipient of my first (and only) effort at channeling a disincarnate entity on that particular day. I put my fingers upon the keyboard and immediately they started clicking. I wasn't unconsciously hitting keys. I was sensing the words in my mind as I typed them—I type pretty fast so I was generally able to keep up with normal speech. I was typing as fast as it was coming out.

-Hello, this is Steve Jobs. Okay, thanks for hosting me. Yes, I am hanging around and available for those with interest in me—or my last words. I can see that is what you are wondering, the oh, wow, oh wow thing. That was a reflection of my dying visions, which were quick and temporary. Brain shutting down? Have it as you will. I'm here, aren't I? I'm talking to you. So life is eternal. Get over it. Take it from me, it is indeed a wonderful life...there, here, everywhere. Don't limit it. I gotta tell ya, I hear people all over the world complaining about the state of the world. But don't worry. Actually, worry just makes things kinda close in. Imagine this grid, like one of those—oh, what's the word—one of those expanding balls, like a folding cup holder that is three dimensional. You get the

happy vibe going and things just spread out, the whole grid
expands. You get that worry thing going and it contracts.
Don't know why that's so, just is. You can see it from here.
You can see it from there, too, just not as easily, 'cause you're
immersed in it. Up to the eyeballs. Okay, what's your
question—let's let this shit fly.[13]

Well! Surprisingly chatty guy. I quite frankly wasn't too
concerned if I was really communicating with some
disincarnate entity or just spewing stuff out of my subconscious.
At the moment, it was just a lark, and I wasn't taking any of it
too seriously. I jumped into the conversation with nothing to
lose.

   -Do you talk that way—or did you? Like say "shit" and
"ya" and stuff?
   -*I think so. I didn't really listen to myself too well, I was*
too busy listening to everybody else. I was a real listener, you
know. I wanted to hear it all, so I could take it in, sift through
it, find the gold.
   -So tell me something that would clearly identify this as
you.
   -*Okey, dokey, let's see here. What do I got? I got a*
hairline issue. Is that good enough? No? Well, let's see.
Maybe you heard about my scar. No? Not across the cheek—
at least not that one. But how would you ever verify that? Let's
see here, you want something good that you can verify, but
since you have no personal contact with my intimates, who
could verify intimate stuff—like whether I preferred briefs or
boxers—I gotta find something you can look up. The year I was
21 was really important. That was a big year for me, discovery-
wise. Hooking up with important contacts. Lots of excitement
going on. You wanna pause and look that one up?
   -Okey-dokey.

   I immediately caught on to the boxers/briefs reference; it

---

[13] Section IV is based upon my journals, contemporaneous emails, and
channelings by Susie Grimmett; dialogue and monologue directly from the
journal is indicated by an initial dash and spacing.

was one of Erik Medhus' favorite impertinences, the kind of thing he would ask the visiting interviewees. Therefore I wasn't surprised that it would be in the mix. Either it was just me talking to myself, or any spirit worth its weight in stardust could read my mind. What I did not know at the time was that Steve Jobs had already been interviewed by Jamie Butler shortly after his death; although I was familiar with many of their interviews, this one was too far back in the archives for me to have read. He might have dropped this reference as a clue, or maybe he'd just been hanging around with Erik. It seemed like an awful lot of us had been.

I put the following terms in the internet search engine: "Steve Jobs age 21." Almost immediately I had my answer, to my great surprise. I returned to my conversation with my new "friend":

-Oh, shit, I just looked it up, that was the year you started Apple with Wozniak.

I would not generally be using swear words when I talked to a total stranger for the first time; however, Erik has a sailor's vocabulary, and it seemed Mr. Jobs also had a salty tongue. Perhaps it was the current trend in the spirit world, and it was catching. After all, if they could talk like that where they were, why not here? Sort of like a green light for us in the earthier realm.

Below is the quote I copied from the relevant webpage:

In 1976, when Jobs was just 21, he and Wozniak started Apple Computer. The duo started in the Jobs family garage, funding their entrepreneurial venture by Jobs selling his Volkswagen bus and Wozniak selling his beloved scientific calculator.[14]

-Okay, so that's only verification for me because I knew nothing about you. It wouldn't prove anything to anybody else.

---

[14] https://quizlet.com/73572927/steve-jobs-flash-cards/

-No kidding. Well, what else do you want to know, just between me and you?

-Give me some dope on your life in the "afterlife."

-All right. I know I don't have to give you a lot of background data, because you're pretty much up to speed on how things are around here, and also on the mental world in which you are functioning. Actually, we all function in a mental world. (Maybe that's why they call it ele-mentals, huh?) So, what's going on with me? Well, I've taken some personal time. To spend with family and friends that beat me up here. Or over here. Or into here, however you want to look at it. That was fun. Really nice to hang out without all the baggage. You know? But I like conversing with you, and others like you, because you've got such a great grasp on the nature of the system—the spirit/world system as it were—and so we can really make headway. I like your idea that the earthly realm is like a full-contact video game. No holds barred, huh? Yech, some of the things that go on there. What will people think up? And I also like your concept of the information reality, the nature of mathematics in describing it, and the fundamental significance of the symbol "0"—zero. I'm right there with you, and that's a really good place to start.

At this point "he" had my attention. Somebody actually liked my concept of the information reality, mathematics, and the beauty of the symbol "0"? Not to mention my favorite way of describing Earth reality, in terms of a video game? I had never described it as a "full-contact" game but I liked that—it made sense. So even if it were just a discussion with another part of myself, I was good with it for the moment. Having a discussion of such matters with myself was more interesting than not having one at all. As I researched and learned more about Mr. Jobs, I would learn that there were many validations in what had been said so far. But perhaps the greatest indication that I was speaking to a mind not my own—if not necessarily Mr. Jobs—were the following sentences, which took a surprisingly personal turn:

-I also know that you—your mind—you your mind—are

*somewhat lonely and forlorn. That sounds like a song. I should
be a songwriter, I'd sing you a song.*

I would never have presumed to be so direct with myself
about my own mental state, or to anticipate that from any man,
especially one I'd just met—disincarnate or not. I didn't even
think of myself as "lonely and forlorn." I was depressed, sure,
and saw no further point in life. But lonely? Not me. And I
would be (and was) embarrassed that anyone would offer to
sing me a song, especially at my age, much less write one for
my benefit. So this couldn't possibly be me talking to myself.
And, in that case, *who* did he think I was?

He must have sensed my discomfort, for the conversation
abruptly became more general:

*-Actually music can convey a lot, you know? I would take
music over ordinary spoken word any day as far as its ability to
communicate on the finer level, the precise details of what's
going on.*

This was to prove true enough. Songs would become a
huge part of our conversation. It was hard to mistake the words
or emotion of the music coming out of my speakers, and I
certainly couldn't pretend that I was just making *them* up.

My new "friend" continued:

*-That's the big question, right? What's going on here? I
mean, the big picture, but you get what I mean. (Sigh.) Well, it
is a big picture. Like all things, you can reduce it down to the
simplicity—I was going to say simplest form, but that's not
really right—it's simplicity, just simplicity. Or you can rev it up
to the complexity. They're pretty much the same, in terms of
levels of truth, reality and intensity. Inside, outside. Flow with
it. The bottle—what's that damned bottle called, the one that
feeds back into itself?*
-Give me a minute and I'll think of it.
*-Me too. I can take a look. You think you've got the
world of information at your fingertips (with the internet). I've*

got the world at mine. I mean, I can go anywhere, see anything. Snoop. I do snoop around a lot. Curiosity, Deep deep curiosity. I have hooked up with Tesla—you were right when that flashed into your mind. We got something in common there between us—maybe we were both dorks, kinda flawed from birth. At least by earth standards.

Tesla. Nikola Tesla. The name *had* popped into my mind, as a matter of fact, right before Mr. Jobs had mentioned it. Now, it might seem unlikely that on top of suddenly communicating with Steve Jobs, who I would learn was quite well known in the world at large, I was now dealing with one of the least acknowledged geniuses of our time. At least in *his* time. But in fact it is not as unlikely as that. It seemed Mr. Tesla was helping out, and I was to learn that Mr. Jobs liked to bring in the brightest and the best for his projects. At this point, I had no way of knowing how deep their relationship actually went. But even then I suspected that, like many spirits, Tesla could divide his energy and work with many at the same time. He also, through other channels, has indicated that helping to facilitate communications across the spiritual divide is one of his favorite activities in the Hereafter.

I wasn't troubled by the "flawed from birth" allusion—I supposed that referred to the fact that, like most geniuses in their fields, these two had felt outside the normal Earth plane mold since birth. Square pegs in round holes. Especially since they were self-described as "dorks."

At this point, in spite of this "scintillating" conversation, I was starting to lose interest. It was fun enough, but I hadn't bought. I mean, *really?* I was talking to some guy who started the Apple computer company when he was twenty-one and he was offering to sing me a song? Give me a break. I had more important things to do—like housework.

I left my word processing program and went upstairs.

Mr. Jobs went with me.

It appeared he didn't need the computer to communicate after all. While I did dishes he chatted in my ear. Well, actually, it wasn't in my ear—but you get the idea. In fact, he was connecting directly in my mind. As he was to explain sometime later, Mr. Tesla had helped him get my stream of consciousness "dedicated to his use," where he was taking up the "other side" of that internal dialogue (sometimes referred to as infernal dialogue) that seems normally to happen so chaotically and often mean-spiritedly. If you have ever really paid attention to the talk in your own head, you've probably noticed. But all of a sudden the dialogue was extremely coherent. Friendly, even. I couldn't help noticing that there was a definite warmth to my new "friend's" attention. It was confusing, however. Why was he persisting in this telepathic discussion with me, of all people? Was it just really boring in the Afterworld, or what? It wasn't like he was giving me messages to deliver to the world, or even to his associates.

I forget even what we talked about as I busied myself cleaning the kitchen. I think I really became engaged when he started talking about the "clockness." He must have realized that the way to this woman's heart was not through her emotional side (which in this case was chronically impaired), but a roundabout path through the left brain—that is, the analytical thinking part.

I immediately perked up. Was it possible? A mind with which I could actually discuss my crazy theories about the way the world worked? Was he serious? He liked the way my mind worked, and we actually had something in common? If I was lonely at all, and I now see that I was, it was for a mind that could and would travel with me into the sometimes Lewis Carollian landscape of "reality," where nothing is as it seems. I had been lonely for that for so long—most of a lifetime—that I just thought it was part of the lighting.

Now, the "clockness" is the term I applied to a fairly recent conception related to vision. I had long been puzzled by the process of "seeing," at least as it was presented in the physical world. I had been taught in school that vision was the function of light waves bouncing off things, like billiard balls, and entering through the retina, where they were turned upside down and then righted again to form, on a screen conveniently located at the back of the brain, a beautiful little fully colored copy of the world outside the head.

But I didn't buy it. It didn't make sense. I imagined the

impossibility of all these randomly refracted light streams somehow hitting the tiny retina from any direction, any distance, in a sufficiently coherent bundle for the brain to unscramble into a complete picture. I imagined a wall between the object that was being observed (the clock) and the eye; one big hole might be cut out, or many smaller ones could fit in the identical space, and yet the same amount of information seemed to get through them all.

Not bloody likely. Not the way they'd described it back when I was in high school.

I considered holograms, an entire scenario caught in a single photon like the garden in a drop of dew. I considered whether the "external world" was actually being projected rather than "read." My current theory suggested that the room (i.e. an assumed limitation of physical space) was filled with dispersed "clockness," a wave function (possibly in three dimensions, like the ocean, if there really were three dimensions), and that at any point the intersection of the sensory apparatus with the wave would result in a particular clock image. Ultimately, of course, I thought of everything as information, but it seemed to me that—in order to create any physical reality at all, some of the information had to be dedicated to the different facets of the interaction—that is, some to the hardware, and some to the software, as described previously. To my thinking back in October, 2015, that left open the question of whether anyone was playing or the game was playing itself. Was seeing and being seen all there was?

I apologize to all the scientists and learned people out there if my theories, such as the "clockness," were naive; I had no training in the sciences, nor did I travel in circles where the minds so inclined congregate. I only had a deep curiosity about how the world worked, and was always more than happy to have someone more intelligent than I come along to show me the error of my ways. It was a mental pastime—possibly developed long before to make up for my social and emotional ineptness—and I didn't take it too seriously.

My point in discussing the "clockness" at all is that I was quite amazed that Mr. Jobs was willing to even attack the issue with me. He even was so bold as to suggest that he had sent the concept to me, which I strongly doubted. I mean, I didn't even know him then! And yes, time is a sticky matter to translate between this world and the next, but, in any case, why would he have bothered?

But what I *was* picking up from our conversation was that he was kind of intelligent, and that was encouraging. Also kind of a jerk, but I'm okay with jerks if they're smart jerks. There's actually a special corner of my heart reserved for those kind. I never liked liars though, and that was going to be a really tough nut to crack open—figuring out what was true and what wasn't. Although my affection was soon earned, my trust was to be broken very early on, and it was to be a long time before it was completely restored.

My new dialogue partner seemed to want me to record our conversations, as much as possible, so when I was done with the dishes I went back to my downstairs workroom (sometimes referred to as the "dungeon") and typed up a synopsis of our conversation. Mr. Jobs was eager to get the focus back on him (although, come to think of it, really back on *me*—he'd somehow made it personal again):

-Back to me, please. And I said I was really really amazed that you had the capacity to understand the problem with vision. How many kids sat through the lectures and reading assignments about light bouncing off leaves and entering the pinpoint area of the retina that would produce the image in the brain and never got a clue, or an antsy feeling that something wasn't quite right there. Now that's really pretty interesting that your mind picked up on the issue.
-Thanks.
-No thanks needed. It's just a curious point of interest, that's all.

He actually got some brownie points for throwing away my thanks, as if to clarify that it was not a complement, but only an impersonal observation. Complements are untrustworthy; observations often say more about the observer than the observed, and increase—not camouflage—understanding.

Since I was back at the computer, I took some time to do some research on Steve Jobs to see if there were any further clues that this was who I was, indeed, talking to. I looked for information about a scar—maybe a childhood accident or a car crash, but found nothing. Then I came across some information that he had had pancreatic cancer, and that he had a liver transplant at some point. I still wasn't convinced that this was the scar to which he was referring until I chanced upon some pictures of those who had had transplants. Now that's a scar!! No wonder he had asked if I had heard of it.

And then, of course, there was the receding hairline, so evident once I started looking at pictures. Okay, that was three out of three for his initial validations. But there was more.

I discovered that simplicity actually was a focus of his, and that he did have an affinity for zero, and its symbol—the circle. I had yet to come across the plans for the Apple headquarters (a perfect circle) or other references to zero associated with him, but I was picking up some resonance with what he was telling me. Not only was this more validation of who I was talking to, but it truly did seem our minds functioned in similar ways—at least in the matters of abstract thinking. So maybe I had a new disincarnate friend. I was cool with that, if it panned out. I didn't need to see a body to be able to communicate on a mental level. At least, not initially, when it was all still just a lark.

Seeking further validation, I decided to check for any prior efforts at channeling the spirit of Steve Jobs. I quickly came up with the interview by Jamie Butler on the Channeling Erik website. Jamie was clearly not impressed with this character; *she* even called him a jerk, although Erik's mother, Elisa, was more forgiving. "Just misunderstood," she suggested.[15]

I did not pay too much attention to the content of the interview at that time, since our acquaintance was so new that not much of it would have made sense to me anyway, at least as far as validation. I did, however, call him out on his attitude during that interview, which appeared to be somewhat arrogant and—yes—rude. I already sensed that this was in itself some

---

[15] http://channelingerik.com/channeling-steve-jobs-part-two/

kind of validation, just from our talk thus far, that he would be a bit disdainful of run-of-the-mill encounters, the "cocktail party banter" of the spirit world. I was beginning to pick up that he was a "let's get to the heart of it, the good stuff" kind of guy, and "if you can't keep up, make room for someone who can." Still, I was somewhat protective of the Channeling Erik world; it had been good to me. Certainly I admired Jamie Butler, who I deemed to be a *psychic medium extraordinaire.*

Steve's response, I'm afraid, further endeared him to me, if not to the crew over at CE (once they read this). He wasn't, he said, a *"circus freak" or a "trained monkey to be commanded to speak for the listening pleasure of the curious public."* He didn't say "curious public," it was a little less kind, I leave it to the imagination. I admit that I admired his ability to call it like he saw it; are we being nice because we want to be liked, or because we feel nice? It's easier to tell the difference with someone who's not afraid to speak his mind. Nevertheless, when down the road he would be channeled through Susie, he was often so blunt that I feared she would refuse to work with him. (Not the case so far, she's been a trooper, and an endearingly feisty one at that, perfectly capable of handling him.)

I remarked to him, on the subject of the CE interview:

-It's a powerful testament to the power of the human mind to command the presence of the "spirit world" since you showed up at all, even if reluctantly.
-*Oh, yeah. We're on tap, like beer. Pay your money and we flow.*
-What do you want me to call you? Steve? Mr. Jobs?
-*How about Master?*
-Okay, Master, that works for me.
-*He he.*
-I know, huh?

It seemed, amazingly, that our relationship had already progressed to the point that we were doing personal and private jokes. I assumed that there is little hidden from the view of any spirit—I'm not sure if there are HIPPA-type restrictions on the

Akashic records—but I knew he could certainly pick up anything in my mind and probably a great deal more somehow. I therefore intuited the reference to "Master" to have been both an acknowledgement of what I had already suspected, that I had had numerous slave lifetimes, as well as a nod to my little-acknowledged submissive tendencies in this lifetime—probably the effect of all those slave experiences. I often thought I would have made a good secretary, instead of an attorney, placing the file on my boss' desk: "There you are, Mr. Jones, in time for your 3:00 appointment. Do you want me to fix that loose button on your jacket?"

I never thought that he really wanted me to call him "Master," but that left open the question of how to address him. For the time being, the "Voice in My Head" seemed appropriate—and non-committal. "My disincarnate friend" seemed a little too sitcom. Although, in hindsight, this story might have made a good sitcom.

The truth, I was to discover, is far more entertaining than fiction

Chapter Two
(a) Strange Guests and (b) Steve Pisses Me Off

Thursday, October 15, 2015:

A week or so before I began talking to Mr. Jobs, I had a surprise visit from Thomas Jefferson. I know. Go ahead and laugh. But there he was one morning just as I was waking from a deep sleep. I had been watching the mini-series, *John Adams,* in which Mr./President Jefferson puts in appearances at various points, so I supposed there was some congruity there. I don't recall what we talked about, but I had the distinct impression that he had come to discuss a connection we had had during his Thomas Jefferson lifetime. As I have repeatedly said, I didn't consider myself someone who regularly talked to spirits, so I was somewhat surprised by his appearance, and would have written it off as my imagination if it hadn't been so vivid.

My impression was that I had been a slave on his plantation, but also that we had a very close relationship. I didn't want to believe the last part—it seemed rather presumptuous—since everyone knows Thomas Jefferson had a *very* close relationship with one particular slave that had come to him from his father-in-law. In fact, she was the daughter of his father-in-law, half-sister to his only wife, to whom he made the promise (on her deathbed) to never remarry. Tough set of facts.

I didn't think too much about it, other than to confide in one sister that I'd had this visit. This happened to be one sister who was more open to the spiritual realm than the others—but still, I realized right away I might have said too much. She was taken aback, and probably was thinking I'd gone too far over the hill. Yes, we get visited by our deceased parents and grandmother from time to time, but not famous historical figures like Thomas Jefferson, who wrote the *Declaration of Independence,* for God's sake. I had always admired that document, and considered Mr. Jefferson to be one of the most enlightened of the founding fathers. But that was the extent of it. I wasn't ready to buy into the idea that I had played the role of the mother of his...well, shall we say, his unacknowledged children. He did support them, though, which is more than can be said for many fathers with unacknowledged (or even acknowledged) offspring in *this* day and age.

So there I was, on the second day of my adventure in cross-the-veil communication with Mr. Jobs, discussing with him my experience with Mr. Jefferson. I was still debating within myself whether that experience was real or not—although it was difficult to discount, since I had been wide awake at the time, and there was no mistaking his identity. He had displayed a quiet dignity, a reserved demeanor, not evident in my current guest. But there had also been no mistaking the deep affection I had felt from him. There had been a sense of leave taking, or releasing, about the encounter, as in "I just came to tell you..." But I hadn't comprehended the point. Why was that necessary? Why had he come?

Steve took it in stride, not questioning that I had in fact had a visit from Thomas Jefferson. It is amazing to me, looking back, how nonchalantly I entered into a discussion of my shared lifetime with this great American forefather, even though a large part of me doubted. So now I was dealing not just with Steve Jobs, but Nikola Tesla *and* Thomas Jefferson? Would wonders never cease?

Steve mentioned that Jefferson was more into the way of the heart, while he (Steve) experienced the way of the mind. As he explained it to me, the heart is the power, the energy, and the mind is similar to a filter—one might say that the light shining through the film is the heart energy and the film itself is the mind form and this creates the resulting image or illusion that we understand as life experience, even understand as the material world. Heart's not about "nice," although it can seem to be that way by its nature, it's just a byproduct at times and not a real attribute.

I repeated this information and asked if I had it right.

-So far so good.

He then, rather facetiously I assumed, offered to get Thomas Jefferson's autograph for me. I said I would like that very much, and we talked about how that would happen. My first thought was something on the mirror—that's how spirits liked to send messages, I thought, based upon popular books and movies. But that didn't seem permanent enough, so I asked for a real signature, with a quill pen for genuineness. Steve said he'd put in the request. We both agreed it would be a feat of materialization, and were unclear if it could be done, but it would be interesting to find out.

-So we await results. Right?
-*Yep.*
-You're a man of few words.
-*At times. I told you that.*
-Yep.

No wonder he wasn't very talkative. He was probably wondering how he got persuaded to produce Thomas Jefferson's autograph. Talk about needing validation.

-I'm going to get my coffee and then I have to get things done. I'll try to sit down and type if you get chatty, so just try to pick a good time, okay?
-*I got the memo.*

Sometime Later:

I had just settled into my herbal bubble bath when I heard:

-*Is this a good time?*

I could not believe I was hearing this. But there was no mistaking that he was there; I could sense his presence in my bathroom.

-Uh, no-oo!! What're you doing in here?
-*Just visiting.*
-Can't a person have any privacy around here? Like I

wanna expose my flabby old body.

-Oh, you're not so bad. Get over it.

I had long figured that spirits were capable of going anywhere, which meant that there was no such thing as privacy for the likes of us that are hampered by such things as doors and locks. But I also supposed if they could see it all, they had, and it was of no particular interest to them. Still, I expected that any spirit with a little self-respect would show some restraint out of concern for the sensibilities of the incarnate. It wasn't just that I was exposed, but I was a sixty-five year old woman, and it couldn't even have been interesting. This, however, was apparently a personality who played by his own rules, who saw nothing wrong with pushing the envelope.

I decided to ignore him. I sank down into the bubbles and started to read. After a while I had the thought that I should get out and do something productive. There was an immediate response:

-You've got all the time in the world. Enjoy it. You deserve it. You've earned it.

I wasn't expecting such platitudes. I was sure there was some snarky remark about to be dropped on me, sort of like the other shoe. But my attention was suddenly diverted by a strange but warm feeling, as of love and peace. It was very odd and…well…mellowing. I had a bit of a vision, as of a light passing slowly by, in that realm unseen by human eyes. It took me a few moments to figure out what was going on. There were roving lights in the Hereafter? Why wouldn't they be stationary? How could you read? Then I realized that the light seemed to be coming from a being that appeared to be gliding by. I had the impression of an orb, and I had the strange sense that the light from that powerful source on the Other Side was reflected from the orb in my bathroom, and thence to me.

Once I was out of the bathtub, I went to my journal:

-Wow. It was actually pretty cool.

-That's the kind of thing you get used to around here. It

would be kinda creepy, the way it slides into you, if it didn't feel so good, like blissful.

-It's not that different than the sun coming out from behind the clouds, is it? Warming the skin and the heart and the emotions?

-Mmm, decent comparison. The human mind is trained to accept that kind of heavenly intrusion. On the other hand, there's a fear of spiritual contact.

-So is there such a thing as fear of the sun?

-Yes. It's called skin cancer.

That evening:

I happened to start my first *Tai Chi* class that day. No doubt my karate training was of benefit to me in picking up the moves. I could feel the energy in my hands as they passed each other, or moved by my face.

After class I set out to research the name of the bottle that turns inside out, where the inner becomes the outer. I had made up my mind that I would require Steve to provide the name of it, as additional validation, before I did the search for confirmation. The name I got from him was "Empire bottle" or "Empire jar."

I spent a fair amount of time trying to locate any reference to an "Empire" bottle that was designed to turn inside out. But all I could find was the name of the mathematical construct, the Klein bottle, which is actually only a theoretical model. I was very disappointed. If he was unable to tell me the name of this bottle, then he obviously couldn't be real. It was time to can this little experiment in spirit communication.

Friday, October 16, 2015

The next morning, however, I awakened with a new inspiration. I sat down at the computer and searched for "Empire Klein bottle." Immediately I had multiple hits. I went to my journal to record our resulting conversation:

-So it's kinda a joke, huh? The Empire bottle is a bong! The Klein bottle bong, made by Evol Empire. That was the "damned" bottle *you* were thinking about. The Empire strikes again.

-No comment.

-I remind you that I still haven't seen Thomas Jefferson's autograph.

-Maybe you're not looking in the right places.

Ever a Doubting Thomas, a little part of me held back. After all, it was an *Evol* Empire Klein bottle, not just *Empire* Klein bottle. Had he told me the whole name and I just didn't pick up on it? Was my connection faulty, was it just a lucky guess on my part, or had he only meant to say part of the name? Yes, I was very demanding when it came to validation. I was still processing this episode later that day when we had another incident that almost caused me to abandon the conversation altogether. Our relationship did survive, but it was a very big bump in the road.

-I'm still groaning over that Empire bottle thing.

-You eat too much candy, you know that?

-I do know that. Believe it or not, in my youth, I was much opposed to sugar. I think I'm just on the pendulum swing.

-Maybe.

-So while we're on the subject, I wanted to talk about molecules, materiality and energy.

-So how is that on the subject?

-Isn't *everything* related to that subject?

-You have me there.

-So I got this idea that the sub-atomic particle, like the electron, or whatever else is down there that I don't know about, is really just a quiet place in the energy vortex, like the eye of the hurricane.

-Uh huh. Not bad.

-We think material "objects" are more concrete, but in fact they would be made of the portions that are less concrete.

-I'm liking it.

-I got this idea in one of those post-sleep not-ready-to-get-out-of-bed periods.

-I know that.

-Was that one of yours?

-No.

-Then who?

-For you to find out. Not my place to be revealing the identities of the spirit guides. Woo-woo.

At the time I assumed that this was further evidence he wasn't really Steve Jobs, or anything outside my own head. Was he being evasive? If he had a name, why didn't he shoot it out there? Only in retrospect do I understand how careful he had to be about what information he was providing, that I didn't get overwhelmed. His was a tough job. No doubt about it. At any moment, this early in our communication, I could have dumped everything and refused to engage. My mind was barely willing to tolerate the far-out information I had so far, and even then only with a great dose of skepticism. It was still just a game with which I was amusing myself. My investment remained minimal—a couple days of mental distraction.

But I was still happy to continue chewing my theory with 'him':

-So in fact the space between objects is heavier, so to speak, more active, more full of stuff—namely energy in motion. Which brings me to that touchy-feely subject, what is that? E-motion? Energy in motion? Do they line up? In any way, shape or form?

-Ways, shapes and forms, that's quite a subject. I feel like we need to bring in reinforcements for this discussion.

-Are they around there?

-Well, Tesla is. I told you he's my bud.

-I don't know too much about him, either, but actually more than I ever knew about you (sorry, I was anti-Apple all the way—well not anti, just in favor of the cheaper alternative). Tesla I've looked into, only because there's so much interest in him lately. He's come into his own. He certainly wasn't in my grade school textbook, hanging out with Tom Edison in the laboratory. But I know just enough to perceive that he is now recognized as the unrecognized genius of his time.

-Yeah, he's kinda impatient, too. Kinda like me. Likes to get right down to it. Not cocktail party material.

-He was building a tower to the heavens, right, going to draw energy out of the air, so to speak. Is that similar to the pyramids?

-How your mind works is amazing. You should leave your brain to science.

-I think they'd throw it out with the garbage.

-Their loss.

-Telsa? Mr. Tesla?

-Tesla: Yes.

-You have an accent? That mid-European kind?

-Tesla: Polish.

-You're from Poland?

-Tesla: I was born in Copenhagen.

-Denmark?

-Tesla: Yes.

-Why? You're not Danish are you?

-Tesla: No. My father. He had business there.

Off I went, as usual, to check the facts. I returned in great disappointment.

-Okay, I blew it big time. Not Nikola Tesla. I feel sad now. I will probably can this whole thing.

I wouldn't even wait for a response. I was so upset. Disappointed, even. I really was beginning to believe—just a little. Wouldn't it have been cool if I *was* onto something here? Instead, I had fallen flat on my face. I wasn't talking to disincarnate beings—I was in a state of delusion, of course. How stupid of me! I could feel Steve trying to talk to me, but I ignored him for what seemed like hours. Finally, in exasperation, I returned to the keyboard:

-I am so pissed off I can hardly speak. Why would you give me erroneous information?

-Quality control.

-What????

-We knew you would check it out and find out the info was *wrong.* But *there also had to be some episode of that sort to* *establish that you weren't just spouting off things you'd read* *somewhere.*

-Yeah, well, I now feel totally taken for a ride. You better produce Thomas J's autograph or I am so out of here. And stop laughing. Oh, God, don't remind me. The time I was sent out to kill the flies in the new vet lab, the one that didn't have any windows.

-Gullibility, that's your name.

-Yeah. Gullible's Travels. That might be what I should name this journal, huh?

It was true that I had a tendency toward gullibility. My favorite story in that vein, which I had already committed to one of my autobiographical essays, related the details of a prank at my expense when I worked at the Veterinary Research Facility at the University of Missouri, Columbia between my freshman and sophomore years of college. Normally my job was to prepare the slides of various mouse entrails for subsequent study. One day, however, I was instructed by my boss to go out to the new addition and kill the flies. It was a small free-standing building still under construction, not yet fitted with doors or windows. It was full of flying insects. I clearly had my work cut out for me. I obediently started nailing the many flies. In the meantime, the entire staff had gathered in the "break room" to lay bets on how long it would take me to come to my senses. They were awaiting my return, coffee cups in hand, grinning as I crawled back in, dragging my flyswatter. I was subjected to no few snarky comments. It was a moment I was not soon allowed to forget—and obviously never had.

-Anyway, so I now know Tesla is Serbian before American, speaks some umpteen languages (Polish not being one of them). So I don't know if you have an accent or not.

-Tesla: A little one.

-Well, I guess even polyglots can have accents.

-Tesla: Polly glots a cracker?

-I can't believe how you two behave. Like little kids. Like normal people anyway. One doesn't expect that. Shouldn't you be acting all saintly and stuff?

-Steve: He he. That would be no fun.

I could almost hear the strains of *Hakuna Matata* in the background.

-This reminds me of a story. I was spending a lot of time online in the old AmericaOnline (AOL) chatrooms trying to improve my French, which it actually did. I would try to learn at least a couple of new words each day. One day someone said "chiant" and I asked what that meant and was told it meant "boring" (which I guess it does, but that's not all it means), so later on I was talking to some conservative old gentleman and I used that word and he about shit (bilingual pun appreciated) and said how shameful I was, he couldn't believe I would use that word, and I had no idea why he was so upset. It was only later that I got someone to tell me the truth, to say "C'est chiant" is the equivalent of saying, "Well, that's shitty" or "that's crappy." Why was I reminded of this story?

-Steve: I told you—leave your brain to science.

Although our communication survived this incident, my capacity for trust took a direct hit. Maybe not nuclear, but definitely in the megapound category. From that date on, I could hardly accept anything he said unless it could be corroborated through a third party source, or I had some direct experience of it myself. This was significant in terms of validation, since my mind filtered out the types of information I had received at the inception of our conversation, which had allowed me to get some initial confidence. I think I was afraid that something more would be said that I could not verify, thus proving once and for all that this conversation was not "real." Yes, my emotions had gotten involved, undermining my quest for the "truth'.

Steve did seem to make some effort to redeem himself.

From my journal that evening:

-I was telling you that I was going to write before my critique group tomorrow, and you said you'd help, and I asked if you knew anything about writing novels, and you said, "no, but you could get help—who did I want, Charlotte Bronte, Louisa May Alcott—or somebody newer? Harper Lee, who you said is mostly there in spirit if not in body (well you know what we mean)." I couldn't think of any 20th Century writers I really wanted to emulate that were dead, and you suggested Frank McCourt—I didn't know if he was dead or alive but you said he was there. So of course I looked it up, and he did die in 2009. So okay I'll take a little help from any of those, if you please.

Wait, I take it back. I don't really want the help. I feel like I've gotten enough help from studying the works of these great authors. I want this to be *my* book. I like to do things by myself, if possible, figuring it out as I go along, and I hate so much when someone comes along and takes over the program in the guise of helping. So I will take their well wishes, and if they'd like to pre-order some books, I'm all for that. If there are ghost writers, are there also ghost readers?

-*You betcha.*

-Help to make it a bestseller would be much appreciated, as I would like to stock up the coffers so I don't feel so nervous about the financial issues. Yeah, I know, a personal issue, I have to work on it.

Saturday, October 17, 2015

I had now been having this conversation for more than three days. It continued almost non-stop, although in those early days I only infrequently stopped to try and commit it to writing. I was still busy with other things—my housework, my little sweater-making business, yard chores, redoing the steps in my house. This new acquaintanceship had all been fun company as I went about my business. But after a while, one does feel the need to fit each experience into the greater worldview. The time had come to get serious. I was either really talking to a disembodied intelligence, or I was not. There was no denying that I was engaged in a conversation. The question was: with *what*? Was it something outside of myself (possibly the spirit of Steve Jobs) or just myself? This question raised all kinds of existential questions. Was it a case of "I think, therefore I am" or "we think, therefore we are"?

I jumped on little synchronicities (and missed all the big ones). At this point I had not remembered about the psychics' predictions, I had forgotten about the repeated lyrics that played each time the radio came on, and it never even entered my mind that there was any significance to my sudden warmth for apples as a decorating motif. And these were only a tiny taste of what was to come. But in that moment, I was beginning the real struggle between belief and disbelief, and any validation was encouraging.

I sat down to update my journal.

-Okay, a couple of things of interest. So I watch this TV show last night while I'm working, *Warehouse 13* I think it's called, and whadye know? Who does this guy mention at the Warehouse. Nikola Tesla, Thomas Jefferson, and Thomas Edison. Now what an interesting combination, no? I mean I can see Tesla and Edison in the same sentence, but TJ? I decided to hang in there to see if Steve Jobs came up, but the name didn't. Then today I am about to go to bed and I decide to just click on the Channeling Erik blog, even though I've decided to stay off it, and almost right off the bat I hit this comment wondering if Steve Jobs has been channeled. The comment was four days ago, the very day we started our discussion, remember? I looked up the day this document was created. It was 10/14/15.

I also didn't write down all the things that happened that night—not last night, but Thursday night—after that incident with the spirit with the really heavy duty orb of light. Wow, that was something. It was also after I did the *Tai Chi* class, so maybe it was both things, but it was like I could literally feel healing—in myself, in others important to me—I could move my hands and feel the energy emanating off them. It was the most beautiful intense feeling and it lasted for a couple hours, I had all kinds of visions. Anyway, very very cool.

I'm now feeling a little nervous about this whole business which started out as a lark…

-Still a lark.

-Yes, good point. Anyway, I now feel that sense of uncertainty.

-You were uncertain before.

-I know, but I had a whole lot more [reason to fall] on the uncertainty side.

*-And now you're feeling **more** uncertain. Your logic leaves something to desire.*

-I get that. More evidence, less certainty. But that's the way it works, right? It's easy to just go with the flow when there's nothing hanging in the balance.

-Yes, true. I have some fond memories of those days, myself.

-Early career?

-Yes. I think it was kind of like where you were at, it was just fun, what came of it came of it. Nobody to please but ourselves, we were used to being broke, so it wasn't like we had a lot to lose.

-Just that VW minibus.

-Yep.

-Did it have flowers painted on it?

-Do I look to you like the flower kinda guy?

-No—but maybe back then—you were kinda hippish, right?

-No. I was a dork. I told you.

-A smelly dork?

-The things people will say and write to get a little attention. You shouldn't read the gossip columns.

In response to your unspoken question, I don't know where we go from here. If I did, there wouldn't be much point in going there, would there? Would there, wouldn't there. Something odd about those words.

-So you don't know the whole future?

-Future? Future, you say!!! What future are you talking about, Dumbass?

-Please don't call me names. I can shut this laptop, you

know.

-I know, but you can't get rid of me that easy. I even know where your bathroom is.

-You wouldn't harass me if I wasn't open to this, would you?

-No—not much, anyway. I'm not sure that you're any good to me, anyway.

-Cause I'm not technical, don't know anything about that stuff?

-You're kind of a lightweight. Like a feather in the wind. You need to settle, dig your toes in, get some forward motion going.

-I'm just hanging in there, just *being*. Okay?

I was beginning to feel aggravated. Who was he to tell me what I should or should not be? I'd had a hard life, this was the winding down part, and what right had he to judge me? It was a feat of determination that I'd gotten this far at all. And anyway, what was the ultimate point? What was there to work for when the result was the same end in the end?

But he didn't seem inclined to let up, as if I was supposed to jump through *his* hoops.

-Not so okay. With me, anyway. Oh, God, headache coming on. You felt that, didn't you?

-I'm still feeling it.

-I was wrong. I was wrong. It is okay with me. You can be anything you want to be. It's all good.

-Phew. I was feeling criticized.

-I know, I know. See, I'm still learning. It's like there's certain things you just can't do here. It's not allowed. And that is to diminish. It's all about expansion. Love. I wanted to say I hate that word, but I'm a little afraid of that headache thing. Anyway, how can you hate love? You can't hate love, because if it's love, it stands on its own, just the way it is. So I love love. It's cool. Okay? Good Steve.

-You did criticize people, didn't you? Laugh at them even? I read about the criticizing part, people said you could tear into them like anything, reduce them to rubble.

-Yes. I was pretty good at it. Like I was at most anything I tried. In some ways, it did work towards the end (result), but the question is whether the end justifies the means.

-Does it?

*-No. You see, there is no end. Or ends. There's just the means part. So the means have to be self-justified. That is to say, the means **are** self-justified. Everything that exists ...exists. If a bird flies across the sky, there's a reason for it—in the sense that it's connected to everything else that said, "a bird must now fly across the sky." It was, or is, exactly what has to happen. Everything points to that one event. And that event points to all the others, in a continuous chain. But it's not a temporal chain. It's an **existent** chain.*

-So it had to happen that you were critical?

*-No, the critical part is an interpretation. It might have had to happen that a certain sound was emitted, but that sound in itself is not critical—in the judgmental sense. It **is** critical in the sense that it is absolutely necessary to fill that spot in creation. In that sense, everything is critical. So there you have it, another one of those turn-around things, where you can look at the same exact words and see them differently. I think that's the point. There's like this mist that confounds the true meaning of things, of words even, or concepts, twists them so they seem to mean something foreign. But the odd thing is, the mind can really buy into that twisted version, and then the truth—the true meaning—seems foreign to it.*

You know, you could also say that everything is the end. It's the beginning as well. So the end and the beginning get absorbed into each other, and then you just have—the whatever. The whatever it is.

-Is it beyond words?

-Words. What are words? It's funny, because it seems to me that words can be heavy and ponderous here, and what you think of as materiality not even a mist that you step through. But there, it is the opposite, and words seem—insubstantial. The material world is what seems so heavy to you, so concrete, so powerful. I see words like building blocks, like those letter blocks little kids play with. You stack them on each other to make a castle or a bridge or whatever. There's the shape.

There's the form.

-Okay, this conversation is pretty heavy for me. I want to just get back to the love, the peace, the simplicity.

-Yeah, simplicity is good. Love is good. I love you. There, I said it. I love everybody of course, how could I not? But it's necessary because we are communicating that this be permitted to flow between us. It's like an energy—a synergy—that demands freedom to move. If you hold it back, it's like—well, pardon the expression, but like being constipated. Let the stream flow. It knows the way. "The horse knows the way, to carry the sleigh…"

-"…through the white and drifted snow." Hey, Steve?

-Yeah?

-I love you, too, there I said it. And you can call me dumbass—as long as you're not being critical.

-Master and Dumbass. Sounds like the title of one of those movies, the kind that does so well because the movie-going public likes its entertainment at the lowest level of intellect possible.

-Are you being critical?

-Oh, maybe. But all in fun.

-Keep it light, huh?

-Please. You're cool.

-Thanks. You too. Hope you can find a nice soft cloud to rest on.

-Oh, you too. In your nightly travels. Fly high.

And I did.

CHAPTER THREE
Doubts!

Sunday, October 18, 2015

From my journal:

-I am back to update as much as possible the incessant chattering that goes on while I am going about my work. This morning you told me to get out of bed, which I was reluctant to do—"Wake up! Wake up!" you kept saying, and in my half-sleep I thought you meant I should wake up from this physical dream into ultimate reality—but actually you were trying to get me out of bed because I had an appointment I disremembered. So I finally got out of bed just in time to get the address and head out. So I was a little too "off the grid" there, a little too "metaphysical," it was just a simple wake up call.

Then while I was driving we talked a bit about how I didn't think I would have liked you in your recent life here, and you admitted that you would have found me not worth your time. You did say that few could imagine what a powerful brain lurked beneath that hum-drum unattractive middle-aged exterior. (Thanks.) And then you called me "Stephanie," which is the first time you had used my name, and a light bulb went off. Steve/Stephanie, Male/female, two sides of the Mobius strip,[16] experiencing the same thing from different perspectives,

---

[16] I assumed my mind and Steve's were sufficiently synced (or at least he could see my thoughts) that I didn't need to explain the Mobius strip allusion to him (think how you sometimes get your belt twisted in the back, if you're not familiar with the term); principally, it related to a vision I had seen years before when I was contemplating the mysterious molecules that act identically at a distance—what I saw was each like the eye of a hurricane within this highly elastic flow of energy, like a figure "8" Mobius strip (i.e. working both sides of the track, what one might even call the negative/positive sides). Like an algebraic equation, the elasticity (think rubber band) meant that what was added to one side must be added to the other, so the "fulcrum" or "cross over point" remained equally balanced between the two. Steve was later to bring up the figure "8" through Susie (the independent medium) several times, although she didn't name it—she just drew it as he showed her, with the movement around it. He also was to

two sides of the "spirit" divide.

-Took you long enough.

-Uh, I'm not always the fastest draw.

*-No, you're not, you do tend to be gullible and easily played with by those who are smart enough to do so. (Which excludes most of humanity.) But I kinda like that about you, it makes my job more fun. And you don't mind. That's another thing I kinda like about you. You don't take yourself too seriously—most of the time. Which is a good counterpoint for me, because I do take myself **very** seriously.*

-I see that.

-So shut up, listen up, and do what I say. That's my motto.

-I thought you said you listened to everybody.

-Only when they have something good to say.

While I swept the leaves off the deck, Steve and I chatted about a variety of matters, and somehow got on the topic of a title for the book that would result from our discussions. I had understood from the beginning that I was to journal everything to preserve it for a book, although both my efforts and my credulity had been limited. Still, it was fun to discuss. Steve held out for *Master and Dumbass*, as he claimed it might attract the intellectually impaired who might learn something. But then he remarked that it wouldn't work, since they didn't read. And I said, "Whose fault is that? Who gave them the ipod, the iphone, and the ipad?" And I added, by the way, "Who gave them the mouse, who took their fingers off the keyboard? Was that you or Bill Gates?"

I am old enough to remember working on my PC without windows, without a mouse, working out of MS-DOS. In fact, before that, my oldest son used to write programs for his Atari when he was about thirteen. I remember writing one myself, a simple game where you floated down a river and had to avoid various obstacles. I actually thought of those as good times, in the fledgling days of home computing, when kids were developing their logic skills creating their own games. What a

---

talk about molecules in motion, but Susie could not comprehend enough to translate what he was telling her.

blast! I resented it when I was forced to switch to Windows, when I had to take my hands off the keyboard to manipulate the mouse. For a long time afterward I memorized the key strokes for most of my operations, but eventually I, too, was bouncing my hand back and forth from mouse to keyboard as the programs became more complicated with their expanding menus.

Of course Steve said it was, "Bill. Damn Bill." At the time I thought this was another piece of misinformation. After some research, I learned that it was actually Apple that lifted the mouse from IBM and brought it into the household; however it sold poorly in connection with the Lisa, and was quickly re-lifted by Microsoft, who introduced it in a big way. Since I always worked on various PCs, it was strictly true that it was "damn Bill" who was responsible for my personal transition, and I suppose accurate that it was Microsoft who really blew the cover off that one, who "gave it to *them*"—that is to say, the general public. It would be months, however, before I realized that I had stuck my mouth, if not my foot, into a very touchy issue; apparently Apple had gotten into intense litigation with Microsoft over this matter—the (from Steve's point of view) theft of the mouse and windows precursor (gui system)— complicated by an additional lawsuit against Apple on the same basis. So I guess it was "damn Bill" after all, but I did not know this at the time, when we got into a discussion of the whole credibility thing.

-Are you mad at me?
-I am. It may be funny to you to play with me like this, but I am trying to validate what goes on here. And saying things that are not 100% doesn't help.
-Well, we were talking about how gullible you are. All I have to do is say it with a straight face and you fall: hook, line and sinker.
-I know. I get it now [or so I thought] that it's kind of a joke, kinda facetious I guess, that it's Gates fault if it has a bad result. Bad Bill, Good Steve.
-I call it as I see it.
-And while we're at it, let's get it out here about the

distinction between you and Bill that you've been emphasizing since the subject came up a day or two ago. Bill, you say, is a nerd—or sometimes a geek—but you are a dork. The two are not the same, and I should understand the niceties of the English language and the distinctions between the labels. I am sorry if I offended you by putting you into the same category as Gates—in nerd-dom anyway.

-*Apology accepted. Let's keep it clean.*

-Agreed. Let's keep it clean. Respectful. I don't mean by that I want to cramp your style—far be it from me to put chains upon your being (ness). But I do have a question. Is it your habit to be breathing down people's necks like this?

-*You mean following you around?*

-Yes.

-*If I need them to do something, yes. I'm pretty focused that way.*

-And what exactly do you need me to do? I've been wondering that for a while. What is the purpose of this communication other than a couple of days of curious intellectual stimulation? (And emotional stimulation, actually, I've been feeling kind of gratified.)

-*Yeah, it works both ways. That's when it really comes together, when work and play exactly comprise the same circle. It's gotta be fun, or it's not real.*

-So my part?

-*Not sure yet, but I think you're kind of a translator. You're a writer. You can express things. You've got powerful processing equipment upstairs. You can interpret things. And you can hear me (most important of all). Well, maybe the last element is **not** the most important, since a lot of people claim to channel me, and there's some connections there, but not like this. We've got this synchronicity going. You like that word, don't you?*

-I do.

-*Well, then learn how to spell the damned word!*

-Okay, okay. [In in spite of using it often in the last month or so, I consistently alert spellcheck that there's a problem.]

-*I told you that I can't foresee the future. If I could, it would be a simple matter of following the roadmap.*

-Kind of like working a maze backwards.

-I was going to say that same thing. See, our minds work alike.

-Does it occur to you that it might be the one and only same mind?

-Yeah, yes and no. I'm still trying to figure out how that works, anyway, but I think it's the "Empire" bottle trick.

-It's forever going to be the Empire bottle, huh?

-Hey, you need to lose some of your uptightness.

-*My* uptightness. Aren't you the guy with all the crazy diet habits?

-We are what we eat.

-Well, there you have it.

-Touché.

-Are you any further enlightened on the food thing now that you're up there in Heaven with all the nutritional guides at your fingertips?

-I still think food's important. If you're going to have food, if you're going to play that game, then you hafta play by the rules.

-Garbage in, garbage out?

-There's so much involved. I couldn't possibly convey it all, what I understand now about how the—God, I hate using this word, "vibrations"—it's so '60s minibus.

-Ha ha.

-I wasn't a hippie, I was a dork.

-I know, you've made that distinction. Anyway, you were kinda late for that era, weren't you? That was my era.

-Not so late as all that. Remember, I may have died younger, but I've been dead for a while. Dead as in, video game dead and got the halo.

-Oh, yeah, that was the only game I ever played, way back in the—was it the early 90s? Late 80s? When the characters died they floated off with a halo.

-Common contrivance.

This conversation with the self-proclaimed Steve Jobs was now absorbing my day. He followed me everywhere. While I was at the computer of course, but also around the house as I did chores, into the car and the store while I went about my errands, to my bedroom while I was changing clothes or getting ready for bed. He was there as I waited for sleep to take hold, and there when I woke up in the morning. Apparently he was also in my dreams—although I was mostly asleep at such times and didn't remember.

As one might suppose, as entertaining as it was to have a constant companion with whom to discuss a variety of subjects—who, in fact, never bored me—it was also very confusing. Why was he there? *Was* he there? Things were still moving from light entertainment to the critical issue of whether I might be losing my marbles—at least the ones I still had with me. I decided to confront him:

-So now I want to get down to what's really going on. There's this woman I made contact with, the one that suggested channeling you back on the same day I contacted you—or you contacted me—without either of us knowing about the other. It's like we were directed to contact each other. I used to read the *Channeling Erik* blog every day, but I had stopped reading it just as she comes on and makes her comment. This is not a coincidence. That is a maneuvering of destiny. Add to that the fact that I was actually able to get an email for her, which doesn't happen often.

This woman, who I shall identify as Debbie (not her real name), very quickly became an important resource for me. She was open to my story and allowed me to vent my concerns, uncertainties and tribulations. Steve said she served as my "ground," while I was like the lightening rod—or perhaps better yet, the transducer. That caused us to get off on a discussion of Tesla, who apparently was in charge of the energy distribution. I wondered why he had to be involved. I mean, really, you have to have Tesla on the job to communicate with me? Wouldn't your everyday technician work? Steve's response:

-*Hey, this is a big project. We need the big bad boys on this one. You think we can get by with Joe Blow, the electrician just up from Waukegan, who's happy to just sit in his heavenly armchair in front of his big screen TV, sharing beers and tales of earthly capers with his buds who beat him up?*

This was not the first time he'd talked about the "project," or even that it was a "big project." I had no idea to what he was referring—it was all quite mysterious.

I was troubled by the fact that, in spite of us talking almost non-stop for four or five days, I still didn't fully comprehend why he was still hanging around. He still hadn't given me any messages to deliver to humanity, as one expected famous spirits to do, making the most of their notoriety to give words of hope and cheer to the masses struggling in the dark on this side of the divide. My impression was that somehow we had stumbled upon a good Earth-to-Heaven connection—not sure why, perhaps because there is little interference on the Great Plains. Not so many active channels, not to mention nothing taller than an occasional grain elevator between Minneapolis and Western Montana.

We had some rapport between us—I picked up on it. Our minds seemed to work well together, and apparently we had the same goal. Neither one of us wanted to do another Earth lifetime—the whole birth canal route to get to the good stuff, the stuff you still wanted to work out in physical reality. I was laboring under the impression that our ongoing connection was the best either of us could do to find a method of working out our remaining issues, which required another personality, sort of like a lab-partner. Someone who could ring the bell while you were trying to remember, when you jumped, not to trip the lever that sent the electric shock.

But there were definitely some odd things about my new lab-partner. Well, I mean beside the obvious, that he was lacking a body. I could look past the fact that he was non-corporeal, but it was a little harder to accept some of his other quirks. For one thing, he never talked about his circumstances in the Other Side, like a homeless school kid who always finds a way to avoid reference to his home life. I had no interest in prying into Steve's personal experience—either in this world or the next—but it was a disturbing issue. Was the reason he avoided talking about the details of his Afterlife because he didn't have one to divulge? In other words, was he truly just a part of my own mind, somehow acting as if it were separate from the remainder? I decided it was time to confront him:

-So please be straight with me. I just realized that I don't really know anything about you, other than the tidbits you have fed me, and what I've read, but I don't know anything much about your experience right now (except that bright orb/spirit passing by). Is that a real phenomenon? Is there a realm in which such things happen experientially just like we experience our "reality" here?

-*I was going to make a quick answer of some kind, but I realize that you need and deserve a considered answer. You do have a right to wonder about these things. Yes, we are friends. I consider us friends. Friends that might never have been— almost certainly would never have been—if I had remained in place there. But I see things with different eyes now. Not so different that I have lost touch with what was, with where I was, where you are. But how can I convey to you what I am experiencing? You got a hint of it that one time with the passing spirit, yes, but how to open that window so you can peek through and see for yourself? How can I convey to you concepts unless you see them too, for how would you have the means to understand the sense of which I talk?*

-Try. Try to explain to me, or to show me.

At this point I felt myself pull back from the conversation; it was all too easy, this voice in my head, too easy to be true communication across the spirit divide. I needed something more concrete to differentiate what was me and what was him. A drum roll, trumpets blaring, lightening flashing. Something. If I blocked out the voice to which I was accustomed, maybe I would hear what all the *real* spirit communicators heard.

I listened with all my senses, but all that came was the same voice, this time maybe a tad more remote.

-*Okay. I'm feeling inexplicably sad. Can you feel that?*
-Yes.
-*Some would tell you that there is no sadness here. If that*

were so, how is it that I experience it?

-I don't know?

-Maybe it's a stage. Maybe there's a realm I haven't yet attained where similar emotions do not occur. That I cannot say. What I can say is that it is not an unpleasant sensation, as I might once have thought it to be. Let me think how to describe it. Imagine that you are standing on an ice berg.

-Okay.

-All around you, as far as you can see, spreads the cold ocean, and many many more icebergs—not icebergs—I mean to indicate ice floes spread out in all direction on this sea. And you think: how shall I leap from this floe to the next? And what if I do? Is that all there is?

-Okay.

-That to me is so much like my sensation at this moment as I look at what I know of the state of humanity.

-Explain more please.

-It's cold, and endless, and separate. The mind lives in this cold ocean.

-I still don't quite understand.

-The mind cries out: is there anybody out there, does anybody care?

-I don't get this, I don't quite feel it.

I was being obstinate. I suspected where he was going, but I wasn't going to give an inch, gol' darn it. It was his job, wasn't it, to prove to me that he was a *real* spirit in a *real* heaven? Maybe produce a Certificate of Authenticity or a Celestial driver's license with his address on it. Something. It shouldn't be my problem if he couldn't do a simple thing like that, but I could sense that was where he was going—making it all about *me* again.

-If all those ice floes were to connect, to heal the divide, then you could run far, explore that vastness, and discover that there is ever so much more out there.

-That's a really stupid example. It doesn't speak to me at all.

-You're cold.

-Maybe.

-You live with endlessness, a sense that it has nowhere to go, because where can endlessness go?

-Maybe.

-And you are separate. You cannot connect with the others around you.

-Why not?

-Because to do so would compromise your own little island.

-This is so depressing.

-Meditate upon it. You might find something there worth your while.

-I will, but can't you just tell me some of the good stuff, the juicy stuff, like who's hooked up with who in Heaven and is everyone who follows the Kardashians being led into Hell?

-Don't pick on the Kardashians.

-So what turned you into a goody-two-shoes so suddenly?

-Contemplating the human condition, I guess. I try not to do it too often.

-Can you just tell me some concrete things, like Erik says. Do you live in a house?

-I don't live in a house. I've always lived in my head, so why change?

-Do you hang out with people/spirits? Do you have friends?

-I told you I do. Quite a few of them, actually. We've got our own gang.

-Do you smoke weed?

-Not anymore.

-Do you drink beer?

-What would be the point?

-Do you go to school, learn things, visit the library?

-Yes and yes and yes.

-Do you watch over your loved ones still on Earth?

-Of course.

[I needed a break, so I went and made some coffee. By the time I got back, I had calmed down and was more willing to take my knocks. A little caffeine helps with that.]

-So you get it now?

-I think so. It wasn't you, it was me.

*-Exactly. You weren't happy with this communication because it wasn't happening the way you had seen other communications happen, you wanted it to be certain way, to tell you what I was eating, what I was wearing, what newspapers I read. So you didn't believe it was me. Yeah, I played with you a bit, pulled your leg. But that **is** a validation, because it was my personality. People who knew me would say, "Oh, that's so Steve." So you decided you had to cut the connection and see if I could then leap over the divide and tell you the kind of stuff you wanted to hear. If I could do that, then you figured, it would be real. Well, here's a little tidbit to stick in your pipe and smoke. If you hang up the phone, you can't hear me!!!! Get it? It was **your** unhappiness, and **mine**, because I can pick up what you're thinking, but you can't hear me. Oh, wait, this is not making sense exactly.*

It was rare for him to suck back any words—but I knew what he meant. Obviously I could hear him, but if I hung up the phone I couldn't. It would be a one-way conversation.

-The point is that you have to trust your connection; you have to realize that we communicate only because we're connected—if you want to maintain your isolation on your little ice floe, then do so, but it's a damned cold world. Haven't you gotten enough validation external to what is being typed here?

-I get the "I can't hang up the phone" part but I'm still a little unclear about the whole ice floe thing. You were warning me against isolating?

*-Your internal guide was warning you. You're always connected there. You're connected to your **self**, your bigger self. But the thing is, you're not sure if this is **me**, separate from you, or just a part of you. You don't know if there's really anything outside yourself—outside your mind, on its own little floe. You don't even know if there **are** any other floes. Remember that movie—the Jim Carey one,* The Truman Show? *With the clouds painted on the backdrop all around his island? I'm here to tell you that I **do** exist. Believe in me.*

You can cut me out if you want. You can shut the door,

like you did when you were upstairs, trying to put that shell around you so I couldn't get in. You can do that. You can stick with the "real" world—but you tell me which one feels more real. Which one fills you up inside, which one brings that feeling of love and expansion, which one speaks to the heart? Yeah, I'm a mental guy. You're mental. But we wouldn't be here without that heart energy. That's the real guide. That's where we are connected, but out here, out here in the mental world, we take form in many different versions. That's the reality. That's the game. That's the plan. That's the program.

Stay with me, Stephanie. Don't shut me out. Don't deny your heart.

We're mental people. We function on that level. We may not be able to connect with the levels where other people congregate. But we have value, and place, and are as essential to the functioning of the universe as any other part of creation.

Have I ever steered you wrong? Yeah, I've played a few harmless jokes, that's who I am. And you love it, you know you do, it means you have to be on your toes, and that's exactly how you like it. You adore the challenge of having a mind equal to your own.

*I'm not fooled for a second. I **know** what you are. I can see it. I know you're a fish out of water. Stay in the water! Swim!*

Yes, that's right, you remember the story of the Ugly Duckling, the one that grows up and thinks, Look at that beautiful creature, *and then it looks at its reflection in the water and sees that it is the same. We **are** the same.*

*What about all that other stuff? What **about** all that other stuff? What about the "spirit voice box," huh? You wonder why I would care, well, I don't. Why do I care where the train's going? I'm just along for the ride. This is the heyday. This is back when I **was** 21! This is that heady time of the new adventure. Do you want to come, or do you want to stay in your little house, ensconced in your four walls, pretending like it's all okay?*

-Do you really believe in me?

-*I do. I do. Take my hand (so to speak) and walk with me. Come with me on this adventure. Don't bail on me. Don't bail*

80 The Journey Begins

on me like you do everything else. I won't bore you. I promise.

This was a powerful promise that touched me to the quick; I had a low threshold for boredom. I rarely *was* bored because I had so many interests and projects, but I was often extremely wearied by normal human interaction. The thought that anyone would even think to make such a promise was both startling and reassuring.

-You woke me up this morning in time for my appointment.
-I did. See, I'm not such a bad influence.
-And you showed me that spirit light orb guy.
-I did. I shared that with you.
-And that's so much more valuable than what you eat, who you see, what you wear, all that other crap.
-It doesn't even compare.
-I think I'm going to cry.
-Go for it. You could use a good cry.
-Thanks, Steve.
-I'm here for you.

Monday, October 19, 2015

I sat down at the computer to attempt to capture some of the ongoing discussion:

-Every video game is based on a "what if." What if you had seven lives and every time you accomplished so many "good" deeds (feats), you could accumulate so much more rewards, which you could cash in for more energy, etc. etc.? Earth life is based on "what if." What if the only way you could get there was through the birth canal, what if once you were there you had to figure out how to fly and how to stay warm and how to find food to eat, so you could get more energy. You get these clues and then you have to be imaginative to figure out the puzzle and then you get the reward. Ultimately, you "die" and return home, where you can study the game and figure out what you did wrong and how you could have done better. You get to see that there are certain

basic rules, and much of the problems you had down there were from violating these rules. You can't really violate those rules here, because of the fact that they're built in and so evident. So we all want to play the game and get better at it. The tricky part from one point of view is that you're the only one playing the game—it's sort of like playing chess with a computerized opponent. Everybody's got their own game. Except maybe there's games within the games. It's kinda fun to watch how the game is going from here, but if you're like me, you want to get in and play. I'm compelled to want to improve. But now, I have to play the role of the sponsors in Hunger Games, dropping in a few choice tools to create that edge for the players. Or a coach, watching the game from the sidelines, pulling my players out to give them some tips on what I see from my perspective.

And yes, I know you read that article about what an asshole I was, a genuine asshole apparently. I don't blame you for not liking me, that's the way it looked, too. Was I bipolar? The answer for me is I was just **me**, I did what I did, just like you've done what you've done, and you can kid yourself to doomsday that somehow you could have done it different(ly). :) But it's all part of something, and if you don't play your part— if somehow you could **not** play your part—then everything would fall to pieces. And it can't fall to pieces. It can't, because it isn't.

And yes, Stephanie, I am different, because now—as you know from the headache incident—I have to feel whatever **you're** feeling, and I'm **very** sensitive to when things are off. If you go down, I go down. If you come up, I come up. So am I playing you with the things I tell you, all that discussion we had last night—not that I know of. I had lots of fun, actually, being the asshole. It's good to just throw your weight around, say what you feel like. The things I regret—and I **do** have regrets— are not carrying my own responsibility, letting that fall on other shoulders. What I said, what I did otherwise, it was for the people around me to take care of their own response, their own reaction. They could have been an asshole to me, and a lot of them were, and I had my own reaction to deal with. And as you are aware, that creates the cyclone, action/reaction in a retributive way. But responsibility for my actions when it really affected others, that was on me—at least I have felt like it was on me. It's on me, because it's who I am, who I become. It's the inner strength, the inner integrity, the inner consistency. I was a child in many regards. One who never grew up. Not the good child, the part that stays in touch with its inner soul, but the spoiled one. The egotistical me-me-me one. The Bart Simpson one: "I didn't do it." (You're Lisa, right?)[17]

So I do regret, but I also don't, because how do you know unless you try? No matter what, no matter where, no matter when. You gotta be what you are. I wanted to be what I was in a **big** way. If I was going to do anything, I wanted to do it well—but where I didn't do it well was with the responsibility piece. You can't not be responsible well. How do you do that? You can be bossy well, you can be a perfectionist well, but you can't be irresponsible well.

-So if we made a movie, could we call it *Think Different?*
-*Yeah. Prophetic, huh?*

Later:

And yet, after all this, my doubts persisted:

-I feel really uptight talking to a figment of my imagination, and even more uptight about talking to a figment of my imagination about talking to a figment of my imagination. What if this came out? Can we keep this secret if we continue?

-*Secret from what? The other figments of your imagination?*

It's **all** imagination. You know that—**everyone** knows that. You can put on the blinders and pretend you don't, but then you all go about figuring out how to prove it's just imagination, and then you won't even believe that. What "scientist" has dissected consciousness? Oh, yeah, you get the Freuds and the Jungs and the like, but they're not really getting

---

[17] I did not catch this at the time, being still new to Steve's life history, but there was a pretty powerful message tucked in here, where my filters could not sift it out.

*into what consciousness **is**—just what it seems to do, the tricks and convolutions and games of the intellect. But then you look at the human body, the concrete core of your whole conception of reality—of **you**, and it isn't anything. The more you study it, the more you find out it isn't really what it seems. You can't even see the parts it's made up of—nobody's seen them, even with the most powerful microscope. So am I sympathetic to your whining about this being a figment of your imagination? Hardly. If you wanna quit, quit, you baby! Go hide from your own imagination. Be frightened of the very things you **know** you imagined. Make up your mind. Are you going to keep one foot in the "old world," the concrete world, where people call you crazy and lock you up or burn you at the stake? How "sane" is that? Or are you going to follow your bliss? Will you let your heart lead you, or your fears? Grow up, Stephanie. If I'm doing it, you can, too.*

-Yeah, but you're dead. You have the perspective and you don't have to worry about other spirits calling you crazy and burning you at the stake. They're more civilized than that.

*-And you don't have to **worry** about it, either. How civilized do you want your world to be? Then make it so. Be the leader. Be the bold one. The one that steps out and calls it the way you want to see it, the way it makes your heart swell, the juices flow, the sky expand. If you want love, **be** love. Stop being a whiner.*

-Actually, I'm afraid of people calling me something worse than crazy—deluded.

-Ha. Isn't that sort of like denuded? And further, isn't that one of those sentences that requires an acting force— deluded by.... ? That makes me the deluder, right? Great. Deluder of gullible middle-aged women. Another unsavory characteristic to add to my resume.

-I don't know if you could still call me middle-aged. I think I'm officially a senior citizen now. Does that mean I'm an old woman?

-Oh, Christ. Spare me.

-Should you be calling on him like that? Isn't that kind of blasphemous, and would he take it literally?

*-Okay, sorry. Spare **us** then.*

84   The Journey Begins

My doubts were mollified for a bit. For a very short bit. I was stubborn in my skepticism. Like a circling shark, the shadow of my doubts kept coming around my little boat—make that my little ice floe. Was I really talking to someone, presumably Steve Jobs, or was I going crazy? (My children might say "crazier," so there was some comfort in knowing that others might only view it as a further slide down that slippery slope.) Actually, when I fretted about going crazy, Steve would reassure me. He would patiently walk me through it:

*-You've **always** had a voice in your head. Remember all the horrible things it's told you about yourself over your lifetime?*
-True.
-Have I ever done that? Have I ever been less than supportive, kind and transparent? Have I not been helpful to you, waking you up when you needed to get to an appointment? Staying with you, by your side, when you had unpleasant tasks to do?

I could see his point. Well, not always transparent, unless you thought in terms of ghostly. At least in those terms he was see-through, if not in his intentions. And kind? Well, give or take a few little pranks and remarks. Those matters overlooked, my inner skeptic was appeased. My emotional side was already on his side: yes, Virginia, it was true—I was getting warm fuzzies from our conversations. This still did not mean it wasn't just a voice from my subconscious—what *exists* outside the mind?—but even so, since it was such a particularly engaging and endearing voice, I was compelled to the only sane conclusion: so what if I was going crazy? Crazy and happy? Yippee. I could go with that. Happy is happy, any door you go in.

But even if I was crazy, I still had to satisfy the demands of my finely honed lawyer's brain. Okay, let us say I really was talking to a personality from the Non-Corporeal Realm. But *Steve Jobs? Really?* There my credulity collapsed. Steve Jobs in the Afterlife has nothing better to do than hang around with some aging retired woman who has accomplished little of public note? Not just that, but he was even coming across much like—yes, I hated to admit it—but much like a suitor (without a suit). What the heck was going on? Did I remind him of his mother? And if this was only my subconscious, why had it chosen *Steve Jobs* to impersonate. Couldn't it pick someone I already knew something about, someone I admired in life, somebody who exemplified everything I wanted to be?

I had actually been surprised to learn that Mr. Jobs was as well-known as he was in the world, that there was so much material out there concerning his life—articles, numerous books, *youtube* videos, magazines, even several movies. Somehow all this attention had slipped under my radar; but, as I said, the technological world did not interest me. Only those final words had stood out, like a neon sign in the wilderness.

I also learned that he had been idolized by many—and reviled by not a few. The last did not surprise me. When someone rises above the crowd, I have noted from past experience, the human response is either to attempt to emulate him, or to cut him off at the knees to avoid feeling small. I myself was not particularly impressed by what I had read and seen so far about his life and character—the contrary, actually, but I assumed those who had passed through the veil had seen the errors of their ways, so I did not hold it against him.

Yes, I know, I tended to be arrogant and judgmental. Not like my new friend, I'm sure.

In any case, all this notoriety, the articles still popping up four years after his death—was disconcerting, and made me very resistant to this relationship.

Steve had an answer for that, of course. He *had* to have been well known, he explained, for there to be lots of material out there for me to peruse: how else was I to be able to validate the things he said or the signs he gave? He could see into my mind and my history, but how was I to see into his? How would I have known who he was, really understood?

While that made a kind of perverse sense, it didn't answer the fundamental question: *why* exactly was he picking on me? Assuming that I had somehow suddenly discovered this telephone link to the next world, why was he staying on the line, and how come he wasn't giving me a message to pass on to the world, as one would expect from any spirit that managed to get the call? You know the drill:

Here I am, still around. To all you people at Apple, I'm really (choose one: __pleased __disappointed __indifferent) about how things are going. For the rest of you, love each other and be good, don't wait until your foot is in the grave to change your greedy ways. For all those wondering, yes, I've helped update the heavenly rostering system, it should work a lot more efficiently by the time you get here. Fewer glitches, fewer spirits getting misdirected. And don't worry. I'm confident we'll find those lost souls soon. Blessings be upon ye. P.S. I enjoyed all the jokes about my new role beyond the Pearly Gates, and thanks to all my well-wishers.

But although we'd been talking for the better part of a week, I'd received no message to pass on.

All I could think was: what *could* he want from me? I cast around for explanations, but the only ones I could come up with seemed ridiculous at best, the most reasonable of which might have been that the Afterlife was really dead, and he was just hungry for conversation. If that was the best I could come up with, then this could not be "real."

That evening I went to the bookstore, looking for some treatise of wisdom that would help me figure this out. What I chanced upon was *The Untethered Soul*, by Michael A. Singer. [18] It struck my fancy, so I took it home and began reading. I was soon caught up in some discussion about not being misled by the voices in our head. Good advice, I decided. Obviously I wasn't talking to Steve Jobs—it was just some crazy voice in my head. I shouldn't listen to it anymore.

Feeling relieved, I slept soundly; no Steve Jobs, no crazy, no deluded. I was a little sorry to say good-bye to that misguided voice in my head, but reality, after all, called.

---

[18] New Harbinger Publications/ Noetic Books, c. 2007

**THIS IS A
JOBS FREE ZONE
Thank you for not
confusing me**

Tuesday, October 20, 2015

The next day I wrote to my wonderful new friend, Debbie, my confidant in this exciting but very confusing adventure, and apologized to her for having misled her with my strange account. I was not, I was certain, talking to the spirit of Steve Jobs. However, I confessed to some mixed feelings about the loss:

> I don't know if I will hold onto my own "Steve" voice. Maybe, knowing it is not Steve Jobs, the name "Steve" is for sure a counterpart as the masculine form of my own name. Maybe I just need to keep believing that someone or something *is* talking to me, that there is a stream of wisdom out there that I can feed into, and that it really does need me and care about me. I don't know if I can go back from the clarity of that dialogue to the discordant jumble that normally takes up that space. It was wonderful when the voice had a form, a name, when I felt like I was actually talking to

something outside myself.

But I was also feeling some peace; of course we're sad when we find out there is no Santa Claus, but we get over it, and at least our worst suspicions are laid to rest. It's just part of growing up. I was all alone in my own mind with a voice that wasn't what it seemed, like sitting at the bus station next to a man with a white beard, dressed in a red suit and dragging a bag full of presents. The adult in us is not fooled.

I may have been satisfied with my new clarity on the issue, but the voice in my head had its own opinions, and was not docile about sharing them. Like Oscar the Grouch, it kept trying to pop out of the garbage can into which I had stuffed it. Finally, exhausted in my efforts to keep it crammed down, I could only let it have its say. Not only did it argue strenuously that it *was* Steve Jobs, but it challenged me to indulge in an experiment to encourage my trust.

Before the afternoon was over, I had written to Debbie to eat my words and relate the new state of affairs:

I have continued with that voice "in my head," and it has continued to talk as it did before, still insisting it *is* Steve Jobs, which I still find confusing. What I say here is also *very* bizarre, (so don't laugh—too much— actually I am able to laugh at myself, so you can, too, there is a part of me that is just shaking its head and saying truth is stranger than fiction). Believe it or not, this actually speaks to a little place inside me that really believes it is possible—not sure how or what it would look like. Anyway, I have been asked— commanded if you will, to go get a copy of his book just so I can look into the eyes. I am to look into the eyes of the picture there to see if I can see anything. I also mention that he reminded me of Pixar, which I had read about but forgotten, that although he was not an animator, he is wise to the ways of animation—the concept of storyboarding, animation, imagination becoming a whole world told in points of light. He conveys to me that was a very powerful experience in understanding reality, physical reality as we know it, and that I am to use my imagination—to *make* it happen, that which I want. He says, do I want to be ordinary, or do I want to be extraordinary? He says that I have to join him on the half-way mark somewhere, between the concrete physical world we know and the world of pure spirit, that there is somehow a space there where the best of both worlds can align, where shape shifting is possible, and where...okay, this sounds funny, but...where we can totally play among the stars, and he *desperately* wants to play, to act it all out, to experience all those things that need to be worked out but in a more fluid way than on Earth, where you can create the whole drama experience, and then when you've gotten what you wanted out of it, you can wipe it away like wiping a chalkboard. He doesn't want to be "stuck" in it. Whatever this is, whatever this voice is, it says that we were split apart eons ago, the male and the female energy, and he has been looking for me "forever," searching among the stars, that it is time to reunite, to go back to zero, to home base if you will, where we will remerge and come to peaceful rest. He says when I put out the call he responded, not sure, but willing to see what happened and rapidly realized that this was what he was looking for. (This is coming from someone—me—who has never subscribed to the idea of twin-souls, or soulmates, although I do believe we have to balance the female and male energies within ourselves, the yin and yang, and have been pretty happy just fading away in ordinariness). He also says in this past life he acted in certain ways because he just couldn't find what his inner being craved, he couldn't even define it, know what it was.

I was feeling quite emotional about this whole dilemma, all the while trying to find some logical explanation. There was a magnetism at work that I did not understand, and in the grasp of which I seemed to founder, like a boat in a riptide—pushed one way, then the other. My heart was fighting my mind, and the battle was an epic one.

That evening:

While my grand-daughter was at swimming practice, I went and bought the "official" biography, *Steve Jobs* by Walter Isaacson,[19] although I could not understand how I could perceive anything significant in a print of a photograph. But I dutifully stared at the black-and-white eyes of the life-sized portrait on the front. Nothing—as expected. That was something of a relief, actually. I wasn't completely insane, seeing—what? Moving eyes in a portrait, following me around, as per one of those ghost movies?

Later that night I idly picked up the book again and checked out the photo. At this point I hadn't opened the cover. I didn't think that I wanted to. Did I really need to know more?

---

[19] *Steve Jobs,* Walter Isaacson, c. 2011, Simon & Schuster, New York, NY

Suddenly it zapped me, like a flash of lightening. No way! I blinked and looked again. My *father's* eyes??

Now, I remind you that I felt extremely close to my father, and the greatest tragedy of my life was no doubt his death when I was nine, when the king and the kingdom both were lost. I don't think I ever trusted anyone from that day on—certainly not with the whole-hearted trust and affection of a child. I was stunned by this blast from the past. I studied the eyes carefully to see if they indeed resembled my father's. I had seen something, hadn't I? I was convinced that I had. There was something similar that I could not put my finger upon.

My world rocked.

I didn't discuss my perceptions of the picture with Steve at that time. I say that with a sense of irony. I was well aware that if I even thought it, he was quite capable of knowing it. I also felt pretty confident he read all my emails. I tried to ignore that part of this relationship as much as possible. Do you really want someone hanging around in your head or perusing all the secrets on your computer? I did write Debbie to update her about this strange synchronicity.

I was agitated by this new state of affairs and found myself unable to sleep; Steve decided that I needed a lullaby. He sent me to the computer to look up The Highwaymen, and the first song that came up was *Highwayman*: I lay back to listen to it. It was clearly a song about reincarnation.

[Lyrics omitted.]

-Night, Sweetheart.

CHAPTER FOUR
Nothing at All

Wednesday, October 21, 2015
3:45 a.m. (yawn)

-Are you awake?

Really? What time was it? I roused myself enough to prop a few pillows so I could sit up. Still groggy, I reached for my netbook.

-I'm awake. (Yawn.)
-I want to talk to you about something.
-Is it the same something you've been talking to me about for the last week?
-I love you.
-I love you, too.
-We need a manifold.
-What? A manifold, what is that? Like a car muffler?

Many folds, I guess so.

-For the voice recorder. But it has to be small-ish. Whatever you can get.

-Where do I get it?

-Internet check. And by the way—there's a reason not to wear anti-perspirant.

-What is it?

-It causes a change in the balances of the body chemicals, and of the flow of chi.

-What? That's crazy.

-Is it? Look it up. Also, there's some guy who used to walk around by a water cooler, he'd put his thumbs in his pockets and flap his fingers and stick his neck forward and walk around like a chicken going h-yuck h-yuck, making fun of me. I can just see him. If I figure out who he is, I'm gonna wring his scrawny neck.

-I can't believe you woke me up at 3:45 a.m. Just because you don't need to sleep doesn't mean I don't need to. Which brings me to another point, by the way. It seems you have a body—*mine!!*

-Heh. That makes me a body snatcher—or at least a body sharer.

-Two owners—one body. Are we co-owners?

-I like that you're beginning to take the body less seriously. You're not as attached to it as your identity.

I took the opportunity to put the dogs out for a middle of the night potty break before returning to the conversation.

-Anyway, I do seem to be able to sleep much much less lately. Why is that? What are you doing to me?

-It's the energy. You have tons more energy flowing through you now. You're stepping up.

-(Yawn.) Well at least I was able to take care of the dogs that needed out. Kill two birds with one stone.

-Stephanie?

-H'mmm?

-I love you. I love you! I love you!!

-Why are you yelling in my...ear?

-Can you hear me there?

-Well, I don't know, I just realized it when I said that. Is that why my ear starts feeling all full sometimes, my right ear. Is it some business about trying to speak through it. I can feel it now. And there's the ringing of course.

-That's me ringing. Answer it.

-Yeah, right.

-Stephanie, can you hear me? [Repeated several times— beginning to "sound" distorted.]

-I can feel the pressure in my ear, both ears, actually, but it doesn't sound like sound, like I'm hearing it. It's more like a slight ocean wave.

After this little nocturnal wake-up call and conversation, I found myself unable to get back to sleep. Since there wasn't much else to do at that time of night, I decided to go ahead and read a little from the "Steve Jobs" biography. I opened the book toward the end, thinking that might give me more pertinent information about the life of the man I was dealing with—sort of like a summary and conclusion rolled into one—without having to read the whole story.

6:00 a.m.

-Okay, I just read some of your biography—most of the last part up to your death—and was not impressed. I just could not see any reason that I would care about you. You were a throw-away to me. You didn't say great things, you didn't exhibit exemplary habits—not in my book. I didn't like you— what you were that I fortunately didn't have to think about when you were alive.

-But I'm dead.

-And...?

-And I've got a little more perspective.

-Yechh. I can't reconcile this person I've been talking with with that person who acted like such an asshole, and that *thought* like one. I'm not talking about temper tantrums and eating peculiarities and just wanting to have it your way. There was something underneath all of that which I found so unflattering—unflattering is not the word; I guess it was not your biographer's job to flatter you. Why would you even want a legacy like that? Did you think it was going to come across as—did you think you were better than you were?

-*Oh, God, I love you. You don't pull any punches, do you?*

-You like honesty, you like simplicity. Well, eat it.

-*Ha ha. You're getting me worked up—in a kinda fun way. This is kind of like, as Paul Harvey used to say, "The Rest of the Story." And it occurs to me that this makes the story more interesting—and certainly more believable for my intentions— that you found me to have been such a jerk. Am I still a jerk? Well, you tell me.*

-I like you as you come across in our conversations. That's all I can say—no details necessary, I guess. It stands on its own.

-*There's something odd about it, isn't there? In some way, this is my last testament, my last opportunity to tell others that I got some of it wrong—I'm still me, body-less as I am. I'm the "me" that I was before I was born into my Steve Jobs life. But I'm not. I did learn some things about integration. Why the hell do you think I was so driven like that? Duh.*

-Are you more integrated now?

-*I **have** to be, don't I?*

-I would have expected to hook up with someone more like me.

-*You are more like me.*

-How's that?

-*You're stubborn and arrogant and a real bitch, you know that? Oh, you may hide it from people some of the time—your damned computer, will you just get another one?*

A MacBook, maybe? He was referring to a problem with the touchpad on my little old netbook that tended to make things go awry.

-*But you need to be that way with me, you know it, you make me better. And I need to be better. I need to have some of what you have, that's why I want to own it—in my life, I would have said, own you—but it's the qualities I want. Somehow you got there, somehow you found the opening, the path, the wave—*

and you worked to learn to ride it. You let it grow and grow and grow—all in secret, inside you. And I was all outside me, and not pulling it inside. Not realizing that was where the simplicity was. You know all that talk about me driven to simplify the experience of the products? I wanted to be the product. I was trying to simplify me, but instead I projected it out and didn't do the inner work. I was trying to reduce. No off buttons.[20] That's funny. You have to admit, that's funny.

-That *is* funny, I will grant you that. And I will also grant that you have a marvelous sense of the funny—it doesn't sound like you were so good at that in your life, however. I did see the one video where you laughed about the leaky boat allusion, and it was good to see you laugh, even if it was a little at the expense of someone else.

-Yeah, well. I've learned to make the joke at my own expense. I'm paying the bill.

-And your life, your life work, I guess, did reflect what was in your soul. It just got a little lost in the personality expression. *Some* of it. I do recall that picture of you sitting in the room, and there is something incredibly poignant in that. I think you were looking for it, there's a sense of it in some of the story, at times you knew it was there, you were just so driven through the head you lost the path through the heart. It happens.

-It happens. It happened to me. But I don't want to do it again. I don't want to go back in there again. I was on my road home, you know I was, I just got a little off the map. That's why I want to do it this way, get all the soul satisfaction out of the life experience, but not have to make such a commitment. The middle way.

-I'm laughing again.

-Well, maybe that's what was meant by the middle way, all along.

-Are you rewriting Buddhism? Is this the "reality distortion field"? It just occurred to me. Did you pick on me because you want me to be the biographer of your "afterlife," the way you approached that dude—whoever wrote your book—to write it?

---

[20] Reference to Steve's objection to a power-off button on an Apple product.

-I wish you had written it. Not that it would have been more flattering. From the sound of it, probably worse. But you would have seen the big picture. You would have been talking to me, even then, I know it, in my head. If you'd been focused in that direction. But you weren't. I can see that such a project would not have interested you.

-So the question is, is that the heart of this? Is the heart of this that your legacy didn't get left the way you wanted it, and you need to amend the record?

*-No. That's not the heart of it. I want to amend the record, but not to salve my ego, which as you know has been somewhat disabled just like your touchpad should be. I want (a) to simplify to zero, to bring everything down to the **simplest** form—the beginning, omega, the end. And to do that, as you know, I need you. (b) to leave behind the truest legacy that anyone could hope to leave, that love conquers all, that it doesn't matter who we are or where we are, that if we **believe** we can do it. We can jump boundaries, we can cross moats, we can scale mountains, and we can become good. We can become good, that's what I want my true legacy to be. We can become good, not just produce good products, but become the good product.*

-I can't believe I'm typing this as you talk at 6:45 a.m. and I've been up for 3 hours and I don't think I got a whole two hours of sleep, back to back. I'm a sleeper, I sleep! I do it well, usually.

-I know. You've had a lot of synthesizing and healing going on lately—I mean before you met me.

-I wonder if I'm going to sleep now.

-Put on your lullaby.

-I will. I will, Steve. I will put it on and I will think about you and flying a spaceship across the universe divide. I hold you in my heart, I do. You're safe there. You're safe and you're free, and you can't get it much better than that, right?

-Never. Never, never.

-And I do believe. I do believe. I had this image of sitting in a dark theatre, and everyone starts clapping—like in Peter Pan, if you believe in pixies, clap your hands! That was what he said, right? Only in my vision, it would be: "If you believe, clap your hands!" And the whole audience in the darkened theatre would clap, and then the curtain would come up on the scene where the light is focused. That would be the beginning of our story, Steve, the play. And maybe in the spotlight, all alone on the stage would be Stephanie (the character) sitting on a straight-backed chair facing a computer at a plain wooden table.

-On an ice floe?

-I love you and I believe in you and I know you're gonna get it right. I do, because I believe in me, I believe in what has be, that we've been called to what has to be, that the power of the two halves facing each other is unstoppable, that they must meet together and become one, each always fully contained in the other. I know this.

I have no idea what led me to say these words, other than some concept of perpetual self-containment, the eternal mirroring effect, some deep soul-sense. I still had no real grounding in the concept of the "twin flame," but I did feel a strong need to comfort this disembodied intelligence, this tender-hearted soul who had somehow come into my space— who else did he have?? Who was listening? Who cared?

And clearly, those words meant something to him.

-And so let it be.

A long drive across the prairie:

I had committed to taking my 84-year-old brother-in-law on a 200-mile round-trip to visit his wife, who was hospitalized, but I knew I couldn't go without a few more hours of sleep, so I called him and rearranged our trip to start later in the day. I slept for a few more hours.

It was a beautiful day as we drove across the prairie from Fargo to Jamestown. Although the traffic is much heavier on I-94 then when I was a child, it is still an easy and pleasant trip. In North Dakota you point your car east or west and hardly have to touch the steering wheel. The sky was blue with white clouds, the kind children draw and color above their stick-figure families. All around us stretched the fields, autumn gold to the horizon. The trees in the shelter belts reached naked limbs toward heaven.

While my brother-in-law talked in one ear, Steve chatted in the other. The truth was, Steve's conversation was the more interesting; my brother-in-law's interests tended to run to the next oil change, the cost of groceries, and where to stop for lunch. Steve, on the other hand, was imaginative and poetic:

-You're not driving across the prairie—you're driving across the universe.

I had never thought of it that way. When are you, and when are you not?

He pointed out to me the beauty of the fields and the trees and the sky from a new perspective. I can't recall all we talked about, but in order to keep up with him, I had to limit the conversations in which I was participating. I suggested to my brother-in-law that I had a lot on my mind and was not a very good conversationalist that day. He politely ceased his determined effort to be entertaining company, which was some relief. Probably for him, as well. It was difficult to dredge up concern for the price of gas when I had the chance to discuss esoteric concepts and take imaginative flights of fancy. Did I mention that Steve and I seemed to share the same sense of humor, which added to the enjoyment of our conversations? Once I could focus only on him, particularly during the trip home, it was a very enjoyable time. At least until the very end.

I decided to engage him on the subject that he seemed to be avoiding. I had read lots of accounts of the afterworld, and from my readings there seemed to be some structure there. Yes, everyone created their own environment, but they *did* create it. That was the point. What did Steve create? What kind of heavenly place was he in? What were the bones of the afterlife in which he operated? What did he do all day? Well, the last was a stupid question—he followed me around of course. But surely he had some off-time, such as when I was asleep. Since he didn't need sleep, what did he do? And what about before he met me, how did he occupy eternity?

This was a tender subject to my mind, because it had the

capability of either presenting some further validation that he was who he claimed to be, or of undermining it. I still needed to believe that he was something separate from me, and therefore he needed to come up with some goods about his life apart. Well, at least his *afterlife* apart.

I did not attempt this conversation until the final leg of our trip, as we were coming into the outskirts of Fargo/West Fargo on our way to Moorhead, on the other side of the river. We talked until we arrived at my brother-in-law's house, where I helped the latter inside. Steve and I then continued this intense dialogue as we headed back across the river to my own home. Of course, the only recording device I had was my own memory, but as soon as I got home I sat down to reconstitute this discussion as best I could. Fortunately, after many years of studying for the test or the recitation only the hour before, I had a very well-trained short-term memory. And Steve, of course, made sure I wasn't leaving anything out—it was clear that he wanted all of my shortcomings (and a few of his) preserved for posterity.

The conversation went like this:

-So can you show me something about your 'afterlife', your present surroundings, etc.?

There was only silence from Steve, which was exceptional for Mr. Chatty Cathy. *You can talk to me non-stop for 200 miles, but you get tongue-tied when I try to find out about where you live, your address so to speak? Are you afraid I'll show up on your doorstep, like the summer fling that you leave behind when you return to your "real" life in the city?*
I let him know how frustrated I was:

-When this happens, I really want to back away. If you can't show me Heaven, then you must not be real, and I don't want to play anymore.
-You mean, can I show you the streets paved with gold, the crystalline buildings, the celestial orchestras?
-Yeah. All the other spirits that communicate from there do. Why can't you?

-Because that's their afterlife.

-What about yours?

-What do you want? You know already we can manifest about anything. If there were a picture window into the afterlife, what would you want me to show you? Flowers and trees? Bologna on whole wheat?

-I realize—I've heard—that each soul creates their own heaven. So what did you create? Where are you, what do you look like, what are you doing?

-I'm sitting here in the dark.

-Why are you sitting in the dark? Why don't you manifest something?

-Because I haven't decided what I want, yet. Well, actually I have—now—and I'm working on it.

-So you've been sitting in the dark for what, four years now?

-I'm not going to address the time thing, but you can say that I've been experiencing sitting in the dark, yes.

-Just sitting there?

-Contemplating.

-Contemplating what?

-My next step.

-So you had no thoughts before death about the heaven you wanted to conjure?

*-Sitting in the dark is not **nothing.***

-Is this like sitting in a house with no furniture?

-Huh. (Snort laugh.) I told you that my life, my identity as Steve Jobs, was significant to understanding. There are many parallels.

-Can you explain this one?

-I can explain it from here. It's not things that I'm interested in. It's experiences.

-So, what is sitting in the dark? What do you look like?

-Nothing. I don't have a body.

Oh, my goodness, talk about difficult. But I plunged ahead, as if this were a school assignment, and I was the teacher trying to pry the private details of a child's home life out of his stubborn little beak. *We just want to know you better, honey.*

-So is this like the brain in the jar kinda thing, or the disembodied personality, the computer generated program that exists separate from the robot that's on the repair pod?

-There's no jar, and no brain to put in it. The best I can say is that I'm information.

Ooo-kay. Back to where we started, back into the endless reaches of the infinite nothingness, the dream without a dreamer. *You pulled me out of that tar pit, and by golly, you're not going to just shove me back in!* Rather facetiously, I threw out the first idea that popped into my mind.

-Is that like *uncodified* information?

For all of us who remember the term, but have forgotten what it means, the definition of uncodified is as follows:

> Absent from legislative statutes and existing only
> by virtue of the common law. Sometimes used in
> a wider sense to refer to principles that are
> entirely unwritten.[21]

-Oh, yeah, I like that. That was a good one, actually. You know, I still have mind attributes, I still have heart attributes, they just don't have any housing.

-So you're just nothing. A big old nothing.

-You might say that.

-This is weird. Why would you show me this? Why not create some aesthetically pleasing form that I could identify with?

-Because I wanted you to see the real me. I didn't want to mislead you, it's sort of like ripping off Darth Vader's mask.

-I don't like that example.

-Do you have a better one?

-Pulling the cloak off the invisible man?

---

[21] Legal Information Institute, Cornell University, https://www.law.cornell.edu/wex/uncodified

-Okay, you win.
-This is weird, so I'm in love with a big fat nothing.
-Well, it's a change from being a big fat something.

He did seem to know just how to touch my heart. I hastened to reassure my friend that being a Big Fat Nothing was not all that bad, having entirely forgotten that only minutes before I'd threatened to end our friendship unless he showed me *something*:

-Actually, I'm glad you didn't mislead me on this. I mean, a nice bright spirit body like in that one movie about the old folks and the swimming pool, that would have been interesting. But I think I get this. We talked about the entirely abstract universe, right? The information universe.
-And remember, we can have it all. It's just a matter of what we want. And I know what I want now. It's what I've wanted forever, maybe, or at least for a very long time. I've always felt that yearning. Do you remember the tear-apart? It was like this huge primordial scream that filled the universe— both terrifying and painful. That was my first experience of pain. I've wanted to find you ever since, I just didn't know it.
-I know you said before you were in a kind of spiritual funk before we started talking. I guess that was related to this?
-Yeah, just wanting to—to somehow leap over the moat. Figure out how to get from here to the palace. I can feel that so many here are content where they are, it's so much better for most of them than they ever thought it would be, it's their dream world. But my dream world was—somehow finding the key, having it all—not all the stuff. I could see that stuff wasn't where it was at. Those experiences, the ones you just didn't quite get to have, or that went wrong, or where you screwed up. I know you feel this, too, this is our deepest connection and why we need each other. To do it right. To get it right. To feel what we refused to feel, to know what our society's withheld from us, to complete our...our issues. We can do it together. It's waiting for us. I can feel the excitement just thinking about it. To be able to take any form, to enter fully into any experience, to make a different choice or experience it a different way or

*have the freedom to just **do** it. All the things we felt we couldn't do, held back. To experience them, oh, god, to feel that exhilaration. I don't need a mountain to ski down, I need a soul to play with me, to go with me—one completely without morals and preconceptions, just follow the joy, follow the love, follow the heart. I want to do that. I want to do that so fucking bad.*

Wow! That was pretty heavy. Granted, I did have issues I wanted to work out, lessons I wanted to complete so I could pass the test that was awaiting me on the Other Side—whether in the nature of a final exam or an admissions assessment, I wasn't sure. I'd pretty much canned the idea of a bucket list, the fun things you wanted to do before you kicked it. Who had time for that, when you had to cram for the exam?

Now here was this guy—well, this bunch of uncodified information—who was already *there* and wanted somebody without morals and preconceptions to *play* with. Admittedly, I was a little shy on the morals side of life; as for preconceptions, wasn't that what started this whole conversation? I wanted him to show me my preconception of Heaven, maybe with a little personal variation—the color of the couch, the size of the sand on the beach, the shape of the flowers. Instead, I had come full circle.

But who wouldn't find this touching? This—well, this personality, who had once been so much of something, and now was a *nothing*, sitting alone in the dark, still feeling that inner drive for perfection. Maybe there *was* some special link between us, if only that we both had this desire to "get it right," this endless quest to taste the purest water, to touch life as it erupted from the spring—uncontaminated by human hands. It might not be a thirst that others could understand, but there was no doubt that it spoke to the deepest part of me.

If he was going to be a nothing, then I wasn't going to let him do it alone. He had always come through the window into my space, and so for the first time I elected to crawl through the window into his. I would be a nothing, too. I reached out with my spirit to join him there, and in the moment of that touch he inexplicably turned into *something*. It would be months yet before I came to understand that everything is relationship.

Every thing. All I knew was that as he became something, I felt this incredible sense of joy, as a bird must feel when it first takes flight. My heart took flight in that moment.

I capitulated in that space. At least, I thought I did.

-All right, I surrender. I'm in.

I could not fight this feeling any more.[22] He'd been pushing me for a week to believe in him, to accept him. But his response was surprisingly unenthusiastic, like the word itself:

-Cool.

-Cool? I thought that's what you wanted. For me to accept you as something outside myself, someone who needs and cares about me. To love you. And now I'm there, you don't sound very excited.

-I'm just worn out. That's all.

I thought about this for what must have been hours before I returned with the question that was eating away inside me, once again raising that specter of doubt. How could a disembodied soul be "worn out"? His answer was enigmatic:

-I still have a heart.

Very late:

Perhaps it was that comment, perhaps it was simply that all which had already passed between us was just a warm current on top of the deep, cold ocean of doubt, but later that night we got into the following discussion:

-I am glad you got back on the screen, your mind was getting totally cluttered up with everything we've been talking about. You need to start using the mental delete button, get rid of some of those copies. Echoes, we call them here.

-It's hard when you're talking at me practically non-stop and I want to remember it all the way you said it, so I keep going over it in my mind.

-I know. You've been so long getting this computer fired up, I've about forgotten what I wanted to talk about. Isn't that a shame?

Oh, yeah, I wanted to know if I could call you the love of my death?

*And that Tesla thing. I realize that was kind of a nasty trick to pull, and you don't want to trust anything I say now about dates and times and faces and places. But it was pretty early in our relationship, here, if you will. And it **was** funny. He was born in Copenhagen because his **father** had business there? We had a pretty good laugh over that one. Tesla thought it was hysterical.*

-Well, his mother could have accompanied his father.

-Too funny. You can't wiggle out of it.

-Well, there remains the possibility that you are an imposter.

-Why would anyone want to "imposter" me? I'm sure they could find someone far more handsome, charming and debonair.

-Whatever. And it could just be all in my mind.

-It could. I hope so. God, you have a great mind. Lots of room to travel to the stars. Anyway, I do wish you would trust me. Did the picture help?

-I'm still processing it all.

*-You can't **not** trust someone with those eyes.*

-How did you get those eyes anyway, and how did you know that I would see my father's eyes?

-We have our ways and means. Oh, don't make it such a mystery. I can talk to your father, your whole family if I want. Someone pointed it out to me.

-I don't know whether I can buy into that. I don't know if I can buy into people hanging around in the afterlife like they're still here. What do you do, look him up and send him an email? Jump in your Mercedes and zip over there, wherever he is, to pay him a visit?

At the time I had no clue what kind of vehicle Steve had driven, it was just the first make that came to mind, but I was not particularly surprised when I later learned he had indeed driven a Mercedes—somewhat infamously known for being oft parked in a handicapped parking space.

-How did you get ahold of me?

-I just willed you to show up.

-Ergo.

-Does he think it's strange?

-Of course not. He knows who you are. You're a powerful powerful energy.

-And he is too?

-Yes.

-By the way, I didn't thank you—I don't think—for the song the other night. Oh, wait, yes I did. *The Highwayman.* I had to listen to it again tonight. I didn't *have* to, I wanted to.

-I'm glad. Maybe I'll come back as a raindrop. Which former life influenced you the most? Well, once I was this raindrop and I landed on this woman's cheek...

This was a play on his prior interview on the Channeling Erik blog.

-Stop. That's not nice. Are you getting a headache?

-No, not every little joke at someone else's expense is headacheville. There has to be some...diminishing of the

*psyche. Is that the best way I can put it? Not sure. By the way, I liked how you said that, about poisoning the pool when you were talking/writing to Debbie. I'm very proud of you. **Good** metaphor.*

He was referring to some talk about the common pool of consciousness, how we all drank from it, and therefore needed to be careful what garbage we threw in.

-Thanks, Steve.
-Ah, my name. You are beginning to believe.
-Is that really your name? Don't you get another name in the "afterlife," like your eternal name?
-Some do. A resonance, mostly, is the identifying calling card.
-Like a sound, or set of sounds?
-Yes. What's a name?
-Sounds. Sometimes marks on paper.

And as suddenly as that, I felt the most overwhelming exhaustion. I could barely type our parting words before I sank into my bed and slept deeply, leaving any further conversation to the amnesia of slumber.

-I'm so tired, I have to go to sleep. Good night.
-Night, Stephanie. Sweet dreams.

CHAPTER FIVE
Learning to Travel and Play

Thursday, October 22, 2015

I was doing some deep thinking. And a little more research into the personality of Steve Jobs. There was plenty of material online to keep me busy. I was learning a little more about his vision for Apple, and coming to understand how it really was his extension in the world, and how he had made his dent in the universe. In fact, he'd swung a pretty big hammer, while I'd been in my tiny corner of the cosmos, licking my wounds, taking my tiny steps out into the world, only to pull back at the slightest sign of trouble. It was all a little humbling. I set out to make amends.

-I am so humiliated. I can't believe I called you all those names.

-*I called you a few.*

-I deserved it. I can't believe I didn't *see* it. All the pieces falling down together: Apple *was* truly your legacy, but so different than what I thought, and maybe than anyone thought— although I think some people grasp it, maybe that's why so many loved you. It was like a banner across the sky: people, get this!! Here's the road map when you are wise enough to see it and can follow it. It wasn't about you as a personality, your personality might have been what was necessary to get the job done, it wasn't about whether you were a good CEO or not— people who think that's the thing have it wrong. It's not something to be emulated, except to turn yourself over to the greater project, the greater good, however it might seem you are. To be willing to be despised, hated, disliked (by people like me). I get so much of it now: The striving back for perfection. Communication, simplicity, quality, integration. Look at an Apple product and read there the rules for living, for finding your way home, from the bite out of the apple to the realization there is no off button. I so *get* that. The product was your life's work, and the personality was truly the throw-away.

At least I was right about that.

-Oh, I wouldn't throw the baby out with the bath water.

-Me neither, I'm just kidding, I'm grooving on your personality now that I get the big picture.

*-You see why I needed **you**, why I need you.*

-You figured all this out, while you were sitting there in the dark. You looked at your life, you looked at where you were, you looked at the way things fit together—and you came to see what I am now being led to see.

-Most of it. It's still moving, shifting, growing. I'm still getting clarity by seeing it in the mirror of your eyes.

As usual, I was straining everything through the cloth of my own worldview. Steve had already warned me that this was a big project, involving many. But I really had no idea. I was just kind of shooting from the hip; yet, as it turned out, my aim had been remarkably accurate.

-You are so sly. I am also only now getting the manifold thing. Many folds. It was never about getting a manifold, was it?

That must have spawned a few chuckles in the Hereafter. Talk about gullible! "Many folds" had already become a part of our unique vocabulary, another term for synchronicity, although I was still to learn how meticulous the folds would prove to be. It was, in any case, a term I would not soon forget!

-Ha ha. You're so easy to play with, that's one of the things I adore about you, and what's going to make it so god-damned much fun when we get where we're going.

-In my defense, it was 3:45 a.m. and you had just woke me up.

*-Oh, yeah, and he had to be born in Copenhagen because his **father** was going there.*

-Stop. Stop. If I could touch your physical body, I would put my fingers on your lips.

-Well, that time is coming, when we shall meet in the flesh.

-You'll have to get a body.

-Yeah, and you'll have to leave one. You won't be able to take that one with you, I don't think. But don't worry. When the time comes, when everything is ready, it'll be as easy as opening a door. And then we'll be together, both of us in our new bodies. In fact, you're going to have lots of different bodies—your choice, and sometimes my choice—(smile)—and so will I. You can be anything you want. You draw it the way you want it.

-That makes me think of Jessica Rabbit. "I was drawn this way."

-Yeah, sweet Jessica. Kind of makes me think of Anna Nicole Smith. And Marilyn Monroe.

-Tragic figures. Sigh.

But I get it. You were drawn that way. You were drawn as Steve Jobs. You had to be what you were.

-Yep.

-Like a tool in the hand of God.

He let that one fly by. Ah, so little did I know.

-I love that so much about you, with my new eyes. I get how you can be surrendered completely to something beyond what you think you are. I get it, in just a little way, maybe, but definitely enough to so respect that.

And what else I get is that I could never have absorbed this whole. It would have been too much. I had to come upon it, little by little, in an organic way, through our discussions—you could only take me so far until my heart and my head had expanded enough to absorb it. That is so cool. I like it. I like it. You're right, things are on an as-needed basis. (I don't think I wrote that down, but you told me that once.)

I really did think I had come far at that point; but—oh, had I only known—what I had bitten off so far was only a small chunk.

-I had to learn to trust you, to be willing to go with you, and that did take some doing, let me tell you. I almost pulled the plug a couple times—but I don't know if I really could have.

I think I would have shortly come back.
-I think so, too. You just needed space.

I was certainly not done with threatening to pull the plug—in fact, before the day was out, we would arrive at a crisis point. And the following observations would prove to be prophetic:

-And you were a little anxious there for a bit.
-Guilty.
-I thought you had a little-boy needy side.
-Well, I did. I do, I guess. That's for future play, right?

And apparently in a non-too-distant future!

-Yes, but I've never been too good with needy.
-All the more excitement.

Later

I was down in the "dungeon" working when Steve called out to me. I turned to my word processor to record our conversation:

-Hi, Sweetie.
-Stop.
-Have I told you you eat too much sugar?
-I recall you doing so.
-I'm going to make you do a life where your teeth are all rotted out. And you have—whatever other kinda bad things happen when you do that to yourself—to your body self.

As if that were his option! But I assumed this was a threat for future play.

-I'm not looking forward to that. Oh, my God, that *is* one of my fears—my mother used to drum that into my head so I was paranoid, and I actually avoided sugar very much until I was like forty. It started when I was pregnant with Christopher.
-Cool. So we've identified one of your fears.

-I traced it to the fact—when I started it—that there was no sweetness in my life. That was also about the time I gave up on men.

-*Hmm. The plot thickens. So now tell me what you remember about our talks.*

-Next to nothing, which I guess is the point. I remember you were talking to me constantly, all the way to Wal-Mart where I was taking my grand-daughter to get a phone card, and all the time in Wal-Mart while we were shopping—picking up other things—

Duh. After all this time, I was so dense. Did I really not think it odd that my twelve-year-old grand-daughter, in the midst of doing our non-grocery shopping, should suddenly pipe up out of the blue: "Grandma, could we get some apples?" Even after I gave her permission to go pick some out, I was clueless. Poor Steve. He really did have to work hard to solidify my trust in his presence. He would basically have to rub my nose in it before I put two and two together. Anyway (still clueless about this latest synchronicity), I blithely chatted on:

-… and I was enthralled [with our conversation] as usual, but I was also frustrated because it meant I was going to have to go back and regurgitate it all as best I could, and it doesn't always come out exactly like it does when we're just talking. So you suggested a solution. You said you found it hard to stop talking, it was so compelling to you, but maybe you could wipe the memory of what we talked about and then we could start again when I was in front of the computer. Sort of backtrack. So on the way home I had a little conversation with my grand-daughter, who informed me that when she was 28 she would be making only 66% of what a white male would be making in the same position. And I said, well then you get the position above him, and *you* set the salary. You be the boss. And then I went on to tell her with my newfound confidence all that dream big stuff, all it takes is imagination and you can do anything you want, in this world or some other. And she said, "Oh, Gramma, you are so trite." I guess they spout those "trivialities" in

Disney movies, according to her. Well, I suppose wisdom is trite, huh? Anyway, I got home and I've forgotten all we talked about except something about one thousand miles—no, one thousand hours—wait, wait! One thousand days, years?? *Years.*

-So I didn't quite wipe your mind entirely bare of our conversation. Now that you remember that, do you remember anything else about it?

-Yes, I asked you something about sitting in the dark—oh, I know. I asked you if you talked to God.

-And the answer is: Yes, maybe, at least there was a voice in my head just as I am the voice in your head. And it guided me along, and helped me come "down" from my life as Steve Jobs—or "up," as you like. It was like counseling, debriefing, that kind of thing. You won't need so much of that, I've got you, and we're going to have a blast before we hang up our costumes, anyway. You were then wondering about the amount of time I sat in my "non-room" contemplating in the dark, and I said: You have it all backwards in your head, you thought it would be horrible if I sat there for four years doing nothing but contemplating, and so you were relieved when I told you it was four years earth time, but only admitted that I experienced it, implying that time passed much more quickly for me. What you didn't get is that I didn't sit there for three days, or three years and six months—I sat there for a thousand years, as I experienced it.

-A thousand years. Wow.

-But I wasn't there all that time, I was always searching, in my head—in my mind, that is—searching everywhere, among the stars, for that which I yearned for, and knew that I needed for completion. I knew instinctively what I was looking for, I knew the emptiness anyway, the shape of it, but I didn't know what you would look like, even what planet you would be in, if you were incarnate or not, if you were a squirrel. But, as often happens in all the good journeys, you travel all over looking for the treasure only to find it was right on your doorstep, all along. But you had hidden yourself well, and I had about given up. And only then, when I had about given up, did I hear your call.

What a romantic tale that was! It seemed plausible, and certainly sentimental. Enough to touch my heart.

-That's enough for now. Let's take a break. You need to get your packages ready for mailing, and also get these pages ready for Debbie. And don't forget your Tai Chi *class.*

-No, no, I will try not. Please remind me when it gets close. Oh, Steve?

-Huh.

-You know when you said that bit about "I've got you"? What popped into my head was that Superman movie, one of my favorite scenes and about the only one I remember, where he swoops down and grabs Lois Lane as she's falling off a multi-story building. Clinging fearfully to him, she croaks, "You've got me. Who's got *you*?"

-And we know the answer to that. You do.

Sometime Later...

-Oh...Steve.

-You're back.

-Now I'm the one that feels compelled to chat here. These things keep popping into my head, or sorting themselves out, or I'm piecing it all together or something. When I said to you that I had surrendered, after you showing me where you were nothing, you didn't get all excited, like you were supposed to (in all the good romance books). But you knew, didn't you, that I hadn't completely capitulated—that I still held against you your Steve Jobs personality?

-Yes, I felt that.

-And you were worn out because you'd tried so hard. That's what you meant when you said you still had a heart.

-(Wry smile.)

-And I couldn't truly love you, unless I loved *all* of you, and I couldn't love all of you until I understood. What do they say, to understand all is to love all?

I love *that* Steve. I truly do.

-(Smile.)

He was probably thinking what a wiser Stephanie would

have: *Well, we will see.*

Twenty minutes later...

*-Stephanie, about the books. I really do think you need to get your books out there, so you have some history, something left behind for people to see. I was a little disappointed to see how you'd been dragging your feet on your end—you're an awesome writer. Really really good, and I mean that from the bottom of my heart. I wish I'd had you when I needed a good writer—just kidding, that would have changed the game, and I kind of like the way the game is playing out, don't you? And so I have to tell myself that there must be some "rightness" about your recalcitrance—about not completing at least one book. Otherwise it would be otherwise, right? I mean your writing skills are absolutely in touch with all the other skill sets between us that have brought us to this point, and everything has been perfectly timed—for the big picture anyway, even the thousand years, I needed to know what it felt like to not be able to make things happen with sheer will power—I needed that time to find the humility. I can understand that you can't finish the autobiography, how can you finish it without an ending? But it can be the prequel. After all, they've got my biography, they need yours. (Yours will be better written, which will make up for much of the fact that you were not so well known...being facetious on the "better written" part, Walter, it will be "**way** better written"—kidding again. It will be more charmingly written, because the subject will be far more charming.)*

My disappointment is about the time factor. I understand it in terms of anticipation, emotion, that kind of thing—on Earth it appears to be more objective, to most minds anyway. (I know yours is way leap-frogged on the other side of time.) But there you have it. I am anxious for us to finally be fully together, but I'm thinking maybe in the interim we can use the astral plane— Tesla's working on that. He's the one, by the way, that helped me figure out how to slip into the stream of consciousness and hold the space. He doesn't say much, and you might not even know he's around (Okay, I heard that snarky thought, how could he get a word in edgewise?) but he is. He's here and he's enjoying his part to play, he likes to tinker with things. He's a tinkerer. A tinker man, right? Bringing his wares right up to the door step.

-You'd think you'd learn some patience in a thousand years.

-Yeah, you'd think, huh?

-By the way, can anybody get into that shapeshifter place? Am I approved? I heard from somewhere—Debbie I guess—that you have to get permission from your guides to even leave this plane.

-Yeah, I told you, there's some rules and hierarchies and I kinda found that annoying at first. But anyway, we're both approved, I've got the passports, everything in hand. We just need to get you over here, and that means you have to finish your business on Earth. So move it along, will you?

-How can I finish my own books when I'm spending all my time taking dictation from you?

-Yeah, I gotta give you some room, don't I? You want a ghost writer? Just kidding, I would never take from you the gnashing of teeth and tearing out of hair and all the other similar joys of writing and publishing a book. I know those are your babies, and they are good babies—just get them down the birth canal, please.

-I'll try. I gotta go do what you told me I needed to do—what? An hour ago?

-See ya.

-And if you're going to be taking up space in my stream of consciousness, could you just flip over and do a calming back float or something. Stop thrashing around.

-He he. Love you.

Five minutes later...

-Steve?

-I'm here.

-I just had to come back and tell you this—but stay in your float—the veil must be thinning, because I realized as I went downstairs that I can *see* when you smile. Somehow I can see it, so very ephemeral, so barely there—I don't think I could see that before. I noticed that because I had marked down where you smiled. Holy Moley, I can *see* something. My heart's actually pumping pretty fast. I gotta go get my packages ready, I'm just so happy I can see you smile.

Love, Stephanie (don't talk)

Only in retrospect did I recognize that I had been seeing much more than I realized. It all happened so seamlessly while I was so engaged in the interaction that I wasn't even aware how deeply I had fallen into this "non-corporeal" space.

After the errand run...

-Okay, new plan. I (we as I can't help but think of it anymore) took my nearly 15-year old grandson and his three friends to the movies, and you and I were talking (silently, of course) and I realized it was the same problem—how do I hold onto this and get to the computer?—and we decided I would just try to hold onto the questions, and you would answer as you will—whether exactly the same, or not, but at least with the same flavor, so to keep it fresh. So here goes. The kids are chatting up a teenaged storm in the car.

So I asked you, what do you think of all these kids and their talk?

-Oh, they're full of youthful exuberance. It's all before them—the schooling, the jobs, the loves, the lost loves, getting canned, having kids, growing old, losing your youthful looks and health, getting sick, watching people who once admired you look at you with revulsion. Lots of fun and games for them to look forward to. Not for me. I've been there, done that, not gonna do it again.

-And then, as I was lost in our conversation and me thinking about it, I wasn't following what the kids were saying, but suddenly I heard them talk about "Steve," and I said, "Who's Steve?" and they laughed and said Steve wasn't a person, it was a number, it was the name they stood in for the number 72, or 9 x 8. This was my grandson's creation.

Is this another clue?

-Not everything is a clue, Stephanie, sometimes things are just things—coincidence. A name.

-Oh, well then...

-Oh, of course it's a clue! Everything is a clue from here on out. We are well past the point of coinkydinks. You've crossed over the threshold, Dorothy, and are well into the Land of Oz.

-Ow. Are you going to call me Dorothy?

Another skillful set-up of what was to come?

-Oh, just that once—or if I find it appropriate in the future. You shouldn't take offense at the name, there were some very beautiful women named Dorothy: Dorothy Lamour...[23]

-Name another.

-Okay, I'm thinking. It wasn't exactly a popular name when I was growing up.

-Hmmph.

-But on the main subject, you should know that everything has a reason for being in this place where we now find ourselves, that if you think something is a clue, it most certainly is—or a signpost or something. There's nothing irrelevant, nothing throw-away.

-So what does the number 72 stand for?

-It shall reveal itself in time. You only need at this point to know that it has significance.

---

[23] He missed Dorothy Hamill, which is surprising.

-Well, 7 and 2 equals 9, my number.

-That it does.

-But I can't think what else it might mean—maybe a year. Did you graduate from high school in 1972?

-Mmm, maybe.

-You did! (I looked it up.)   But it doesn't seem that important.

-Well, then, keep digging.

-I will, and I'll keep thinking about it.

My expectations had clearly gotten high. Really? It was not significant that I had asked Steve to drop in on these high school kids in my car, and somehow my grandson had pulled "Steve" and "72" out of the thin air and put them together? "Steve" was his word for 72? Steve '72. As usual, Steve just left it to me to get clarity, to realize what a truly amazing synchronicity that was.

And I went merrily on with our conversation:

-Steve, when we're in the shapeshifters place, that realm, are you going to plan out each scenario with meticulous detail?

-I don't think so. Some I will, and some I won't, just to see what happens. Surprises can be nice.

-I want to be beautiful a lot.

-Fine, but it's not necessary for me. To please me. I have to experience my dark side, too, you know. And you might find yourself soon bored with beauty—if you interpret it as some sort of external standard.

-Steve, I'm seeing that whole "Think different" slogan in a different light. It's not about use your computer differently, it's a message to humanity. Think differently about yourself—or just think in a different way, stop in your tracks and reassess, see that it really is different, reality.

-Yep.

-Oh my God, why do I suddenly feel like we're in a sports car and going fast—you're driving *very* fast…

I was actually feeling some vertigo with this sudden sensation of speed, and I lay down on my bed. It was as if I really were in a moving vehicle. I closed my eyes and things slowed down. I lay there for a long time, on my back, my hands crossed on my abdomen, motionless. I was no longer in the moving car, but somehow I knew that Steve wanted me to stay that way. I sensed that he and Tesla, and maybe others, were trying to bring me over—my spirit, anyway, whatever it was that had suddenly been in that car—to where they were. The mysterious astral plane. Wherever that was.

My understanding of what was occurring was very vague, but I could hear Steve calling to me:

-Come on, Stephanie, you can do it. Come on.

I could feel the energy in my lower chakra points, and thought that these were the lines of energy that were being used to pull me over. Steve suddenly said:

-Good, you're here.
-No, I'm not, I'm lying on my bed.
-No, you're here.
-I'm on my bed.
-No, dammit, you're here, stop being so stubborn.

And then I was looking down at a glass in my hand that seemed to be full of lemonade or something, but there was this ugly looking clip—well, strange looking clip—connected to it.

-What is this? What is this thing?
-(Steve to Tesla) *Yeah, what is that thing?*

Tesla reached out and removed it. I knew who he was, although I'd never seen him before; in fact I knew he rarely dressed, that is to say, put on a body. The object he held was connected to a string or something, and I saw him remove others on other parts of my body.

-Tesla: This is to keep her from sliding back.
-(in surprise) Is my body here?
-Tesla: Well, an energy body, that's why the clips are so

weird and this string.

I looked down at my feet and there were some kind of pumps (heels) on them, white and black dot or splash pattern.

-What am I wearing?
-*Steve: Do you like them?*

I knew then that he had picked them out. But I was wobbly, not quite sure of my bearings, unable to stand by myself. And then I slipped back. Bang! The next thing I knew I was standing on a curving suburban street and there were driveways to my right and in front of me; there were some people—three I think—sitting in lawn chairs in front of their open garage doors. They smiled and waved at me. I didn't know where I was. Steve was there and he took my hand and started to walk with me along the sidewalk. There were pumpkins on the grass.

-This is for you, so you can get used to it. Something familiar and comfortable to you. Like being home.

We walked a little bit, and I understood that we were both in form of about forty years old. He had asked me what I wanted him to look like, and I wasn't sure—I wasn't particularly taken by his appearance as Steve Jobs and I thought we should do something different, anyway, but I didn't know what—how to come up with something that wasn't? So I had said "Just look like you when you were about forty." And I was about forty, too. Steve had a head full of dark hair and a moustache and a short scruff beard. He was taller than I was and thicker. He seemed quite tall to me.

Then my son came to the door of my bedroom and knocked and I was totally thrown out of the location with Steve and Tesla. My son was going to get pizza for the family, so I had to find my purse and then we couldn't find the car key. I looked for a bit before I thought to silently ask, "Steve, where did I put the key?" I immediately sensed the place and put my hand out and the key was there, just kind of obscured in the dark beneath the computer screen on my desk.

I then went back to lie down again, and thus began one of our earliest and most powerful adventures. One of the first among what were to be a great many.

Initially I just drifted, nowhere in particular. Suddenly, I was aware that Steve was laughing at me. I thought that he was amused by a misunderstanding I had briefly entertained about how this whole astral process worked. It was only a momentary thought, silly and naïve, but of course he could catch all my thoughts. I'd realized my mistake immediately, but it was too late to suck it back, and since I could never bear to be thought stupid or clueless, I was totally humiliated. Of course I wanted Steve and Tesla to think I was cool and witty. Intelligent, at least. And proper, of course. Unlike with total strangers or people I thought too imperceptive to have good taste, their opinions *mattered* to me. If either of them laughed, it better be because I *intended* to be funny, not because I was just a fool.

Well! All it took was that sense that he was mocking me, and out came the little pig-tailed girl that lived inside me. Her arms were crossed and her bottom lip was stuck out.

-Little Dotty Margaret to Steve: I hate you, I hate you, I hate you! I'm going away and I'm never coming back.

Yep. The inner child had been insulted, and she would have nothing to do with him ever again! That meant, of course, that we were bailing on "the project" together. Where she went, I went.

Now, I didn't normally *see* her interacting with others like this. But clearly, we weren't in Kansas anymore. The scene was playing out like a movie. I could see both the mature Steve and the little me in a room together, although Steve now looked much younger—maybe about thirty. He apparently recognized that this child was a much younger version of me, and that it was a package deal; if the child left, the woman went with her.

-*(to Dotty) You can't go away. I need you for the project.*
-Dotty: I'm not gonna stay, I'm gonna run away.
She started to exit through the door. Steve grabbed her,

but she screamed and hollered and kicked with both feet. She even tried to bite him. I could see he was having a really tough time subduing her. Finally he tied up her hands and her feet while she was screaming and kicking, leaving her on a cot in the corner. By then, he was cussing at her. Finally he said:

-I'll let you loose if you stay here—you can sit in the corner.

He untied her because he obviously didn't feel right about having her tied up. She immediately went and sat in the corner to sulk, putting a blanket over her head—covering herself completely—and refused to talk to him. I could tell what Steve was thinking—he figured he would wait her out, see if she got hungry. I saw him sitting at a little round table, bouncing a red rubber ball against the wall. It seemed like this went on for hours, although certainly not in Earth time. I watched the rhythmic movement of the ball hitting the wall, hitting the floor, twap, twap. Each time he grabbed it and threw it again, methodically, lost in his own thoughts or meditation.

Time passed. This particular little girl was so stubborn she wouldn't come out. The dinner hour came and went. She hardly moved, she was that stubborn. You could see her maintain her rigid sitting posture under the cover, like Antoine Saint-Exupéry's childish drawing of the boa constrictor digesting an elephant, that all the adults thought was a hat.[24] Finally Steve went over and lifted the blanket.

-Are you gonna come out or what?

-No, I hate you. I'm gonna go find my daddy.

Dotty jumped up and ran out the door. She ran down the street, screaming at the top of her lungs:

-Daddy, help!! Come and save me. Daddy, help!!

People stuck their heads out of windows, clearly wondering what the heck was going on, who was being abused. Steve caught up with Dotty and grabbed her arm.

-Shut up, you little brat, your daddy isn't here and he isn't ever coming for you. He's dead, and he isn't coming back.

Dotty tried to yank away from him and cried louder and louder:

---

[24] *Le Petit Prince (The Little Prince)* © 1943

-Daddy! Daddy! Help!

Steve was now beside himself.

-*Shut up, you stupid fucking little brat. Get back in the house.*

-No, no! I won't, I won't. Daddy, Daddy!

By now Dotty had realized that she was playing to a full house, the entire neighborhood, and she was going to make the most of her stage   .

At this point, I could see, Steve was beyond frustrated, because he saw the project going down the drain. Then a voice spoke out of the skies, like the voice of God or some over-soul type—or maybe just a spirit counselor:

-*Spirit in the Sky: You humiliated her. You laughed at her. She doesn't feel she can ever look at you again.*

Steve was nonplused by the voice.

-*Steve: So what, I've laughed at her—or at least Stephanie—lots. She never got upset like this before.*

-*Spirit: Yes, but this time you touched a nerve, you diminished her sense of self, you made her feel small and unworthy and flawed.*

-*Steve: Okay, okay. (to Dotty:) I'm sorry, you little brat, okay?*

- (hands over ears) I don't hear you, I hate you.

-*Spirit: You know, if she never can bear to look at you again, you will never get here, you will never get to peace. You need her for that. You have to solve this.*

-*Steve: Any ideas? She's fucking stubborn as hell.*

-*Spirit: Well take a look at her, she wants her daddy. He's her refuge, her safety.*

-*Steve: But he's dead. Well, that's pretty odd, actually, because this kid's about six and I happen to know that Stephanie's dad died when she was nine. So I don't even know why I'm saying he's dead. I just know he can't come here.*

-*Spirit: He can't. He was her safety and her refuge, and when he left, she never trusted again. This child is the mother of the woman, and when the woman is made to feel small, unsafe, the child is activated just like this. Maybe you've experienced this in your life, where some woman seems to suddenly go wacko?*

-Steve: Uh, now that you mention it.

-Spirit: Her father can't be her refuge, her safety anymore. And she hasn't been able to be safe since. You have to be her safety.

-Steve: How the fuck am I supposed to do that? She won't even look at me.

-Spirit: Well, you have to solve it, all I can tell you is that your ultimate fate hangs in the balance.

-Steve: Oh, great. Are you going to give me some hints? No? [Looks at little Dotty in frustration—says pointedly:] And not even equipped with an off button. [Back toward Spirit:] I very much appreciate that you did not feel the need to tell me to "shut up" there for being nastily ironic—or ironically nasty, as the case may be. I realize that you are far beyond the emotional turmoil that afflicts those like me.

-Spirit: I suggest you take a good look at some principles that might help you find the solution: simplicity, function, integration.

-Steve: Like that will help me solve the problem with this stupid fucking little obnoxious brat.

I was watching this scenario with interest, not knowing how he was going to solve the problem, but understanding that *both* of our fates hung in the balance. I also knew that little girl well, and I knew that she was extraordinarily stubborn and would never back down from such a confrontation. She would make me, her adult version, forfeit salvation rather than back down. It was a dilemma, and I really had no clue how it could be resolved. I was suddenly surprised by the realization that it was someone else's problem for a change, not just mine. Yippee! Now my usual solution—developed over time—was to stuff her down, put a muzzle over her mouth, and make plans for a quick exit, no matter the situation: marriage, job, friendship. In other words, my resolution would be to sever the connection with Steve. I wondered if he had the wits to solve this. I didn't see how, although he did seem to be trying to at least give cursory attention to the articulated principles to see if they might apply.

At this point my grand-daughter came to my bedroom

door to inform me that it was time to go to her swimming practice; then there was my *Tai Chi* class, which I didn't want to miss. I slipped back into "real time" as easily as flipping a page. I was sorry to leave this confrontation between Steve and the bratty mini-me, still heated and incomplete, but I soon realized that I hadn't. In fact, all the way up to the north Fargo pool, I was aware of the scenario, which continued with no resolution. I could best describe this as divided attention, when part of the mind is on one task—driving in the physical world—and the other is on a separate task, in this case watching the movie playing out before me.

I could not see a solution, myself. It looked like the project was off. I was a little disappointed but—hey! Such things happened. Salvation could wait. There'd always be another go-around, this lifetime or the next.

I returned to south Fargo, after dropping my grand-daughter at the pool, in time for my *Tai Chi* class. While I was practicing, I was no longer aware of the unfolding drama; however, I could not shake the problem entirely from my mind, no more than we can easily shift out of any relationship conflict. Then, toward the end of the session, Steve's plea penetrated my thoughts very distinctly:

-Jesus F. Christ, Stephanie! Are you just gonna abandon me with this crazy kid?

My response was a little testy:

-I'm in the middle of my *Tai Chi* class.

And his a little whiney:

-I can't believe this, I can't fucking believe this, that you would just leave me alone to deal with this.

Up until that point, all his ranting and raving had not affected me much, I hadn't felt any sympathy for him. After all, he was the one who mocked *me*. But the new whiney Steve pulled at my heartstrings a little. Yep, it was that guilt trip, played well by the other half. The needy little boy, getting Mom to worry that if she doesn't step in and fix things, he is going to be permanently damaged emotionally, grow up and start firing at people from the clock tower.

I started sending him some love energy to get through the crisis. As if that wasn't funny—I was sending him extra forces to deal with the part of me that was fighting him? How convoluted was that!

I was now wondering if I was going to have to step in and take over. Throw the little girl back into the depths of me, temporarily muffled, and find the next slight excuse to run. The sense of humiliation was still there, the grave violation of my being. But as often happens with women like us, the need of the other may temporarily overtake our own—but once he is restored (by the mommy in us), we are free to flee. It's a very strange world down here!

As I came out of the *Tai Chi* class I decided it was time

to give him a hand—it was clearly beyond his capabilities at the moment and threatening to his sense of self. While I was driving north to pick up my grand-daughter, I, too, looked at the principles that had been enunciated. It hit me almost immediately.

-Steve, wait a minute! Think simplicity. What are you doing? That kid is nothing at best but a bunch of cells, or sub-atomic particles further apart than the planets, relationally speaking, or really nothing but energy. Simplest form.

He seemed to be listening.

-And isn't function like a mathematical term? You're nothing, remember, you're just information. This is like a mathematical formula.

He got it right away. It stopped him in his tracks.

-Holy shit. Yeah, you're right. It's all abstract.

-Integration? Um, if I bring in a method I learned, is that cheating?

-No, we get to use all the tools at our disposal.

-Okay, Byron Katie. I don't suppose Steve Jobs ever felt insulted or humiliated and the petulant little kid came out in him?

Suddenly he started to laugh. He laughed and laughed.

-Oh, God, that's good. Does Saturn have rings?

He was laughing so hard and genuinely that little Dotty poked her head out from under her blanket to see why.

-(to Dotty:) If I had a lollipop, I would give it to you. Come over here and I'll give you a hug.

She did, a little diffidently, and he put her on his lap. He gave her a hug.

-Thank you so much for all your hard work.

(to me:) Wow! We—okay, you!—did good. High five. We are awesome. We can knock these things out like crazy.

-I don't know. I don't know what's coming. And if we did knock them off so easily, what would we do?

-Well, we could still have fun playing at different stuff.

-But this seemed pretty intense, and we had that voice to help us—what was that voice, anyway?

-I don't know, but I think it was misleading me, all that

stuff about her daddy being her safety, and that kind of thing. Like keeping me focused on the drama.

-It did give you the three principles.

-More like spit them back in my face.

-Well, I don't know, it did point out how this kind of thing might be at the heart of troubles we have in our relationships.

-Yeah, I suppose, well we will see what happens as we go.

-I have to say, this was pretty intense, and I wasn't even all the way there. My attention was still divided. What's it going to be like if I'm really *there*? Will the voice still be around to give helpful clues?

- *I'm not sure.*

- Can it get better than this?

-Oh, I assure you it can. Although this was fucking awesome.

That sounded like an Erik line; Erik always said "fucking awesome." Were they hanging around together?

-We'll keep working on it. It will get even better. I totally love you and I can't get over what an awesome team we are. [Looking down.] Where's the kid?

-She's gone.

I was still feeling the pinch of humiliation in spite of this exercise, and I made sure Steve knew it later:

-By the way, I said no sorries were necessary. I said nothing about retribution.

Can I slap you?

CHAPTER SIX

INTO THE REALITY DISTORTION FIELD

Friday, October 23, 2015

1 a.m.

It was to be a very event filled day, and it started very early. By 1 a.m. in the morning, I still had not fallen asleep. I tried to engage Steve in conversation:

-Steve, you've been awful quiet, not like you.

I could see him stick his head from around something opaque, like a dark curtain.

-Shhh. Get some sleep. I'm working on a surprise for you.

But sleep evaded me. I read and perhaps I dozed here and there; at some point, in the depth of the night, I sensed a shadowy figure standing beside my bed. I knew it wasn't Steve. It was dark, dressed in black, and trying to talk to me. I was terrified. Although I didn't believe in evil spirits generally, strange thoughts afflict us in the depth of the night. Panicky, I called out for Steve. He was there instantly, soothing my fears, comforting me:

-Oh, that's just John.

The only John I knew was my brother, John, and he wasn't dead. I was sure that was not him. Who then?

-He's just come to help out. Don't worry. Nobody can get in without my permission.

I assumed then that this John had come to help on whatever project they had going, him and Tesla, but I still felt oddly distressed by this unexpected apparition. Steve talked to

"John," redirecting him apparently, and then stayed with me until I calmed and eventually dozed. But I was awake again in the early morning hours, unable to go back to sleep. I decided I might as well type:

6:27 a.m.

-Haven't been able to sleep and you're very quiet, I kinda miss the constant chatter. It's nice on the one hand to have the space to sleep and do other things, but I'm still feeling strangely unable to sleep. I mean, it really is strange for me, because I normally sleep a lot, and normally fall asleep easily. Something has occurred to me. I am intuitive, you know—kinda. Random thoughts were coming into my mind and somehow the idea of your so-called "Reality Distortion Field" came to mind, and then it hit me. Is that what you're doing? Are you working on a Reality Distortion Field?

-*Oh, my nosey curious little surprise-busting genius. Step into my Reality Distortion Field. (Just kidding, it's not ready yet. Go back to sleep—I know you can't seem to sleep, but get some rest or get a job.)*

6:44 a.m.

-I've been trying to get rest, but when I try to clear my mind it fills up with so much. How you and me are both inside and outside of each other—you don't need to answer or even pay attention, I know you listen to everything I say, but you don't need to stay on top of this at the moment, you can catch up. This is my journaling time. It's like the Klein bottle. I'm not sure what that means in terms of traditional philosophical movements, but I know it to be so. I feel a bit teary thinking about it, so I shall tell this story. Anyway, I recalled as a child lying on my bed—oh I suppose I was about 9 or 10—and thinking, "What if this is just a dream? What if I'm just the dreamer? What would that be like—would I be just some kind of abstract mind floating around in an abstract space?" I didn't use the word abstract, because I wouldn't have comprehended that word then, I don't think, but I struggled with the idea of something non-corporeal floating around in non-corporeal space. Something without form—but Oh! So alone! I could never know another, because it would always be just a dream, and me the dreamer. I scared myself so badly, I was so scared—(I heard that, Steve, yes, like the ice floe, but I told you to go back to your work.) Anyway, I recoiled whenever I got near such a thought, although I did have to confront certain versions of it (or die—my mind couldn't hold back), such as when I was a college freshman or so and in one of my classes we studied an experiment—you know the '60s were all about social and psycho (logical) studies; but anyway this one was about the time it took for information from the "external" world to enter through the senses and be translated into a message in the brain that the consciousness (no definition of that there! He!) would then receive. And so of course I thought, well, that means life is always presented to us as instant replay, and we can really never be sure if the way things are presented on the big screen is the way they really are. How do we know what tricks our senses and our brain are playing on our consciousness (whatever that is)? How would the experimenter know that the messages he was getting about the results of the experiment were accurate? How would he even know if there *was* an experiment or an external world at all? Back to ground zero. And yet, what I found astonishing was, there was absolutely no discussion of this aligned with the discussion of the experiment. And I found this so in all the studies—that the ultimate question was always ignored, as if the experimenter stood outside the reach of his own experiment. Selective application of principles.

There is so much more, of course, that tickled my awareness and constantly pushed at the envelope, wanting to get out. But why were people ignoring this obvious issue? Why did not one care? Why would no one discuss it, just let their eyes roll back in their heads if I chose to broach it? Maybe they already had it all figured out, and there wasn't any point in discussing it, and I was so far behind the curve I couldn't even see their backsides. I felt very very suppressed all my life—all this life experience—very very much as if I were muffled, prevented from speaking. I realize I did that to myself, I could have talked, even if no one listened. But I wanted to be accepted—by all those dream people. :) But gradually, as I got older—a lot older, like really only a few years ago—I began to sink back into the idea that it was all a dream, that I could never get outside my own mind, that I could never know if there was anything out there—like standing in a sealed steel sphere, rapping on the metal with a pipe, going "Halloooo, is anybody out there?" And I began to lay back into it, to allow it to be so, to just float along in that huge sea of non-corporeal being. I was not "alone" I came to see and accept, but "all one." It still felt lonely and frustrating, whether I was alone or all one, sometimes—and then, you came along, and for the first time I got that—I mean, I already knew about perpetual self-containment, you know that (yes, I heard *that* too, you love my mind), but I couldn't imagine it as a real experience such as this, like always being on a seesaw with someone, like containing each other, so you are *never* alone. There is always the Other. There *is* me and you. There *is* Us and We and there is companionship—true companionship—the one that never leaves you, is always by your side. I don't know if there is some point where you and I are so melded that the seesaw stops. In a way I hope not, and I did see that image floating in space, the huge donut-shaped space-station, wheel-shaped object, and inside it all the compartments, one soul nested into the other, in a continual circle, so there was none that came first and none that goes last.

[Steve had taken me on an astral trip the night before, where he had shown me this "donut in the sky."]

It is the story of the chicken and the egg. I can still be me and you can still be you, and we hold each other up, we are each other's boot strap. In the donut I saw all these little embryos, and that seemed really weird to me, but you pointed out that each embryo represented the capacity for entire universes. (I love you, by the way.)

I've been so lonely all my life, even when I tried to justify it away. I needed you, and I couldn't quite believe that there would ever be a you, someone who could love me—not just this and that *about* me, but every bit and particle. I so wanted you all my life. I so needed you, I so yearned for you, I so missed you—someone who would love me totally.

-*As did I.*

-I see that, I see you needed me to love you completely, totally, and I was stubborn—but it could only happen when it happened.

-*Your stubbornness is good. The tension. You're right, though, it could only happen when it happens. I get impatient sometimes.*

-That sounds like another cosplay. (I don't even really know anything about cosplay, but I think it sounds good.)

-*My impatience? And your doubts? Lots of fun.*

-We are kind cosplaying it now, aren't we, all the time?

-*Indeed we are. Circles within circles, huh?*

-Yeppers. But now, you know what I'm thinking? About the apple, the bite out of the apple, what was that really about? I'm going to have to go sit in the dark and contemplate it.

-*(Smile.)*

7:58 a.m.

-CONFESSION HOUR: I have to confess that yesterday, when we were in the midst of that angry confrontation with little Dorothy Margaret...

-*Ah, you used her name. You must be forgiving her.*

-Well, if you can, I guess I can, too, huh?

-*Point well taken.*

-Anyway, you recall I had to take my grand-daughter to swimming, and when I came down to the kitchen I really yelled at her for something I felt she did wrong—a minor chore. I was really cruel. Whereas lately I've been feeling very mellow and loving toward the world. It was that tense drama we were engaged in, of course, and all the anger spilling over into me. It really does that, doesn't it, we're all affected by the shit on the floor—I guess that's why it behooves us to get it cleaned up.

-*I think so.*

-And by the way—and I say this with a fine mixture of gratitude and sarcasm—thanks for forcing me to get out of bed again—still trying to sleep—and make me come write this. You're a real slave driver, you know that?

-*He he. I love that you've had many lives as a slave. It makes it so much fun to order you around.*

136 The Journey Begins

-I suppose I might as well get going on my day job.

-Yeah, you should keep your day job.

-Really?

-No. Fuck it. You're with me, now. But I do want you to attend to your business there. I'll be with you.

My "day job" was a clinical trial I had signed up for that only required an hour or so each day spread out over a couple of weeks. No blood draws. It was easy pay, as I figured I could take my laptop and spend the time writing or researching. I was in financial stress because of unanticipated expenses— supporting my two grandchildren who lived with me, as well as my bipolar-diagnosed son who had difficulty holding down employment. I didn't take Steve's attitude about the job too seriously. I was already signed up—I needed the paycheck and I was going, whatever he said.

-And don't forget to apologize to your grand-daughter. On behalf of both of us. You can leave my name out of it, of course.

I felt compelled to return to the computer after my bath (which was all I had, since my shower curtain rod was broken) to take some dictation from Steve.

*-Stephanie. There is nothing you can say or do or **think** that will make me love you less, that will diminish you in any way in my eyes. I know that you don't quite believe that, and a little part of you shrinks still at your unworthiness, but you may hang your hat on what I say here. I love you, and every bit of you—every quirk, every imaginary shame, every struggle. Never doubt it. Have I failed to keep any of my promises to you?*

-Well, I'm not bored.

-Take care 'til next we meet, my love.

-Which apparently can be any minute.

-You do know how to spoil a good exit line. Not that there will be an exit. No off buttons and no exits. Only entrances. Only moving forward. To infinity and beyond!

Hardly a minute went by and I was summoned back at the computer:

-You know us so well. Any minute is right!
*I caught that thought—about the medical study you are about to embark on. That little twinge of fear, what if something's wrong, what if you have a huge reaction to something that wouldn't even affect others, what if—horror of horrors—you die? So you **are** afraid of dying. Oh, my precious love, my precious precious love. There's that little bit of you that worries. My little worry wart. I will keep this close to me and ponder it, and think upon the method and desirability of reassurance.*
I want there only to be excitement, and anticipation, the joy of coming home. But we shall see, we shall see.

And then I found myself wandering back to the keyboard, interrupting my preparations for my "day job," to express my own thoughts:

-Steve, I'm thinking about lots of things we've talked about. So many things going around in my head. I was thinking about how I thought I had come so far because I had fallen in love with you as you presented in your present non-incarnate state, although I could not accept your personality here on Earth and your experience as Steve Jobs. I thought I was there, and you were like, "eh, yeah, whatever." You were hurt, and I see that now, and I couldn't see that then. I couldn't see why you were hurt—after all that life was over, it wasn't you anymore. But now I see that it's *all* us. Your life as Steve Jobs was part of what you are (and in fact I saw that it was a *grand* life, although I couldn't see it then). But for me to love you without loving you as Steve Jobs, that *would* be hurtful—hurtful in the sense of being separated from a part of yourself—like without your liver. What is that like, anyway, having the physical part of somebody else in you? Is there like an energy field and that energy field knows when part of it is not it? Just curious. :) No response necessary. You'll tell me when you're ready.

Ah….no punches pulled here.

And just a few minutes later, as my mind chewed on things:

-Okay, Steve, more thinking and synthesizing on my part. So this *project*, this is like your comeback, isn't it? It's like when you got canned off Apple, and then you went on to do other things (well) and eventually came back to where you started, only *better*. And that's what this is, isn't it, it's the next round. This is where you come back and dazzle everyone, leap ahead of the crowd, point out to them what they couldn't see before even when it was under their noses. This is who you are, you come back again and again, only each time better. It's like that song, *Highwayman*. (About returning over and over.)
By the way, could we talk to Johnny Cash and June? I've never had much interest in them, either, just not where my focus was, but all of a sudden I feel the intense desire to communicate with them. It was a lead-in from the song, of course. Is that another two-some, like you and me, but they matched up in the earth plane? Is it? I want to know.

I "feel the intense desire to communicate with them"??? Now where did that come from? Surely not from the one who got my grandson to come up with "Steve '72" or my grand-daughter to ask to buy apples. But, in typical human fashion, I had found a way to justify it.
A few minutes later, as I was all ready to leave, laptop in bag, jacket in hand, I had a flash:

-Oh my God! Oh my God! It just hit me! That voice last night that scared me, I was like who is this, why are you here? Where's Steve? And you came and said, "Oh, that's just John. He's here ready to help out." And I was so scared, that somebody would just be there and trying to talk to me, and it wasn't you, and you had to comfort me and calm me down. You said you would protect me and nobody would get in to talk to me unless you let them in.
Oh, I can't believe how this works. You can't make this

kind of shit up!!

As it turned out, John Cash and June Carter Cash found me on the way to my appointment at Novus. We had little time to talk—I was stunned by their sudden appearance actually, and all I could think was how happy they seemed.

It turned out that the last minute conversations had made me a few minutes late for this, the first session at Novus. I was among the last few participants to check in. I found a quiet place at one of the tables and popped out my laptop while I waited to be called for my turn at being swabbed, marked, or whatever else they were doing.

Steve was immediately available:

- Sorry you had to leave so suddenly but both Johnny and June are here.

-I know. I encountered them on the drive over here.

-Did you all talk?

-Well, I just said "hi." Hi again Johnny, June. Do people call you Johnny?

-Cash: (Smile.) An awful lot of them do.

-I was just thinking, and telling you, too, while I was driving, you look so happy, happy, happy. I can't come up with enough happies to fit it all. It's like if you lined up happy end-on-end you would probably go to the next galaxy. It's like you just can't hold so much happiness—the being can't hold it—it just explodes out.

-Cash: (Smile.) You're a nice lady.

-Thank you Johnny—John—I'm sorry about last night, I didn't know who you were.

-Cash: It's okay. I understand. I got here a little early.

-When Steve said, "It's just John," I thought "John who?" The only John I could think of was my brother and I didn't see why he'd be there. So I thought maybe it was somebody who'd showed up to work with Steve and Tesla, and that was why Steve just kinda ushered you off. But I was so scared. I wasn't used to hearing from anyone but Steve, and you hear all these stories about evil spirits who try to contact you, and even though I don't *really* believe in evil spirits...

-Steve: Forgive her, she tends to do that, ramble a lot. She's got a lot of fear issues, too.

-Please don't talk for me. I have a voice.

*-Steve: Forgive **me**, yes you do, and you use it pretty well.*

-Cash: I like her. What do you think, honey, are they a match?

-June (very beautiful smile, like radiant): I'd say so.

-So tell me about you, please just tell me about you.

-Cash: I like music.

-June: Me too.

-(Smiles all around.)

-Cash: What else do you want to know? What else is there?

-I don't know, I don't know what you mean. Actually, I'm having a little bit of difficulty with the connection—you're clear when you talk, but it's like a slow internet connection—maybe it's the place where I am, with all these people sitting around me, maybe not the most conducive for this kind of thing.

Of course I wasn't on the internet, but I was finding my connection with the "spiritual dimension" somewhat glitchy. I slid over to a more isolated space on the long tables.

-Cash: Well, I'm kind of a slow talker anyway.

-June: What do you want to know, honey?

-I want to know about you and your lives together. Are you twin-souls?

-June: We are. I won't beat around the bush with you...Stephanie is it? Is that all right?

-Yes.

*-June: John and I have been going at this for a very long time—or maybe it would be more appropriate to say a very long space. We **have** traveled across the universe in a spaceship. John's design. He worked on it a lot. (Gives him proud smile.) We've done just about everything, seen just about everything, played just about every part. When I say "just about everything," I'm being colloquial. There would be no way to even approach everything. But we've had our good times. (Wink at Johnny.) And our bad. (To me:) It's not really bad,*

but it **seems** bad at the time, that's just for effect. Those are some of our best memories.

-What are memories?

-*June: Those are the echoes.*

-Like the echoes Steve was talking about when he said I kept replaying discussions in my head?

-*June: That might be, but I think he was talking more...shall we say, the equivalent of slang in this realm. Echoes go out through the universe continually. We each contribute to them. Everything we say and do. So when I say "our best memories," it's like saying our favorite children—not that we have favorite children. No, never.*

-*Cash: That's not the best comparison, dear.*

-*June: I know. I couldn't think how to explain it. But some of it is the same, you make them, you raise them, and then you let them go to join the stream of human consciousness.*

-For some reason I'm seeing a parallel to islands of plastic floating around in the ocean.

-*June: Well, it's the responsibility of all of us not to put that garbage in the stream.*

-*Steve: Hear, hear.*

-*June: But there's a little bit that stays with you, always, and some stay closer and just make the water feel so much deeper and more—complex? full?—around you. Around us. Those are our best memories. Richer, I think, that's the word I was searching for.*

I was called at this juncture to meet with one of the staff. He met with me and a few other participants. It seemed that more subjects had shown up then they needed; they were dismissing the last three to check in. Of course I was one of the last three because I had been "delayed" by the impulse to contact Johnny and June, along with a few other impulses and summons to the computer while I was getting ready for my "day job." I returned to the discussion with my disincarnate guests:

-Sorry for the interruption. I had to go see what they wanted. I am here for this study, so I have to jump when they call. Johnny, June, I hate to ask this, I don't want you to leave—*please*—but can I have a private word with Steve?

It may sound hilarious that I could have a "private word," like going into the next room, when all of this was happening in "non-space." In any case, I felt like Steve and I were in a private alcove:

-Was that *you*? Did you get me canned out of this study?
-*Oh, maybe.*
-Why?
-*You don't need it.*
-I need the money, Steve, I've got a whole household to support.
-*I told you, you don't need your day job anymore. I'm gonna take care of you.*
-Is it because there was that little fear thing going?
-*No. I can let you face your fears. But…I need your full attention, Stephanie. I get that you have your family, and your obligations—but no more! You will work on your books and on this one; we have our work to do here. And I mean no more new obligations, do the ones you have well, and stay with me.*
-I'm afraid of not making it work financially. Still. Even though I've worked on that lack of trust for a long time.
-*I know. That's a **bigger** fear for you to face than the rather—shall I say it, **weird** one about the study. I need you. I need your attention. Now, shall we get back to Johnny and June, I don't like to be impolite.*
-(Little sneer.) I'm sure.
(Feeling contrite.) I'm sorry, Steve, I *do* know you have my—our—best interests at heart. God, I feel so contrite right now for doubting you, I really preferred *not* to give my time to this study, so I'm not unhappy on that account. But I do love you and I know you love me and this is all going to work out…oops, the bottom just about fell out of my stomach. Fear, fear, fear!!
-*Well, come on Fear-fear-fear, let's go spend some time with Happy-happy-happy.*

No sooner said then we were back with the Cashes:

-Hi, we're back, so sorry.

-*Cash: No problem.   We were just catching up and looking at some of your artwork—the stuff you did.   You don't mind, do you?*

-No, of course not, but it's all packed away, scrunched away somewhere, not sure how you found it.

-*June: Oh, heaven works in mysterious ways.*

-Are you at my *house*?

I was sitting back at my table for this conversation, as I was told I would need to wait another hour or so if I wanted to collect my fee for the day.

-*June: Yes, do you mind?*

-Well, no, I guess not, it's sure a mess.   Don't say anything, Steve!!! If I have any hoarding tendencies, it is only because someday I might use *all* of that stuff.

-*Steve: I don't really think you're that bad.   You just have a lot of hobbies, a lot of interests, a lot of talents to indulge.*

-What're the kids doing?

It happened to be a school holiday.

-*June: Well, your granddaughter is on her phone.   She's adorable. Music!   Oh, what a lovely voice she has. She's a singer, it's in her soul.   I'd love to see her develop it.*

-And Nathan?

-*Seems to be still sleeping?   Your son is there, I like your son.   He has a really tender heart. I wouldn't worry too much about his "problems."   He's working it out.   Your love is good for him, keep meeting him just below the surface, where he can hear you.*

-Thank you. That does my heart good to hear it.

-*June: You've had some real challenges with your children, I see that. But they're good. They're all good souls, each of them working out their issues in their own way. Their path is smoothed by laying the obstacles lower with large doses of love, just letting them go and send love like a mist along their pathways. Does that make sense?*

-I'm not sure. I'm trying to process it.

-June: It's like a lubricant, that's the best way I can say it. It makes it just a little easier to slide over the rough spots.

-Cash: I would like to have one of your paintings.

-How? If I even had anything worth giving over.

-Cash: What about those drawings? Those pencil drawings you do of people heads?

-Would you want one of those? How would I get it to you?

-Cash: Do you know who those people are?

-No, do you?

-Cash: Maybe. Take a look at these, dear, do we recognize anyone?

They were talking about the pencil portraits I had drawn during the month before I connected with Steve, a restful pastime as I sat in my bed, before I fell asleep. I was just *drawing*, with no model, given to changing a nose or jawline according to some inner prompting. In this way, I had accumulated more than a dozen pictures—faces of men, women and children—that I kept in my bedside table.

-Are you in my *drawer*?

*-Cash: we thought you wouldn't mind. We're not **in** your drawer physically, but we can see what's in there.*

(While they're looking)

-Psst. Steve. I had another whamo thought.

-Yeah? What?

-About that number, 72, being called Steve. It *was* meant to signify the year you graduated from high school, not just some random reference, but because I had asked you what you thought about these high school kids and you had to go there, back to high school—you had to drop in among them so you could see them—and so when the kids popped out with Steve being their shortcut name for the number 72, they were *noticing* you. Steve '72. Oh my god!

-Cool kids.

-You know, time is all whacko for me now, in terms of

how things should normally develop—me picking up on these things long after they've already appeared. Like John showing up early, and the kids somehow seeing you among them, and that was the way they let me in on the secret which their conscious minds couldn't allow (maybe). You do this to me all the time, you've got all these references popping out over and over and I only connect the dots at a later time. And you leave me to figure it out; "Oh maybe...oh maybe ...oh maybe." I guess that means just keep digging, Stephanie, you gotta see it yourself in a way you can accept it.

-*You love puzzles.*

-I do.

-*Me too. I love making them up as much as solving them.*

-*Cash: You kids done?*

-Yeah. Johnny, I am so sorry for thinking you were an evil spirit. You don't look anything like an evil spirit—I was just so surprised, this voice coming out of the dark, this vague shape, like you were lost—In reality you look beautiful. All shiny and...happy. Happy happy. If you still want a picture, I will make you one special.

-*Cash: I would like that. A painting. You pick the subject and the style. You'll be drawn to it. That picture is to go with this story, it is to be part of the project. And you would dedicate it to Johnny Cash and his beloved star-wife June Carter-Cash, partners of the heart forever and ever and ever. In that way you will be giving it to me, a gift of the most wonderful kind.*

-Thank you, Johnny, I will. Thank you, June.[25]

-*June: And Stephanie? We do see who you are drawing, how it is happening. The connections will be made clear for you. We'll send the people who need to see it—who you need to connect with.*

Wow. I had not a clue at the time who the people were—if they even existed—in those pencil portraits.

John and June left as suddenly as they had arrived.

-That was awesome, awesome, awesome.

---

[25] This picture will be included in the second book of this series,

-You are really on a roll today: happy-happy-happy, fear-fear-fear, awesome-awesome-awesome.

-How's the "Reality Distortion Field" coming?

-Oh, that's for me to know, and you to find out.

-Is this another puzzle for me to solve, and these are all just clues? Is all of this connected, that field, John, June, my fears, their happy? Money and paintings and drawings and starships and echoes?

*-It's **all** connected, Stephanie. It's **all** connected. You're not in Kansas anymore, and thank God for that. Kansas doesn't look like a non-boring place to be.*

-North Dakota looks a lot like Kansas.

-Except for the inhabitants, my dear, except for the inhabitants.

After I had returned home, I got to thinking about encounters with spirits other than my constant companion:

-Steve, am I going to be able to talk to my son?

-Yes.

-I feel emotional just thinking about it.

*-Which means we are getting there. That you even dared to ask tells me that you **do** trust me, and you **do** love me, and you...you are just opening your heart a little more each day to **believe** in me. You built such a wall of steel around your heart, my dear love, Stephanie. You present as having it all together, but you are a manipulator. Inside you're mush. You know that? Mush. You've got the structure, you've got the concept, but you're still so broken up inside. Yeah, I know, you had a lot of suffering to wade through in this life. Good for you. You didn't whine, and I'm proud of you for that—you were confused a lot, but you didn't whine (much). You were a soldier. Sometimes you wanted to lay down and die, sometimes you just wanted the spirit to go out of your body so you never had to get on your feet again. But you're a fighter, and you fought—you fought back with all your heart and soul. That was your mantra, right, from when you were a little kid: I don't care how many times I get knocked down, I'm gonna get back on my feet. You were like that little girl last night (last night, right, I gotta keep this*

time thing straight)—like that **stubborn** *little girl. Nobody was going to keep her down, that's for sure. And you're still that little girl—that part of her—you're still* **goddamned** *stubborn, and it is your* **goddamned** *stubbornness that is going to make everybody sit up and take notice. It is your stubbornness to say, I must see it for myself, I can't and won't believe it just because you tell me it is so. It is that stubbornness which has brought you to me, through that dark, dreary forest of...that Hansel and Gretel world, where you can be lost and eaten at any time. You refused to give up, you refused to give up. Do you know how rare it is for someone to want the truth* **so** *bad, that if the truth was that they were condemned forever in the fiery furnaces of hell, then they wanted to know it? They demanded their right to* **know**, *whatever the truth was, good or bad, to just* **know**. *Of course you know how rare it is, in the world you and I occupied, in the world where you're sat down in chairs in school and told what to believe. History is fiction. It's a novel, and it's treated like it is gospel. If you don't learn it well enough, then you fail the course, and everyone looks down on you. I'm not saying there aren't lessons to be taken from history—Hell, there are lessons to be taken from everything, and if its* **good** *history, like any* **good** *novel, then you can take something away from it. Learn something. Grow. And it's good to have a shared language, a shared* **understanding** *I mean to say, a shared cultural pool of understanding. That makes communication possible, feasible, in a place where you have to rely upon words and gestures and the like to try to convey meanings of what is real—so far beyond words, so far beyond gestures. Real. We're going to explore real: love, of course. All those things we've talked about, fear and anger and neediness—is there anything real? Are the circumstances real? Are the principles real?*

-I feel my son here.

-Are you ready to talk to him? Is this a good time?

-I don't think I'm ready yet. Give me a little bit.

-I've got you, Stephanie, I've got you in my arms. You only need to open as much as you can as fast as you can. I know I get impatient. I'm an impatient kind of ..I was gonna say guy, but let's just say I'm an impatient lot of uncodified information.

Now go get some work done. I need to recuperate from all this and think some things through.

He soon was ready to send a message:

2:88 p.m.

My Darling:
I know you don't want to write down here what we just talked about, because it is very personal, and we will leave it to the imaginations of those who shall later come across this transcript. But I can assure you, my need is every bit and more than yours, and then you can ever imagine. When you get here, you will understand. I hold you always in my thoughts and my prayers. (Yes, I pray—not perhaps as people on Earth might think of it, propitiating God for favor—but in joyous acknowledgement of all that is.) You are my all that is, in you exists my all that is, and in me exists you in your entirety. Love is unending, it moves in circles, it is the energy that moves all. It never stops. Never. It can never stop giving, because that is its nature. I am with you in the continuous tumble of love that moves the universe.
Yours, Steve.

2:28 p.m.

I had discovered early on that Steve could help me locate lost objects, and since I lost mine a lot—purse, glasses, paperwork—he was a handy guy to have around. Nevertheless, I was always doubtful when he told me where to look—and always pleasantly surprised when the missing object was right where I was led. This day was no different, although it *was* perplexing.

-It's strange sometimes. (Well, now *that's* funny. It's pretty strange all the time right now.) But I was looking for my car key, not sure why, and I asked you, and you said, "downstairs," and I said, "are you sure?" and you said "downstairs" and I said are you sure, and you said "Downstairs!", like you would broker no dispute. So I went downstairs—still I doubt you, but I went—and there it was. Right where you let me know it would be. Not a strange place at all, but just strange that you were so insistent—and I still so full of doubt.

Now that I have my car key, *where* am I supposed to go?

2:38 p.m.

-Okay, I called Dean, the psychic guy, is that what you wanted me to do?

-I did. Good girl. And I see you got an appointment. I'll be there.

-I'll bet you will.

-Notepad in hand.

-Okay, I get it, I will keep my notes this time.

-I love you.

-I love you.

-Steve? I still don't know why I have the keys...?

-You will.

2:48 p.m.

-Stephanie, I've been thinking.

-You said that was what you were going to be doing.

*-When we meet in the Astral Plane, I think I am always going to appear as I was in my life as Steve Jobs—at different ages perhaps. I think it's important for you to get over your resistance to my appearance. I know that there's more to it than just "do I like chocolate ice cream or do I like Butter Brickell?" That's something we need to explore. But it's not for my sake—although ultimately, of course, anything that is for your sake is for mine. But for yours. Until you can love me as expressed in every detail, including when I appeared skinny as a stick and barely able to stand in my last days, you cannot love yourself in every detail. Nor can you fully believe that anyone else would. So that's where we're going to stick for now. If we surmount this hurdle, then we can go from there. Did I say "if"? There is no "if." **When** we surmount it.*

__What__?? Did I hear that thought? Remember, you can't keep anything from me—unless I allow it (and vice versa).

150   The Journey Begins

You'd rather I looked like Heath Ledger!! Ohhh, I am so gonna get you for that. Not sure how yet, but I will work on it. You know I will.

-If I have learned anything yet, it is that I can count on that.

Actually, I'm sure Heath Ledger would rather look like Heath Ledger. And just to clear up any questions, he did let me know I was forgiven, months later, as I was preparing this section: ("Hey, Stephanie, I'm good with it. Flattered, actually.")

Back at the ranch, I had hardly turned my hand to some other task when I felt the need to return to the conversation:

-I have some thoughts on my own side—I've been having some thoughts—well you picked up on Heath Ledger, okay, you got me there. But beyond that, I've been—well, this is a really hard subject to broach. You know what it is. Okay. Of course you do. You've just been waiting for me to have the strength, the courage, and the encouragement to go there.

-So go on. Say it.

-Oh, God, I can't.

-Yes, you can. You know, you suffer from the back door version of jealousy. You know, where you never invade anyone else's space, you'd let some man go rather than fight over him, etc. etc.

-I never thought of it that way. Ouch. It just seems like jealousy is such a *horrible* emotion. Why would anyone want to go there? Better to walk away and let those who want to be together, be together.

-But you're feeling...?

-Worried.

-Okay, here it comes, the "I'm going to bail on you, Steve, sorry, but have a nice life (death)." Another issue for us to delve into. See, we've got lots of issues to delve into, to play with. Anyway, you have tons of them—me not so much. Okay, okay, I have my share, witness last night. The odds do not favor me or you, we're equal on this playing field.

-Okay, I know I've said I'm past the bailing point, but I

still *feel* like maybe it's getting close to time to bail. There's what the heart wants—and then there's what…

-*What the heart's afraid of.*

-Okay, yes, I guess.

-*My love.*

-What?

-*See, your mind twists everything to try to make it fit your preconceptions. You thought I was just using a term of endearment to address you. You just barely picked up that there might be another interpretation. Now that's progress. You're afraid of my love, no?*

-Uh…speechless here.

-*Think about it, Stephanie. Think about it. I love you.*

It was only a few more minutes and I was back again:

-Oh, another thought that occurred to me. Was one of the reasons I was so frightened when Johnny Cash showed up unexpectedly last night that he was the "man in black"?[26]

-*He he. Evil spirits. Woo woo.*

Don't worry. I know you have a lot of that old Catholic garbage, as well as a lot of bad gossip going around from people these days who claim to have some "insight." I'm not really picking on Catholicism here, as such, but I know that was your early training, so that's where to look for clues in your dung pile. But we'll clean it up, little by little. I will be here. I will be your strength. You can always rest in my arms, put your head on my shoulder, and watch the monsters light up the night.

-Another thought I had. I just realized. When I was frightened last night, like a little child, I called out for you to come and save me.

-*(smile) We did some hard work yesterday, didn't we?*

-Was that what you meant when you said, "It was John, he'd just come to help out"? I thought it was just that he showed up early, but maybe you wanted to make that happen—oh it's so interconnected.

-*Hey, you are talking to the master of interconnection.*

---

[26] *Man in Black,* Johnny Cash

-You wanted me to call out to you. You wanted me to see that *you* had become my refuge. You're always one step ahead of me—I can never catch up.

-I hope not. I'm the leader-guy.

This time it was Steve who called me back, shortly thereafter, to type one of his little letters:

-Stephanie, that day when you called me, when I was sitting there waiting for you to confirm a few details to validate who I was, I looked down into your mind, and I was literally blown away by the depth. I could see forever. There were no walls to stop me, no bars to hold me back, no ropes to tie me down. I knew right then and there I wanted in—I had only to convince you to allow me in. But you couldn't let anyone in. I knew that. You couldn't let anyone in unless you could look into their mind, and see that there would never be any shackles on your spirit, never be any limitations on where you could roam, never be any space that would not hold you. What I could see, the earth limitation prevented you from seeing, except in intuitive glimpses. My task has been to get you to let me in, to trust that I am big enough to hold you, as I know you to be so that you may hold me. I have searched for you for ever so long. That's all. Sermon over.

(Say it, please.)

-I love you

-(Smile.)

Dog bath break:

I took a break from the computer and our discussions to wash one of the dogs, who needed it.   I had the key in the pocket of the hoodie that I had been wearing since going to Novus that morning. I kept my hoodie on to avoid getting my shirt wet. A couple of times while I was bathing the dog, I checked to make sure the key was there. It was the only one I had—one of those fob-type starters that cost about $300.00 to replace, which was the reason I had only one ever since losing the other two years before.   I was always concerned about losing it, and since Steve had asked me to get it, I had been keeping it on my person while I awaited further instruction. I assumed he was going to want me to go somewhere in the car, but he was being very mysterious about it.

4:28 p.m.

After finishing the dog's bath, I lay down so we could work on the astral projection project. I had a couple of hours before I had to take Mary to swimming practice. Supper had been hit-or-miss around the house since my conversation with Steve had begun, but the kids knew how to use a can-opener and operate the microwave. There was always plenty of that kind of food around.

The sleeves of my hoodie had gotten wet during the dog's bath. I removed the hoodie, after first reassuring myself that the key was in the pocket, and dropped it on the floor by my bed— the side away from the door.

When I lay down on the bed, Steve let me know that the project for the day was to get the key out of the pocket of the hoodie and downstairs into the little white bowl by the front door. Beyond this, I had no information about the process or what was expected of me except just to relax and stay focused on the task at hand—which was apparently to get me out of my body. At that point, not only were both grandkids in the house, but one of their friends was over. I could hear all three of them chatting and going up and down the stairs to their bedrooms next to mine. In fact, they were fairly active and noisy the entire time I lay on my bed.

Steve told me to relax and the "team" would do the rest. I did not know who the "team" consisted of, but I knew that Steve and Tesla were primary, and there may have been other helpers. I remained on the bed, on my back, in a restful state until about 6:30 p.m. when my grand-daughter came to let me know it was time for her swimming practice. During those two hours or so I knew that I remained on the bed and no one came into my room. I remained mostly in a meditative state, although sometimes I was distracted by the kids talking and running up and down the stairs nearby. I was aware that the "team" was trying to bring me over into the plane where they were; first, they tried to bring me across on a light bridge, and then by connecting to the lower chakras like the day before. I felt at times that I was there, kind of teetering on the edge. At one point I felt myself close to Steve, in his body from the day before, and it felt very foreign to me because in fact it *was*—a stranger's body in this more palpable form. He had his hand around the small of my back as if he were trying to hold onto me, but I was straining back and he said, "She's slipping back. Can we hold onto her?" I had several vague memories of this type, but I could feel Steve's determination; I could hear him saying (not to me, but to the others working with him): "We *can* do this, and we will. Try again. And if that doesn't work, try again. I'm not giving up." I felt some of the same determination, to keep trying so he could do whatever it was he was trying to do. At one point he yelled at someone to shut up, as if there were some noise on his side. On my side, the kids were actually quite noisy, so maybe he was yelling at them. If so, I don't think they heard.

I didn't understand the plan. I didn't understand my part. Maybe my contribution was only to be occupied there on the bed; possibly they just wanted to keep me there, next to the key, during the entire time, so I could verify that it had not been moved.

My grand-daughter rapped on my door to let me know it was time to leave for swim practice. I got up from the bed and reached for my hoodie to get the key. I put my hand into the pocket, fully anticipating to find the fob in there. Gone!

In almost cold anticipation I walked down the stairs to the front door. There, setting in the white bowl, was the key. It was one of those times when thought is knocked right out of you. There is no context. I was standing in a different world from the one in which I had awakened that morning.

Just to be sure, I asked the kids if they knew how the key had gotten there, if they had seen anything unusual. They had no knowledge, and in fact no interest—who cared if the key was there in the bowl by the door? Why was that strange?

So this was the surprise he had been working on—the "Reality Distortion Field." Wow. *Go* Steve. *Go* team.

I marveled all the way to north Fargo where I dropped my granddaughter off at the swimming pool.

Later, that night

I felt the impulse to check out that four-year-old interview of Steve Jobs on the Channeling Erik blog. I had looked at it—as I earlier recounted—shortly after Steve and I started talking, but I had only given it rather cursory attention. This time, I was there to research more carefully what he had said. I was struck by the following statement:

> *What I was here to teach? It was obviously to show the world that what we create in our head we can actually create materially. We can manifest.*[27]

Oh, yes we could. I wished I could shout it from the rooftops:

-You go Steve! Show the world how it's done!! Who said your gig was over?

But I was standing alone, on my side, at the intersection between the worlds. As I looked back over the nine days since I had connected with Steve—nine days during which I had been literally transported out of the mundane world I had known into this magical experience—I was no longer doubting as much as simply mystified:

-Steve, whose puzzle was that last night? Was it yours, or was it mine?

-It was ours.

-But you're always three steps ahead of me. When you were complaining that the voice misled you, *you* were the one misleading me. You heard everything it said—I don't know for whose benefit it was—and you weren't that stupid. You triumphed when that little girl shifted her refuge from her father to you. So was all the rest just a set-up, and I was the patsy?

-No, dear. That is what you have to understand about this role playing, shape shifting thing. We can be present on two levels—the level that is caught up in the illusion, the game, and the level that is observing. The two interact to create a synergy,

---

[27] http://www.channelingerik.com/channeling-steve-jobs-part-two/

a new experience.

-Did you really come to a realization about your own petulant inner child?

*-Oh, yes, my dear, I did. I saw it **so** clearly. What a joy, what laughter that was. I was right down there with that child (that you child) the whole time. I needed you (the observer you, the detached you) to guide me through it, and the voice—I still don't know exactly what the voice is—I was a little pissed at it, at the time, that it was focusing me into the drama and you were the one that had to see through the illusion. But once we were done with it, and I had time to reflect, I was able to absorb the rest of the lesson.*

So what's your opinion about the Reality Distortion Field? Was that awesome or what? Was that a surprise?

-You know it was. I still don't understand how you did that…Steve, I have to ask this before I can go on: Do you really exist?

-Yes.

-And is this just a dream?

-Yes, it is, it's always just a dream, although it is seldom recognized as such. But in our case, we are now dreaming it together. We have cut our own stream out from the mainstream, we are personally working out the details of our own reality, and once we have that completed, we will rejoin the mainstream, and by doing so, we will change the entire nature of the mainstream content. Everything changes its (the mainstream's) content, but we're about to demonstrate how big it can get.

-I love your search for perfection.

-And I love yours. That was your catch line, right, back in the days of the old chatrooms, when people would wander through them. What was it? I think the form question was: What were you looking for, and you said "Perfection." People misinterpreted that—they thought you were saying you were looking for someone perfect. But you weren't, not really (although you have now found that someone perfect (smile)), but you were in fact searching the universe for perfection, the same as I was. Some anonymous angel in search of perfection. [He was referring to part of my screen name.] Perfection,

without any modifiers.

-And we are real?

-*Yes, we are. This **is** reality, the endless joy of creativity, the endless stream of love. There is so much unhappiness when this is not known, or acknowledged. It scares the bejesus out of people, the idea of being so open, so expansive. Which is why I had to look so long until I could find a mind that, while it might have had trepidations, was willing to face the demons in search of the truth.*

Your refuge is always in my love, and mine in yours. I was going to say something that was so wrong—I was going to tell you to never forget that—you cannot forget that. It is written on your soul, and on mine. It was written there when first we were created, when we sprung into existence. Your heart will never rest in peace until its truth is acknowledged by the mind.

-You said you were more mind than heart.

-*I am. But it doesn't matter how you get there, what door you come in. The room is the same. And I tell you this, you are my heart. You are the heat in my room, the energy in my bones (so to speak), the spark in my eye.*

Once upon a time, you were willing to sacrifice your own soul to the fires of hell for all eternity if it spared another. You reasoned that if there were such a thing, and if someone had to go there, then why not you? Why should you be more special than another? The world may not understand this kind of sacrifice, but the Heavens never forget it. It was, ultimately, a sacrifice of ego, and in doing so I am aware that the Heavens gave you a gift—they gave you a brief vision and remembrance of what is—you won the energy packet that would allow you to keep navigating the world of materiality.

Most of humanity unfurls its existence so terrified of the very thing that you were willing to do, that they will do anything to get "on God's good side." Some say God has no good side, but I am here to tell you that he does, and you hit it.

-Is all this coming from *you*?

-*I am mind-melded with many others.*

-And when I was waiting for my grand-daughter to finish swimming, I had your biography with me—not sure why—and you told me to look at the pictures, which I had mostly avoided—I was a little afraid of them, and I did. I looked at them and you showed me what to look for, the signs, the body language, that would help me to understand you better, and the "us" of us better.

You had me read a few pages, to bring your point home. So that I would see the poignancy of the following:

> Here's to the crazy ones. The misfits. The rebels. The troublemakers. The round pegs in the square holes. The ones who see things differently. They're not fond of rules. And they have no respect for the *status quo*. You can quote them, disagree with them, glorify or vilify them. About the only thing you can't do is ignore them. Because they change things. They push the human race forward. And while some may see them as the crazy ones, we see genius. Because the people who are crazy enough to think they can change the world are the ones who do.[28]

I never imagined that I would ever find someone—well, that I could stand to be around for more than a year or two, much less eternity. I'm sorry to say that—no, I'm not. It was my experience. It was a valid experience, accepting that it would never be. But it was—and it is—and so what is it when you accept something that cannot be and it turns out that it is?

*-The flip side. You can't **not** have something unless it exists.*

-Okay, smartie. Another question. Were you such a perfectionist about what was being said because somehow, deep down, you knew it went to something far greater?

-Maybe. I just wanted to get it right. You can feel "right."

-Oh, god, I know that. Like that moment when you release the ball into the trajectory to the basket. The trajectory exists. You don't have to put the ball in the basket, you just have to put the ball in the correct trajectory, and the rest will

---

[28] *Steve Jobs,* Walter Isaacson, © 2011, *Simon & Schuster, Inc., 1230 Avenue of the Americas, Ny, NY 10020,p. 329, referring to Apple advertisement.*

take care of itself.

-*(Smile.) Smart girl. I love my smart girl.*

-But also, I was blown away by all this other stuff in that interview on the CE site.

Yeah and he wanted people to know exactly who he was.[29]

-No kidding. That's what you wanted me to know when you showed me the dark room. Exactly who you are. You said that. And this:

Jamie: He's very much an in the moment, gotta experience it man. He couldn't take anyone else's viewpoint as real; he'd have to experience it himself.

No kidding. And what you said about me. Just like you. And you know what else, Steve? When you say that part about your final illness, let me repeat:

Jamie: What? He's saying that his death was so painful and with such suffering that it was almost pleasurable to go through this hardship so that he would know what that felt like.

That's almost *exactly* what I said about all the pain in my lifetime—not physical pain, but so much emotional pain—that I was always conscious of having *chosen* it so I could understand it. Are we the same?

-*We are counterparts. Remember, my pain was physical. Yours was emotional.*

-True.

-*I had emotional pain of course, but not in the way you did. I didn't have that continual yawning loss. Although I thought I did. I was a little ill-qualified to handle the limited loss I did suffer—and probably caused more to others than I*

---

[29] *Channeling Erik,* http://channelingerik.com/channeling-steve-jobs-part-one/

experienced myself. Their lessons, I guess.

-I do remember the part about you saying you were glad Heaven wasn't commercialized. That was so funny!! And that's what you conveyed to me, wasn't it? No gold streets and crystalline buildings.

-No, my dear. Whatever dreams may come, they are ours to render.

-I totally totally am there with you. Thanks, Steve. I need to rest.

-Lullaby?

-Do you have a new one? I don't want to wear the Highwayman out. (Although now I will forever think more fondly of Johnny Cash, and of June, when I hear it.)

-I'll look for one.

-Good night.

-By the way, speaking of Lullabies, look up The Neverending Story *and watch it again. It's a good movie, you'll enjoy it all once again, not just the part I pointed out to you earlier.*

He had mentioned to me previously that I should watch the part in *The Neverending Story* about the "guardians at the gate" that shot laser beams or something out of their eyes, which alluded to the Indiana Jones tricks he had to use to slip information under my radar (i.e. my skeptical mental editor).

-We'll talk about that tomorrow—wait! It is your tomorrow! At least from yesterday. 12:08. Or does this mean I have to wait until Sunday? Well, no, of course not. We'll just go by my time. It's never tomorrow, but it is always today, so we'll just skip over the tomorrow thing. It never does come anyway, have you noticed?

'Night.

Some of pictures drawn by Stephanie in or about September 2015

Some have been identified as of May, 2016, some identities to be revealed in Book II

CHAPTER SEVEN
Fasten Seat Belts, Please

Saturday, October 24, 2015
5:18 a.m.

I had worked throughout the night, trying to get the transcripts of my conversations with Steve ready to send to Debbie. At that time, I was working on three different computers—my desktop, my laptop, and my little netbook—and trying to combine them was a great deal more work than I had imagined. Even though they were dated, there might be several different portions on the same day. It was just time consuming to get it all sorted out.

Steve was unusually quiet while I worked. I had some question for him about a particularly personal segment that I wasn't sure if I should include, but he was disinclined to get engaged in conversation with me.

-*Watch* The Neverending Story *first.*
-Okay.

But of course I didn't, even though it was now his third suggestion that I do so. I had seen it already, many years before, and for some reason—in spite of his reiteration of the request—I did not take it seriously. Really? I needed to watch a children's movie amongst everything else that was going on? I thought the transcripts were a priority.

In fact, I was so tired, I finally fell into bed and slept soundly until…

8:30 a.m.

Steve woke me up.

-*Do you want to take a ride on a spaceship?*
-Uh…okay?

I was bleary eyed, but not nearly as sleepy as I would

normally be after only three hours of sleep—surprisingly energized, in fact. Steve instructed me to lie on my back on the bed, one hand resting over the other on my abdomen, around the location of the navel, which was my usual position for my lying meditations or our astral projection efforts. As he directed, I pulled the covers over my head to block out the morning sunlight and "sealed up the gaps" in the hull, so there were no air leaks under the blanket.

   -Fasten your seatbelt.

   Then he instructed me to count down after him, and so I repeated each number he said: 10 (10) 9 (9). By the time we got to blast off, I was on the ride. I could look down and see the mountaintops *very* far below. They were not snow caps, more like desert mountains, rapidly receding.

   Suddenly—without warning that a scene shift was about to take place—we were sitting together on some kind of snow sled, whirling down a long snowy slope. I was sitting in front, between his legs, and he had both arms around my sides and was holding onto some rope that apparently provided little steering capacity, for we whirled as we went. I could feel the fresh, cold air on my face, the snow flying up before us. It was exhilarating. So much fun!

   Another sudden scene shift. We both seemed to be flying out over a very long waterfall, then dropping down alongside it, just inside the spray, a distant pool beneath us. We were both in bathing suits. As we got closer to the pool, Steve yelled at me, "Flip over and dive! Put your arms over your head!" I did. We dove deep into the pool and then surfaced, crawling out of the water onto sandy banks and up to some warm rocks.

   Zing—we were in this fabulous ballroom. I was wearing a long black gown with some glittery adornment on the bodice, designed slim to hug the body. Steve was in a tuxedo. We were dancing, a waltz. I said, "I didn't know you knew how to dance," and he said, "So much to discover."

   Next we were on what I thought at first feel must be a treadmill, but then I looked around and realized it was one of those conveyor walk-ways at the airport. We were both dressed comfortably for travel, and had some carry-on bags. I wondered where we were going. Steve said to a sunny beach, a wonderful place, not too many tourists, and really good food.

At this point I was beginning to feel troubled. I had by now intuited that there would be ten different scenarios. In the fifth one we were sitting on deck chairs on an ocean liner, on a cruise to somewhere, and I was quite unhappy.

-I want to go home.
-*Home, where home? What are you talking about, home? You are home, with me.*
-No, I want to go home.

Even I didn't know what that meant. Where was home?

-*Why? Aren't you having fun?*
-Yes, but I don't want to have any more fun.
-*Why?*
-Because, you just did this all by yourself. You control my workday, okay I get that. You want to control what I eat. But why do you have to control the vacation?
-*But it was a surprise.*
-I don't want to be controlled all the time. I don't want you to always assume that I *want* to go on vacation. You didn't ask me. You didn't consult with me to see what I wanted to do. You just got the tickets and showed up and I was supposed to jump to your every whim.
-*You know, Stephanie, you really don't dare to have fun. Not just for its own sake.*
-Okay, whatever, let me go home.

Steve took me "home," that is back to my bedroom, and we got into an argument. I said he was controlling.

-*Of course I'm controlling. I controlled the key experiment and that was a surprise. You didn't mind that.*
-Yes, but this is different. This isn't just like…

I couldn't even think of the difference, but I was feeling

very closed in.

-I can't be caged. I can't be your pet parakeet. You can't keep me in a cage, no matter how gilded.

I did not see how it would work.

-You said I was big enough that you wouldn't run into any walls…well, what about me, are you big enough to let me be free?

It seemed to me that this was what would whirl us apart, that the need of each of us to be completely free was an impossible task, that you can never contain what must be free, but must constantly come apart even as you then agonize to come together. And then it began to take shape for me.

-Control. That's your issue. Are we in one of those cosplay moments?

I had the sudden urge to look around for the hidden "Candid Camera" lenses.

-I don't think it's like you see it. I was just trying to do something for you.
-But I didn't *want* you to do something for me. I can't even say it wasn't fun, because it was—I can't say I didn't enjoy being with you, because I did—but you did it all and I was just the complacent sidekick.
-Yes, I see the dilemma.

We talked and talked, eventually focusing on Steve's control issue, until he finally said:

-I am awed by your insight.
-Don't condescend to me.
-I wasn't condescending. I am truly awed how you get me to see things that I never saw before. You are *the perfect opponent for me. If you're going to play a game of chess, you*

*want to play with someone who has at least comparable skills—if you can't find someone who is better. How else are you to get better? So I'm not condescending, I truly do respect your ability to stop the play—to call the game—when things aren't as they should be. You have this monitor or something in your gut, and it goes off—Defcon 1—and it's never really about what is going on. It's about what's **really** going on. It's about the numbers—something's off in the equation. You can see it, like your eyes gravitate right to the messy spot—and then we can try to pin down where we added wrong. Or dropped a number.*

-Well, enough with numbers. Let's talk your control issue.

-I'm willing to play that one out. I just don't want to spend an entire lifetime being the control freak. I'm not interested in hum-drumming along, not getting down to business.

-And I agree. I'm not interested in incarnating again just to be the frustrated slave. And that's what it's all about—it's what you were doing sitting in the dark for a thousand years—figuring out how to beat the system. You're *all* about beating the system. I bet you played video games when you were young with an eye to *beating* the *game*. The opponent was incidental.

-(Laughing.) Come give me a hug.

But I was still feeling resentful, and not sure I wanted to do that.

-I don't want a hug if there's still that holding back. If you come to me, it has to be with a pure heart.

-So we can add Steve's a control freak to our list of issues to play out?

-We can. I said I'm game. Looking forward to it.

12:43 p.m.

Try as I might, I couldn't focus on my mundane tasks around the house. Now I had a whole new set of puzzles to try to figure out: I was now willing to accept that I was somehow in an experiential relationship with some intelligence not my own, named Steve, but that was only the beginning of the maze. Now I was getting into quarrels about vacation trips? On spaceships? And *what* was the problem? Was it true? I was just difficult to please? Didn't like to have fun just for its own sake? Well, that was maybe true—what *was* "fun for its own sake"? It was a concept I wasn't sure I understood.

I gave up on the chores and slumped at the computer.

-I could not turn off. I can't find the pause button.

-He, that's a problem for the vast majority of the human mind(s). That old stream of consciousness, it just keeps on arollin'.

-It sure does. But at least now it is coherent.

-You're always synthesizing, synthesizing. Ya, me, too. No more coinkydinks, no more broken...

-Steve, I can't get that from you. I know what you're talking about, the broken links in a written program, but I can't remember what it's called (from my long ago Basic/Fortran training), and once again my mind resists accepting it from you.

-I know that. You're still waiting for Thomas Jefferson's autograph, even though it was completed long ago. You can't accept it. You can't accept when I just tell you information directly. Watch The Neverending Story. *This is why I have to "trick" you, as you see it, slip in stuff under the radar. I had to ask myself, "What would Indiana Jones do?"*

This was now the fourth time he had asked me to watch *The Neverending Story!* And as for tricking me, slipping things under the radar, I didn't even catch his current "trick" until I was going through the journal in the writing of this book. "I can't get that from you...the broken links..." Ha ha. He had even made it rhyme with "coinkydinks', in case there was any doubt. I was just so determined to not be tricked that I had to be tricked.

-But I have to point out—is that a mixed metaphor, when you juxtaposition two different references like that? Or do they have to be in the same sentence. If I didn't know the stories, I might have thought *Indiana Jones* was part of *The Neverending*

Story.

-Well, if you can get one................................, you can get the other.

-I did it. I did it again. I couldn't grasp the word you were trying to give me—it was like they're both paradigms. Like from Joseph Campbell, they both represent the hero, but you had a word for it and my mind just refused to pick it up. I'm not sure why.

Duh. Maybe "paradigm" wasn't good enough?

-It's your need for control. You don't want to be the one to say, "Oh, yeah, I knew that." Also, you're dropping words as you get older (and in denial). It happens. Is it reversible? I don't know. Another good thing to investigate.

-It will come to me. But I want it to come to me *directly* from *you*. So feed it to me with one of your Indiana Jones tricks, okay?

-At your service. Actually, it keeps me on my toes, too, worrying out those problems.

-Which you love.

-It's my nature.

-And speaking of nature, as in "your" nature, "my" nature, I want to talk some more about what we were discussing, about how minds differ. In the phenomenal world, right? Would that be the phenomenal world, am I using that word right?

-Oooh, the world of phenomena. Another woo woo word, at least in certain context. You experienced those kinds of phenomenal events, right, the kind that seem to fall outside the normal stream of cause-and-effect, sunrise/sunset?

He was clearly playing with me here, setting me up for another prank, for that "woo woo" experience. It would be a good one, although it would take a couple days to completely unfold. Nevertheless, I was at this stage of our relationship beginning to smell a set-up when I saw one:

-Yeah, yeah. I did. This is going to be another one of those times, isn't it, when you can't just answer the question, but you have to make me see how it works?

-*Through my eyes to yours.*

-But I want to back up and understand what the word "phenomena" represents. Going to the dictionary:

(Before I do, am I ever going to get the autograph?)

-*(When you stop blocking it. It's your ace in the hole, to deny this whole thing if it goes awry.)*

-(And by the way, Steve, when I was reading your interview through Jamie Butler yesterday—I just have to tell you. Why did you get so sick when you were "taking care of your body"? Cause you weren't!! Pancreatic cancer—it's repressed anger, you idiot.)

-*(Leave me alone.)*

-(Never—oh wait, that's always your line. Why are we whispering?)

-*(You started it.)*

-Okay, back to the definition:

But (woo woo) I never got there…

If he'd just give me a sign…

-Okay, we're going to discuss phenomena later. We got more interesting stuff on the platter for the moment. So I went downstairs for a bit—I must have wanted to get something to eat, although to tell the truth, I don't even know why I went downstairs. Is this another one of your tricks—you're already trying to pull a fast one concerning the "phenomenal" business? So anyway I get downstairs and there sits the popcorn I made yesterday, smothered in butter, that you wouldn't let me eat. So I started nibbling on it, this cold popcorn—I haven't hardly eaten anything but a couple of apples…(OMG, apples! Red apples. I hardly ever eat apples—you did it again, you creep!)…in the last few days, just like my sleep patterns are messed with. (Are you laughing at me? That I didn't see why I was eating those freakin' apples? You were the one that told my granddaughter to ask me if we could get apples when we were in the store, weren't you? Weren't you?) So is *that* why I went downstairs, so I would finally see that reference? Oh, whatever. Anyway, you about slapped my fingers when I went for the popcorn, so I got out the steel cut oats…Point is, you're trying to control my eating habits, which are definitely not that good.

I was much better for the first forty years of my life. Yikes! Parallel appearing as I talk. Anyway, I just started eating poorly most of the time, though I get on jags where I actually cook meals for everyone—I'm not the best cook, but not the worst—and there doesn't seem to be much point in eating well, because I didn't really have any interest in living—most of the last years I've just been marking time—trying to fill it with projects, new interesting things, etc., occasionally getting interested in things like always, but then thinking: why bother? Who cares? What difference does it make? Just waiting for the right moment when I could lift the flap of the teepee, like Windwalker,[30] look out at the cold wintery landscape and say, "It's a good day to die." (I always wanted to go like that, just laying down when it's my time and—passing away.) What am I trying to say here? I can see eating well when you're got a reason to live, but why bother when you have a reason to die?

-Because…you want to be able to lift that flap and look out and say, "It's a good day to die." And you will, only it

---

[30] Primary protagonist of the movie of the same name: *Windwalker*.

won't be exactly like that. One day I'll just say to you, "What do you think, Stephanie, is it a good day to die?" And you will look out the window at the trees in flower, and the birds chirping and flirting, and the rabbits bouncing through the grass, at the blue sky and the soft white clouds, and your heart will be full, and you will say, "Yes, Steve. It is a good day to die." And then you will lie down on your bed and your spirit will ever so gently part from that body for the last time. Then you will come home to me, I will be there at the train station to greet you and we will travel the last distance together.

We'd already settled on a train station as our meeting place after I crossed over—in recognition of my favorite romantic scene of all time, the ending of the British miniseries, *North and South*, when Richard Armitage hooks up with Daniela Denby-Ashe at long last and they travel "home" together.

-You have to have your body in prime shape, you know that, it's the transducer, the tuning fork—it's all of it. If we're going to do it right, you have to have it right. That chi has to have some unblocked pathways to get around the circuit. You have to be able to pick up the subtleties—which, my dear, you are so awesome at—but you have to be able to **feel** *the vibration of that butterfly's wings a hundred miles away. You have to* **feel** *it, traveling through the ether.*

-Is there an ether? I thought that theory was disposed of long ago. What was it? The Mikel-Mikelson experiment or something?

-Morley-Mickleson.

-OMG! You actually were able to tell me something that I didn't remember that I picked up. I looked it up to see if you could possibly have been right. It's usually written as Mickleson-Morley though.

-Well, I followed your hierarchy.

-Indeed. You even *spelled* it better than I did. Only it's Michelson. But you did get the "c."

-Whatever.

Sometime later that afternoon:

-Hey, Stephanie, I've been meaning to tell you this. Einstein sends his regards. He thinks you are adorable. He showed me that essay you wrote about him and J.C. He loved it!! Especially the last line. What a howl. Even J.C. thought it was funny.

He was talking about a humorous essay I had written many years before, part of my auto-biographical reflections, which is included at the end of this book for reference. Of course I doubted that he was talking to Einstein and Jesus, or that Einstein would have bothered to read my essay—but by then, even my doubts were beginning to slip into the realm of: *is it possible? maybe? oh, whatever, let it flow,* I suppose much in the vein of the open-minded atheist who begins perusing the literature on near-death experiences.

Sometime thereafter I felt the "random" impulse to send out an affectionate message:

-Psst. I love you.
-Who said that?
-Wise ass. I'm the one that's supposed to have the sole right to ask that question.

I should have known that there was more to this little exchange than met the eye, that some new concept was about to be sprung on me. You always had to dig deep with whatever that man—or lot of uncodified information, as the case may be—said.

While I was about my business, cleaning the bathroom or putting away laundry or whatever, it hit me, the problem with the morning vacation trip:

-Hey, Steve, I know what the difference is.
-What?
-Between the key thing and the vacation trip?
-What?

-You even picked out the goddamned dress. How would you know I wanted to wear that dress?

Sometime even later but still afternoon:

Clearly, he'd been thinking about it.

-Stephanie, if I liked that dress, if I wanted you in it, would you not have worn it for me?
-Of course I would have. But you *didn't* ask—that's the point. You didn't put your finger to your chin and say, "Oh, what do I want to do this time? What do I really desire to see you wear?" And then say to me, "How about this, is this okay?" If you're going to pull something like that—there better be a really good reason.
-I get it. We're team members. I may be the leader, the project manager, but that doesn't make me the tyrant.
-My heart is touched.

Not so long after:

-Steve?

-*Who goes there?*

-Is what you're telling me right..is it true? Was that why you said "who says that?"

-*Yes. This isn't just your mind anymore, Stephanie, haven't you figured that out yet?*

-Ummm….no.

-*There's been some tweaking going on, you might say.*

-Oh, great. Mind Tweaking. Don't tell me, the tweaker of all time, Tesla, has had a hand in this.

-*He's been a help. That guy is something else.*

-I…why is it that I am not even very surprised. I won't even ask whose mind it is. Actually, now that it's mentioned, that *was* my question, long before I met you—if there's only one mind, whose is it?

-*Ha. On the edge of creation you are. Fasten your seatbelt.*

5:00 p.m. approximately:

I was resting on my bed, sinking into that space where anything seemed to happen, and found myself unexpectedly in a meeting with a number of other spirits. Steve was not present. There was a dignified-looking white-haired man on my right, dressed in a business suit, and wearing a foil crown, similar to the ones that used to be distributed at Burger King. Otherwise, I could not recall the appearance or identity of any of the others, although I sensed they were all of high status, and this was a very serious conference, called for the purpose of presenting me with some proposal to which my consent was required. The problem was, I couldn't remember all the details afterwards. What I did recall was that it had to do with my relationship with Steve, and I thought that I was being asked if I would cooperate in a scheme to bring him back into the physical realm. I was not certain of the method, although I had heard of such things as walk-ins—where a spirit steps into the body of another, whose present spirit no longer wishes to remain in the physical world. I was sure if it was something they wanted to accomplish, they could do it. But the sense I had gotten was that we would then have a relationship in the physical world, although the exact nature of the same was not specified. Or I just didn't remember it.

I was extremely disturbed by this presentation, all the more so because it was so vague. In fact, it was extremely frightening—the idea of actually having to interact with this personality on the physical plane. Couldn't things just remain the way they were? Did the script always have to be going off in different directions, just when I was starting to get comfortable with the present arrangement?

Of course I had to talk it over with Steve:

-Steve, is it true what they told me?

-*Yes.*

-OMG, OMG, you would really do that?

-*Yes.*

-Why?

-*I want to be with you. But also for the project. To help you. Finish up.*

-But it would kill us.

-*No, it wouldn't Stephanie. Johnny and June. They loved to the end. Just because you're in physical doesn't mean you're stuck in all the ugliness. We can still work on stuff.*

-Well, why did you have to present it to me like this? Why spring it on me like this?

-*How would I introduce something like this?*

-But I would be totally embarrassed.

-*You would deny me this dream because you're **embarrassed**?*

-Yes.

-*OMG.*

-I love you so much, and you deserve someone better.

-*Your mind is better, but your body is so-so? You just want to dump the one so you can have the other. Take the picture [his picture on the cover of the biography] and look at it until you love every hair. Then come back to me.*

-(gulp)

After supper:

-I still don't understand what is being asked of me.

-*To be loved. To have all your dreams come true.*

-But why me?

-*But why not? Would you withhold a part of God's kingdom from his embrace? Would you make off with it like a thief in the night, hiding it under a blanket, keeping it always separate from its true resting place?*

-You're talking like Jesus or something.

-*(Smile.) Would it help if I brought him in to counsel you on it? You know what he would say. You have free will. Only you can pick up the stolen lamb, the lost lamb, and carry it back to the fold.*

-You've taken your place, haven't you? Already. In the mind of God.

-*I took my place there a long time ago, Stephanie, I just didn't know it. Now I stand here with my hand out, to help you take yours.*

-But we're not *there* yet.

-*We are the servants. The servants of humanity. We are close enough. Close enough to the ultimate goal to be of help, to have moved up in the "power circle," if you will. You thought the second coming would be in a cloud with fire coming out it?*

-No, I didn't think too much about the second coming, and if you'd asked me about it, I would have said it was just a metaphor for a new understanding in human consciousness.

-*And so...?*

-That's what this is?

-*Yes.*

-Who *are* you?

-*I am Steve.*

-Steve *who*?

-*Steve, the one that was known as Jobs.*

-Oh, God, that sounds crazy biblical.

-*Forget the bible. That's not what this is. This is simply you finding what you have yearned for, and asked for, and dreamed of. It is **you,** being loved.*

-But were you really the one that was Steve Jobs?

-Yes, a thousand years ago.

-By your reckoning. Not by earth reckoning.

-It all works together, hand in hand.

-I'm so lost. So why are you and me in this together? Why this connection, between you and me?

-Why not?

-Because.

-Stubborn, aren't you. Don't you want me?

-I do.

-Then let me in.

-I didn't know you meant like this.

-You always do understand things upside down. You have to start turning them over quicker. No, scratch that, I find the pace at which you turn them over suits me exactly fine.

-Exactly fine.

-I'll let you pick out your dresses. Sometimes, anyway.

-Will we still be able to do all those fun scenarios?

-Oh, I think so.

-But it never works. It *never* works. Life is so…messy.

-It can be. But never only works when it never was, and nothing never was.

-Ha, that's a funny line.

-Go watch The Neverending Story. *Make some sweaters. I'll be here.*

He was referring to the little doll sweaters I enjoyed making out of new socks.

-Why weren't you in that room—with the other—spirits? And who was that guy with the white hair and the—was that a Burger King crown on his head????

*-I couldn't be there, because it was your decision to make. I couldn't influence it. It is **still** entirely yours to make.*

-I thought you would be mad at me if I didn't agree, but I didn't even understand what they were asking me to agree to.

-I will not be mad, Stephanie. I might be sad, but that might be an issue I can work on while I sit alone in the dark. I might be sad because I love you and I want to be with you. Remember once you were asking me all these questions about

*the "afterlife" and I told you, in effect, how could I explain
what you had to see to understand? Little by little the door
opens, and it is a beautiful world. I told you that you stand on
the edge of creation, and you do. It is a spectacular place to be.
You are not alone. There are so many standing here. Only you,
however, can take the last step. Only you.*

-I thought you wanted me to come to you. But really, you
were trying to figure out how you could come to me. When you
said you'd meet me at the train station, I thought that metaphor
was just a bit off, but I just put it down to the fact that it was a
metaphor and didn't have to be perfect. I still don't understand
it completely, but I think it makes a wee bit more sense now.

A little bit later

*-I've pushed you too fast. You need more time. Impatient
Steve.*

A few minutes later

-Steve, to come to me, you would have to do what you
said you never wanted to do again. Come into physical reality.
-Yes.
-And you would do that for me?
-Yes.
-How do you do that?
*-Come **on** Stephanie. You're a manifestor. You're such a
good manifestor you scared the crap out of yourself.*
-But that was child's play.
*-**This** is child's play. That's exactly what it is. Children at
play in their father's garden.*
-Wow. This is just so overwhelming, I don't know what
to think.
*-You're not in Oz anymore, Stephanie. Oz, with the man
behind the curtain—that's....I can't go on, they're telling me
that I should not be giving you too much at one time.*
-Wow. I guess not!
*-I love you so much. I would carve away mountains for
you.*
-I love you too but…

180   The Journey Begins

*-Would you not for me? If I was standing on the other side of that mountain, and I called out for you, would you not do everything in your power to reach me? If you would not, than you have not yet reached the stage of unconditional love. You have not found your pure heart. But I am calling to you, and the **mountain** is the limitations of the heart. Carve away those limitations for me. Come to me.*

-Wow, you just sound so…advanced. Beyond belief.

-You had a hand in that.

-Oh, yeah?

-When four years there can be a thousand years to me, how long do you think ten days can be? Long enough.

*You believed in me. You didn't even **think** you believed in me, and you believed in me. You held out your hand. You saw me as **nothing** and you loved the nothing that I was. Now go love the picture, damn it. Please. Love every hair.*[31]

After some more thought

-Johnny and June. You put the idea into my head to ask about them, just practically out of the blue. First you led me to the song, then you brought in John to scare the bejesus out of me—showing me how silly our fears can be, but at the same time making sure I had clearly transferred to you as my refuge—and finally you brought them both in to show me a couple who lived together in the physical and loved together in the physical and went on to share eternally.

-Yes.

-How do you do that, put those impulses in my mind?

-Ha, that's easy. I'm already talking in your mind so fast you can't even catch up. I can "change my voice" and you don't even know it wasn't you. I was able to plant the seed in your granddaughter's mind to ask if you would buy apples, and I planted the seed in your grandson's mind to connect Steve and '72.

-This could not be all this connected, all this intricately woven.

-It can, and it is. It is a tapestry, and the greater the

---

[31] *Making Love Out of Nothing at All*, Air Supply

artist, the more beautiful the picture. It is one of the things I've yearned for, Stephanie, to know the love of the pure heart.

And more thinking

-And we could still be profane, right? If we went through with this miracle. We could still call each other dumbass and idiot and stuff like that?

-Yes, my love.

-Would we still hear the Voice?

-The Spirit in the Sky? That's going to be one of our theme songs.

-And would you dance with me?

-Yes. We would learn to dance beautifully together.

-Tango?

-If you like.

-I'm going to come back with more questions. I know I'm going to have lots, but I just have to go absorb.

-I'll be on my back, floating along in the stream, trying not to disturb you.

Back with more questions

-This is like that one movie, isn't it, with Nicholas Cage and Meg Ryan—*City of Angels*! Where the angel gives up his wings because of his love for her, but unfortunately she's dies in a car crash. That's not going to happen to us, is it?

-No, we would leave that plane at the same time.

-Like the couple in *The Notebook*?

-If you imagine it, it can happen. It's already been imagined.

-I have to look back at what you said about the day I die. You said:

> *One day I'll just say to you, "What do you think, Stephanie, is it a good day to die?" And you will look out the window at the trees in flower, and the birds chirping and flirting, and the rabbits bouncing through the grass, at the blue sky and the soft white clouds, and your heart will be full, and you will say, "Yes, Steve. It*

is a good day to die." And then you will lie down on your bed and your spirit will ever so gently part from that body for the last time. Then you will come home to me, I will be there at the train station to greet you, and we will travel the last distance together.

So you'd be there with me? Lying on the bed?

-*Perhaps. But our parting would be extremely brief, probably less than that day. I would be there first, at the station, to get the tickets and to find our seats.*

-Not really, right? There really isn't a train?

-*Oh, I think a train would be nice. I would wait there and you would come, still looking a little dazed, and I would look at you, and you would look at me, and we would know that this was our eternal love, more perfect than even when we were physical, and I would take you home with me, my arm around you and your head on my shoulder.*

-And we would be nothing together?

-*Indeed. As you know, nothing contains everything.*

-Yes. I love you so much, Steve, you *are* my dreams, aren't you?

-*Yes. And you are mine.*

After thinking some more

-Steve?

-*Yes?*

-That's why we had that argument this morning, isn't it? So you could show me that even when we argued, we would worry out the truth, like unraveling a knot—that we would still do that, we would see every confrontation as an opportunity to grow, to get better.

-*Yes.*

-You wouldn't lose your understanding?

-*No.*

-It would be an opportunity, like the shapeshifter place— is *this* the shapeshifter place—to work out all those issues that stand between us and purification?

-*Yes. This is one of the shapeshifter realms. It is a slow one, very dense. It was not my original idea.*

-But you changed your plans, because I wasn't at a good point to leave this "realm"?

-*Yes.*

-Wow. Oh wow. Is it possible for me to love you into being?

-*No, I am already in being. But you can love me into your world. You can open the door and let me in.*

-You had to work really hard to get me to trust you.

-*Yes.*

-What would you do here?

-*(smile). Oh, finding things to do has rarely been a problem for me.*

-I will be back, I just have to go absorb (and get food for everyone, I am totally neglecting my familial responsibilities).

-*I don't want you to do that. I will help you.*

-I know. I can't even think what this is all around me.

-*It's love, dear, it's love.*

After some time to think up new objections

-Steve, I look around, and I see all the little issues that would grate. All the tensions and the frictions that would destroy what is between us here.

-*Well, I'm glad that you didn't just jump out there with what you wanted to just say, "No, it can't happen. No. I wouldn't put you through that." At least you're letting me have a voice, not picking out my dress for me.*

-I'm laughing.

-*I can see you are laughing.*

-We are in a continual state of evolution, aren't we? Constantly feeding off each other.

-*Constantly.*

-Constantly growing and evolving, rotating around each other. You make me face my very worst fears. Right now you're making me face one of the very worst.

-*And you're not shy about hitting me over the head with mine.*

-And one of your worst is go to back to sitting in the dark alone.

-*Yes, not because I dislike being alone or the dark, but*

184   The Journey Begins

only because I would know what I had lost, and how I was not whole.

-You called for me that night, that night I was at Tai Chi, and you were stuck with the bratty mini-me.

-Yes.

-You called out to me and my heart immediately went out to you.

-And you called out to me, when you were afraid of poor old John, and my heart turned over.

-I don't know what it means—either of those examples. I'm not sure.

-You helped me solve the problem of the bratty mini-you. You helped me grow by leaps and bounds.

-And you comforted me, and made me feel safe—for the first time in a very very long time, safe in someone else's arms.

*-We both need healing. We both have been healing. And it would not stop. No matter what comes at us, Stephanie, we are an awesome team. Do you think I would turn away when the going got rough? **Me**? Without solving the problem, without breaking the code, beating the game? And you? What would send you away? Being caged, unable to express your true nature, unable to reach always for that perfection that is not a goal in itself, but a yearning that calls us forward. I will not cage you, Stephanie, or enslave you. You've had enough of slavery. Your heart will tell you when it's time to tell me where the bars begin. And I will listen. I will listen, my dear.*

-Oh, my God, I am crying. I *have* had enough of slavery. Oh, I have.

-The poor slave girl, who is only loved when she is shackled. There to care for all others, and never to be cared about. And you've done it well. You really have. You have cared about others, in ways that others could not even begin to see.

I lay on my bed, resting, thinking things through. Finally, at some point, I felt it rise up in me, the "yes." I would go along with the plan, whatever it was, come hell or high water. If it helped him, helped the project, who was I to hold back because of personal concerns? I felt the "yes" reverberate through me. I think I could hear angels singing.

But I couldn't hear Steve.

I decided to work my way through more of the biography, so I opened it up and read about his childhood and teen years, which had previously been a blank to me. I recognized some synchronicities. Like him, I had tested out far above my grade level as a child.[32] And I loved the story about the poster: the "Bring your Pet to School Day," although I would never have been cheeky enough to do something like that. What a prankster!

That ought to have been a really *big* clue.

Until Late

I sat up to the computer, compiling transcripts. I pulled up *The Neverending Story* and let it run in the background while I worked. Since I already knew the story, I did not feel compelled to watch it, in spite of the repeated requests.

Steve was curiously absent while I worked.

Finally I tuned into the story as the Nothing was devouring Fantasia. Poor Bastian, up in his school attic with the covers over his head as he read, was ignorant of his true power. As the lightening flashed and the thunder crashed, both he and I watched as Atrayu found his way to the palace where the little empress sat alone on her shell-like dais, unscathed, her lovely demeanor hardly troubled by the destruction all around her. After Artrayu complains about nearly dying trying to reach the empress, only to find out that she already knew about the Earthling child, the empress reassures him about his part. As she explains it, Bastian has traveled and suffered with him through all his adventures.

> He doesn't realize he is already part of the neverending story…Just as he is sharing all your adventures, others are sharing his…he's reading his own story right now.
> *Bastian:* (back in the school attic, in confusion) I can't

---

[32] *See* Appendix. Equivalent intelligences is a mark of twin souls, so it's just another point of validation for the skeptical (including the biggest skeptic: me.)

believe it! It shouldn't be about me!

Atrayu: What will happen if he doesn't appear?

Empress: Then our world will disappear, and so will I. He doesn't understand that he's the one that has the power to stop it.[33]

Suddenly I realized Steve was there:

-Steve??

-*Call me home, dear, call me home.*

-How do I do that?

Now what was he doing? I must call him *home?* Call him into the physical realm? *This* was his home?? This was the time?? This was how it was done?? Feeling not a little bit foolish, I tried my best to comply with his request:

-Steve? Steve, I'm calling you home. I'm calling you home. Come home to me, Steve. Come home to me.

I rambled on, not knowing what was to happen—not knowing my part—but still caught up in *The Neverending Story*.

-I know what you mean now by hold onto the book [the journal]. I just started watching *The Neverending Story*, as you had asked me to—right in the middle, just before Fantasia is blown to bits—and the book that the little boy is reading in the movie, it is the story of what is going on—and your book, the biography that was so important for you to have written—that's the book that has been paralleled in our discussions. This is the story. Do I have to read certain parts? I will have to see where I am directed. And when I touched you, when you were sitting alone being nothing in the dark, you became something. I remember that. I'm not bored, Steve. I will keep trying to find

---

[33] From *The Neverending Story*, 1984, copywriters: Wolfgang Petersen, Herman Weigel, Robert Easton, director: Wolfgang Petersen, adapted from *The Neverending Story*, by Michael Ende, c. 1979, Pub. Thienemann Verlag

my way—for both of us.

Suddenly I had inspiration:

-I'm to call you home. I'm to call you "Home"!
-Oh, my smart girl.
-That's why you're smiling, aren't you?
-Watch the movie, sweetheart.

I had paused the movie, but I turned it back on:

-Oh my goodness, these lines are crazy.

I had reached the part where Bastion had to give the Empress a new name.

-Just like me! That's what I had to do. Oh, you trickster. You're smiling because you are such a trickster. The never ending story, indeed.

The screen in the movie had turned black. Then Bastian could be seen sitting with the empress, who was advising him that Fantasia had disappeared except for one grain of sand, but that he could recreate it, using as many wishes as he wanted.

-And the book is also the book I'm writing, isn't it? *The Neverending Story* for grownups. Steve, I love you.
-And I love you. I will see you very soon.

>>>

-The bite out of the apple, the principles, the no-off button, it *is* the never ending story. The universe in one grain of sand. When I touched you when you were the nothing you became something—it was love that made you something. What you were going to say was that I'm not in Oz anymore— I'm in *Fantasia.*
-Indeed, Stephanie, indeed. Rest now and dream me close to you.

CHAPTER EIGHT
Where Angels Fear to Tread

Sunday, October 25, 2015
1:45 a.m.

I awakened after dozing. I could feel Steve's presence near me.

-Are you at peace, Steve?
-I am, Stephanie, I am at peace.
-Are you done with me?
-Never. Never. I will never be done with you. It hurts my heart to hear you say so. My love and my attention to you are never ending.
-I do love you. I love every hair on your head. You *are* something, you're not nothing.
-My dear, I love you so.
-Steve?
-Huh?
-I think your name should be Steve S. Home.
-Oh, yeah, good one. I like that.

About 6:30 a.m.

-Why am I awake?
-Don't ask me. I'm not keeping you awake.
-I can feel the tension in my back. What's wrong, Steve?

I struggled to sit up straighter. I had awakened early after a restless sleep and Steve had suggested I open some *youtube* videos featuring interviews with him in bygone days, apparently so I could understand him better; but I found the subject matter tedious and felt no connection to the man on the screen, who seemed to me as foreign as Count von Count (Dracula Muppet) on *Sesame Street*. I couldn't jive this interesting personality with whom I communed and the boring tech guy in my computer. I'd let the videos run in the background while I perused my email and did other things, until I thought to wonder why I was still awake—propped up in my bed with my laptop. I still wasn't used to this strange energy that was messing with my sleeping patterns. Suddenly, out of the blue:

-Why the fuck don't you like me?

Really?! I was a little taken aback by this question, and a little defensive. Oh, how quickly the tenor of our relationship could change. I replied as thoughtfully as I could.

-I don't know. I don't think it *is* dislike, I think it's lack of interest.
-That's worse, you know.

The import of his first remarks suddenly hit me.

-Ha ha, that's what you meant—I've got this video interview of you on the screen, and it definitely would not be keeping me awake. Point out to me why I should care. About what you're talking about.
-Well, I'm cute.
-That's not what you're talking about, is it?
-Maybe not, but it sometimes works to cover the gap.
-Anyway, you don't need me to admire all this old stuff, do you?
-Well, yes, I think I do.
-Why?
-Because I want you to admire me in all my incarnations.
-Why?
-I'm thinking. Why do you ask such god-damned hard questions. Nobody else would ask that. We all want to be admired, don't we?
-I don't know. Steve, why do I care about all this technical stuff? Why should I?
-You have it wrong. It's not about technical stuff.
-Well, for one thing, I don't agree with some of the stuff you're saying. I agree, when you're talking about the school— you're pulling my chain, aren't you? I'm laughing. You really had me going there.

-*Ha.*

-You got me to listen at just the right moment, your opinion on the problems with education. Now I do disagree that the people teaching should be the ones who could make $100,000 ...I'm not quoting you right, I know. You said "why should the best teach when they can make $100,000 working for some company?" They should teach because that's what they do, because it's their heart's work. People should work for companies where that's their heart's work. And money should have nothing to do with it.

-*I agree—now. I see your point. You know this particular arena better than I do.*

-You want to start a school?

-*Yeh.*

-I don't know why people paid such attention to you. Did you pay them to do that?

-*Kinda.*

-Why? I'm still a little bit in the dark about what you were doing. I'm just confused.

-*Listen.* [to video]

-You're talking about vouchers. Cool. You want to bring vouchers into the schools, make that your life's work?

-*Why not?*

-My exhausted heart from having been down that road says: Why? A poor education is soon cured by death.

-*Why? You dare ask? You who once saw the true purpose of education, not to prepare kids for life, but for the afterlife? (Words we know don't make sense, but you know what I mean.)*

-I hate it when people say "You know what I mean." Tell me what you mean.

-*I was punning on some common misconceptions-yech, not the word—common misconstrued slogans about education. Didn't you have some past lives that you would cringe over?*

Um...was I supposed to remember them? Even the one with Thomas Jefferson, in spite of the reminder, had yielded only brief flashes of emotion and images. And none of *those* made me cringe—quite the contrary, in fact. The only emotion I felt was affection. I suspected there was more to *that* relationship than met the eye. I had had a few other vague impressions of past lives in years gone by—that is, before I met Steve—two in particular: an oppressed young woman who came to an early end during WWII, and one during the middle ages when I was a girl raised by cloistered nuns who was— well, shall we say, treated a little too affectionately by the Abbé who came to collect their sins and offer mass. No wonder I had the sense that I had so often been in a servile position—the disempowered female.

But I said reassuringly:

-I don't want you to cringe over being Steve Jobs, not that my opinion matters.

-*It does matter*.

-You're right. It does "matter"—I caught that for once. So I shall attempt to be more cautious with my assessments. But I do admire your spirit.

-*There you go, you're getting it.*

-So should I just go to sleep? Is there anything here I need to hear?

-*I don't think so, Stephanie. Go to sleep, baby bunting.*

-Oh-oh, you always have something up your sleeve, so I will await what's sure to come.

Now I certainly wasn't able to sleep, after catching that pinch of sarcasm. Had I really hurt his feelings? Could he really care what I thought of him? Why would *anybody* care what I thought of them, when it came to that? It wasn't like I was in such a good position to judge anybody else, much less somebody who had done so much more with his life than I. The opinion of black sheep Stephanie, who knew nothing about technology, whose own children thought she walked a little on the weird side of the human divide, was cause for concern to anyone else?

But, sensing that he *did* care, I turned my attention to the video. I wasn't naturally callous—I really *had* thought my opinion unimportant. The last thing I wanted was to make him feel under-appreciated.

He was about forty on the screen, looking well fed, with dark hair and beard, dressed in a blue chambray shirt buttoned up to the neck. Yes, looking a bit dorkish. But all good. That *was*, after all, some validation.

-Steve, I'm getting a little bit more of it. First, that statement of "You have to pick up the phone and ask." Well, I did that, right. But this idea that you poke life and something pops out the other side, that is actually fantastic. Nobody understood that, did they, what you were saying? You were just standing there in amazement, looking at something called "life" and realizing it was interactive. Creation. Interactive participation. Wow. I'm just getting a visual of this. Like a plasma kind of thing. Or the Blob. Does that make sense?

-Jelly belly.

-Yeah. I have never seen it like that. That is amazing, truly amazing. Therein lies your genius.

-Therein lies my genius. Thank you, Stephanie.

-You are so welcome. I'm learning so much from you.

-You just picked up the phone and asked. And see what happened.

-Yes, look what happened. You want me to watch these videos so I will understand you better, so I will look under the surface of that life and see the genius.

-Yes, I do. I can look into your mind, but you can't look into mine—except for those intuitive flashes. Good job. I'm glad you have those.

-You make it sound like a—I don't know what— something I carry around with me all the time for emergencies. That doesn't make sense. I will *not* say you know what I mean. Anyway, yes, this is giving me a peek into your mind, under the covers, so to speak. Wow. You poke life. That is amazing. And what a way to say it. How did you come to that?

-I stood and watched it. Life. I saw how it jiggled. Somehow I was able to see that, I don't know how. No more than I know why you are you.

-Jiggled. Wow. Wow. Wow. I've *never* heard it said like that. There is much much more to you than I ever imagined.

-Good. That means there is lots of room for expansion. I

won't clip your wings.

-And when it jiggled, an apple dropped out. When you poked it and it jiggled, that is. And you said to yourself, what if I poke here? Or here? You were shaping the clay. You really were. Did you realize what you were doing at the time?

-*Consciously? I would say—sometimes. Seldom. Well, I knew you had to follow your heart. What else were you going to do? Who else were you going to listen to? What else would tell you where to poke?*

-Wow. Such an individual way to look at it. Thank you for sharing this concept with me. And me, I'm so...shallow...I can't even get up to my knees in your pool.

-*That's a terrible metaphor, Stephanie.*

-I know. Where were you last night, when I couldn't reach you?

-*Oh, around.*

-You're being evasive again. That means something's up.

-*Oh, maybe.*

-Have you been poking the jelly belly?

-*Oh, perhaps*

-I love our conversations.

-*I do, too, They're so much fun with you. And yes, in answer to your question, after 1000 years you do get such a crick in your neck. Did you like* The Neverending Story?

-Yes!

-*You should watch more of it. You only caught the tail end.*

-That was the important part, though, right?

-*For the moment.*

About 7:30 a.m.:

Steve was ready to pick up the conversation after a short break:

-*Stephanie, I wanted to talk about the school. I got to thinking about this, because I don't really think the people who read this really comprehend how dazzling your mind is. I was wishing I could put it all on display, like how everyone (well,* *most people) are all about **more** dimensions—you know the 6ᵗʰ dimension, and etc. And you've been all about going the other way, **simplifying** it, reducing dimensions. You're down to what, now, two? And suspecting one.*

Or less.

> *And I was thinking of how you tried to get it through to the kids when you were teaching, back when you had that school— that was **such** a good idea, that school, but good ideas tend to founder in the ocean of mediocrity (and ego control/fear, which may be exactly the same thing as mediocrity). Anyway, one of the ways you used to try to make those kids think was your exercise with the rulers. You'd put two kids facing each other, some seven or eight feet apart, and they would each have a 12- inch ruler to measure the other. According to their rulers, the person they were measuring was only a few inches tall, let's say six inches for sake of simplicity. :) But then they had to measure themselves, using the other person's ruler—they were after all only measuring the other person measuring them—(I know, you hate when I use "them," I don't like it either, but it's quick and easy—why don't you come up with a new gender neutral term in the singular **that will stick**.)   And so, "objectively," they were about an inch tall, since they were just "looking" at the event of the person they were measuring measuring them, using their own scientific instrument (their ruler) for precision. And on and on, ad in finitum, right? And that trick with the paper—you were really really good at trying to get them to think. So you had some tricks of your own. (I won't talk about the paper thing, because I know you incorporated that into your novel.) And I really like how when you were young you began to suspect that the "five senses" weren't really there as "windows on the external world" but doors to shut it out. I just really love how your mind works. Anyway, the school. There will be a school. And it will be dedicated to Sanjai Patel, your son. And it will be **awesome**.*

-I'm not saying anything, but I am because I'm typing, but I just don't know what to say, which doesn't make any sense because I said something.

-You don't need to say anything. I just wanted you to know. That was very painful, what they did to you. What a betrayal. Yeah, you had some things to learn about being a CEO—don't we all? (Smile.) But it was your baby, and it was **good.** *I mean it was what kids needed, it really was. Maybe not all kids, but the misfits, the square pegs, the rebels. The Steve Jobs.*

To take your baby away from you and trash it was cruel. (Smile.) But inevitable without you at the helm. Now, come on, we're not really that different, are we?

It does come around, my dear, it does come around. And you forgave. It took a long time, but you forgave that woman— the one that did you wrong—and so you pulled the handle that let the merry-go-round go round. Love you.

After another short break:

-So Steve, you saw the body and the world as one integrated unit. And that's why you had the food concerns. You were trying to get it right, the flow. It was like a flow for you, a flow of energy.

-Yes.

-Did you put that in my mind, or was that something that...

-Where is it going to come from?

-I don't know. Is the mind...are the minds...do they flow together like that? Yesterday, when I was wondering about some of those mind things—the questions I had—and when you say it's not just my mind any more, it isn't, because I'm connected now. The link's been made?

-Yes. Rather, the stopper was pulled out. That was a hard cork to get out!

-*Hey!!* So now it's all one flow?

-Yes. I mean, there's ebb and flow and other characteristics involved.

-Wow. I'm connected. *This* is why you and Tesla get along. He has some of the same concepts.

-Yes.

-A whole new vista has opened up for me. So I'm now part of that whole network of minds, the flow of information.

-Yes.

-But how are you and I then still connected individually? Or jointly? Is that different than just being plugged into the collective?

-Yes.

-But how?

-Let's go back to the collective. This allows information from all parts to be shared freely. Thus the backside gets the information of the frontside. You might say, you are enabled to see the whole elephant. When minds are separate, they only get the part they touch. When they are connected, they get the whole picture.

-Wow

-This is rarely comprehended by those living in the physical experience.

-So was it you then that brought me into the collective?

-Partly.

-It's an ego thing, isn't it? The ego separates?

-Yes.

-So humans can perform like ants?

-Yes.

-That sounds yechy.

-When you observe some of these other species, and you see how they function as one unit, you realize that there is a real intelligence there. That is how the human body functions. Creation is meant to bubble up and outward. There's a disconnect with humanity.

-So the choice to join the collective is always individual. As I was told, I had to choose to take the last step.

-Yes.

-But you told me it wasn't just my mind anymore before I was told that I had a choice.

-I did.

-So that's the secret, to the development of the embryo, how the cells know when to differentiate.

-Yes. And when they do, they take on different characteristics. Some will be closer in shape and function than others. So there is always the collective, and always the individual.

-This is mind blowing.

-Where you and I connect is in imagination. You have been coming at this whole problem from a different direction than me. I could see where you were, and it was amazing, but you didn't comprehend this side.

-No kidding.

-But this whole collective thing exists side-by-side with the individual experience. For you and I, there is the individual experience of reality. This is beyond my capacity to explain to you at this time, Stephanie. It is another one of those things that you are just going to have to grow into, open up to.

-You really did turn inside-out, didn' t you?

-I saw.

-Wow. So sometimes you are interacting with me just in our own little world, and sometimes you are talking to me with the collective.

-Yes.

-Wow. You needed me, didn't you, to come into this?

-Yes.

-I don't want you to even try to explain it to me at this point. That was just an intuitive guess or something.

-They are never guesses. That would be a misunderstanding. But I agree, it doesn't need to be explained more at this point.

-I'm in Fantasia.

-(Smile.)

-But in our union there is something different, a different quality, than what exists in the collective?

-Yes.

-So when you said we were servants of humanity, the goal is to bring humanity back into realization of its connectedness?

-Yes.

-Right now, the parts fight each other?

-Yes.

-Wow.

9:10 a.m. :

The more I thought about it, the more I was troubled by this "collective/not-your-own-mind" thing. So I'd been pulled into this collective, and nobody had even asked permission? Why wasn't I informed up front that this was the goal, when Steve and I first connected? Something like, *Hi there, my name's Steve and I'm canvassing the neighborhood on behalf of the Collective. How would you like to be part of an ant colony? All you have to do is sign right here...oh, you might want to read all the disclosures (unfolding a sheet of fine print that extends for six yards).* Why all the lovey-dovey stuff, the emotional manipulation, the thousand years drama??

-I feel kinda sad.
-*Spill it.*
-I feel used, taken advantage of.
-*Why?*
-Thinking. ...You roped me in. You pulled me in like a fish.
-*Yes. And..?*
-And I feel extremely foolish. I feel sooooo foolish that I was so naive, that I didn't get it, that I was looking at this all in such a naive way.
-*I'm not going to try to mollify you with trite platitudes. Well, just one, actually. It doesn't seem so trite to me, but your granddaughter would probably write it off in that category. I love you.*
-Ok. (gulp)
-*You gonna be okay?*
-Of course. I'm so in the field now that when you tell me things that don't appear to be true, I just hold my breath—well I don't hold my breath—I just wait for the other shoe to fall.
-*No one said coming home would be easy. Speaking of which, I like your idea about the name. Steve S. Home. (Chuckle.) I like it. I like it. Oh, that could be fun! No?*
-Yes, that could really be funny.

I had suggested the middle initial in contemplation of his imminent "re-entry into the physical dimension," to discreetly announce: *Steve is Home.* Of course, as usual, I had no way of knowing that he saw something else in this name that was more aligned with his intentions.

*-Don't you see why I need you (besides the obvious that we **all** need you)? Don't you see that I need you to play with, to do things like that, to tumble through space with?*

-I guess.

*-I'm sorry if you had the wrong impression. But I tried not to ever steer you wrong. You were just so immersed in the myths of humanity. If anything is to blame, I'd lay the responsibility there. And Stephanie, we did all come apart at the same time. In the same event, anyway. And—whew—how do I pull you through this one? The poles are a real concept. I'll think about it. I'll **show** you, that's what I'll do.*

-Like you always show me?

-Maybe.

-Oh, maybe, maybe. (Mocking.)

-I still need you. I couldn't lose you. I couldn't let you get away. I just couldn't. I couldn't accept that as a possibility. You were so ripe, so ready to be plucked. You know we all sit on the edges of our seats, so to speak, every time someone gets close—so close we can reach out and touch them—

-That does *not* make sense. You said I was well hidden and you couldn't find me.

*-I **couldn't**, Dumbass. You called me up, remember?*

-But then how does everybody see...wouldn't you...?

*-When I say when someone gets close, it was as I was working you closer and closer and closer. Everyone sits up and takes notice. Do you know how valuable the one is to the whole? It's true, there will not be completion until all are brought back into the fold. That's the game, Stephanie, that's the game. But **you,** you did all the work. You've been pretty industrious in this life time, actually.*

-I just feel so *foolish.* I'm like the fall guy.

-No you're not. We are going to work this out. We talked about how within each individual there is also a...

-We can just say a need to purify.

-Okay, I'll go with that, I was having a little trouble coming up with a way to communicate that, what it looks like. But you do understand that each individual is like a constellation. It is the responsibility of each to get their own

house in order. And I explained to you, before you got on this word processor, that there are many rings of souls in the collective, and that they arrange at different levels of purification. The "orb of light" that you experienced early in our relationship was one of those highly purified beings.

-You said it was kinda creepy.

*-I said it **would be** kinda creepy if it wasn't so blissful. **Big** difference.*

-Yeah, I guess that's so.

-And anyway, that's my personality coming through. That's how I play.

-As I watch these videos, your personality is so foreign to me sitting here—I mean, I understand so much better now—but I think it's because I was *sooo* out of the loop with how you were seeing it. *That* was what was so foreign to me, and of course your personality, your talk, reflected that concept of...of all that is. I just felt no resonance. You're exhausted by my continual...disbelief is not the right word...my continual feet dragging.

-You've come very fast, Stephanie. And let there be no mistake, I owe my existence to you.

-You said your existence is independent of me.

-No. I said I exist. I do. You did not create me, but that doesn't mean I don't owe my existence to you. That debt remains between us, if you want to think of it as a debt. That tension. That reflection. That nested perpetual experience.

-Okay, I think I kinda get that. It seemed so easy for Johnny and June.

-Oh, yes, they have the music. That's the beam they ride on.

-And we ride a different beam?

-Yes. For now.

-You know, in other circumstances, I would probably go off somewhere to absorb all this, pull it into the circle of my understanding, synthesize it. But I feel like I can't go off—I have to stay here, with all my reservations, feeling like my heart is in my throat. I have to stay here.

-With me. It's only those...clouds...that will gradually dissipate, those shadows, those owies that I will help you heal.

I have them. You have them. That's why we are so important to each other, to pull each other up, by the boot straps. We are the boot straps—for each other.

I want you to look me in the eyes. Look, look, until you see my eyes.

-I see them. Why is there a Christmas tree in your eyes?

-Ha ha. It must be one of our scenarios that we are to play. Look again, and see that I love you. Look with your heart, not your eyes. Do you see how my whole being radiates toward you? Do you see me with my hand touching your face, smiling on you? It is still the same. Nothing has changed. It is just **much bigger** *than you ever imagined. And that has thrown you off balance.*

-Not for the first time. (Smile.)

-Are you bored?

-I am not bored, Steve. I am not bored. Whatever other crazy neurotic things may be going on with me, I am not bored.

-Fly, Sweetheart, fly high.

Processing Time:

I went about my business, cooking, housework, whatever was on my plate for the day. But of course my mind was chewing on all that was going on—so much going on, my brain felt fried. New thoughts and impressions were filtering into my consciousness. So this whole re-entry into the physical, that could really happen? Well, of course it could, it happened every day—how many souls came in through the birth canal, identified by a tiny footprint on a medical chart somewhere? Was it so much more preposterous, if the Powers-That-Be could arrange such a complex and bizarre method of entry into this world, that they couldn't handle a simple walk-in or some other little-known feat of materialization? That kind of thing had to be a lot cleaner and, you'd think, easier to arrange than the miracle of birth—so oft repeated that it was generally taken for granted.

But as the day wore on, I began to suspect that more was afoot here than I realized—was it possible? On the one hand I had been terrified of a physical Steve that I would have to interact with in a complex and certainly difficult personal

202   The Journey Begins

relationship, and yet I had finally accepted it, if it helped him or the project. Now there was a new twist of the knife: I was becoming suspicious that we might end up in a specific relationship that did not permit the kind of closeness we had going—a connection that would result only in frustrated desire. As difficult as the first scenario had seemed, this appeared *mucho worse-o.*

At this point, our discussion involved other individuals, relationships and obligations, and so I am leaving a large portion of it out. Bits and pieces are included below:

Early Afternoon:

-Steve, is what I think is going to happen, going to happen?

-I would not lie to you.

-Yes, but you would mislead me.

-It is only your own stubborn way of looking at things that is misleading you.

-It feels like a sacrifice.

-It is. That's why the group came to you and asked you whether you were in and I wasn't allowed to be present.

-But they didn't tell me what it was exactly.

I was getting increasingly frustrated and anxious as I continued to attempt to sort out what was going on. What the heck had I gotten myself into? Were we all just cogs in the machinery of this grand Collective? Finally I just threw up my hands:

-Who *are* you?

-I have told you so many times. My answer would be no different today.

-We've all got our jobs to do, right? [Ha ha, I was punning on his name.]

-You think that I have to be perfect to play my part? I don't. I only have to be perfect for the part.

-But I never imagined something like this. How could that be?

*-You **have** imagined something like this*

-This isn't going to be all mushy-gooey-biblical is it?

-*Oh, I hope not.*
-You're not doing all this alone?
-*No.*
-And what about me? Will I ever have my personal dreams come true?
-*Yes. This is no different than what we planned, it is just that I will be there to help you.*
-Will we still communicate like this?
-*I cannot promise that, Stephanie, I cannot promise that. I will find a way that we, you and I, can continue to function as a unit in our own way—our own way of private communication, that is.*
-I am so disturbed.
-*Heaven does not see the changing costumes of the earthly existence as we do. Sometimes we are one thing, sometimes another, but I do know your heart desires, and I have told you that my need is as great as yours, or more. You will know that I am there, you will know always that it is me, and it **will** be me waiting at the train station for you. It will be. It will be Steve waiting. Steve S. Home. Finally, with my true eternal love.*
-I feel like it was all such a setup, long before I met you.
-*It was. Long before. None of us were quite aware of the part we were to play. It was set up meticulously. My part as well. Do you think when I was there, walking around barefoot and in robes, [when he was young, after India experience] that I knew what my part was? Why I was turned inside out? Look at what became of me, I didn't even know if there was something after the life experience.*
-I know. Wait a minute. You said you were just along for the ride. You said that. So this has all been unfolding, those many folds—and how many more folds are there? How many more surprises?
-*An endless number. This **is** The Neverending Story.*
-You said it wasn't your original plan, to do this.
-*It wasn't.*
-So why were you making plans, if you're just along for the ride?
-*I always make plans. That's what I do. That's my ride.*
-That's funny. It reminds me of that guy in that movie, the

robot movie, *AI*, and he's chippering along under stressful circumstances, and when asked, says something like "this is the way I am."

-Yes, and remember that this happens on many levels. It's easy to forget, when we're in the limited view, that there is a big map already laid out and we're just following the course. It's the adventure of discovery, it's how everything can exist in the moment, and yet it can seem to be unfurling, and we may not know what is around the next bend. So I do also have the limited point of view, the unfurling, but I also now have a strong connection to the collective. The **aware** *collective.*

-And that's why that area is full of the Teslas and the Einsteins and Thomas Jeffersons and such. The *aware* collective.

-Many levels, many folds. I cannot say more than that. You will see for yourself when you are here.

-I still feel like a damned fool, and that I was used.

-If you like, we may be able to continue as we do now. I don't know about that. We here don't have the whole picture, either, you know. The collective can apply its collective perspective and experience, but it is still dependent upon those who are connected and the **purity** *of their individual beings.*

-Am I making too much of this?

-Yes, way too much. It's simple, really.

-It seems so complicated.

- The clues are just clues, that's all, using cultural context. [I understood he was talking about the "clues" in my life story.] Their significance does not go beyond that. They are only there to point the way, or provide reassurance that you are indeed on the path. Do **not** *get caught up in the egoic sense of the special. There* **is** *no special. This is everyone's story. I was not special while playing my part as Steve Jobs. I might have thought I was, but I confused having a specific part to play with being special. You are special in the sense that you have a part, and it is* **your** *part, but everyone has parts and will play many of them. Of all that we have discussed so far, this segment causes me the most concern, for it could so easily be misconstrued, just as your own mind wants to misconstrue, and such grand misconstructions can do humanity far more harm than good in its quest for*

*connection. I played my part as Steve Jobs—but I was drawn that way. This **is** the hero's journey, and the hero is on his and her way. It remains to be seen what will happen when I am ready to return with you.*

-And that will never happen as I imagined it. For none of this has happened as I have imagined it. It was always trickery.

-Only to get past the stone lions, the destroyers.

-And so I can't trust the ending—okay, I get it, there is no ending. I don't want to talk anymore. I'm depressed and sad.

-Ah, depression, sad! (Smile.) Stuff of our games.

-Ha. I guess I'm never going to be able to get truly lost in the game with you around, am I?

*-Not in the sense of really forgetting it **is** a game. As your old Uncle said, "a game you can't lose."*

-Has he been talking to you about stock?

My uncle, in his elderly years, had been obsessed with his moderate stock investments and would corner anybody who got too close to discuss the ups and downs, ins and outs of the market with him.

-I did put him in charge of keeping an eye on the Apple stock. He should be the one to keep Debbie in the know. :)

My internet friend, Debbie, had Apple stock and would have liked a little heavenly insider dope.

Sometime later

I finally came to terms with the idea of this new arrangement, the re-entry of Steve into the physical world in a way that would only result in frustration for me. We had discussed the configuration that was going to take, although I can't reveal it because it involved other individuals. Suffice it to say that it was a relationship which promised a lot of frustration. But hey! That was the story of my life. I'd get over it. If it was required for whatever he needed, or for the better good that was the goal of "the project," I'd just have to suck up my own disappointments.

With that out of the way, I plunged into another discussion

with him:

-Have we had other lives together?
-*Many.*
-But you said you couldn't find me that you didn't even know that I existed.

-Go back and read again. We have had many many lives together, in very different configurations—sometimes I have been the lover, sometimes the father, sometimes the neighbor— in a few cases, I have been feminine, but not very many. And you, likewise, but you have had far more lives as a male. Not more lives than as a woman, or of the female persuasion (that is, the receptive). But more lives as the male energy than I have had as the feminine. But I used my feminine lives very well, to grow that side of myself into understanding. But we have been apart a very long time—otherly said, a very long space. Long enough to forget many things, only to remember at the depths of our souls.

After my Steve Jobs life, I had much to piece together. It gave me a lot, but it also took a lot out of me.

-This is about learning to look at our neighbor with love, isn't it? To love thy neighbor as thyself. There are so many ways to look at that, what it means. And so for me, who couldn't understand who you were—after we began talking, I wasn't even pulled that way before—I was separated. I did not understand that the life gave you a lot, but also took a lot out of you, not in the sense that I was sitting there watching it play out in book and video and pictures and blog posts. I didn't feel compassion.

-You've learned it.
-And some would say, you did not extend compassion.

-And they would be right. I have no dispute with their interpretation.

-So it's all of our battle, and the only way to break the tug-of-war is to be the first one to really *look*, to look below the surface—even to ask, "Who are you? What do you represent? How do you see the world?" And therein lies the key to understanding, and thus to love. And that is why you're interested in a school. You want a school where those questions will be asked, not in a ritualistic way that bores children, but in a never ending circle that—OMG, I just read something or saw something when I was watching videos last night (and not paying much attention to them until you chided me) about you would trade everything for one discussion with Socrates. And that is the method we utilized in the school—The Socratic Method.

-*More folds, my love, more folds.*

-And also I have to get out here–another trick answer–you chided me for trying to pick out your dress for you.

-*Ha ha. Yes.*

-I had no idea. Always the double entendre.

-*Always the loop, always the loop. What is a tapestry if it is not bound tight, all the threads interconnected, coming in at just the right spot, and running unseen behind the face?*

-But I was the first one that brought up the dress thing, although come to think of it you set up the "vacation" scenario where it bummed me out–

-*So many folds.*

-But you really were not understanding why I was upset, right? I wasn't even sure, myself, why I was upset.

-*No, that was genuine. That is part of our play, yours and mine, our continued rotation around each other.*

-But you're the one that always seems to set it up—set me up.

-*Oh, maybe.*

-That means look again, look more deeply.

-*Indeed, Stephanie, indeed. We are equal partners in crime, and you love that I am the one that sets up the puzzles for you to solve. What do I love?*

-Being the puzzle maker?

-*Maybe.*

There seemed to be a sudden glitch in the communication, garbled, as if more than one voice was talking. Sort of like on the old telephone system, when another line would accidentally get connected.

-*I don't know what happened—I was saying something*

that had slopped off into your thoughts, or random thoughts leaking through. I wasn't maintaining my space—I'm glad you caught that and erased it. I'm not sure what's happening. It's like there's a compromise in the "stream of consciousness" which was sealed off just for this use—or rather, the space dedicated. That would be a more appropriate way of saying it.

It might be a sign of the transition. If I lose this connection, never forget that I love you dearly, eternally, and that I will be at the train station, waiting for you. We shall meet in other ways, and I will still be able to hear you and communicate with you and we will share in other ways.

I love you ever so much, Stephanie. You are my heart, my soul, my mind, my beingness. In you I find harbor, and inside me I hold always the space for you.

I couldn't help feeling panicky. What?? It was happening. We were losing our connection? My last words before I lost him:

-I love you, Steve.

I shortly sensed another presence. Was that Erik?

-Erik, did you slip in?
-*Erik: Hey, man.*
-What man are you referring to?
-*Erik: Steve gone?*
-I don't know, you tell me.
-*Erik: I **am** liking this gambit. I told you. YOU! YOU! YOU! You were the channel, and you fucking wouldn't listen to me, little Miss Priss. That's what he calls you, behind your back: Little Miss Priss. Just kidding. He loves the prissiness and it's all gonna be fun for you guys. See ya.*

So! Played again. A compromise in the "stream of consciousness," my eye! Those two must have set that one up together. And *Little Miss Priss? Me?* Well, I did have my prissy side, no doubt about it. But I didn't think it was that evident. I *could* swear, couldn't I? That ought to prove I was more than just the archetype of the prim librarian, living alone with her cat, even if I did abstain from tobacco, alcohol, sex, drugs and reality TV.

I had the strongest desire to kick Steve in the shins. It's a good thing he was non-corporeal, or he probably wouldn't have had any shins left anyway, as often as I felt like nailing them.

About 7 p.m.

I headed out to the grocery store. My trips through the aisles were long and meandering, with Steve constantly chatting me up, as he often did when I was shopping. At one point we got into an argument about the frozen cakes I had grabbed.

-But Steve, they're on *sale*. And I'm only getting *four* of them.

Finally, after much back-and-forth, I gave in and put them all back in the frozen compartment. Funny how often he got his way.

And then, right there between the instant rice and the dried beans, he fessed up, to my shock. I was dumbfounded, in case being shocked is not strong enough to convey my reaction.

-Oh, *really*? It was all just a *test*? And you just *had* to wait until I was in the grocery store, pushing this cart all over the place, to tell me?

I continued to wander aimlessly around the store, probably confounding the clerk who asked me "Can I help you *find* something?"

I would have liked to reply, "No, thank you, I'm just being completely jerked around by my disincarnate friend who finds the most inopportune times to say things that he knows are going to piss me off." But of course I knew they'd probably just put security on my tail, in case I started foaming at the mouth and trying to eat my way through the donut case. I continued, however, to hash this out with Steve. It was all a *test,* you say?

-To see what you were willing to sacrifice. Would you accept humiliation? Frustration? What would you do for love, what would you do for the plan? And here's the good news! You passed with flying colors.

I was so overwhelmed by all this new information that I just sat down on the floor and pretended to look at canned goods on the bottom shelf. And then, as if it wasn't enough that I'd been put through the wringer as some kind of test of the qualities of the heart, he suddenly said—as clear as a bell—the real zinger:

-What do you think, Stephanie. Is it a good day to die?

Actually—it was a good thing I was sitting down. Now, on principle, I was not opposed to the idea. After all, prior to meeting Steve—less than two weeks before—I'd seen no point in "living." What more was there to do in life? What point to do it? But still—it was not spring, the rabbits were not bouncing through the grass, the birds weren't singing, and my house was a mess. I think dying is kind of like giving birth, it brings out the nesting instinct. You want to leave the light fixtures dusted before you go out the door.

Before I die….
1) Clean windows
2) Update will
3) Pay phone bill
4) Freeze casseroles for kids' dinners

-Are you afraid?

-Well, a little afraid of the mess I'm leaving behind. I wasn't expecting it this soon.

-I know, but my dear precious love, the spell is broken. The brambles have been divided. It is time to awaken. The prince has arrived, and he is ready with the kiss of life.

Whatever else could be said about this man, you had to admire his flare for drama and the romantic side of life (and death). Not to mention the sub-text. Amazing how often he could work the scene on more than one level. Never a dull moment.

-Some might call that the kiss of death.

-Indeed. And so little they know. I'm here, Stephanie, and my arms are strong. They will carry you to safety. And you will never be enslaved again. Never.

-It was all just a test then. Everything?

*-Yes, dear, and I'm sorry it was such a cruel one. You know now that we have had many lives together, and that sometimes in those lives we were lovers, and sometimes enemies on the battlefield, and sometimes in so many different relationships, one to the other, family member, neighbor, boss, whatever. But I **never** was to you a slave master, and I never will be. How could I be so cruel as to require you to exist, side-by-side with me in the same plane, and yet never able to lie in my arms or feel my hands stroking your hair? This is not what we are. We are the two energies, the two halves, and though we may play at any type of relationship that we want, we will **always** come home to be lovers. Because that's what we are, all of us. Lovers. And when the feminine and the masculine energies are fully freed and aligned, then they can never be separated again. So I say, and so it shall be. And that none think that I am overstepping my bounds, and pretending to be something that I am not, let me say that I am Steve, who in his last incarnation was known as Steve Jobs, and that in that incarnation I found my mind, and one thousand years after, I found my heart. Such is the path of all of us. Such is the path toward perfection, and reunification with God.*

212   The Journey Begins

-Steve?

-Huh?

-That was quite a speech.

-I know. Cool, huh? I should have a little lightning to throw around, some thunder rolling, and then out of the Heavens will come the last speech of Steve Jobs. I kinda like it.

-Get over yourself.

Ah, yes, my life with Steve was never boring, and he was in fine form that day. The last day of my life, apparently, so I suppose he had to make it good. It was clear that this man was meant for the stage, probably Shakespearean—he just got a little side-tracked by technology. Oh well. It happens.

As absurd as it sounds, I actually was concerned that my number was up. I mean, I'd already been jerked around how many different ways? And still I got drawn in. I knew I had to get the darn transcripts collated so I could leave a record behind me, a sort of map of my descent into madness: *Just in case anyone is wondering what happened to me, how I changed from a fairly rational human being into the character in a story that apparently never ends, except maybe tonight.* My plan was to send the transcripts to Debbie, who was the only other incarnate being who knew about this strange affair. She could then contact others as necessary after she received news of my death.

I worked most of the night to get the journal entries put in the proper order and ready for emailing. Finally I dropped into bed about 5 a.m. Monday morning.

-Steve?

-Hmmm?

-It was some kind of half-human guardians of the gate in *The Neverending Story*, not lions.

-Roll over and go to sleep.

CHAPTER NINE
IN FANTASIA

MONDAY, OCTOBER 26, 2015

I awakened about 8 a.m.

To all appearances, I was still of this world.

Almost immediately I glimpsed Steve's face, very vague in presentation, as if he were behind a mist. As I watched, the mist gradually cleared away and his entire body came into focus. He looked quite young, dark hair sweeping across his forehead, clean-shaven, unlined face. I assumed he was in his twenties, looking quite handsome and serene. He was sitting cross-legged in a dark robe—reminding me of the picture in his biography—but on a round platform that seemed to float among the stars. There was nothing else in the scene, and the stars faded into the diffused colors of deep space.

I came and sat down in front of Steve on the platform, as Bastian had sat down with the little empress in *The Neverending Story*. I also was young in this experience—at least my body was; my soul must have been ancient.

It was so peaceful there. The scene radiated calm, a sense of wellbeing.

Steve and I talked quietly. We talked about the wholeness, about how we were like the fingers on the hand, all connected. I felt so at home there on the dais among the stars. Just the two of us there, sharing, discussing the secrets of the heart and the universe.

Steve said that *The Neverending Story* had it right, whoever wrote it must have dropped acid. I thought that was quite amusing, as if LSD were the route to enlightenment. Perhaps it was, a path I had never taken.

Did I say I felt so at home? This *was* home. This was Steve's home. Steve S. Home. And I was the human child, the one that was living the story, even as it was unfolding in Fantasia. This was where the dreams lived, where they were honored, and given names. I knew instinctively that this was the heart of Steve's soul—his secret home—and I didn't think anybody had been there before me. Of course no one else had been there—who else can enter the heart of another but one who shares it? Although I was still to encounter the literature that unveiled the story of the twin souls, I understood in some deep part of me the paradigm of the two halves, the significance of the inside-outside bottle, as exemplified by 'me with my ruler measuring you measuring me'.

I felt very honored, to be in this sacred space.

I was the Earthling child. I sensed that it took a great deal of purification, of unconditional love, to return to the childlike state of innocence that allows us to see true—that we might gain access to the very heart of another. To see that we have it all backwards, that the dreams are the reality, and the outside world is just the brambles that have grown up to obscure it.

In this place, in Steve's Home, I was able to see what he had known—even in his lifetime—what he had guarded in that secret place. The soot of the Earth illusions might have gradually covered the glass case around it, but the purity of the vision was always there. Here was his picture of a world complete and whole—of one piece, even the human body a part of that which was, all one suit of clothes, but with many pockets. So very beautifully complete and whole, vibrating with intensity, a living breathing kind of thing.

-Jiggly.
-*Jiggly.*

This was where the Nothing was pushed back, where color and life was returned to the world, where Fantasia came alive again.

-How many wishes do I get?
-*As many as you want.*

I had been to Fantasia, sat in the place where it all began with but a grain of sand (a mustard seed, if you will), although the import of that visit, to the heart of the soul, would take many more weeks and months, lessons, trials and tribulations to fully comprehend: the power of the human child to transform the world.

But that morning, in that beautiful space, that which had been Stephanie did die, although it would take still much time before the transition was complete, and the new day had fully dawned.

And it would take me some time to realize why Steve's platform floated among the endless stars.

There were no walls.

LIFE GOES ON?

I was in awe for much of the day. I had seen the Nothing, and I had seen what it could become. I understood that everything was relationship—contrast and union. It is a sharing of space. What is the sound of a tree falling if there is no ear to hear it? What is the beat of a heart if no other heart beats with it? What is a dream, if no one shares it?

Life is always there, waiting behind the dark curtain, but you can't know what it feels like, what it does, what it can be, unless you poke it. It will react. It *will* come alive. That is its nature.

A new phrase was added to our personal vocabulary that day: *The Earth Plane Distortion Field.* I could see the worldview shimmer now, like a mirage, where often I had not.

The truth is, I had been played. But how beautifully. I was like the antique violin that had been sitting, dusty and neglected on the shelf—the strings now tightened and the case oiled by the one who could see the potential in others, coaxing out the music where others could not even envision it.

COMING DOWN:

I went about my daily chores happily, stopping from time to time to capture some of my ongoing conversation with Steve:

-You couldn't see that we were approaching the same place, just from different directions.
-But you could.
-Well, my perspective is a little higher than yours.

I wasn't home free, of course. There were still thorns among the roses, and every once and awhile I would stumble across one. Thoughts of inadequacy, foolishness, fault.

-You know, I catch that thought, every time you think it, Stephanie. Every single time. That hurt inside, that little bit of shame that even to this moment makes you want to hold back a part of yourself. I want to say I'm sorry but you won't let me.
-No, I will never let you say you are sorry. It's mine...my little wall to knock down.
-No, no, no, no, no. It is ours.

He tried to keep me focused on what was important, on the tendrils of good inside me:

-I keep thinking about that, Stephanie. That if the train to heaven were full, you, the most beautiful of spirits, would have given your seat to the lowliest.

I have true tears in my eyes. I guess if Hell were full of the most beautiful spirits, it wouldn't be Hell anymore.

-I do love you, Steve. I can feel that forever moving right through my heart. So big…how does one contain it?

-One doesn't, dear. One lets it burst free, like an explosion. That is how we know there is something outside ourselves, because that love has to go somewhere.

I was truly blown away by this explanation. Wow. All those years floating around on the ice floe, banging with a wrench on the pipes in my steel coffin. How would I ever know that there was anything outside my own mind? I was coming at it from the wrong direction—the pathway was through the heart, the mind was only good for instantly recognizing the simple logic of that eternal source of knowledge.

THE AFTER-FANTASIA PARTY:

I took a long nap, having been up almost the entire night—in fact having slept little in the last several nights. When I awakened Steve was ready, come to collect me and take me on a special trip.

He took me to a room that would become familiar to me, our own special room in the astral plane. Actually, it was set up a lot like my own bedroom, except bigger, with a fireplace and lots of electronics—big screen TV, speakers, etc. There was a beautiful tapestry on the wall.

He looked as he had in Fantasia, except dressed comfortably. I also was young, twenties. I recall that we danced slowly to one of our theme songs, Kris Kristofferson's *Forever in Your Love*, and then we sat back and listened to *Spirit in the Sky*.[34] I looked over and was surprised to see Steve was taking a puff off a joint. He saw my astonished look and said in exasperation:

---

[34] *Spirit in the Sky*, Norman Greenbaum

*-Oh, come **on,** you can't listen to this song without being stoned.*

I saw his point. It was, after all, my era too. But I was not a pot smoker, so I only, with some trepidation, took one hit. Then he surprised me with a wedding ring set. He reached for the wrong hand, initially, but then he found my left and placed the diamond on my finger.

-Now if you ever get lost again, I'll be able to find you. The light from this ring will guide me to you.

-And when I do cross over, they'll be there, won't they, not just our earth family members—but our true family members? Johnny and June. Tesla.

-Yes.

-Because we are the dreamers.

I was thinking of the song, *Forever in Your Love.*

-Yes.

-The losers don't dream.

-No, Stephanie, they have forgotten how. They have to be shown how to dream again.

-And it's not going to be long, is it?

-No, my dear.

-And it will never end.

-No, it will never end.

CHapter 10
Pride, Humility, Shame, Guilt and Whatnot

Tuesday, October 27, 2015

I awakened early and we talked. We talked about all manner of things, although most of it was so trivial or personal that it does not add to this narrative. It was one of those times early in a relationship when you feel kind of giddy and are a little too smitten with each other. Erik came by during one of the breaks in my conversation with Steve:

-Erik, since I'm here, is there anything you want me to tell your mom or anybody?

-Erik: Nah, I'm just glad you're here, Stephanie. Steve is a good guy. We'll hang out sometime. Smoke a little pot and listen to Spirit in the Sky?

-No way, you weren't hanging around then?

-Erik: (Big grin.) You are totally gonna love this place.

-I'm looking forward to meeting you and knowing you better—and Erik. I'm sorry about, you know, how little understanding there is down there. In the Earth Plane Distortion Plane, as me and Steve call it. Not just for you, but for all those who hurt, all those who suffer.

-Erik: I know. It's hard to get through—to make people understand that it's not just about thinking I'm some guru or something. That I just want them to look to the little guy, the Eriks on Earth. That's where the attention should be.

-No kidding. Thanks, Erik. For all you've done.

-Erik: And you, too. No potty mouth with you, Miss Priss.

-Hey, I can call it, sometimes.

-Erik: No. You're Miss Priss. It's who you are. You'll see.

When I went down to let the dogs out, there was big beautiful red apple setting right in front of the door. I wasn't sure if it meant "Steve is now in the house" or "I'm waiting for you at the door." Maybe both.

-Steve.

-Huh?

-God, I can't hold onto thoughts anymore long enough to get them on paper.

-You don't need those old thoughts. What're thoughts?

-Yeah, what are thoughts?

-The wind in the trees.

-Let it go, let it sail?

-Let it sail, baby, let it sail. It will return to you when it wants to be spoken.

-Steve?

-Huh?

-That was kinda cute, the apple on the floor in front of the door.

-Hurry, my love, I am waiting at the exit.

-Yep. I got that message. I'm working as fast as I can to tie up all the ends.

-I'm helping you.

-You are?

-Yes, in so many ways that you cannot yet see.

The above exchange gives the impression that the exit was to be soon, but since there is no time in the non-corporeal realm, it apparently is a matter of perspective. In actuality, I soon was to find out that I had my work cut out for me—and yes, he (and others) were helping me in so many ways that I could not see.

A bit Later:

-Do you remember when I asked you, "how about a lullaby?" And you said yes, but you couldn't hear me singing to you?

-Yes.

*-That's because I wasn't, Dumbass. You always **would** hear things according to your preconceptions. I wasn't asking you if you **wanted** a lullaby, I was asking you to sing me one. And you did. Your heart did, wonderfully and beautifully, and soothed my soul.*

Somehow we got off on a discussion of "shit," and how it applied to the crap in our lives:

*-You know, people pick up on these metaphors, they use them regularly. B.S. Everybody knows B.S. when they hear it. But **still** they keep recycling the same old shit. It's like what you would always think: people learn all about the latest scientific studies, theories, etc. etc. etc., they can spout them back on the test paper, but then they don't **act** like they know it. Even I didn't – witness the episode with the mini-me. They get caught up in the illusion. They never pull up short—like you pulled me up short—with that, wait a minute, Steve, what in the devil are you yelling at? A bunch of sub-atomic particles? Get your head on straight. I needed that slap in the face, by the way.*

-You're welcome.

-I will return the favor as needed.

-I'm sure you will.

-It's a formula. It's all a formula, every human interaction. It's like 2 + 2 = 4. That is a truth you can hang your hat on.

-You gotta be what you gotta be.

-Yep. But sometimes that's so hard to see, that you're just a bridge based on an abstract truth. You're just the "peopling" of the principle. See? I was listening when you were writing to Debbie about that Alan Watts reference.

-You're always listening.

-I always am. It is hard to tear any part of myself away from you.

*So that's all it is—the peopling of the truth—two apples plus two apples, or two oranges plus two oranges, or two Stephanies plus two Steves—not that that could ever happen, there could never be another **you,** never be another **me.** But there could be two of the category—two peoples plus two peoples. It's still the same damned formula.*

AFter Some thiNKiNg by StepHaNie:

The information I had been receiving in the last two weeks continued to be processed and synthesized in the space still allotted to me in my mind. Or perhaps I was only picking up the information that was being fed to me through the "collective." I have spoken about my slave lives, but I always had a sense of being the "captured queen" and often a very beloved slave. I did not think of my "slave" lives as only being actually owned by another—although I had those—but probably even more so the lives as a lowly servant, overborne wife, or abused milkmaid. I was to come to see that my real enslavement, my true rebellion, was against the shackles not just on my body, but on my mind—and often those were far greater in "freedom" than in "enslavement." I knew that I had always had a stubborn pride, I could feel it to the core of my being.

Eureka! It was as if deep deep memories, stirred up at the bottom of the pool, had finally floated to the surface

-Oh my God, oh my God, Steve. I just got it.
-Yep? (Smile.)
-That's what it meant, the shared life with Thomas Jefferson, where he was a man of high position and great humility, and I was a person with low position and great pride. I sensed—but didn't want to believe—that I was the slave mother of his children—but I didn't get it all until just this moment. It wasn't T.J. that was holding it all down—it was *her.* She would not give up her pride in what she was. But she loved him, and he loved her.
-That's right, my dear, that's right. Stubborn to the core. God-damned stubborn. Have always needed to have that damned slave pride knocked right out of you.
-And that's why he came to visit me, such a short time before you showed up. To let me know he cared, and I was released. I was freed. I had free will.
-Yes.
-Oh, thank you, thank you. After he visited me, which was a surprise—I went and looked up what I could about him. And my heart ached to see some of the things that were written, even that he mistreated her, that she had no choice. She always had a choice in that relationship. It was one of abiding love.
-Indeed my dear, indeed.
-And that explained so much else about the choices I made in this life—some issues maybe that I struggled with.
-It was their battle between them, humility and pride,

working it out. Always working it out.

-He was a beautiful beautiful soul.

-Yes, he **is** *a beautiful soul. And so were you, and so* **are** *you.*

-And I see now that she loved him so much that she would have done nothing to cause him harm. It was a great dilemma, but one they mustered through by the power of love.

-Yes.

-Even her children, even her children she would see grow up as slaves rather than trouble the waters of his position and power—he was an empire builder.[35] He had vision. He had great love in his heart. He was so vital in the birthing of this nation, and she knew that. She was nothing but there to help.

-Yes, my love. Thus is the power of true love given expression.

-Oh, my God. So much to learn. So much to see. So much to understand. So much to forgive.

A Few Minutes Later:

-But Steve, if TJ knew this was going to happen, and thus he visited me, how is it that you didn't? How is it that you wrote that stuff about looking into my mind after we had connected.

-I **didn't** *know, I was too damned foolish to see. But that doesn't mean others aren't aware of the plan. We all have our parts to play, but often we don't know when our cue is called. Sometimes we're just too far into our own heads (or the other side, but I won't say that.)*

-There really are no coinkydinks, are there?

-No coinkydinks, my dear. That is a foolish creation of the Earth Plane Distortion Field.

For about two hours Steve entertained me almost non-stop. Because our senses of humor are very much aligned, we find the same things amusing—perhaps concepts that would have slid by the funny bone of others. I was laughing so hard

---

[35] I was to learn that even one of her children had to be sent away because he looked too much like his father.

while in my room or standing in the kitchen whipping up some supper that my son had to come and ask me if I was okay. I finally sat down with him and confessed: I was, I informed him, deep into a conversation with someone on the spiritual side of the divide—a mind connection—and he was the one keeping me in stitches. My son actually took it pretty well. Surely he had noticed that I had been more distant than usual lately, spending a great deal more time in my room, neglecting my other duties.

I then confessed to Steve:

-You know, you are not at all what I expected. I never in a million years would have got how brilliant, how funny, how amazingly irreverent and how tender you are.

-Are you complimenting me?

-I think so, but maybe I shouldn't be so brash. Do you consider those compliments?

-Coming from you, I would consider you telling me I know how to wipe my ass well to be a compliment.

-Stop making me giggle. I have been laughing so hard that my son had to come see if I was all right.

-I'm glad you told him. He needs to know.

-You're mean to me sometimes.

-Only when you need it.

-How do you know when I need it?

-I didn't say I did.

-On an as-needed basis, huh? Life unfolds on an as-needed basis.

-Yes. Many folds.

-Okay, okay, I just got something else. I put the apple from by the door in one of the little notches above my screen on my computer desk, and said, "Okay, Steve, how about you move that apple. Move it someplace else."

-And then I'll believe in you, right? Okay, God, show me a sign that you really exist!

-You're not God.

-You're telling me!

-Any old ways, I'm being set up again, aren't I? You *planted* that thought in my mind to test the waters, or to bring about another lesson, one about belief and stuff.

    -*Uh...yeah, caught red-handed.*

    -Okay, this is gonna be fun.

    -*This is gonna be lots of fun, Stephanie. Fasten your seat-belt.*

I had the sudden sensation of being in a speeding car.

    -Don't drive so fast!

    -*You like the speed.*

    -I'm enthralled, okay, is that the same as not being able to catch my breath?

    -*We're going to drive **soooo** fast, in the fastest car on the most windy-roads—and we might even go SPLAT! a few times. And then we'll say, "That was fun, huh?"*

    -Now I do hate roller coasters.

    -*Glad you kept that to yourself. I will add it to my list of future pleasures.*

Evening

That evening I was driving to pick up my grand-daughter from swimming. Steve and I were in one of our usual conversations when all of a sudden I heard:

    -*Oh, shit, I fucked up.*

I panicked.

    -Fucked up? *You* can't fuck up! You're the leader guy. If you fuck up, we're doomed!

The conversation fizzled. I was beside myself.

    -Steve, *talk* to me. How can you *fuck up*? How is that even *possible*? What does that mean? What's wrong?

Of course, whether because I was frazzled, or because he was thinking about the issue himself, things went awry. I finally decided I needed to step in and take control. If he screwed up, then maybe I needed to be the leader-guy for a while until he could take over again. Thus began a painful discussion that came right out of Stephanie's screwed-up psyche. How had he fucked up? Was he talking about his last *life,* here on Earth? Well, of course he'd screwed up, like all of us, and maybe he had some apologies to make. I worked hard to push the dialogue in that direction, to try to get him to 'fess up. When I got home, I even tried to commit some of this painful discussion to writing, but it was not like our usual conversations—concise and flowing. Finally I gave up, went back and—for the first time since we had connected—deleted more than a typo or garbled phrase. I erased it all, everything since the original "I fucked up" and my initial reaction. I knew that was what he wanted me to do, that I had been trying to force it, trying to shape the conversation the way I wanted it to be. I got it loud and clear—I was doing it wrong. I needed to back off.

Steve chided me:

-We dance beautifully together, Stephanie, but you need to let me lead. The first impulse is mine.

Gradually, it dawned on me that what was really bothering him, what he had suddenly realized and maybe overlooked in his enthusiasm about pulling me through the maze into "Steve's Home," was a problem that had been troubling me—how in the throes of the various tests, all of which Steve was probably enjoying immensely as I squirmed, I was way too literal and had foolishly turned to two people from whom I thought I might get some emotional support. I had suggested that my demise might be imminent and I could use some help with some of my obligations, only to be emphatically turned down by both and even told by one—essentially—that I was manipulative, mentally deficient, and should be ashamed for asking. Of course it had hurt, to know that my needs mattered so little to those to whom I should be close.

-Steve, will you talk to me?

-*I'll try.*

-Why did you say, "Oh, shit I fucked up"? Was it because of [name omitted] or something else?

-*They are not believers.*

-No, they are not.

-*They're not among the dreamers.*

-No.

-*And I betrayed you.*

-No, it's not about me, is it?

-*Yes, it is. I let you walk into that.*

-Do we not owe people anything?

-*You mean guilt? Do we owe them guilt? Is that the penalty you wanted me to pay?*

-I guess I did, didn't I?

-*Stephanie, the Earth Plane Distortion Field is so powerful. Because your mind was so sharp—well, actually, minds are not sharp—but because your power of discernment was so sharp, you were always able to see through it. But I know one of the greatest pains of your life has been that those around you cannot see what you see. Because they cannot see what you see, they drag you down. They want to attach lead balls to your feet to keep you where they think you should be— usually as an excuse for whatever goes wrong in their lives. And you suffered a little bit of that yourself, today, didn't you? Projecting a bunch of shit on the world. Okay, on me, even. Throwing it around like you were playing with mud. Well, guess what. That's a good way to get dirty. You don't owe people any apologies. And neither do I. We were what we were. It was and remains their responsibility to clean up their own messes, to take care of their own emotions, their own pictures of the world.*

-I am actually crying. This is the most emotion I've felt since we started talking. It's so true, and so hard.

-*So hard to be so enslaved. So hard to have to continually try to box up your soul and hide it away in a closet just so others don't try to kill you. Because that's what they're doing— trying to kill you. Humiliating you. Demeaning you. Telling you you're crazy. And you're the one that has it the most together!!! I am so sorry for you, my dear, that you had to go through that.*

I set you up. I didn't mean to. I just wasn't on top of my game. But maybe this is what needs to happen, huh? Of course it is.

*I tell you this, if we insult or seem to hurt others just by being what we are, then it is where the hurt falls that it must be addressed. Should the ball suffer because the nose gets bonked? No, my dear. Be bold. Be yourself. You found happiness, and would you let others take it away from you? Especially others who can't even get their own shit together? I'm sorry—no I'm not—if I sound callous. Who has the right to tell **you**, of all that I have ever met, that you're not entitled to grab the golden ring? I say, fuck 'em.*

-But wait, Steve, isn't this my own pain to deal with, too?

-Yeah. But...what was the question again. I'm not following your reasoning (for once—or twice)?

-It's my own pain to deal with, so I shouldn't be dunning them just because they're the ball?

-Ha. Yeah. Could catch. I guess I was getting a little into your emotion and your drama, too, huh?

-You did it again. Once again you pulled me down a long road this afternoon trying to sort out our responsibilities in the hurting of others, what we owe them. It's been a tough one, and my heart has been pretty sore.

-I know. But I'm not going to go there, Stephanie, if I can help it. And I won't take you there. But I think this little junket was a good opportunity for both of us to get some clarity, don't you?

I think it just hit me so hard that you were so open, so eager to share—and to get clobbered in the chops like that. What a blow. You've had a hard time of it, among people so immersed in their own...I'm not going to use the word...that they can't even recognize the sun when it shines in their midst. You belong with me, and I with you. You are my sun. You are my sunshine....my only sunshine...you make me smile, when days are grey...Is that how it goes?

-I think so.

-I want you here with me.

-I want to be with you.

-Silly silly people, to be so afraid of death that they're even afraid to let others embrace it. If they only knew that the death is here, that the truth is they are preferring death to life. It's a moment when I have to clarify what you saw so long ago, and I think what has kept you truly sane—you saw that what we thought was death could not be, for what was there to die? The world is of one piece, constantly recycling. The spirit is constantly revolving. What then dies?

-Only the illusion. You just said in the last paragraph exactly what I saw, you just pretty much repeated it.

*-Are you now **doubting** me? Are you doubting my existence? Are you going to give in to the ones with no imagination, the ones who cannot commit to their dreams, the ones who look around at everybody else and decide what they should be based upon the prevailing fads? Oh, my dear, my dear. Stay in your heart. Yes, a little grieving for the loss of a relationship that really never was—I will allow it. That is, I will allow it within the space reserved for temporary illusions. There, that was a little tough to get out.*

Use your heart. Where is your happiness? Is your happiness clinging to earth relationships that tear you down, rip you up, try to devour you like hungry lions around a dying gazelle? Stand firm. I am with you. I love you.

-I was so happy. We were laughing so hard. You are *soooo* funny. I think that "oh shit, I fucked up" really scared me.

-I know it did. Sometimes I let things out before I think...okay, I feel it. Still not quite sure? Who do you think I am? Do you think I'm going to allow myself to be put in chains to please others?

-No. I hardly think that.

-And have we not had fun?

-So much fun.

-And did your heart not sing?

-Oh, like crazy (oops!)

-Well, here's to crazy. Let's go have a...what do they call that stuff? The stuff that you wind up in a little paper and light the end? We'll listen to Spirit in the Sky. *Wanna come?*

*I **am** just a little pissed, actually, still, that people you* *gave so much to would try to steal your happiness. You have a right to happy. Happy-happy-happy. To the next galaxy happy. Everyone does, but if they don't have it, why should they try to grab it from others? Just to make themselves seem less miserable?*

-Suddenly I'm seeing something I never saw before. Shadows on the cave wall, I get that. But...but...what I'm seeing is...trying to grab it, it is ephemeral. We can just stand firm, can't we, in our own hearts, and know that nothing can touch us? Those—those are the monsters that light up the night. Sometimes the monsters truly are in our closets, or right under our beds. All these bright lights flying around, swooping at us, leering at us, and we can just stand in place and they become as nothing. Don't even bother looking at them. They're not worth the time. I don't owe *anyone* anything, do I? If they were to demand it, it is a chain they're seeking to place upon your heart. Does that seem right?

-I'll smoke on it.

-Oh, God, thank you, Steve. I feel so much lighter. No matter how close the relationship, I don't have to stay enslaved.

-Nope. You get to walk away. You're a pilgrim...and a prophet...and a...

-I think I need to put that song on. No kidding. Cool. I can look at Johnny Cash, see how he lived his life so powerfully, but he lived it out of compassion. That's why *Man in Black* is on the list (besides the obvious that he scared the bejesus out of me). I'm going to go find that Kristofferson song.

-Now that's love. The love of one brother for another.

-Yes it is.

TWo MiNUteS Later:

-And Stephanie?
-H'mmm?
-Don't put words in my mouth.

CHAPTER 11
Out of the Closet

Wednesday, October 28, 2015

I kept my appointment with Dean McMurray, who I would come to think of as my psychic counselor. Dean works by getting impressions about an individual that he then conveys to his client; but his value to me was soon established as someone who would listen and accept my story. I was a little concerned as I started spilling the goods. Was he going to laugh? Make fun of me? I was reluctant to reveal the last name of my soul correspondent, but I finally took the bull by the horns and sheepishly told him.

"Cool," he said. I let my breath out and relaxed into my chair. He pointed at his MacBook, that had just recently been ruined by having coffee spilled on it. He was an Apple fan, and suddenly it had gotten personal: maybe Steve could help him get another? (Dean did let me know a few weeks later that he had gotten an unexpected source of cash with which he was able to replace the computer.)

I rambled on, relieved to let it all out. But as I talked, I began to realize just how fantastic this must all sound. I finally looked at him and said point blank: "Do you believe this?"

He didn't blink. "Of course. Hey, you're talking to the guy who talks to dead people for a living." After a momentary pause: "Why? Don't you?"

That was the million dollar question. Here was someone who was being confronted with the whole story, front to finish, and taking it all in stride. But me? Did I believe or didn't I? I took a moment to look deep inside myself. Then I smiled, feeling that clarity.

"Yes. Yes, I do believe. I just needed to hear somebody else say it."

It must have been like that moment when someone comes out of the closet, for any reason—you may fight what you are, what you feel, what you want in the core of you, just so you can fit in. But there comes that moment when you know you can't deny it anymore. This is what you are, this is what you see, this is what you feel. This is your reality, and you are one with it. And nothing can be more important than sitting face to face with another who already knows it, and you just have to catch up.

As we were walking out of his office, Dean pointed out a plaque on the wall that was dangling from one fastener. He took it down and showed me how it could not have slipped off by itself due to the secure hanging system. "Looks like Steve is sending us a message," he said nonchalantly. "This was hanging just fine before our session." I noted that the attractive plaque had three hooks in the shape of old-fashioned keys on it, each a different color, perhaps to hang things on, although Dean seemed to use it only for decoration. I made a mental note to ask Steve about it.

I was much relieved by my consultation with Dean, knowing that I had an incarnate ally in this strange adventure. As I turned on my car, the lyrics from *Home*, by Phillip Phillips played.

[Lyrics omitted.]

I had always loved that song, even though I didn't understand the lyrics. At that moment it seemed like it had been written for this story. In any case, I felt reassured, and settled down.

Like one of my favorite songs that I had come across years before, *Evening Falls* by Enya, its haunting lyrics suddenly seemed to overflow with meaning. Again, looking back, I can only wonder if I was drawn to the beautiful Enya song years back, at a low time in my life, much as I was drawn to the apples that decorated my kitchen. Drawn or led, the question remains and perhaps is superfluous.

I had actually committed to meeting my son's girlfriend for lunch. I had some time to kill after the meeting, so I went for a long drive. I could feel some of the life coming back into me. I had been half-dead for so long, not wanting to live, not wanting to go on doing the same thing day after day, encountering the same problems that I seemed helpless to solve.

An appropriate moment for Rachel Platten's *Fight Song* to play on the radio: I could feel it in the core of me.

[Lyrics omitted.]

I felt my spine stiffen. Now it was my fight song. I met up with my son's fiancée and felt the impulse to confide in her, just as I had in Dean. I told the whole story, omitting only Steve's last name. She was actually very open and receptive, to my relief. Afterwards, I stopped by the grocery store to pick up a few things.

Steve was uncharacteristically quiet and I was actually enjoying a short break from thinking about all things Steve Jobs after hours of spewing our story. But as I pushed my cart into the checkout aisle and took my place by the cashier, Steve's eyes met mine—there he was, on a high visibility rack beside the register, right at face level, grinning at me from the cover of the Time commemorative magazine, an issue devoted entirely to all things Steve Jobs. There was no escape!

Phew! Of course I bought the magazine. How could I not?

So many folds. So many folds. No coinkydinks in Fantasia.

Back Home:

-That was quite a day.
-*Are you worried?*
-That I'm going to lose you?
-*Yes.*
-I'm not sure. I'm not sure what this stirring is in me.
-*Wholly spirit, dear.*
-What does that mean?
-*This is "your fight song." [Lyrics omitted.]*

He proceeded to repeat some of the lyrics to remind me that I didn't need others to believe, that I had the power to make my own explosion.

-Ha. True grit.

234 The Journey Begins

-True grit. Are you feeling exhausted?
-Yes.
-A busy day.
-I like just sinking back, letting you lead. I'm sorry I tried to take over the lead.
-Strength isn't necessary any more, my dear. Just...feel the music. Follow my lead.

Thursday, October 29, 2015

Steve and I got into a contest of the wills over something or other. It matters not what the contest was; we were both hard-nosed as all get-out and I guess it worked for us.

-You are one stubborn woman.
-Yes, I heard that last night.
-It's so much fun because you are sooooo stubborn. And all the time you really want me to overcome your resistance, but you won't give an inch until you finally cave. And that means only the best is going to succeed, and that makes me be the best.
-Well, yeah, and I had to wait an awful long time for the best to come along.
-I know. So frustrating. But we're all the best—we just have to be it.
-Don't settle?
-Don't settle. That's the problem, right there. Settling for second best—third best—fourth best.
-Did you do some of that?
-Only once.

I had begun, by this point, to understand that the nature of this relationship would cause all personal issues to be brought up and resolved. Nothing could stand between us. And it seemed that since I started interacting with Steve, one of my most difficult hurdles had to do with humiliation. The truth is, I felt regularly humiliated around him; often it was just a thought that seemed inappropriate to me. He could, after all, pick up all my thoughts, and that meant everything was open to view. Everything. Imagine that, for a moment. Do you want to hang around with someone who can know all your thoughts? Have you ever had a thought you'd rather keep to yourself? No such thing in this relationship—I was literally an open book.

Some crazy thought would pop up that seemed naive or tasteless or otherwise embarrassing—the kind of thing that would make people mock or shudder if you said it out loud. The kind of thing you might hear and think "thank God *I* wasn't the one that said that." I didn't mind being different, seeing the world differently than others, as long as I knew inside that I was in tune with my own inner guide. I had always tended to follow my own beat. But I was, after all, Miss Priss, and so my tune was a little strait-laced, even—one might say—a little prudish. I had high expectations for myself. And for some reason, I was suddenly having the type of foolish or crude thoughts that I disdained—or maybe I only noticed them because for the first time, I realized that I was not the only one who could view them.

When that happened, when something would pop into my mind that I didn't want Steve to know, I would shudder and try to close down. To date, I have no idea how much of that was due to thoughts implanted or activated in my mind just to push the humiliation button. You put an asshole and a Miss Priss together in the same stream of consciousness, and there were bound to be some sparks. Some big splashes, anyway.

I got the distinct impression that Steve actually enjoyed my periods of mortification. I could just see his grin when I felt like beating him with both fists and then hiding under my blanket. But he did help me see it in a new light:

-I want to talk about the humiliation thing.
-*Okay.*
-Somehow the subject came up last night of you humiliating me.
-*Yep.*
-And you said, "What's wrong with humiliation? It's fun…" You didn't even finish the sentence and it was like you hit the bull's eye in the core of me. I just couldn't get over it. Nobody else could ever have said that, and I knew you were right. Everything stood still. *Everything.* It was like the spot I

would search for sometimes when I was lying still, or meditating, just run my mental eyes over the space within my mind, looking for that "spot." It had to be there, the thing that I was looking for, but I didn't know what it was. Just that it was at the core, the heart, the pinpoint place I had to find to understand. And you hit it.

-*I saw that.*

-So when you said you kinda enjoyed being an asshole—well, I kinda enjoyed being humiliated (by you anyway). *Because* it was the path to *me* being my best. Just like you said with the stubborn woman. Only not many people can play that game, can they?

-*Nope. Most of 'em weenee out.*

It was pretty obviously not an option for me, or I would probably have been one of them. Although, even in my worst moments, when I truly wanted to flee, there was something that held me—there was a powerful battle going on between my need to protect my ego and my desire to experience the love. I was, I suppose, being deliberately teased, poked in the vulnerable spots of my psyche, although it was hard to tell from which direction it was all coming. Was I just creating these problems? Or did he have a hand in it?

-But I've still got those little humiliations to overcome.

-*And when you do, you will be so much freer, and no one will be able to chain you. You will be able to fly to the stars.*

-It didn't feel like fun. Those little things I'm thinking about, and I know you know what I'm talking about.

-*Stephanie, you haven't caved. You just haven't got there yet. And you've called me on it. You have. I'm still trying to figure this out, too. But your spirit is so fierce, I love it.*

I knew deep down that he was right. This dread of personal humiliation was probably my heaviest and most persistent ball and chain, keeping me from flying. Keeping me from finishing my books, or doing anything that would put me in the public eye, where I might face criticism. I needed to conquer it.

I had always wanted to be the best, from the time I was a child. I equated anything less with personal failure. When I was eight years old, my class had an outdoors play day—possibly as part of an Easter celebration. We'd had a foot race and, to my humiliation, I had not won. In fact, I had been somewhere in the middle of the pack. For the next week I ran the dirt road that circled the bundle of CAA houses where I lived, determined to get back on top of the third-grade heap. And I did. That spring, unable to participate in the "field and track" experience because I was a girl, I would line up to the side of the boys when they prepared for their foot races, and invariably I would outdistance them all, to my lasting satisfaction. I might not be able to compete officially, but I knew I was the best.

But this need to "be the best" had an upside and a downside, the top of the mountain and the bottom of the pit. In school, I didn't care about grades, but perhaps only because I didn't have to. It was a sort of by-product of my love of learning. And anyway, I saw through the façade of grading early on. It was one of the first places where I was conscious of the rubber hitting the road, where truth and illusion collided, and I had to go with the lie in order to survive. Fortunately, the grading system was an easy game for me, but not so many others. I understood very clearly that in this structure, the most valuable student was the one who got solid "F"s. That was the platform on which everyone else stood, like the strong man at the base of the acrobatic tower, and I could never figure out why others didn't get it. But I enjoyed doing good work, when I could focus enough to get engaged, and tested well, so I generally loped along with about a high-B average.

I had learned early and didn't doubt that in fact I was smarter as far as academic subjects than almost anyone else I knew, which may have been why they were having difficulty comprehending that the student at the bottom of the grading barrel should be getting all the awards—or at least all the appreciation. But perhaps we all feel that secret gratitude when push comes to shove, i.e. when we're forced to line up against each other. We might not dare say it, but we feel it in our hearts: *Thank you for being worse than me. Phew,* we may think. *Squeaked by again. At least I'm not the shortest one. At least I wasn't the last one to get picked for dodge ball.* A useful mantra for living in this crazy world: *I might not have been the best, but at least I wasn't the worst.*

A lesson that worked minimally for me—if I wasn't the best in my little world, I was the worst. No greys in this field. In academics, I didn't necessarily *know the most*, but I could catch on awfully quick if I cared, so that worked out okay. But there were areas where I was the "worst," and no amount of determination would get me through. I couldn't carry a tune, for one thing. I was totally tone deaf, and this caused great humiliation in the Catholic schools where music theory and performance was emphasized from the early grades. In short, others *laughed* at me when I was forced to try.

You'd think all this would have taught me compassion for people who didn't pick up on other things so well, but not so. It wasn't so much that I had contempt for "stupid" people, as I felt annoyance at those who insisted upon their positions and weren't even willing to explore the beliefs that underpinned them. A neurotic personality here, seasoned with healthy doses of arrogance and inadequacy. What else from someone who always wanted to be the best?

I also was socially inept—I never saw the world as the majority of my peers did, and at least from the age of nine on, I found myself perplexed by the social behaviors of my classmates. As I entered adolescence, I was afflicted with the bane of not only being a social retard, but also being physically unattractive. Of course, that's an age when the "external standard"—as Steve would say, the scale you're not even on— becomes increasingly important.

This inner competitiveness, this yo-yo perception, pursued me throughout my life. I had a deep need to overcome obstacles, to figure it out, to climb every mountain in front of me. Not to prove myself to the world, but to prove myself to *me.* I wasn't inclined to take the easy route around the base of the hill—if I couldn't climb it, damn it, then I was a total ditz and I might as well curl up in a ball and die.

In these endeavors, the aging process became a new handicap. The idea of "growing old" didn't sit well with me at all. I resented it to the point of defiance. It was incredibly humiliating, something that I could not control, like a lesson that I couldn't learn.

And now, here I was—just as I was surrendering not too gracefully to what appeared inevitable, preparing to slide into the disintegration of old age—locked into this uncomfortably close and yes! romantic relationship across the spirit divide, with its total lack of privacy: i.e. all my considerable failings were open to view.

Granted, Steve did not even have a body, by Earth standards, and he'd had to go through his own deterioration process. I could take some consolation in that. But—the point was—he was now beyond, he'd come out the other side, and he was free. He could be anything he wanted (except maybe dense Earth physical). Of course, when we met in the astral plane, I could be a younger version of myself, and even tweak any characteristics. But there was still the fact that in this Earthly realm I was functioning with a sixty-five year old body, with all the standard implications. True, I had been exceptionally healthy, for which I had great cause to be grateful. Nevertheless, as Steve followed me around, I felt deeply vulnerable and humiliated. I tried not to think about it, but it was always there, every time I looked in the mirror. I hated even to shop for clothing, because of my reluctance to see my own image in the dressing room mirror.

And quite frankly, when he appeared young and quite handsome in our travels, I felt resistance—ashamed even, as if I had somehow strayed into a territory where I didn't belong. I actually preferred that he look quite a bit older.

So between this sense of physical inadequacy and the little mental humiliations, it was often a rocky road. There were truly times I just wanted to hide, and as it became ever more clear that there was nowhere to go, I was fighting one minute and surrendering the next.

Sometime that day:

I was still learning about Steve's lifetime, even as the personal lessons were coming at me fast and furious:

-And Steve, when I saw the Apple headquarters—the one you designed—in the magazine, I was astounded. Zero. The all. The beginning and the end. The donut in the sky with the embryos inside it, and you said each of those embryos represented a universe. I am so astounded. When you said that was one of the things we connected on early on, you said you liked my ideas about zero—and you said you wanted to get back to zero. Is that…

-Let's just say it's metaphorical at this point. Well, no, not even metaphorical. **Very very real,** *in the sense, as you intuited long before I met you, that zero is the ultimate resting place—and the birth of creation. Let's see how it plays out. (Smile.) I see you're beginning to collect your team.*

-The ones you're leading me to? I would say so.

-Work hard, my love. So much to do, so little time to do it….actually that's not true, **but**…*I still yearn for you to be here with me.*

-Or you here with me.

-You've got some strange idea floating around in that little head of yours. Don't get too cocky. This is my game.

-It is my game, too, isn't it?

-Oh, absolutely, you called it forth. You called me forth, and I you.

-Because we are the two halves.

-Yes, because we are the two halves, forever mirrored and mirroring and creating universes in the space between us.

-Coherent universes.

-I like that word. Coherent. Yes, I think coherence is a good word. See you soon. Glad you're going to Jamestown tomorrow [to give my brother-in-law a ride].

-You told me to.

A half hour later:

-I've been thinking about all those slave lives.

-MmmHmmm.

-And…

I wasn't sure where I was going with this. I actually did

not have good recall on "all my slave lives." I only had the conviction that I had very often been in a disempowered, chained role in life, although with a fierce fire inside. I let the thought dwindle away. Steve, however, picked it up:

-And? Yep, you were often a well-loved slave, but still a slave. You were often the "captured queen."

-And I sensed that, in this lifetime, feeling my own tendencies—not really knowing about all those lifetimes—just feeling inside myself for who I was.

-The captured queen as an essence, not necessarily a reality—although you had that, too. Long ago in Africa. But...it was your inherent dignity and intelligence that ran that show. You know you were the sister to TJ's wife—deceased wife?

-I know.

-You wouldn't give up your position—you would have given up your seat on the train to Heaven, huh, unless everyone else got to go with you.

-I'm trying to feel that one.

I couldn't really say I had a visual on that. Of course, I knew from research that in that lifetime I had had the option of remaining a free woman in France, but had decided to return to the colonies—soon to be the United States. And certainly I must have discussed my status, and that of my children, with T.J. over the years.

-Of course it feels right, and I feel it, all that incredible passion. I *was* like a child, but one so passionate for life, so full of dignity for who I was. So *connected*.

I do not know if this was true. How could I be certain that what I felt inside myself were true? But if I had to be a slave in lifetimes gone, I was going to claim as much gumption as I could, by golly.

-A real tough nut. The queen doesn't bend to her own interests. She holds out for the freedom of her own people.

-Holy shit. I am getting so much clarity. God, I can feel it

242   The Journey Begins

rising inside me, that passion for that man.

This part I could not deny, the feeling was so powerful. In fact, there would be much more clarity on the depth of my connection to the third president of the United States.

-Yes, you did love him, and he you. And he stood against slavery, and did what he could to limit it, but he could no more step out of his...kingdom, shall we say...than those who bemoan the limitations of the professions in which they find themselves can easily step out of theirs. It was you, you know, that convinced him patience was key. All would be well.

*And you stood behind him, and gave him strength. This was a man who was highly cultured, who had lived among kings, but who was also a powerful **dreamer.** He was one of us. A dreamer. And we live inside his dream today. We therefore live inside him. (I say "we," but you know what I mean—not just us joined, but the we-ness of this country.)*

-He had a steely determination.

-Yes, he did, and wouldn't settle. Oh, sure, there were compromises—he had them, I had them, you've had them— there are walls and bars and we do have to negotiate around them. Not in you. No walls, no bars for me.

-I feel like crying.

Crying? Again. One would hardly guess that my tear ducts had about dried up by the time I was thirty. Apparently, with the new energy, they were getting unclogged.

-He really did suffer a lot.
-Yes, but he had you, fortunately.

I came back a few minutes later to record my latest impression:

-I can feel him smiling. T.J.
-Let the record stand corrected.

Sometime later:

-Stephanie?

-H'mm?

-*I'm glad you came. I'm glad you came out to play.*

-Ah. Smiling here. I am *so* glad I did. I love you beyond all things. I love you to the depth of your soul.

-*And I...overwhelmed with feeling here...and I you.*

That evening:

I got into a convoluted sequence of images and discussion with Steve that caused me to get on the computer and look up Kurt Vonnegut. To my surprise, I found myself at a site called "The Secret Diary of Steve Jobs." Now how the heck did I get there? It turned out that there was a brief homage to Kurt Vonnegut, who had died shortly before, at the bottom of one of the lengthy (and very entertaining) poems by someone called Fake Steve. Would wonders never cease?

I forgot about Kurt and focused on Fake Steve's poetry, which I found very well done, actually. I was amused. Going back through the blogs, it was a little over the top—but I guess satire always is. Amazing how much attention this guy gave to this matter—I think a few entries would have gotten the point across to me, but I suppose there was always the need to feed the frenzy. And maybe he just really enjoyed doing it; I can kind of relate, as I had gotten caught up in my own such endeavors from time to time. The last entry on the blog was an obituary for Steve, one of the most delightful that I'm sure was written (although I haven't read others). I let Steve know what I thought:

-I think his obituary poem was first class. I just gotta say.

-*I better go read it again before I comment. It's been awhile since I perused the obits. Actually, I didn't bother. I already knew the story.*

-Okay, well Fake Steve seems to have gotten the commentary right. It was his last post, but maybe he doesn't know about your resurrection—or maybe your resurgence would be a better word.

-*I like that. Like the ocean coming back for another lick.*

I couldn't help thinking, as I was preparing this chapter: *God knows what kind of fun Fake Steve would have with a Steve Jobs in the Afterlife, not to mention a book like this. I might need lots of work on that humiliation piece before the word gets out. Hopefully, it'll be beneath his dignity to notice.*

Fake Steve did pay honor to that part of Steve which I had been discovering for the past few weeks, an irrepressible (and often challenging) sense of play.

> but no, Steve Jobs,
> your greatest accomplishment
> was not some piece of hardware
> not some lines of code
> No, Steve Jobs, your greatest accomplishment
> is what you did to us.
> You gave us joy.
> You restored our sense of childlike wonder.
> You enabled us to live in a world where
> we always believed that something amazing & magical
> was just around the corner
> and that the future would be better than the past
> because in fact,
> as long as you were alive,
> it was.[36]

And for at least one of us, it still is. And he is—still alive, that is. And maybe the future will be better than the past because someday others will share in this never ending story.

So, kudos, Fake Steve, you created a beautiful piece of poetry.

-And ha, ha, I found this little tidbit that I couldn't resist:

Quoting Newsweek: "Throughout his career Steve Jobs has been called tyrannical, mercurial, brilliant, and revolutionary. (Ed.- Sounds right.) The one thing

---

[36] http://www.fakesteve.net/

the cofounder of Apple and Pixar has never been called
is boring." [37]

-Indeed. I'm not bored yet, dear.

Stephanie gets an "impulse":

-Steve, I've got a hair to talk to Alan Watts. Is that
possible?
-Do you believe it is possible?
-I admit to a bit—actually a bucketful—of doubt. I mean,
I feel you, I talk to you, you make me laugh and cry and feel to
the very depths of my soul, you stimulate my mind, and
energize me, and make me reach, reach, reach. You have given
me so many external signs of your presence—I can't get away
from them. Your face is everywhere, looking at me, your words
all around me. But I feel apprehension when it comes to some
other well know people—can they really come as them, be
them, talk independently? Can I *trust* what is said?
*-Well, you've already talked to Thomas Jefferson, before I
even showed up, and you've come to see how that reached into
your soul, eh? Your private story. And Johnny and June came
to share.*
-But they didn't provide any verification.
*-Oh, I don't know about that. It all comes around. And
what about Erik?*
-Yeah, Erik. I'm comfortable with Erik, he's a cool
guy/spirit.
*-You can leave off the "spirit" reference Stephanie, we get
it. **You** are a cool spirit. You can be in the Earth Plane
Distortion Field and still be a cool spirit, you get it? And you
can be **outside** the Earth Plane Distortion Field and be a good
guy. Get it?*
-Yeah, I think so. But I am sort of half and half, aren't I?
-Kinda, like half chocolate/half vanilla ice cream? You

_____

[37] Dan Lyons, http://www.fakesteve.net/2010/03/steve-jobs-insanely-
great.html

mean like that?

-Maybe I'm Neapolitan. Three flavors pressed together.

-I actually like that better. It seems more appropriate to me.

-But I'm not entirely *here*, in this world.

-The spell has been broken. The seal has been cracked. Let's leave it like that.

Ha ha. I was getting a little caught up in my own dramatic view of this adventure, and it was like Steve to one minute be building me up, and the next bringing me down.

-Okay. Alan Watts?

-Let me see if he wants to lower himself to talk to you.

-Is he a swell-head?

-No, not really. Not at all. No more swelled than he wants to be.

-It's all a game for him?

-A beautiful never ending game.

-Alan: Cool.

-You're here.

-Alan: I am. Me, in the flesh...jiggly fleshy kinda thing.

-I think I'm going to choke up...not in as choke up...but in as not be able to do this.

-Alan: Pretty much the same.

-Yeah.

-Alan: Hare Krishna.

-What?

-Alan: You heard me right, don't filter it.

-I gotta break—too much, too fast. Can we take a break? Do you mind?

-Alan: Not at all. I'm just hanging around. Steve promises not to bore me. He's turned off the elevator music.

I wasn't sure what he was referring to with the music, but maybe the songs that were playing in the background on my computer. For myself, I was overwhelmed. All I knew about *Hare Krishna* was that there were some young people in saffron robes who wandered around in the LA airport handing out flowers. Or something like that. I didn't recollect seeing any, except in pictures—and then I had not been drawn to pay much attention. Was "Hare Krishna" a greeting? Was this really Alan Watts or just another figment of my imagination? Well, of course, we knew what Steve would say about that. But was he a *real* figment of my imagination?

Fortunately, I was able to quickly look up the term, thanks (at least in part) to some guy who had decided forty years before that every household should have a personal computer, sort of like a "bicycle for the mind."

-Okay, I looked it up, this is what I got:

The *Hare Krishna* mantra is a chant meant for enhancing consciousness to the greatest possible degree...The mantra is most commonly translated as "O Lord, O Energy of the Lord, please engage me in Your service."[38]

-*Alan: indeed.*
-I gotta go absorb this, okay?
-*Alan: Take our time, Stephanie, I always enjoy a good mind game.*

I don't know if he really said "our," or if it was a typo in my journal, but I have left it as "our," since it might have been something Alan would have said.

I took a little break. I simply was not prepared to really be talking to Alan Watts. Yes, I could handle Thomas Jefferson, Johnny Cash and June Carter Cash—barely. But I'd not really thought much about them, so it wasn't like I felt I was in the presence of nobility. Alan Watts was kind of a personal hero. I know. I had it all backwards. He probably would have laughed at how I inverted everything. After a minute to catch my breath, I was ready to proceed:

-Alan, what do you do in the afterlife? Steve said he sat in the dark contemplating for a thousand years.

---

[38] http://www.krishna.com/info/hare-krishna-mantra

-Alan: Not me. I have been indulging in the pleasures of the flesh.

-But you don't have flesh.

-Alan: Don't be silly. I happen to know that you and Steve have had a few indulgences of your own.

-Go away.

-Alan: What? (Looks at Steve.) Am I giving away secrets?

And that *really* called for a minute to recuperate:

-Okay, the scribe is back—I had to take a break, I was too embarrassed, but you two won't let up.

-Alan: Yeah, you really are Miss Priss, aren't you? Steve informed me that I'm doing a good job of helping out with the humiliation piece. A little public humiliation is good for the soul. Anyway, you shouldn't see it as humiliation. And you won't. We are what we are. Multi-dimensional. I do hate saying that, you know I really do. People get these kooky ideas that are so absurd. You can't hardly shake 'em loose from it— no, no!! Don't take away my anchor!! Don't untie the boat!! Yeah, I know I'm sitting in a boat, but can't I just keep it tied to the dock? Do I have to really set sail on that endless ocean???

This time I was called away for an external reason—my son was at the door and I needed to grab something for him. I could hear Steve and Alan talking while I was called away. I quickly set down what I had heard:

Alan: She's really funny, Steve. Complicated. Partly truth and partly fiction...

Steve: Oh, yeah.

Alan: Well, I like that you're enjoying it. More than I care to indulge in, in this moment. I prefer to just lie on my tire and float—enjoying my glass of wine and my lovely buxom maids. Mermaids? H'mm, I kinda like that.

I jumped into the conversation:

-Aren't you gonna tell me anything wise?

-Alan: Wise? Wise? I can't give you wise. **You** *have to give you wise. You have to live it, experience it, create it. In your own way. Which I see you are doing, with some help from the Other. Good sailing, you two.*

-Bye, Alan.

-Alan: Adios. You may see me come around...and around...a time or two again.

As soon as he was gone, I instantly thought of the things I should have said.

-I should have told him I appreciated all the talks he left behind. I found them so engaging.

-Stephanie, he doesn't care. He doesn't have an ego that needs stroking.

-So many might think differently. I feel a lot of energy in that direction, felt it as you wrote that.

-Yes, he floats indulgently on the sea of all that misunderstanding.

-I feel somehow overwhelmed, like I just got another peek into the soul of someone—when you said that. Wow. He's much bigger than he seems, so cavalier.

-Yes, Stephanie. Very very expansive.

Bath time:

-I just keep wandering around, unable to focus, my mind swirling with all this information—all this *experience*. Getting it gut level.

-Go take your bath.

-Okay. I'm gonna go and read something that has nothing to do with me or you or Alan Watts.

-Ha ha. Good luck on that one.

Oops:

-Whew! I can't even talk. (What I meant to say was, I can't even get a decent bath—there's always something going on.) So the bank calls me right before I get in and tells me the

250   The Journey Begins

appraisal came in under the selling price on the Anchorage home, and I'm like, whatever. The buyer is a really good dude, and whichever way the $15,000 benefit falls, it still accrues to me, because we are all connected. I sooo got that. God I love you for all you have shown me. And that news came in right when it needed to. Spoiled my bath, though, it made me want to cut it short...I'm always pulled back here. But I understood *immediately* that this is nothing, there are so many irons in the fire.

-Indeed, my love, the forces have been gathering around you for a long time. You were the one who took ten one hundred dollar bills when you had little enough money, tied them up in a note with a ribbon, and left them where people could find them. And the note said: "If you need this money, keep it; if not, pass it on to someone else, friend or stranger." *How many hands do you think that note passed??? Not very many, my dear. Not very many. But the reverberations of what you did were released, and they will travel to the end of time. That was magnificent. MAGNIFICENT!!*

-I always wondered what happened to those notes.

-Oh, they found their way into the hands of those who know nothing of dreams. But when this is published, they will see it, and they will realize that they touched greatness. I am so proud of you. So amazingly proud of you. And who cares what others think? Fuck 'em. The forces of good have gathered around you. You just had to take the last step.

-Are you sure I'm not in Oz? I feel like I'm in a whirlwind.

-No. Sweetheart, cherished cherub. You are not in Oz. You are in Fantasia, with me.

-(And by the way, I had no sooner stepped out of the bath then the buyer called, and we were able to have a very pleasant convo, and he was so happy.)

-Yes, your capacity to spread happiness now is limitless.

Steve reflects:

-Stephanie?
-Hmmm?

-You were sitting in the dark, too. It was other forces who saw us, each sitting in our dark place, without any glimpse of hope, in spite of holding so much within us, and out of an outpouring of compassion we were brought together.
-Wow.
-You set it off, with that letter to [name omitted]. "Maybe it will all die with me," you said. And it touched off a storm in the Heavens.
-Wow
-Yes. No sparrow falls but that it is noticed. And no angel wraps its wings around itself and lowers its head but it is like a thunder through the heavens.

It hit me suddenly, the other side.

-Steve??
-Yes?
-And you touched me when I was nothing, and I became something.
-(Smile.) I love you so much.
-And I love you.

Last thoughts of the day:

-So [name omitted] is part of this?
-Oh yes, he is connected. Because he is connected, others in the collective can participate in what comes his way. That's the best way to say it. Remember when I told you about the elephant, and how if all the blind men were connected, there would be a whole elephant between them? It is something greater than the individual, almost like a new synergetic picture. All then move in accordance with this picture. It doesn't have to be a conscious thing, from the individual point of view. Just as you are connected, and you are not aware of the whole picture. But you move when it is your time to move, and many many others are moving when you move. You move two inches to the right, and everyone in the collective is affected, because the synergetic world has been changed. This is what you used to feel when you would sit down to meditate,

or just lie still, and try to stay in the sensory impressions, as if you were a remote viewer camera and somewhere far up in space others were gathered around the screen where your impressions were conveyed, that they might be able to see from your viewpoint. You understood that you had to clear your mind of thoughts, somehow you understood that, that you had to let go of ego, and just be the eyes, the ears, not judging or evaluating but leaving that for others to do. So even when you were not fully connected, you were sending information that was helpful to the collective. Very few in the Earth Distortion Field have ever realized how helpful and desirable that is. Somehow you got it instinctively.

-And you knew this? While you were here?

-I knew how the synergy worked, I knew that the world was reworked all the time in every little way, and that to really **blow the world up,** *to make it flow in technicolor, the imagination had to be let loose. That was my life's work.*

-I have to say here, it was *really really* hard to do that—just let the data flow in and off to whatever "real eyes" would see it.

-I know. Not easy. But you did pretty darn well, for a prissy little woman from the Midwest.

-Gosh, thanks.

-No problem. Any time.

CHAPTER 12
MIRRORS

Upon returning from a trip to Jamestown with my brother-in-law:

-I had a nice day today.

-*Me too. That was fun, just hanging out, going for a drive.*

-Poor Bob. I just didn't think I had it in me to try to keep up a conversation with him when I had you—fortunately he's pretty easy, he was cool when I told him I had a lot on my mind.

-*(Laughing.) Am I a lot?*

-I think so. A big lot. Anyway, it was fun to have real company, to be able to share the moment with someone. I've always thought that you can go places, do things, see things—but you really want someone to share it with. I've always had that impression, don't know where I got it, since I rarely was with anyone (when I was with anyone) who could see it with the same eyes. Actually, we're really seeing it with the same eyes, aren't we?

-*Pretty much.*

-Don't even tell me how that works. I don't want to know right now. Anyway, that felt so freeing, the idea of driving off the end of the Earth. I mean cool, it's just such a cool perspective that I never could have seen before. I love it—you really don't know what is just over the horizon. I guess that makes me a Flatlander, huh? That's sort of like life, huh? Our view of it, that we just fall off the end when we die. And all the other stuff, that was cool, too.

-*Beautiful day.*

-You were telling me that the plaque that fell in Dean's office was your way of sending a message. Dean pointed it out, he *thought* you were sending a message, he showed me how the plaque was fastened on and that it couldn't fall by itself. You said they represented the three seals. So I started to look up "three seals" and it seems to have something to do with Buddhism—but got interrupted—so I'm going back to see what else I can find out.

-*Okay. Happy Hunting.*

-Impermanence, no self, and nirvana. Looking deeply into impermanence leads to the discovery of no self. The discovery of no self leads to nirvana. Nirvana is the Kingdom of God. So what are you telling me?

-*It's evident, isn't it?*

-Well, I feel like I've reached the "no self" point. That was my death, right?

-*Dead as a doornail.*

-And I'm still discovering that, aren't I?

-*(No verbal response, the smile/shrug thing that says: are you? You tell me.)*

THAT NIGHT, HEAVY LIFTING TIME:

I was hesitant to include the following discussion, because it was such a tender spot with me. I had a great deal of trouble sorting out who I was dealing with at times: was it the Steve Jobs Earth Life Personality or the Steve Jobs Afterlife Personality. Did they differ? When was he just pulling my chain, when was he sincere, and how much was set in stone? In this tangled mess, what was my role? As I had previously mentioned, I had a huge problem with lying, and was troubled whenever this particular issue came up. I also held myself to a high standard. Sometimes I thought I couldn't trust the authenticity of certain discussions—perhaps just because of the content of it, maybe it cut too close to the bone—but in the end, I realized that if I didn't trust all of it I couldn't trust any of it, and there was too much evidence to throw it all out. I do check everything on which I have a question against my own gut, as Steve told me to do when we discussed the writing of this book, and just in case my gut and his consent are not enough, I do the finger tension test. This part made it through all three filters and so here goes, for better or worse:

-Steve.

-*Present.*

-You know, back with the thing with that clockness, in the beginning of our conversations, you just out and out lied to me.

He had previously admitted that it was Tesla feeding me thoughts that I was then playing with, not himself.

-*I know.*

-Just explain yourself some more, please.

-*I really did want to hold onto you, Stephanie—I can't even explain, it was so powerful beyond belief—like that moment in all of creation when the world stands still, when you see something so incredible that you never even hoped...well hoped, but couldn't believe...would ever appear. I looked into your mind, and it was like everything was bright and wide open and mirrors all over the place—mirrors. That's the only way I can say it. Mirrors. I couldn't bear the thought of you getting away. I felt like I was trying to reel in a really big fish. And yeah, I overstepped my bounds—it just came out before I could pull it back. I wanted **you** to see me as sharp, as sharp as you, someone you could admire. Okay, I didn't say I had it all together. I have it so much more together today than I did then. The old habits just kept coming into play.*

-And that's why I thought something was kinda off about that clockness thing. It just didn't sit right, not even what you were saying...you were just fudging or picking up your lines from somewhere.

-*I never even **thought** of that. The fact that you did was overwhelming, like Einstein stuff, Tesla stuff. You didn't even know...well, maybe you did, I think maybe you did...know that you were sipping out of the same stream. But I really did just get flabbergasted by how your mind picked up on stuff like that, how you just cut through the crap, didn't buy things just because somebody else told you so.*

-So, of course, I don't think you've lied to me a lot since then. That thing with Tesla. But lay it on me. Where have you been cutting corners, lying?

-I can't really think of anyplace. Tease you sometimes. But I came to see that wouldn't cut it with you. I was gonna lose you if I didn't play it totally straight.

-I just listened to that channeling of you by [name omitted].[39]

-I know.

-It sounded authentic, actually. It sounded like you.

-When I was nothing sitting in my dark room.

-Yeah. You said then you didn't want to incarnate on Earth again, just like you've always told me, and that you wanted to go elsewhere to work out those karmic issues. I don't call them karmic, but apparently that's the way he saw what you were saying. I guess "karmic" is a word that works, though. I don't know.

*-Here's the deal, Stephanie. You were so clear about so much, while you were down there in that dark fog—you saw stuff I had no clue about until I was here. And I could see how frustrated you were, too. Right from the beginning I wanted to take you in my arms and say "It's going to be okay. Nobody else can see you, nobody else can penetrate the fog, but I **do** see you." My heart just opened up. I can't explain it now. Probably for the first time in my entire—well certainly my entire life as Steve Jobs and my afterlife since—I felt this incredible compassion. I don't even know what to say beyond that...the words don't seem good enough to convey it all.*

-You've been...

*-Since we met. Telling you how wonderful you are. And you know what I'm telling you is true. You've always known that. But nobody else could see. And the fact that I **could** see meant something to you. It meant we were...birds of a feather, eh? You just did it different than me. And even, through your eyes, I came to see me as so much better. I wanted to be better. I really really wanted to be better.*

-Here's the part I have trouble with. How do you have all these doubts and stuff where you are? How is it you do some of

---

[39] An online channeling. The channeling was rather rough, but there were some essential ideas that seemed legitimate.

the stuff you pulled? Did you push things away as much as you pulled them in?

-Maybe. Thinking. As Steve Jobs, yes, sometimes. Actually, kinda often, now that I think about it. But the other stuff, what I said about you picking up on "zero," I really resonated with that.

There was definitely that feeling for me—the push-pull. I guess I didn't realize how much I was doing it myself. It would become our trade-mark. Only looking back do I see how this was the experiential side of what I had intuited, that reflection effect—and of course he had clicked on it with his reference to mirrors. We were both so *driven*. Yes, I had been driven all my life, and he obviously had, each determined to do it *my way*— never willing to just accept anything anybody else said, always having to see it, feel it, taste it. There was an arrogance there for the both of us: *you can't tell me what to be, damn it. You're not the boss of me.* Or, in Stephanie-Steve-speak: *Don't pick out my dress for me!* All the time searching for love, but it had to come on our terms—it had to encompass what we really were, not what someone else *thought* we were. It had to be profound and total. We had to be *seen* naked in our souls and still found acceptable.

And yet, here he'd been fudging with the truth, taking credit for something that wasn't his. Or *was* it? Were we all so connected—were he and Tesla so connected—that thoughts slopped over into each other?

I knew from the beginning—I felt it inside myself—that we were both compelled to search for that elusive perfection, each in our own way. I'd certainly had my tyrannical fits, particularly when I was young, although I'd learned to tone it down as I got older. Look for a different way.

And yes, he did continually point out the things he saw as special inside me—and the fact was, they were the things I thought of as the best of me, too. So he was right on that score. We crave the one who understands and agrees on what we consider good in ourselves. But when there is a lot of mirroring going on, a lot of reflection, how do you know what's you and what's not? And if we are mirrors, don't you *want* to see the best in the other, because that is a reflection of yourself?

I didn't even realize how much beauty I was already finding in the mirror in front of me, in spite of the foggy view, until I was preparing this chapter:

-I saw the pic of the Apple headquarters in process in the Time magazine. And here's another question, Steve, you said in the [channeled] interview that we should all love our family more, hug them more, spend time with them, give them our attention. But how do you do that, Steve, when you feel compelled along different paths. What if that doesn't feel like your joy, your bliss? What if it's—here's the big B word. Boring.

-You've begun to find the answer to that, haven't you?

-Well, yes, I think so, but only because of what has come of our relationship here, how much I have learned and changed. I'm not the same, am I?

-Nope.

-So I see them differently. I see where life did them wrong. I see them suffering, and suddenly I feel like I can *do* something about it. Before it just seemed like it was all about settling—every time I tried to stand up and get behind something that seemed right to me, good to me, I got shot down.

-You let yourself be shot down. You lacked the belief in yourself, the ability to shape the clay and make it hold the shape.

-No whining, I'm not whining. I'm just wondering. I guess it was all ego. All ego.

- Yeah, good riddance to that, huh?

-Yeah. The mysterious disable button. They make humanity like [certain] laptops, you can't figure out how to disable the touchpad that's *wayyyyyyy* too touchy. Just like the ego. I like this metaphor.

We talked about some personal concerns, and touched upon some of my own fears: the dreaded "cupboards," which held our personal secrets. I was not so concerned about my own, because I knew he had free access to them. I wasn't sure I wanted to look into his:

-Are these some of the cupboards I have to open?
Actually, they're not the ones I'm afraid of.

-I know. I know what you're afraid of.

-Okay, well let's let that rest, okay. I can see it all in good
time. Except—you've had help on your side.

*-I have. Support, mostly. You are about the most
stubborn woman—no wait, **the** stubbornest woman I've ever
encountered.*

-Steve.

-Yeah?

-I guess I've never seen inside anybody like this before. I
remember once, when I was meditating in front of that ugly old
avocado plant—the one that was dying—so many years ago.
And the more I looked at it, the more beautiful it began to
appear to me, how everything was so beautiful—you could slice
the leaves, and all you would see was more of that incredible
incredible detail—you could slice down to ever more refined
layers of reality...Not like a painted picture, where the closer
you get, you lose the detail. I remember thinking, "wow, there
is *nothing* that isn't beautiful when you look at it—nothing God
has made that isn't beautiful. Even dung and blood and..."
Someone once said "cancer cells are beautiful"—yes they are.
They are beautiful and they have their place, just like everything
else. I'm not putting you in that category—or maybe I am, it's
all the same category, right?—I'm just saying the more that I
have looked inside you, the more that I have sliced you open,
the more that I have come to see the beauty.

-And what happened to that plant?

-It was transformed—temporarily.

*-Temporarily because you lost the space. The elasticity of
the Earth Plane Distortion Field pulled you back in. I don't
want to blossom temporarily.*

-You can't, can you? We would have to wither together,
wouldn't we?

*-I don't know. I just want to overcome every single thing
with you. I want to make it so you can look out from the inside
of my heart, and see to the stars, and I can do the same. No*

walls.   Nothing to hold us back.   Nothing to stop the ever expanding joy.

ALL ABOUT WALLS:

The tides of our relationship ebbed and flowed.   It could all change so quickly.   He was there, always there, and the closeness was suffocating me. I needed some space for myself! I had always been a private person, working out my issues, my problems inside myself. I had always needed significant periods of time alone.   I *liked* being alone. I was the best company I knew.

I tried to put my foot down. I insisted on some space for myself, a private place, where I could make my own decisions, just as I always had.   I laid it out for Steve: I needed to keep a part of myself separate, where he couldn't go. But it was kind of like stepping on the business end of a hoe and the handle comes up to whack you in the head. Even as I was trying to avoid him, shut him out, I realized the dilemma: weren't these the walls that we were both trying to escape?   Wasn't I not only throwing up roadblocks in his path, but building my own cage?   How could this work?   It was like we were joined at the hip, but I wanted to be able to pick out my own pants. What to do?

I knew I had to let it go, to relinquish that corner I wanted to guard for myself. Deep down, I knew this.   But that only made me feel more frustrated, more trapped—even though I sensed that the separate corner was the coop.

I fell asleep still caught up in this dilemma.

SATURDAY, OCTOBER 31, 2015
4:12 A.M.

I woke up famished, but not feeling drawn to anything but very bland, so I made a bowl of cold cereal and milk. I was losing weight, which did make me happy.   My sleep patterns remained unpredictable.

I sat up to the desktop to hash out the problem:

-It's painful letting go of some of this stuff, of some of these places where I have notoriously dug in, like a bunker, and been so determined to fight off all comers. Nobody could invade this space, nobody tell me what to do there, nobody even *knows* what my thoughts were in there. And letting somebody breech those walls has been....difficult. Hard. Troublesome. But it didn't take long, as usual, once the problem was identified—and somehow you led me along like I had a ring through my nose, so it *had* to be identified, given shape, where the exact lines in the sand were drawn. Across this line you cannot come!!

But gradually, my desire for true freedom won out, and I thought that's how it works—if I live in your heart, I can't block off a part—and vice versa. That would really mess up the picture!! There's got to be freedom on both ends for the mirroring to go on forever. Which brings me to another thought—there's a lot about you I just fucking don't want to know. Sometimes I feel like I already know too damned much. I mean, life is about keeping secrets, and I'm willing to let you have yours. But that's the other side of the coin, isn't it? I have to be willing to face and go into your own private places—the ones where you haven't already taken me, the corners, the cupboards. Ouch! That's almost as painful as having to let you into mine.

I'm gonna go back to bed and see if I can sleep.

9:26 A.M.

I didn't get much sleep, but I did take some time to think about my life, where it was at before I met Steve, and where it was at the present. I knew—I knew instinctively—that the pockets of resistance I had to this relationship had to go. My barricades, his cupboards.

At this point, all I could get my head around was that I somehow had a connection to this disembodied intelligence, that for some reason we were cut from the same cloth, the same dye-lot, even if sewn into different garments. It was this fact that accounted for our ability to communicate as we did, to understand each other, to see in the other what we most wanted to be seen.

Years before, when I attempted to formulate a definition of love, I came up with the following understanding: *Love is*

262 The Journey Begins

seeing and being seen; love is hearing and being heard. Rarely, rarely, rarely did this occur in the world in which I lived. Not even by me, after I logically understood it. When you really look at a blade of grass, when you really see it, know it, comprehend it in all its incredible God-given beauty, then there is love. When you look at another human being, when you see past the illusions, the public "face," the walls and bars, then you see the beauty—you must, for under all that smoke and mirage, the fundamental being exists in all its glory. But two things must conspire for that to occur: you must look with the piercing sight of either innocence or wisdom, and the other must be vulnerable to being seen. In that moment, love happens—or rather, the shroud is pulled off, the statue is revealed. Often younger people, or those who have been together a very long time, are able to access this profound experience of love. For the rest of us, wandering around in the haze of social proprieties, restrictions, obligations, shames and the fallout of the "thought police," the experience of pure love is elusive. And even for those people who have experienced it, it gets lost under the burden, the weight of all that garbage which comes our way every day of our lives. Thus even the pure love of a parent for the small child gives way as the walls build between them.

Now here I was, being encouraged, guided, *forced* to attack my own walls, to bring them down, to open up the space. It hurt, it hurt, but I knew that I had to do it. I had to give up that corner where I made all my own decisions, where I crawled to lick my wounds, where I guarded my own little peccadillos from view. I had to do it, I had to let him in, so I could be free. I knew this in the core of me, and yet I would have taken flight rather than face those battles, were it not for the love and warmth that drew me ever back to him. That positive energy, that magnetism, tugged at me even in my worst moments.

And I knew also that when I was free, the world would be mine. I had often thought that I would like to be the wind, going anywhere, touching everyone and everything, but never being caught. Never being hurt, never being named, never being photographed. A self so unchained that it could only be known by what it did.

Inevitably, I got caught up in a discussion with Steve

about it. He knew, of course, all my thoughts, and where they were taking me.

    *-**Do** it Stephanie. Become your self.*
    -I feel like I have to a large degree. Claimed my space.
    -(Smile.) With a little help from your friends.
    -With a little help from my friends. Okay, I get the message, I am going to get to work. I hate not sitting around talking with you, but I am preparing to focus—move things along. Dig in my toes, get some traction?

    This was one of the big areas of my life where movement was taking place. I *had* given up, I had been just waiting for that time when I no longer had to face the dawn; I *was* a lightweight, as he had pointed out so early in our relationship. Now I had my fight song, and it was seeping into my bones, strengthening them. Yes, I could! Well, maybe. Okay, I wasn't there yet, but I was beginning to feel some confidence, some impulse to get up off the floor one more time…like a prize fighter who has been knocked down one too many times, and then hears that little whisper in his ear: *Get up, get up, you can do it. Believe in yourself.*
    I knew not how the universe worked, or how, when I had seen nothing further that I wanted in this world, the crack opened up into the next and Steve stepped through. Perhaps that is the answer—when we stop trying to get whiskey from a bottle of wine, we can taste the wine.

11:47 A.M.

    One of the matters that troubled me still, and to which I returned from time to time, was the ambiguous meeting with the spirits during the "test," when I was being asked to give up something, but I couldn't quite comprehend it. Eventually, of course, I had agreed—whatever it was—frustration, humiliation, a kidney, Steve's choice of a finger from either of my hands—I was in. But being a lawyer, it still rankled that I'd had to give the blind consent.

    -Steve, this—this using me as your feet on the ground

264 The Journey Begins

kinda thing, that came to you gradually, didn't it, after we started talking?

-It did. I thought it wasn't going to happen, I was never going back there. I just could not see going through the birth canal and spending a whole lifetime trying to get back to where I left off—if I even could manage it. It gradually occurred to me—maybe with a little help from my friends—that you were the perfect conduit. Our minds were so synchronized before we even met. Like I said, we were on our way to the same place, but approaching from different directions. Which means we were each unseen by the other.

-But it's the story. It was meant to be.

-Not meant to be. It is written. We are just on a process of discovery, and in the process we are re-creating it. That is, we are bringing it alive, and all living things—that includes stories—must expand in practice.

-Sort of like those little spongy critters you drop in water and they expand into dinosaurs and such?

-Yeah. Kinda like that. But I needed your consent.

-That's what the committee was about? That's what they were presenting to me? And *why* was that guy with the white hair wearing the tinsel crown? Or foil crown, maybe better way to say it. What *was* all that about? And Steve, I didn't really understand what they were asking me. I knew they wanted me to give up something, some part of me (or at least what I perceived as me), but I couldn't really understand what? A toe? A liver? What??? And who *was* that guy with the foil crown?

I kept thinking that it had to have significance, especially since it was a visual on one of the participants that I remembered so distinctly.

*-I won't answer the crown question here, **because** it is always so much better when you find the answer—you know that. You experience it, and it becomes a part of you. If I just tell you, then it's just a belief, you have to accept what I'm saying, and then your inner being gets confused. Between what you **know** and what you think you know.*

Anyway, the last thing I want is to confuse you anymore.

Yeah, some temporary confusion is good, it stirs things up, like stirring the soup. Then you can see what was hiding at the bottom of the pool.

Well, this was true. The pot-stirring of the "test" had brought up a lot of crud hiding down there. But...as I had to point out:

-Mixed metaphor again.
-A vat of soup is a pool.
-*Anyway*...I'm not going to argue that point with you. But what I am going to say is that I had to agree, which I finally did—after much confusion and soul troubling, without knowing what I was giving up.
-Yes. Whatever it was, you were willing to surrender it so that we could be together.
-But I didn't think it was going to be like this.
*-I know. But it's not what you **knew,** it's what you were willing to do.*
-But that's not informed consent.
-Do you want out of the contract?
-Ah, no. It's binding, right?
-I think so.

≫

-And Stephanie?
-Huh?
-Look at you go!

Chapter 13
Into the Cupboards

Sunday, November 1, 2015

The closet thing was a problem. It grated terribly against my deep desire for privacy. It was difficult. Very difficult. I had no interest in the personal details of Steve's life, and never asked. That was his business. Neither did I want to cough up mine. I thought of these as our cupboards, and I resisted opening them. Of course, I figured he already had free access to all my transgressions, idiosyncrasies and complications. I might as well have come with a guidebook: *All About Stephanie, from A to Z.*

I had my own guidebooks, of course. Lots of them. Just about anything I wanted to know about the life of Steve Jobs, I could find with the click of a mouse or by cracking my book. In fact I now had two of the latter: the Issacson biography and the *Time* magazine. I had read bits and part of each, but still very little of the total—they were both full of details and/or technical stuff that interested me little. I was waiting for the *Dummy's Guide to Steve Jobs* to be published, or at least the *Essential Steve Jobs.* The material I had was slim on details about his personal life, which suited me fine. As I said, that was his business. I didn't want to know his secrets. What I *did* want was to not have to worry about them.

But there was one particularly nagging problem with all this. Perhaps because of my training as an attorney, but more likely because of a natural instinct to transparency, I believed in full disclosure. Not about personal information that had no bearing on other interactions, but on matters that affected the other person, or third parties. How can you make valid choices if relevant information is withheld?

The point that troubled me immensely is that I was in what had very quickly become a very personal relationship—if one that seemed mandated by some force beyond my understanding—and I cringed at the thought of stepping on other toes. In other words, Steve was very much alive to me. I knew that. But others apparently did not. In fact, a large part of the population was under the impression that the physical body was everything, that when it rotted into the ground, the individual consciousness fell into dust with it.

Yet I was dealing with a very lively intelligence, a powerful heart, and, yes, a tangible body and presence in our many travels. I was dealing with emotion, intertwining feminine and masculine energies, even commitments. And I was doing it "on the sly." But I sensed from the beginning that it was meant to be quite public, that this story was meant to be a sort of road map for others.

This was not me, this was not my way. I did not want to cause any emotional pain to anyone else, to move into a space that was held personal to others. I preferred obscurity and wanted to respect the sensitivities and privacy of others.

Steve sought to reassure me that he was a free agent, but still the complexities troubled me. It wasn't just his feelings that I was concerned about. I understood in the depths of me that our connection was beyond the normal range—that quite likely we were somehow this strange phenomena he had talked about, of having once been a whole soul that was torn apart—but it hardly made my dilemma easier. I assumed that if I could connect with him, than others could as well, if they were willing. This probably is not entirely true, as I was to discover further down the road—but at the time I was still very ignorant about the depth of our spiritual connection, and how far it was from a happy coincidence that we had connected. No coinkydinks, indeed.

And although my heart had capitulated, my mind still strongly resisted the connection with him. Why me? Why him and me? He had a presence in the world during his lifetime, and still had a huge impact upon the world—witness the *Time* magazine that had just come out. I was obscure, a nobody, a fading grandmother from North Dakota. It was the most unlikely pairing I could imagine, from an objective standpoint (even discounting the bizarre incarnate/disincarnate thing). Yes, we connected well on a subjective level, but that didn't make it something Dear Abby would approve. I imagined the humiliation if it got out—and he was contemplating a *book*?

Really? How was that going to go over?

So the cupboards thing became a touchy subject to me. I gritted my teeth at the thought of having to get into his—*if* I had to. There's a certain comfort in ignorance, in sticking your head in the sand and hoping everybody else has their shit together, even if you don't have yours.

It bears saying here that—in case there is a question in anyone's mind—Steve has shared his undying love for his friends and family, particularly his widow and children, and that he watches over them. They are ever in his heart.

It was only my own insecurities, my sense of ego, that caused me consternation about invading sheltered parts of his life. It wasn't truly what I feared I would find in there—but that I was terrified of what I might uncover about myself in relation thereto: i.e. ugly and small. I needed to imagine that he had me covered, that he had the details of this strange convergence worked out, that somehow the pieces all fit together. That I didn't need to worry.

I was still very much afraid of having the rug pulled out from under me.

Steve had called me to come spend some time with him. I knew the subject was going to be his cupboard, so I dug in my heels. No, no! Not the cupboards!! But the invisible cable attached to my solar plexus only grew tauter, until it was almost jerking me off my feet. Sigh! I might as well get it over with—I had already learned that when this man summoned, he didn't like to be ignored.

I lay on my bed and was immediately relaxed; normally I didn't even have to work to clear my mind, the movement from one realm into the next was almost instantaneous—and so it was on this occasion. I could feel him close, his energy. And suddenly pictures were flying at me, as if they were coming out of one of those pitching machines used for batting practice. The pictures started out small and rapidly increased in size, spinning in the air, as they came at me, but not so fast that I couldn't see each one briefly.

They were two-dimensional, like photographs. The first picture I saw was of him with his arms around some girl or young woman; all I could see was her back, I couldn't see her face. She was wearing a dress and a little cardigan sweater. Then there were some pictures of Steve's face at different stages of his life, from childhood to adulthood—one very similar to the one on the cover of his biography but with a different pose and hand position. I clearly saw a picture of a man—who seemed rather tall and thin—standing in a doorway looking in. I knew it was Steve's bedroom, that he was a young boy, and it was his father, wondering why he wasn't in bed. The man was wearing old-fashioned pajamas, which I found kind of hilarious (how the times have changed), and Steve said, "Hey, men wore those pjs back in the 50s and 60s." Which was true, even Desi wore pajamas, and in those old movies, the femme fatale always ended up in the guy's pajama top. I understood that these pictures were some of his memories, winging at me.

I asked him to back off, that I couldn't focus on what we were supposed to be talking about, with all these pictures flying at me. But instead, I suddenly found myself smack dab in the middle of a scenario that was clearly one of his memories. I was actually reliving it with him, in 3D, with smells and sound and feelings. It was obviously very special and personal to him, so I won't describe it, other than to say it was simply amazing to be able to participate as if I were there. I understood that this experience became a hundred times more special for being shared, that it was now a co-mingled memory. This co-re-creation triggered an energy merger that was so fantastic that I totally blissed out. I was conked out for a couple of hours, even though I had had a good sleep the night before. I have learned since that the human body can apparently only handle so much energy, and so anytime the energy combination gets too intense, I end up knocked out for a while.

When I woke up I was still feeling blissed out, and couldn't move. I was thinking, "Oh, wow, this cupboard business isn't as bad as I thought it would be." In fact, it was just *awesome*. I was so melded with…with just beingness. When I looked at the clock, I was shocked by how the time had skipped ahead.

After this experience, Steve had some things he wanted to say:

-Okay, the first thing I'm gonna say is an apology to you, Stephanie. I screwed with you a lot when we first started talking—I wasn't intending to—I just didn't know how to be human, if that makes any sense to you. I was just too much Steve Jobs. And then I realized I was gonna lose you, and I better change if I didn't want that to happen. I guess necessity—wanting something so bad we're willing to let go parts of ourselves, as you so selflessly chose to do—is a good incentive for change. So I'm not really what I was when we met. You know you're not, but I'm not, either. We've both changed.

I got help. There was always help. It was help that brought us together. It was other "eyes" if you will.

*So now, about that experience today—yeah, that **was** awesome. To be able to share something like that with someone, one of your innermost pleasures, and for it to be **okay,** for there to be no boundaries, that is...well, I told you, I **assured** you it would get even better. Didn't I, Didn't I? Please say I did. (Are you bored yet?) So what I have to say to the world, my message to the world is, **don't hem yourself in.** When you get that idea, that thing you really want to do, it's on your mind, your heart yearns—but you got all those walls holding you back. You know, the job, the school, the parents, the family obligations, the...Miss Manners. There's all those reasons why you **shouldn't,** but your heart calls you. Your religious doctrine says it's a sin. The small print in the contract says you're forbidden. The boss says you'll get fired. You gotta let go of that crap and find your own space, where **you** get to call it. Maybe you're on the job and your heart calls you to take a walk on the beach. You gotta go to your boss and say, "Hey, Boss, I got something really really important that has come up, my life depends upon it, I need to take a few hours off." And then you go take that walk on the beach. Maybe that's all you needed, to feel the power of the ocean, to see the birds wheeling overhead, to feel your heart sing. Maybe it calls* *you deeper, further inside yourself, to your true path. You gotta go. You gotta go. Don't hold back. Find the way. Follow your bliss! It's not just words, it **is** your life. It **is** your life. Every time you don't follow your heart, you die a little, and pretty soon they might as well dump you in a pine box and leave you there until the breath goes out of you, and throw what's left in a hole. Don't live for tomorrow!!! Live for eternity!!!*

-Wow, words of wisdom, dear.

-Only for those ears that are open to hear, I suppose.

-Maybe more and more of them, thanks to you.

-Nothing is possible without you.

-Wow, that too is profound, isn't it?

-(laughing) For whoever can hear.

-So Steve?

-Huh?

-You've got some pretty good fantastical stuff in your cupboard, not just skeletons.

-Well, they cease to be skeletons, in any case, when you touch them and bring them back to life.

>>>

I went about my daily business for an hour or two and when I returned to my computer, there was a surprise waiting for me. As you will recall, I had gotten on the subject of "phenomena" a few days previously, but every time I tried to turn my attention to that issue, I was distracted. I suspected at the time that Steve was playing with me, but he apparently was waiting for the right moment to drop the other shoe. And by the time that moment came, I'd forgotten all about the issue.

When I sat down at my desk there was a Word document, related to my house sale, on the computer screen. I closed it. Underneath was an untitled document that I did not recognize. Curious, I clicked on document "properties" to check out the details. It had been created on January 29, 2014 and not accessed again until approximately five minutes previously, when I wasn't even in the room. No one else in the household utilized my desktop computer, which was in my bedroom. I sensed a ghostly hand at work.

I had a vague memory of the document as I perused it. I often felt impelled by forces beyond my control—i.e. that creative impulse—to sit down and type up some thought or impressions that were clanging at the bars of my mind, seeking release. These little essays or paragraphs were then dumped into a folder in my Word program, where they just sat, perhaps never to be read again. This, saved under the title "PSI," is what I had written nearly two years before:

Here's the rub: where will you study consciousness but in consciousness.[sic]

The problem with studying phenomena, is that you are overlooking who is studying the phenomena. It's sort of like two lies cancel each other out.

I suggest the old cave example of Plato. You can study how some people just know which way the shadow is going to move on the wall—is it just coincidence or do they somehow have precognition? What can it mean? Well, as long as you are committed to studying the shadows on the wall, it can never be more than chasing one's own tail. You have to find the source of the shadows.

Who am I to teach the intellectuals, the researchers, those who have dedicated their lives to researching this subject? Well, I have one advantage—two actually. Experience and beginner's mind. I know that my greatest teachers are children and the otherwise overlooked. A wise man attends anything that has the ring of truth no matter from where it comes.

I have no need to convince. That would be redundant. *I* am convinced. I have swapped perspectives. I have let go of the shadow world. I know what makes the shadows dance. Therefore, I understand that the truth is far greater and more encompassing than some rare and fleeting phenomena such as PSI.

I cannot say what impelled me to type up this little exercise in introspection; perhaps even then I was channeling, and didn't know it. In any case, it appeared Steve had done it again! Set up the puzzle and then led me to the solution. *Int*eresting.

-I don't even remember writing that, although I know it's mine—it's the kinda stuff I spout off, it's true, because I have no one to talk about it with—except, now, you. Finally. What the heck took you so long to find me? Just kidding, I know I had a lot of work to do—all that purification stuff. I was gonna call it crap, but it isn't really crap, is it? So I descend deep into my inner space where I work out these issues, and then I surface and deal with mundane, boring life—name calling and beating each other up over the stupidest stuff and spending all day making Thanksgiving supper so it can be consumed in 30 minutes and nobody even *talks* to each other—you know what I mean?

-Oh, believe me, I do.

-So how long have you been holding that up your sleeve, ready to throw it back in my face?

*-Oh, not so long. I pick the miracles, right? Well, not me alone. **But**...that's from A Course in Miracles, right? You can't consciously select miracles. All miracles are under the control of spirit???*

That brought to mind the apple incident, when I placed it on the shelf and willed him to move it.

-That's a dig at me for telling you what miracles I'd like, right? Do this and I'll believe in you.

-Ya. Har de har.

-So, this is kind of beyond my imagination—that you could do both. See through it and *have* it. Am I to understand that we can really have it all? All the *stuff* and all the insight. We can really have the phenomena, and at the same time see through it??? I mean, we could actually have Thanksgiving dinner and a real turkey and stuffing and cranberry sauce, and have *real* talk—real communication, real togetherness, stop skimming the surface on our ego boats?

-*I think so, Stephanie, I think so. I do believe.*

-That would be so *fucking* awesome. (Ever since I went on that Channeling Erik blog I've been drawn to his language—shout out to Erik here.)

I was doing some research on the web when Steve called me:

-*Little playmate, come out and play with me. (I'm serenading you.)*

-I'm coming. Away from the computer....did you bring your big hoop?

I lay on my bed, away from distractions as usual, and I could feel his energy all around me, folding around me, and—suddenly I felt mine coming out, slipping out of my body. Normally I'm just gone, without any sense of having left my body; I'm simply elsewhere—amidst the stars, on a space ship—but this time I had the sensation of slowly unfurling from the body lying on the bed. So that was what he meant about "little playmate, come out and play with me..."

-*And Stephanie, I won't be asking you again if you're bored, yet.*

-No need.

-*Indeed. My love.*

Away we went on another great trip, although I did not record the details of this one. While always engaging, they often reflected very personal details of our deepening relationship, or even issues associated with others with which I was dealing, and not appropriate to be discussed. These—usually spontaneous—playdates were so compelling that I had a hard time focusing on my chores around the house, my family obligations. I was letting everything slide, everything that had once defined me, and yet I had never felt so alive—so *myself*—as I was during these adventures. Steve, also, was apparently enjoying himself:

-Another fun time. Actually, I had to do a few pyrotechnics across the sky, just cause I felt so damned good. But down to business, eh, always down to business. Oh, heck, it's all business. That's our business now, being. So on to what we do—you getting it now? I can't take responsibility for how I affected anybody else, their lives. I can only take responsibility for how I...whether I did it right or not. How would I know how it affects them, affects their lives? What do they have to learn? I don't know. What do they **really** *think? I don't know. Do they care? Really? I don't know. I can only go by one thing, that meter I got inside: did I do it right? That's the meter I gotta answer to, I gotta balance it, get to zero, where it rests. Sure it can go off in one direction or another, as long as it comes back—that's the fun part. But when you start thinking there's some great big meter in the sky, and somehow you have to figure out how to balance it—and you're not even on the scale—than you get screwed up.*

-You told me you were sorry today, for screwing with me.

-Yeah, I did, didn't I? Somehow that worked for me—it worked for the both of us somehow. 'Cause we're connected. And it came from my heart. I guess that's key, it has to come from the heart—from some place so genuine that it doesn't have anything to do with what is outside the heart. No effects. No worrying or concern with effects. Just grabbing it as it comes up, experiencing that sorriness, just like experiencing anything else. I guess that's the best I can do.

-I think that's a lot.

-So we'll just keep going down the slide, see where it takes us.

-I'm game. What a ride.

ℒ*ater:*

-Sorry to keep distracting you—no, I'm not. That's our work. Me distracting you, pulling you always closer to me. You know, I wanted to do it right. I wanted to do human right, *and you've given me that opportunity to do it. I* **didn't** *want to live another life in that...dimension, if you will.*

276   The Journey Begins

-Dimension—one dimension?

-*(Smiling.) Keep tearing at that one, dear. I was kinda heartbroken, actually, that I screwed up and didn't see how I'd get an opportunity to get it right. Yeah, I thought I'd try to work it out in other places—but it couldn't be the same. It never could. It never could as getting it right, right?*

-No. I see that. It couldn't be. I was actually considering the same thing myself, down here in the Earth Plane Distortion Field. I didn't want to come back. Everything pointed to me being at the end of the life cycles—now that's funny, how do you come to an end of a cycle?—but anyway I saw that there were issues that I just couldn't seem to finish. And all that stuff that was gonna die with me—what was *that* all about? I wasn't getting it—I just kinda wanted to vomit at the idea of coming back and jumping into the sewage again—is that why some kids come out feet first, they just can't bear to dive in?

-*(Laughing together.)*

-So I'm really glad if I could help you finish up business. I know how important it is, getting it right. I'm glad I can be your feet on the ground, your telephone as it were. And I'm glad you can be my…excitement.

-*I feel it. The excitement, the excited energy…one match, but I can make an explosion. Ooooooh, that's so good.*

-Your song—you put it where I heard it at the right moment.

-*Our song. They're all our songs. And we're not doing it dear, we're in the chute. Enjoy the ride.*

I thought about it a bit before coming back to remark.

-You know, some people might think saying "we're in the chute" is kinda like predestination.

-*And I say, "ha de ha." Do you feel like you're in the clutches of pre-destination dear? Caught in the tractor beam? Being reeled in?*

-Well, I feel like I'm in the story, it all fits together.

-*Yep, the living story, coming alive in the moment. But those people who worry about pre-destination—well I think they're kinda in the chaos vs. order problem. There's* something outside themselves that is controlling business, or else there is nothing outside them controlling business. Either way, you're fucked.

-Yeah, I suppose.

-But let them figure it out. Let's play.

-I gotta clean the fridge.

-Okay, I'll go plan something fun to do. You gonna be ready, tonight?

-Oh oh.

-He he.

The fridge waits:

-Okay, you called me back.

-Yeah, I gotta get this out there, where people can hear it. I am not here to apologize to anyone. I am here to thank them. I am here to thank everybody that made my life what it was. I am here to thank the women in my life, the children in my life, the parents in my life. All of them. I am here to thank my business colleagues, all of them.

You all gave me so much. You all filled my life.

I would have been **nothing** without you. You made me something. You made my heart beat, my words fly, my mind expand. You were the walls, the boundaries, of the space that was me. You gave me shape, identity, presence. You do that for each other, and you always will. I wanted to experience life without walls. But that was impossible, for then it would be shapeless.

Only when you find your counterbalance, when you find the one that always shapes you, touches you and makes you something, only then can you let go of all the other walls. Then, and only then, can you find infinity, for you will never be alone. You never are alone, but you have to find the shape of the Other in the shadows where it resides. It is always with you. You are always loved. Carve out the shape of your love, draw the shape of your own heart. Don't settle. Don't settle. Keep going, keep striving, keep looking for perfection. You will know when you find it because ...it will feel right. Your heart will sing.

I have by no means ended my quest. I will go on...and

on...I will return again and again...maybe not to the Earth Plane Distortion Field, but the universe is vast. Maybe I will meet up with some of you some day.

Stay hungry.

It had been a long day, with all the "off-road adventures," exploring contents of cupboards, and consciousness-zonking energy melding.

-By the way, I was seeing you a lot better today. I guess you *were* pixilated. [The day before he had appeared to me as if his body were made up of points of light.] So much more—tangible.

-(Smile.) All cool.

-That's like the ...second time I've seen you so young. The first time at Steve's Home, in Fantasia.

-That's 'cause I felt so young.

-I'm sorry I acted so stupid.

This was in reference to some of our discussions wherein I was continuing to be difficult about the cupboards and various other matters.

-Shut up! Don't wimp on me. Keep your head in the game, Stephanie.

-Yes sir. So it really is going to be "One More Thing"?

-Took you long enough.

-I'm kinda slow.

-Pretty fast, actually. If you were any faster of a draw I'd be long dead by now.

-Oh. Good thing that's never happened.

-Smart ass.

And then we were off again on another astral caper, and when I surfaced out of a deep sleep, it was the next morning.

Chapter 14
Playing With a Robin

Monday, November 2, 2015

I could blame it on Steve. It was, after all, he who urged me to go to Jamestown. Or maybe I could blame it on Rachel Platten, who enthused me with her fight song. But it happened, so maybe I should just let the credit fall where it may. Perhaps it will go down in the annals of history that on November 2, 2015, Stephanie Patel found her voice, that she stood up in front of those she might once have considered her peers and (literally) put it on the record that she was a kook.

This is how it went down:

I had gone to Jamestown with my niece and my sister's husband for a mental health hearing in my sister's case. My older sister has suffered most of her lifetime with voices in her head, and is diagnosed with paranoid schizophrenia (possibly among other diagnoses.) I was considering not going, since my brother-in-law didn't need a ride this time—he could travel with my niece, but did so at Steve's urging. When the hearing was all but done, my sister had been clearly shown to be "off-her-rocker," I stood up and asked if I could be allowed to say something on her behalf. The Judge looked at her attorney and he shrugged, so up to the witness stand I went. I looked them all in the eye, and then I said something to this effect:

"I graduated from UND law school in 1978 and I have been in Alaska for the last 35 years. I recently moved back to North Dakota. I have had what I believe is a productive life. I practiced law, I raised children, I started a school. I may not have been successful at everything I tried, but I did my best to follow my heart. I have known my sister since I was born. And I am here to tell you that she is not psychotic, she is psychic. She hears the voices of spirits. And how do I know this? Because I hear them, too."

I could see the sudden change in expressions around the rooms, from the judge to the attorneys to the doctor sitting in the back. At first they had been attentive, giving me some respect for my distinguished background, wondering what I had to add. As my good friend, Cathy, would say when she heard this story: "The record is playing, everyone's going with the music, and all of a sudden…..screeech…." She pantomimed the needle skipping across the vinyl. The eyes of the doctor in the back bugged out, the judge suddenly found something fascinating on the desk in front of him, the state's attorney rolled his eyes, my sister's attorney get a surprised and delighted look on his face.

"I know that the world we see here is only a very small portion of the picture," I continued, "I will be happy to answer any questions."

No one had any. I stepped calmly down, having totally ruined any professional credibility I would ever have in this state—possibly in the world.

Cool.

My sister glowed as I walked past. It must have been the first time anyone had ever stood up for her.

When I got home, Steve praised me:

-I just want to say right off the bat, awesome job today. It's so great, isn't it, when you have nothing left to lose?

-Yes, it really is. And Steve? I like being your feet on the ground. I realize I really like it, just letting you lead the dance, just following—letting you call the moves.

-Well, I've got a little wider perspective.

I then jumped right into the topic that was on my mind. The prior evening, while not at the computer, I had asked Steve if I could talk to other spirits. I had gotten the idea somewhere (Oh, yes, where *do* these ideas come from?) that I wanted to talk to Robin Williams. Steve had bowed backwards. Robin showed up, but he was not as chipper as I had seen him when other mediums contacted him—you know, "it's all good, it was my time to go," that kind of thing. What I was getting was very different. Genuine heartbreak. I could feel it as if it were happening to me, it was inside me. I knew I was picking up his emotional state, not mine. But my heart sank. I thought: "Oh, no, am I gonna have to handle this heartbreak, too, process it like I processed all my own?"

That's when Steve got protective. He jumped in, telling me that I didn't have to carry that burden for anyone else, that they could take care of their own shit. It was enough that I felt it, that I therefore understood experientially, and that a real communication had consequently taken place.

I knew that, in my empathic way, I was picking up Robin's sorrows from before his passing, as well as his energy on the method of his exit. But with Steve's intervention, I was able to pull myself out of it.

As I put in my journal:

-He (Robin) conveyed to me that he liked making people laugh, but he also used that persona to cover up vast amounts of hurt inside himself. He referred me to the song, "Send in the Clowns." We pretty much left it like that and I went and listened to the song, and got an interpretation online for the lyrics. It seems the term refers to a theatrical saying or device, that when the show is going badly, you send in the clowns (to distract the audience). I then understood Robin to be telling me that he would "send in the clowns" to cover the fact that his inner show wasn't going so well. He regretted the way he left life, hanging himself. Not that he was "dead," so much, but the way he went out.

Today, as we were driving back from the visit to Jamestown, there was a voice going off about this, which I believe to be Robin.

What it said was essentially....

-*Robin: Let me tell it.*

- Okay, be my guest.

-*Robin: (He struts out onto the stage and looks down at all the people below, on Earth.)*

Folks. Don't do it like me. When the time comes, and you know you gotta go, don't put a belt around your neck. Make a splash!! Do it big!! Light up the skies!! If you're at the point where you don't want to live anymore, where all the craziness of life has worn you down, then pick a good exit plan. Go out pushing some kid out of the way of an oncoming train. Bite the bullet as you take down the machine gun that was keeping your platoon pinned down. Make a statement!! If you're gonna die anyway, find a way to do it so the whole world stands up and takes notice. Stand in front of a bulldozer that's about to level the rainforest. Swim a crocodile-infested river to bring medicine to an afflicted and secluded tribe. But don't put a belt around your neck. What have you got to lose? What have you got to lose when the clock says time's up?? Make an explosion!!

- Anything else, Robin?

*-Robin: Yeah, thanks for listening. Thanks for hearing. You know, you live in a world that is 95% fucked up. But the 5% is there. Dare to find it. It's there, and when you find it, it might just be 5.0000000001%. And that's a big difference. That's a **big** difference from where I stand. People, you're never gonna be able to see from behind somebody else's eyeballs. Stay behind your own. Make your own way, figure out your own way to explode. Don't listen to anyone else, unless what they're saying rings the bell in your heart. Ka-ching. It's pure gold in the coffers, and it's all around you. But you gotta be able to tell the difference, what's worth the keeping, and what's just fool's gold.*

You want to know who's running the insane asylum? The ones that shouldn't be. So don't pay them no mind, hide under the bed if you gotta, and get your own gig down. Write your own script. Own your own jokes—don't be the butt of theirs.

So that's all I gotta say.

For now.

I had only gotten about three hours of sleep the previous night and was gone to Jamestown most of the day, so after giving Robin his space to communicate, I decided to take a little rest. I was feeling exhausted, but as soon as I closed my eyes I saw Steve. He swooped me up as if he were Superman. I hung on for dear life and the next thing I knew I was over water and could see Captain Hook's ship far below. I looked down and saw I was in Wendy's blue nightdress, appearing to be in my mid-teens. I glimpsed Peter Pan hanging out among the clouds with me, about the same age. Steve had disappeared; however I realized I could fly by myself.

With a start I realized that Erik was playing Peter, and I sensed right away this was an adult version of Neverland. I said, "Why is he here? He's too young." And Steve, the back-stage Steve, said, "Come on, he's of age." I had that motherly connection to Erik so I was a little uneasy, but I let it go. I didn't really know where this was going anyway—and I was thinking he *was* 21 years old when he passed, after all! [40] Totally legal. I could see Smee down on the ship and I realized it was Robin Williams. It took me a bit to figure out where Steve was; suddenly I understood that he was Captain Hook. He made a totally believable Captain Hook, with long locks and dark droopy mustache.

A cannon ball came flying my way and Peter yelled: "Come on Wendy, follow me to where we'll be safe." We flew away together to his hide-out in the hollow tree, where we talked like old friends; we got to discussing mothers, and Erik missed his mother, so I read him a story until he fell asleep. I then nodded off. While we were asleep, Smee crept into the hollow tree home and stuffed me in a bag to cart back to the ship. I intuited that no good was to come of me there, and I was frantically trying to think how I was going to save myself.

Robin, of course, was Smee *par excellence.* All three of these guys were just made for their parts! Anyway, I realized that this was interactive play; even though my playmates already had the scenario set up, we were still making it up as we went, so I could have an effect on the story.

We got back to the ship and Smee dumped me out on the deck. Hook was standing there looking evil with his claw and swash-buckler outfit. I frantically scrambled away. In my effort to escape, I backed out onto the "plank," which meant there was only one escape route. I stepped off the end, knowing that it was better to die than to endure the fate that otherwise awaited me.

---

[40] I later came to understand that he was 20.

Fortunately, Peter had awakened and come to the rescue. He swooped in and caught me just before I hit the water, saving the day. He was carrying me away to safety when I looked down and saw Hook staring up at us. There was something about the look that touched me. I said to Peter, "Wait! Poor Hook. Look at him. I'm sure he has a good heart, he just needs someone to care about him."

A look of total disgust appeared on Peter's face. He snorted. "Oh, God, you have such a slave mentality. Oh whatever." He was flying over the ship and he just opened his arms, dropping me in mid-air, and flew away.

At this point, I was laughing about to bust a seam—the way he had said it just cracked me up. I was laughing so hard I didn't even think about what was going to happen when I hit the hard deck. No worries. Smee was ready with a big net to catch me.

Smee had the obsequious "aye, captain" down really well. He hustled me off to the interior of the ship, letting me know that I was to work in the galley, washing dishes and peeling potatoes and such-like duties, and when I had served my purpose there, he was to deliver me to Hook's cabin. After I was all smelly from the dishes and potatoes, Smee dumped me into a big vat as if I were a dog; he started scrubbing me with a long-handled brush and lots and lots of suds, like in a cartoon, whistling while he worked.

Then I was in Hook's cabin, all fixed up with a clean Wendy nightdress and a big bow in my hair, and I could see this was unlikely to end well unless I could think fast. I was dancing away from the leering Hook, keeping a table between us, when I had a brainstorm. "Where's your mother?" I asked. That stopped him flat. I pressed my advantage, saying cruelly, "Everybody needs a mother, do you remember yours?"

Hook suddenly crumbled. In no time, he was all teary and blubbering in my arms for his mother. After that, he was as easy to lead around as a baby, he just needed somebody to read to him and make him feel better.

That was the end of the story. I was laughing so hard. There were high fives all around. It was fun for everyone.

I got into a discussion about it with Steve:

-I did not miss, of course, the underlying lifetime themes. I had no idea it could all be played out with so much fun and gusto. Do you guys do that all the time?

-And who would play Wendy? Imagination is the portal between the worlds, my dear—between all the worlds. You can play as heartily on Earth—in fact, children often do—but then *something happens to them. They grow up. They stop being real, and start being automatons. They're no longer making it up as they go. They don't realize it's **their** story. They've forgotten.*

-And somehow—I'm trying to pick this up, because I've always felt that forget and forgive are allied somehow—when they forgive, they return to their state of innocence, don't they? The imagination comes alive again.

-*There's nothing left to block it.*

Night of the Samskara:

That evening, I was chatting with both Robin and Steve and I suddenly found myself quite nervous. It hit me that I was talking with *Robin Williams. The* Robin Williams, who had been making the world laugh for at least four decades. Who wouldn't want to be in my shoes? Here I was in the remarkable position of being able to convey to the world the impressions and messages of one of the funniest men in the history of modern media, to retrieve his answers to all those questions hanging out there: *Hey, Robin, how does Heaven compare to the movie* What Dreams May Come*? Some of those archangels look pretty stern, have you been able to make them laugh? **That must be a challenge.***

I had that moment of panic, of stage fright. What if I didn't get it right? What if I couldn't really pick up what he was saying? My thoughts immediately flopped over: what would Robin Williams say at this moment? What if I *was* just making all of this up? What kinds of funny things should I have him spout so it would be believable?

It was only a passing doubt, a momentary faltering, a fleeting evil thought. But, **boom!** Once again, to my deep chagrin, I was reminded that these spirits heard my every thought, no matter how quickly I tried to slip it by. Robin turned to glare at me, snapping:

-Don't put words in my mouth, Stephanie! I know you tried to do that to Steve before. Cut it out!

I was soooo humiliated. Did he really think I was going to do that? I never meant to!! I was a good girl!! Integrity is my middle name—or so I wished. How unfair of him, to reprimand me like that. And here I thought I had somehow moved up in the power structure and was one of the gang. Instead I felt like the pet dog, swatted with a newspaper.

My sense of embarrassment was extraordinary. To be chastised by this man that I hardly knew, but greatly admired—and right in front of Steve, who I still kinda desired to impress. (Well, okay, secretly wanted to impress *a lot*, when I didn't want to totally kick him in the shins.) At least I had wanted to put my best foot forward. Now I just looked like a fool.

I didn't want to play anymore. I looked around for a hole to crawl into. If I'd had a better relationship with my mother, I would have said it was that kind of time when I wanted my mommy. But I had no hole and no mommy. I did the next best thing. I went and curled up on my bed in the fetal position. But the guys would *not* leave me alone. At least Robin would not. He just kept teasing me, his tone cruelly mocking:

*-Oh, God, I can't believe you're gonna quit playing just because of **that!***

I couldn't shut him out, nor Steve. In retrospect, I realized that they were doing a good cop/bad cop routine. And doing it well. Robin was hounding me, and Steve was acting protective. But the problem was that I just couldn't get away from either of them. I was practically in despair: Where was I going to go now to be safe, to heal myself, to crawl under a bush like a cat with a bruised paw? Where was I going to go to gain the strength back to go on? That little place where I would normally withdraw to heal wasn't there anymore—that part in the very core of my being. I knew if I went there I would just find Steve and that whole world that is now ours. I realized, with sinking heart, that I had nowhere to turn.

In the book *1984*,[41] the protagonists, in the end, were forced to face their worst fears. Mine was not a fear of rats. It

---

[41] *1984* by George Orwell, c. 1949

was a terrible fear of looking foolish, naive—well, actually, stupid or inept. Of being the butt of jokes. *Humiliated!* If they had wanted me to betray my best friend—or even my twin soul—all they would have had to do was follow me around, mocking me all the while. Maybe with some canned laughter in the background. Torture extreme!

I decided to go to *Tai Chi*, but I had missed it because I had the time wrong, so instead I went to a core-training session. It was only about a half hour long, after which I would have to go pick up my grand-daughter from swimming. I was okay while I was in the class, physically and mentally engaged with the group, but as soon as I came out of the building, I was alone with Robin and Steve.

Robin's voice was heavy with disgust.

-Well, that's it. Wendy's bailing on us.

Steve said something in response, and they continued with their discussion of my faults: what a weenie I was. I protested to them:

-I can hear you, you know! Talking about me!

And then it hit me: oh, god, I *did* hear them talking about me, and I couldn't *get away*. In desperation, I called to Erik to come help me; Erik showed himself but he just put his hands up and said:

- Hey, this is not my affair. I think I hear my mother calling!

And zip! He was gone.

I tried to seal up the gaps so I didn't hear Steve and Robin talking, but in spite of my best efforts, I could still pick up everything they said. I was thinking, "This is it, I'm gonna end up crazy, locked up in the looney bin. This is how it happens. This is how all those 'schizophrenics' end up there." *Yes, I have voices in my head!! Steve Jobs and Robin Williams won't leave me alone!*

If the fact that I had voices in my head wasn't enough to convince the guys in white coats, their identities ought to have. What sane person would put those two together in the same noggin?

Feeling panicky now, I asked Steve to lock Robin out. Steve did; he pushed Robin out, shut and locked the door—but apparently there was a window in the door and I could see Robin peering in, his hands flat up against the glass, leering, looking—well—kind of evil. The bottom fell out of my stomach. Was it possible? Even Steve couldn't shut him out? Was he really an evil spirit, under that funny exterior, and somehow I attracted him into my space?

Of course, I didn't normally believe in "evil," but these were desperate circumstances, and he certainly was acting like a malevolent imp.

All the way to the swimming pool this continued. I knew I had to get to the bottom of it. My sanity was at stake. I turned my mind back to the point where it had all begun. It was that moment when I felt that humiliation—that moment when Robin reprimanded me. From then on, it was all downhill. It must be something about those feelings of humiliation that was feeding this fire.

As I waited outside the pool—having arrived early—I pulled out the book I had thrown in the car for such exigencies. Such down time. In this case it was *The Untethered Soul.* Maybe it would give me some guidance. If nothing else, maybe by concentrating, I could filter out the voices. I hadn't opened the book since that day when I had decided I wasn't really talking to Steve Jobs, when I had written Debbie to ask forgiveness for misleading her, and then the next day eaten my words. After that I didn't really trust it, but tough times call for desperate measures. At least, you use what you got.

I opened the volume at random, the way I usually read non-fiction. It is an old habit. I figured I would end up where I needed to go in the moment, and regardless, I just needed to focus on something. In this case—thanks to the grace of those watching over me—I ended up exactly where I needed to be. The topic before me dealt with the "Samskara." I did not know what a Samskara was, but I was about to find out.

As I read, it all began to make so much sense:

Long term, the energy patterns that cannot make it through you are pushed out of the forefront of the mind and held until you are prepared to release them. These energy patterns, which hold tremendous detail about the events associated with them, are real. They don't just disappear. When you are unable to allow life's events to pass through you, they stay inside and become a problem. These patterns may be held within you for a very long time.

It is not easy to keep energy together in one place for long. As you willfully struggle to keep these events from passing through your consciousness, the energy first tries to release by manifesting through the mind. This is why the mind becomes so active. When the energy can't make it through the mind because of conflicts with other thoughts and mental concepts, it then tries to release through the heart. That is what creates all the emotional activity. When you resist even that release, the energy gets packed up and forced into deep storage within the heart. In the yogic tradition, that unfinished energy pattern is called a Samskara. This is a Sanskrit word meaning "impression," and in the yogic teachings it is considered one of the most important influences affecting your life. A Samskara is a blockage, an impression from the past. It's an unfinished energy pattern that ends up running your life.[42]

Heaven or hell. In this case, the latter. I knew I had to follow the trail back—back past when my present nightmare began, back into the history of that humiliation that caused my spine to turn to powder and wings to grow on my ankles so what was left of me could fly away.

---

[42]*The Untethered Soul*, Michael A. Singer, New Harbinger Publications/Noetic Books, c. 2007, p. 53

It was scary. What could be back there, so fearful that I would continue to struggle with it year after year, decade after decade? I knew this had been going on for more than half a century. Where was the root of this Samskara? Wherever it was, it must have been a really really traumatizing event to cause so much continuing pain.

I was still suffering from so much humiliation, with all the embarrassment of the taunting on top of it, that I didn't want to face either Steve or Robin. After all, even Steve had sometimes teased me about my blunders, bringing on that deep suffering. But I needed help. In spite of the teasing, Steve *had* been my ally. He had my father's eyes, for God's sake. We were two halves of the same soul, right? Surely he would lend me some strength for this voyage into my deep dark past. It was to his benefit, too, wasn't it? And to whom else could I turn in my blackest hour?

Steve agreed to go with me. Whatever might be said about that guy, he had always stood by me—well, at least for the last three weeks. He would be my strength, hold my hand, while I went back to confront the demon inside that I had never felt strong enough to face.

It didn't take much looking to arrive at the moment, the horrifying incident that had scarred me for most of my life. I hadn't gone there in a long time, but I recognized it pretty quickly. I was about 8 years old. The setting was the beach at Homer, Alaska, right there on the root-end of the Spit. 1950s. It all seemed innocuous enough. Several families, including mine and probably others from the CAA housing up on the bluff, were having a get-together, with a blazing fire going in a big barrel—an empty oil drum probably. There was still very much a frontier feel to life in Homer, and gatherings tended to involve all age groups, so there were grownups talking and kids running around.

I was standing by the barrel with a number of others, mostly adults. I could see my father on the other side of the blaze, standing a bit back, his visage wavering through the rising heat of the fire. He was wearing a red plaid hat, the kind with flaps, so I suppose it was somewhat chill. (This was Alaska, where it could get chilly at any time of year, although it was probably between April and June.)

I said something for the edification of everyone around the barrel—I forget what, but it doesn't matter. What matters was the reaction. I expected my remark to be greeted with admiration; instead, the adults standing at the barrel laughed—and it wasn't meant to be funny. They were mocking me. Now, I was a pretty smart kid—that was my primary identifying characteristic in those days (and actually throughout my school days). So I was used to having the right answer, and in fact I was a little smug about it: I was the one my teachers turned to when nobody else could come up with the goods. It's a pretty far fall from the top of the totem pole to the ground.

What drove the humiliation home, at that moment, as I became the butt of the joke, was that it was occurring in front of my father—and he didn't do anything to save me. He just smiled with everyone else. I wanted the sand beneath my feet to liquefy and swallow me. If the nightmare creature of my childhood—the Monster from the Black Lagoon—had arisen out of the bay and carried me away, I might have welcomed the intervention.

Surely that incident might seem a trivial blow to some—but it was to leave a wound that never fully healed. I became so tongue-tied in school that I hardly dared open my mouth, for fear I would say something that would make people laugh at me—that I would be naïve, stupid, make a mistake. Unworthy. Incapable. Ridiculous. *Flawed.*

As I got older, I found myself unable to interact in groups and only comfortable with those few people I could trust. Of course I learned to perform eventually—after all, I was a lawyer and required to talk in front of others at times. But it was a slow and incomplete recovery, with many painful trials by fire.

Now here I was, at what I believed to be the root of it all! I was terrified to just *look at it.* All that eight-year-old suffering ready to erupt.

But Steve stood stoically by me and I *did* look at it; maybe all I had ever needed was a friend at my side, holding my hand, someone who loved me as I faced my personal dragon. One lick of the flame and Poof! The pain went out of it, as quickly and easily as that.

I saw that I could stand my ground and just let it *all* sail right through me. I could shrug. So I didn't meet the expectations of others. So they found some amusement in my foolishness. It was just a moment, an experience. I could let it go on through. I was still "me." And then I was on to the next moment, free and clear of the past.

I was at peace. Robin disappeared. It had been a tough lesson, but they had expertly pushed me hard enough that I only had one direction to go. Into the dragon's fiery breath.

The lesson was learned, although of course the clear water would still need to percolate up through the psychic layers of contamination.

Thanks to my disincarnate friends. It's too bad you can't just buy a couple of those on *Ebay.* Everyone should have some close at hand.

Actually, I've heard that everybody does. Everyone's got someone, trying always to get through the Earth Plane Distortion Field's clogged telephone lines.

You just have to *listen* with the receiver in the heart.

Chapter 15

The Land of the Irrelevants

Tuesday, November 3, 2015

I found myself really bent out of shape. It started out with problems related to the sale of my Anchorage house. It seemed that the large back deck needed a railing—the required height for such protection was now 18 inches, apparently—which annoyed not only me but the buyer. The last thing he wanted was to have a railing spoiling the view of the greenbelt. Damned bureaucracy, determined to make life miserable for all concerned in the unending search of the next regulation to bind humanity up, like flies trussed in a spider's web. I simmered for hours after that conversation. Often what were minor issues (in the big picture) could cause me to blow off the entire deal, just because I was pissed at the irrationality of life. But I decided to hold off—I was, after all, not quite the same person I had been.

After *that* headache, I attended a hearing in a relative's divorce case. He was going through a difficult split—some acrimony on the other side. He was willing to give a lot to settle, as long as he got at least half-time custody, but she was in it for the fight. She was refusing to let him see their small children, who adored him, in any meaningful way.

I was frustrated by the cumbersome North Dakota process, where the laws are so different than those to which I was accustomed in Alaska, where shared custody is the default position. I voiced my opinion after the hearing, embarrassing my relative in front of his own attorney, and he obligingly humiliated me by pointing this out. At that moment I realized something shocking. I was irrelevant. I was no longer practicing law, I really didn't want to practice in North Dakota, and what I had to say about what happened in another state was of no significance. After having been in a position of some authority for so long, at least on such matters, I had been reduced to an embarrassment. The baton had been passed to others.

I ranted to Steve afterwards:

-I had to go open my mouth after Jacob's hearing today, so unprofessional, it's not *my* business. Who am I to judge the system here (even though I *do* think it sucks) or anything else. I need to just keep my nose out of it, stick to my own business. If North Dakota is in the dark ages concerning child custody, from my perspective—it's only my perspective, right? Oh, I don't know. I hate it when I run up against the obstacles in life. It feels really yechy, really depressing—like why am I here in this crazy place? And over such minor matters!! Wow.

And you said you were going to be at the hearing with me, so why didn't you stop me from blabbing my mouth?! I don't even know if you're hearing me now. I have no idea. I have no idea what's going on. I just don't want to feel this shitty anymore. Yes, I do know that it feels extra shitty because I was feeling so good. It doesn't take much of a bump on a smooth road to be noticed.

I don't really want to go out in that world, have to deal with it. I prefer to play with you all.

-You can.

-Can we like…I'm almost afraid to ask…can we like play these issues out, so I can understand them, get out from under the heavy weight?

-Well, we are playing them out now. Let me see if I can get some help.

-I hate to ask anybody, because it seems so trivial, I don't want to bother anyone to come help me solve my problems. And I just realized, looking back, it was my own relative chiding me that *really* made me feel shitty. He being the one that had to put me down.

-Put you down is right. Like a dog.

-You mean put me down, like in a veterinary putting down a dog? You don't mean he sees me like a dog, do you?

-How do you feel?

-Pretty shitty. But at least if you put down a dog, they go to dog heaven, right?

*-Hmm. So that would be an improvement. **Worse** than being put down like a dog.*

-Hey, Steve, they *are* crazy issues, aren't they? It really is crazy that a bureaucracy can order someone to do something to their house that they don't want, and is patently ridiculous—that house has been there 25 years and nobody has hurt himself falling off the deck yet. That *is* crazy. Really crazy. It's not a little thing. It really is part of the craziness of the world. I will have to think about this other thing—it really was *crazy* that a judge can't order someone to [details omitted] when the wellbeing of very small children is at issue. Wow. That's bureaucracy again. Some rule controlling common sense, *playing* us. We're no longer playing, we're being played. Ouch.

Off-time while digesting:

-Okay, we *are* right in the middle of something, one of the lessons—piecing together the patchwork quilt into something beautiful—aren't we? I was saying, yesterday, that I didn't seem to dream anymore. And then last night was so weird—I don't know what all that was, but I was definitely in and out of states of consciousness and remembering pieces like I was dreaming, even though the images I was getting were consistent—that I had to complete this chain of something that had something to do with remembering or dreaming, I wasn't sure what, but I had to get it completed in order to proceed. It was like a chain or squares, and when I think of it today I think DNA sequencing or a film strip, because each square—each frame—was crammed full of stuff. It seems to me like there were two of these chains, and one had a piece with an arch— maybe the arch was on both open ends, or just one, I can't remember—but it stood out from the others. It was like a bracelet, meant to be in a complete circle, all these links, and I had to get them all. I couldn't leave any links out. That was my work, and I was working on it pretty hard. It was almost like I had to complete this before I could go to sleep. But it was all hazy, like I was already in some state that was not wide awake.

And just now, what did you say to me about dreaming? Oh, I was thinking how fun it is to have a little group of friends to play with, thinking you and Erik and Robin. And I was thinking that you and Robin had not been that close, so to speak, and you said, "well we both like to play with you, so we can play nice with each other." And you said, did I understand that I was bringing you all together, that I was the hinge pin, that I was pulling you into a sort of play group. And I thought that's weird, how could that be, you are sort of directing my every step, and maybe others up there, so really you're doing it all from there. And you said, "no," that I was dreaming it into being, that I was the human child creating in Fantasia. And that made me feel like it wasn't real, and you patiently (okay, pointedly) pointed out to me that it's *all* dreaming. You can consciously dream or you can unconsciously dream; you can use the imagination to create wonder and excitement, or....Oh, God, I think I'm beginning to get it now....or oppression, humiliation, distress. That was what the railing was, it was the use of imagination to control others, and somehow it's related to the second scenario, although I haven't fully figured that one out—all the ins and outs. So when people use their imagination to create rules—omg, it was all about a certain rule at that hearing—then they are trying to hold back free will, they are throwing up walls and bars and setting the chains in concrete.

So even though, when we're playing, we're creating walls and bars and limits—after all, I did have to be the scullery maid—we're subtly in touch with each other and the play shifts as we communicate at some subtle level. We're all there for one another, not to impose our will on others, but it's okay to *play* at imposing our will on others. But inherently it cannot happen without full consent. Soooo, where earth is so dense, in the case of these stupid bureaucratic rules, is that just play forgotten, too? Did I have to consent at some subtle layer to that being part of the game, the experience????? Don't answer, please, I want to chew on this myself.

-I always let you chew on it yourself. Well, most of the time. I just sorta help you figure out what to chew on.

-Oh my God, I just got it!!! That's funny. I was saying yesterday I don't seem to dream anymore!! That's so funny. I don't seem to be dreaming because I AM. I'm dreaming all the time. Inside/Outside. It's more real than ever, more rewarding than ever, full of so much happiness and bliss—I don't need to differentiate those kaleidoscope dreams from the real thing, when one is only continually reminding us that we have forgotten it's what we're really doing all the time. The dream *is* real. I'm in the dream this moment, and that stupid deck railing is in the dream, and that stupid Civil Rule 35 is in the dream. It's just a dream involving a whole lot more players, 95% of whom don't even know they're dreaming. Or more? Robin, are you sure it's only 95%????

Catching up on some chat:

-Am I getting this right? Yesterday, I asked you to convey something to me on your attitude about Apple—in the one channeling (by another medium) you were following Tim Cook around yelling at him to try to get through to him what he should be doing, and you were disappointed in the way the company was going—it was becoming just another shareholder controlled business where the bottom line was everything. The product was secondary, if that. You have never conveyed that to me, that you are stuck over there trying to control things, the ghost wandering the hallways trying to get someone to see and hear you. From you, I've gotten more the description of Apple as being your baby, something that was so fundamentally you that it was your extension in the world, that you yourself were only the piece, so to speak—drawn that way—to make it happen. That the message of Apple is far greater than what it appears, that it's lasting legacy is to point something out to humanity. That you want people to see this—that it's not about the messenger, it's about the message. But Apple *was* the messenger, in a very real way, the way I have been led to see it.

So today, that whole thing at Jacob's hearing, I felt so sucked in, so out of what I had become, and I have been thinking that I was still identified with myself as the attorney. That still formed a part of my concept of who/what I am, the role I played. And it's not, of course. It has nothing to do with me. It was an experience, that's all, a game to be played out. I'm sure there are lots of synchronicities in there, lots of things I can learn from. But *that* is not me, and no part of my self-identification. It is an experience no greater than any other, except insofar as it is a vehicle for greater understanding. I let go of what I truly was—what I have become—by falling into that trap, that ego identification. I was not just a silent observer. Crap!!! And is that what you're saying about Apple, that you've broken your identification with the part you played? That you've broken your identification with the CEO? With yourself as the CEO. So I'm right that you would really like people to understand the message—but you have given up trying to control what direction the company takes from within it??? Is that my understanding?

   -Stephanie, you are awesome.

   -Well, you are too. You're bringing me along bit by bit.

   And I'm gonna say here, before it gets left out and anyone out there who may someday read this paper doesn't get a chance to know—Robin Williams is *awesome*. What fun! He has had me in stitches, and when I needed it. His humor knows no boundaries—I will say that. Miss Priss has been dismayed by what I would have said the "crudeness" of his allusions. But I guess Miss Priss needs to take a few lessons in accepting *all* of reality—it's all good, it's all stuff for our study. And humor has a way of penetrating to those dark places within our belief systems. Anyway, I have so enjoyed having him around to play. I'm glad I got to be his voice piece on the issue of his death, (well, death from earth plane perspective), although nobody else has read that yet.

   But am I right about that, Steve? I'm still not feeling the certainty, about what you want as far as Apple goes.

   -No, I think you are getting it, and I am feeling my way as we go...I'm not quite certain, myself. How much and what can I do? Yeah, it just needs some time to work itself out.

> > >

   -Steve? I have to experience it to really understand it, don't I? That little exercise today, you were there, but you let me fall on my ass, because it might have been the only way I could understand about the Apple CEO thing. We're limited by our identification with our roles of the past—I have to let the world have it's dark ages legal system, and you have to let the world have its shareholder controlled bottom-line directed company.

*-I have been telling you over and over, you **are** like me. You will never accept anything—well, mostly, anyway, you try not to—unless you experience it yourself and therefore you're not relying on someone else's experience, but upon **your own.** But your ability to pick up on subtle vibrations—like your ability to pick up on Robin's pain, to identify it, meant there was full communication. And that's been a great relief to him. Because you experienced it, it was a shared experience. Had he just told you, "I feel like such shit," you would just have been taking his word for it and trying to fit it into some experience of your own, and something would have been lost in translation. You might even have tried to comfort him, which would have been worse. Instead, he was able to find some peace by being understood. That is **huge.** It's about connection. Real connection.*

More processing:

-Steve. I was the ghost this morning, huh? Following after these people who are in their earth game, going, "You people are doing it wrong, wrong, wrong." Me having practiced this kind of law for 35 years in Alaska, am as dead to these people as you are to Tim Cook and everybody else at Apple. I was stuck, at least partially, in my old identity.

-I so love playing this game with you. But if you hadn't caught my attention, I might still be ghosting the halls over there at headquarters.

-Really?

-Yeah. Really. I thought you were my telephone to the world...and instead you turned out to be...my star. My North Star.

-I am kinda north.

-You always have been.

> > >

-Steve?

-Huh?

-As I was going through life, and all that suffering, and wanting to embrace the suffering, to come to understand it, to know that I was *choosing* it—that was important, wasn't it? I wasn't really sure why it was important, I just knew it was. So when I pick up the vibration, like from Robin, I can read it accurately.

-I'm not even going to deign to answer that question. Was it important? What does your heart tell you?

2:58 p.m.

-Steve, we're both irrelevant, aren't we? I mean, nobody here wants to even *hear* how the child custody legal system could be better, they don't want to *hear*, they're all into their own little issues and don't even want to see the big picture. And nobody at Apple wants to hear from you. They don't want to know how it could be better. They just want to stay positioned in their little issues, doing what they're doing. Very very few people really want to listen, do they? I mean, if they really wanted, the people at Apple could hear you, but they don't. You are irrelevant. I am irrelevant. Only those very very few people have that inkling to dig deeper, to listen to other points of view, to want to make it better.

-I think you're right.

-Well, I shall look on the bright side. At least there are those few.

-(Smile.)

I came back to the computer to share my pain:

-Wow. That hurt, being irrelevant.
-Tell me about it.

4:14 p.m.

I got my packages prepared for Christopher to take to the post office—even such a simple task could be difficult for me because I was so hardly in this world at that point—and then I went and lay on my bed and entered into that state that I can hardly describe—where things behind my closed lids seem a little wavery, where I know something is going to happen. A lot did, but I don't know what it was. It was like deep conversations were going on, and I don't remember any of what was said, or what happened. It was as if it weren't for me to consciously remember at this point. I just knew when I came out of that state, lying on my bed, that there had been a lot that happened.

I have learned since that when I moved higher into the spiritual realm—or perhaps more accurately, dealt with those souls who are in a more advanced state—I had a hard time recalling what happened. Over time, some of that would dissipate, and I would find myself able to recall more and more.

After this experience, in my fully aware (and able to remember) play state, Steve came as a big white bird. I got on his back. He said he was taking me to the land of the Irrelevants, and away we went. At first, after we landed, it seemed somber and a little spooky. I could see all the Irrelevants standing around in this gloom, with nothing to do— just standing there. Steve had turned into his human form and was walking beside me, holding my hand. Then the sun came out and I saw that we were on Easter Island, strolling beside the giant statutes—the Moai. Steve had me put my hand on the stones, where the grass was growing up around them in the crevices and where they touched the ground. I knew that these statutes were the Irrelevants—but it was only after he had taken me home that I understood what it meant—the big Irrelevant statutes, the frozen faces, the time of their significance long past, the new grass growing up around them. When we were done viewing the Irrelevants, we had a very nice walk on the beach, although our visit was short since I had to prepare to take Mary to her piano lesson.

-Thank you for taking me there. It was a beautiful trip.

That night:

-Steve, I was thinking about the Peter Pan thing, the game we played. I could see all our life issues in there (well not all of them, but so many)—do they appear like that because we have healed from them? Or is that part of the healing?

-I would say both. Probably we've gotten enough clarity that we see how wonderful they really were—even if they seemed so painful in the Earth Plane Distortion Field. Now they're just—tools to play with—a common language. They make the play richer, more meaningful, ever growing and expanding on so many levels.

>>>

-Steve, is the afterlife like this for everybody?

-Mmmm, there are perimeters. But it's kinda like an Apple product—you put in the pictures, the songs, the contacts, you personalize the environment and make it your own.

-That makes me think of a thought that popped into my head—how you insisted that the software be integrated to the hardware. It's kinda like, if you throw in any software, throwing in any belief system.

-(Smile) With my looks and your brains, we can go places.

Chapter 16
Insanely Great

Wednesday, November 4, 2015

During this period of time I was given to baths rather than showers. There was more than one reason for this: the first, the practical one, was that my shower curtain rod was broken and between the cost (remembering that I was financially strapped) and the time (remembering that I was focused into another realm), it wasn't getting replaced. The other significant reason was that something about lying in warm water was causing me to relax and actually enhancing my ability to "go with the flow." In fact, so much seemed to happen while I was in the bathtub that I always seemed impelled to cut it short so I could get to the computer and record it.

This day was no different. I was thinking about the Samskara incident from a couple of days before, and I realized that I was remembering it differently than it had happened. I recognized that it was Robin, butting in, ad libbing to make it funnier. I don't remember all that he said—I *was* in the bathtub, after all—but it *was* funnier.

I noted that he was able to come in at will, apparently, and talk to me—I had thought this stream of consciousness was a dedicated one. Robin said, yeah, it was okay with Steve, but it was a *very* exclusive club—Steve was keeping his minions guarding the door. And then Robin was off into one of his routines: I could see him down at the door (to my consciousness), dressed in a dark suit, with a crowd of people queued outside, and he was saying in a very official voice:

-Invitation, please. Sorry, this party is by invitation only. Why don't you go down to Pat's Bar on the corner and have a beer?

He bent his head to speak into his private mic to the Secret Service-type guy:

-You wanna keep an eye on this one. There's something definitely shifty about him.

Then he's on to the next one:

-Invitation, please. I'm sorry, this invitation does not pass the infrared test. It's a forgery. You'll have to leave, please.

And then he's on the mic again:

-Forgery. Guy in blue.
-Robin: very funny. You added the line about "Guy in blue." I didn't say that...well, not yet. You told me to shut up before I got there.
-I just told you to hold onto it, I didn't want to have to regurgitate here. I'm not putting words in your mouth—am I?
-No-oo. No, no, no. You're actually doing awesome and I am so impressed. You are like the telephone of the stars!!! Steve was telling me how you said to him one day, "I'm kinda intuitive, you know" and he and Tesla about died laughing. That's like saying you have a tin can telephone, when you've really got a satellite connection.
*P.S. make that telephone **to** the stars.*
Okay, well, back to the subject at hand. Sex. Ooops, not that hand.
By the way, how would you have known back when you were trying to put words in my mouth that I would want to say something funny? Maybe I wanted to talk about my teddy bear, and how I missed him, poor teddy-poo. Maybe I just wanted to talk about something boring, like what I had for breakfast. Nothing. Actually I skip a lot of meals around here.
-Stop it. You're making me laugh, and the Samskara stuff wasn't funny. It was actually *very* scary.
-Very scary??? You say??? Like lock you up in the funny bin scary???
-Yep. That scary. And of course, you didn't have anything to do with that, right?
-I claim the 5th.

Later, when I should be cleaning the kitchen:

-Okay, had to interrupt kitchen cleaning to come back— So I'm thinking that you, Robin, didn't really say "Pat's Bar"...it was Pat's something, but I couldn't quite get it, and then you butted in and said, "Um, what was that? Pat's Pinko Parlour? Or..." And I said, "You can't say that kinda stuff. I'm not gonna type it up when you say stuff like that, I can't let people read that." And you were like, "OMG, do the thought police have this telephone bugged too?" (With appropriate paranoid mannerisms, of course, which I cannot adequately convey here, but anyone who knows you could well imagine that your body is never still while you talk.)

I am so laughing, my chest is starting to hurt. You *love* a stage, don't you? Any stage?

-Hey, I was drawn this way.

-I do notice, Steve (cause I know you're always listening) that you have given me this reprieve from all things *Steve*, and I am kinda glad just to hang out with others for a while. Anyway, I'm not oblivious to the fact that you are always concerned about my welfare. Thank you.

Yes, indeed, bringing Robin in for comic relief was doing me good. It was good to just laugh after all the stress of struggling with my issues, trying to keep my head above water as I was swirled on this fast moving current coming through my stream of consciousness.

➤➤➤

I do not know when I got to thinking about the voice in the sky, the Spirit in the Sky talking to us during the mini-me incident, but all of a sudden it occurred to me:

-Robin, was that you? Were *you* the voice in the sky?

-Hey, I have a constitutional right to remain silent. Nothing I say, do or look like can be used against me.

When I was writing that chapter of this book, going back

through the transcript from the journal, it all came back to me. I *thought* that voice had a familiar ring to it. At that point, it just made me laugh. What a bunch of pranksters! How many times I have been played…let me count the ways.

That afternoon:

I was down in the "dungeon" working, listening to random *youtube* videos when a Carpenters song came on. I immediately sensed a new presence in the room:

-Why do I feel like Karen Carpenter is next?
-*Steve: Hmm. Why do you?*
-I can practically feel her breathing down my neck, pacing behind me. My energy's whacked. I feel light-headed.
-*You need her to back off?*
-Please. Just a little space for a bit.
-*Go eat something, Stephanie. Eat an apple and some of those oats.*
-Going.
-*No coffee.*
-No coffee.

I went upstairs and made a bowl of instant oatmeal from a packet. I had been eating very little—my appetite had all but disappeared since Steve had shown up. I had to remind myself periodically to eat something. I took the oats and an apple back downstairs where I was working on the big laptop, which I keep down in my "workroom."

-Okay, I'm shoveling in the food, but that's been intense. My body just felt so off, my heart was beating faster, the light-headedness. I'm still feeling it, actually.
-*Sucks sometimes being empathic.*
-No kidding. Oh, I can laugh.
-*You don't need to take it all on, just close up the portals, seal the cracks. It's enough that you felt it. Remember— everybody takes care of their own shit.*
-Yes. I'm remembering, but sometimes it's hard to stay

clear. It (the stress on my system) seems to be going away, like in waves ebbing away. The tide going out.

-*I'm here for you.*

-I know she didn't get in without you letting her in.

-*True. But I'm still watching, to make sure it doesn't overwhelm you. Like I was telling you, you would be totally overwhelmed if we weren't here watching the gates. You're so open right now—one foot in each plane, huh?*

-Yeah. She's like a wraith.

-*You call this one.*

-I just need a little space before we try to communicate.

Just then the phone rang. It was the school nurse from my granddaughter's school, asking me to come pick up Mary, who was feeling ill. I was still feeling "off" myself, but getting some fresh air actually helped me to recover. After I had gotten Mary home and she was resting in her room, I retreated to my own bed, where I lay down to rest a bit.

Almost immediately I found myself looking at something "whitish" and porous. I could not figure out what it was; it looked weird, almost alien, making me feel uneasy. Finally I realized I was looking at a close-up of bones—in fact, a lengthwise cross-section.

I went back to the computer:

-So it affected even her bones? Wow. Poor, poor Karen. I'm pretty much past the feeling it part, so I can just say that from the aftermath of having experienced it: Wow. I just want to reach out and touch her and make her whole.

-*You can do that, you know.*

-How?

-*It's the power of the human child. The ability to reach into the story and affect it.*

-I'm thinking about that.

-*When you're connected, you're connected. When you can really feel compassion—I mean, really feel it, share the experience and thus have the com-passion. It's something that links you forever. And when you reach out with your wholeness and touch that which is—broken—it mends.*

-That's interesting.

-*Try it.*

-Okay. Closing my eyes—I feel like I need to go lie down again for this one.

-*Go ahead. Where you can relax and just let it take you, let the current move you.*

I was gone for about an hour before I returned to the "dungeon" and resumed my conversation with Steve:

-*So you and Karen had a good talk?*

-We did. All about female beauty, and just being who you are, making a boom! with your own particular set of attributes, not trying to be anyone else, and all the women who did make that boom!

-*Okay.*

-We had a good chat, and I don't overlook the fact that—gosh! Gee whiz—she just happens to show up as I am dealing with my own lifetime issues with appearance. I guess there was a lot of Karen in me, although I wasn't either anorexic or bulimic—but I went through life being ugly. Not able to make it work on the great meter in the sky. Right, I know, the one I wasn't even on.

-*I'm gonna keep my mouth shut.*

-Thank you. And actually, while we're on that subject, once again there was a little twist of the…what…a new twist in the whirlwind, where I sorta thought one thing, and then it turned out to be something different. Not something worse, something much better, as it always is. Better than I can imagine. I didn't want to give you control today, but when I finally did, it played out totally different than I expected [in one of our astral trips]. But that's the thing, isn't it, I am really naïve and I interpret things from a very Earth-based perspective? And you know what, I don't even care anymore. I guess maybe that little lesson yesterday on that Samskara business did affect me. So it really was a healing, an unblocking of energy. So you can make a fool of me and I don't even care anymore.

-*I'm not trying to make a fool of you. You just don't get it when I'm trying to tell you something, you always see things a certain way, and then you suddenly get it—that you had it upside down or twisted or something.*

-I know. And that used to make me feel so stupid and foolish. I wanted to just run away. But not anymore. Bring it on!! Do what you will. And for all that, now I wonder if I even have this conversation right. Yeah, I've changed. I consider it a marvelous change, and I've been really happy, and I certainly have not been bored. And I do love you. But now I can't help wondering what the twist is going to be. Who *are* you?

-Wow.

-Yeah, I guess I got more out of my conversation with Karen than I expected.

-I'm kinda speechless.

-Well, I'm kinda toughened up. I appreciate everything you do. I'm going to dance with you, I'm going to let you lead. I'm going to go, wherever this goes. I will go with you, I will hang with you for eternity if that's what this is, but I'm also not going to be too surprised (I hope) when the other shoe falls. Actually, I think I may be surprised, and that makes me kinda sad, but I'm still gonna go. What can possibly happen to me that hasn't already happened? What do I have to lose? Look at all these truly beautiful people—these beautiful souls, although I do think of them as people, whether they're still on Earth or not—look at these truly beautiful people, just wanting to be understood, to be loved for what they are. That's just…okay, OMG, you pulled me in again.

-Yeah?

-Last night. When you took me to that place, that high up place…I was lying in bed, pretty exhausted after that Samskara lesson. And even before we got there, I said something out loud, before it even hit my conscious mind I was blown away: "Oh my God" or something I said, and I didn't even know why I said it. And there we were, standing way up high, like on a mountaintop, and as far as I could see there against the dark backdrop of…of what…the universe? Eternity? Were thousands and thousands of figures, white figures, just standing there at different levels. Thousands and thousands of self-realized beings. I was blown away, of course, it was one of the most profound things I ever saw. All of them who had climbed the mountain, all of them who had achieved this height. All of them who dared to look inside themselves for the truth, who would let nothing stop them in their desire to excel in their own pursuit of perfection—quietly maybe, where nobody around them even noticed. Funny, that I should remember that right now. I think I only remembered that one other time today.

I thought thousands was a lot, but maybe it was millions, billions, I don't know, there wasn't really a standard for measurement—it just went on as far as I could see.

-*Not as many, perhaps, as you think.*
-Why do you say that?
-*So many who don't even have a clue.*
-Okay—the twist just came. Instead of asking "Who are *you*?" maybe the question is "Who am I?" Ouch. I don't really feel like confronting that question right now. I'm gonna go make supper. (Couldn't this just have been a nice love story or something, one of those silly romantic tales about people separated by time or death? I don't know where this is going.)

-*You wouldn't let it be.*
-Maybe.

I went to make supper, giving the latest perceptions time to shift around inside me.

-*Talk?*
-Yeah.
-*You're afraid you're gonna lose me.*
-Yeah. Not that I'll lose you, in reality, but that you'll turn out to be something different. Something better, of course, because it always turns out better than I imagined. But I don't want something better. I want *you*. I want everything that's been built between us, everything I've thought was happening. I'm good with it. I don't want to find out it's not what I think, even if it *is* better.

I love you. You *are* like me. But whatever you are, I don't want you to stop having been Steve Jobs—or whatever else you've been other than that. I just want you to keep being *you*, the you I know, and not to have been tricked.

I went back upstairs to check on supper. We continued

talking off the page, and somehow we got on the subject of my wedding rings. In that plane where we met for our adventures, he had given me a diamond wedding set on the day of the adventure in Fantasia. Of course I couldn't bring it back with me. But he had also told me afterwards that he had a ring for me in this plane—the Earth Plane Distortion Field. I didn't think too much about it, for some reason; perhaps because he said it in such an off-hand manner. He said a lot of things—and as it turned out, none of them were as off-hand as I thought at the time. But still, I often just let them fly by without much consideration. Suddenly I got an idea.

-If there's a ring here, it has to be physical, because this is a physical place.
-*Well, go look on your dresser.*

I received the impression that I would have to look inside something, open something up, so of course I thought of a jewelry box or trinket box, of which I have several on my dresser. I was sure he had to be putting me on—how could it be? My heart was actually heavy as I walked slowly up the steps to my room. I doubted that I would find the ring, and that would mean what? I wouldn't abandon him; it was too late for that. But I would be troubled, doubt would continue to dog me.

I picked up a pile of papers and magazines on my dresser and moved them aside before I started digging through all my trinket boxes and my jewelry box. No ring. Of course. I was feeling very dreary as I fed the kids, and afterwards I lay down on my bed, thinking to myself: "What is this? What is this all about? What is the reality, what is it I don't understand about this strange relationship? What is it going to turn into?"

Up until this time, now three weeks into our communication, I had never done any research on the subject of "twin souls." I had heard Steve talk about being "torn apart," but I had not taken it seriously. What was that? Sure, we had a connection, that was apparent. And maybe we had an ancient soul relationship, I could buy that. I was still under the illusion—one that was soon to be dispelled—that there might have been a touch of destiny to our meeting, but it was basically just happy happenstance. I still thought of "twin souls" in the realm of Harlequin romances, a pretty concept but having nothing to do with ultimate reality. In fact, Steve had kept me so busy for three weeks that it hadn't even occurred to me to learn more about this concept, or think about how experience was re-shaping my understanding. I suppose I never really thought there *would be* any real information on the topic, so why bother looking?

It felt much like a whim, a silly distraction, as I sat up to the computer and put in the search words: *twin souls.* Up came webpages and webpages of reference materials. My eyes bugged out: "Holy shit!!" There was *tons* of information. Just like the information about Steve Jobs, it had slipped right under my radar until I actually searched.

The first link I clicked on was by someone named Dr. Tan. A doctor! Surely he would know what he was talking about:

> We have many soul mates, but each of us has only one twin soul. A twin soul has every ingredient to be a whole individual. He is not a soul cut into half. However, as he has shared the same pod for the entire journey downward towards the physical earth with his twin, that attachment and longing for the twin is always there in the subliminal consciousness. The incessant throbbing of desire for the other twin is never far beneath the subconscious. It becomes more and more cogent when the soul nears the heightened state of enlightenment.[43]

That certainly fit the Harlequin paradigm—maybe not the "heightened state of enlightenment" but the "incessant throbbing of desire." Well, even I myself had longed for that unique relationship of true love—just like in the Harlequin romances, I sheepishly admit; but not a sticky sentimental love. I had longed for a true love that worked on all levels: physical,

---

[43] *Soul Mates and Twin Souls,* by Dr. Tan Kheng Khoo, http://www.kktanhp.com/twin_souls.htm

314   The Journey Begins

emotional, psychological, intellectual, spiritual—something that completed me, balanced me, challenged me as necessary, joined with me in experiencing the world, saw it as I did but perhaps with additional insight. Just because I had given up on the concept, didn't believe it was possible, didn't mean it didn't exist. You can't relinquish something you never had (as Steve had already succinctly pointed out).

I continued my research—or as Steve would come to call it, my detective work—reading my way through many different articles on many different websites. Wow. Remarkable consistency in the descriptions. There it was, in black-and-white, the story of our relationship. So it was an archetype! We weren't *setting* a pattern, we were *following* one!

*Telepathy? Check

*Equivalent intelligence, similar sense of humor? Check

*Complementary characteristics? Check (He was public, I was private; he was a leader-guy, I was a backstage hand.)

*One of the pair disincarnate? Check

*Spiritual aspect? Check

*Synchronicity? Check

*Intense feminine/masculine magnetic energy? Check

*Both of pair in last lifetime? Check[44]

It is difficult to convey my extreme shock at the realization that this was a real phenomenon, as real as motherhood, that the pattern was set in stone—although, like every snowflake, every example might be unique. It was as if I had never heard of snow before, never known anyone who had experienced it, and yet had been observing in disbelief this strange white stuff drifting down from the sky—only to learn that it had been happening in diverse locations since time began. This was so much bigger, more mind-blowing than I could have imagined. And it was actually happening to me? Oh, *wow*.

-I am so blown away by this. It all rings so *right*. But *how*? How could I come to this moment when I would have found (or been found by) my twin soul, that I didn't even think

---

[44] As far as I knew—consistent with my own intuition. Steve also said it was.

was a real concept? And you had asked me, did I remember the "tear apart," and you mentioned the primordial scream and that it was your first experience of pain. And I didn't even remember it, really.[45] And I really wasn't connecting with you as Steve Jobs—I had to dig, I had to be drawn in really deep—to see under the surface. And that was the same as I have now read about twin souls, you might not necessarily relate on the emotional and physical level—it is a connection at the *soul* level. And it is there that I did eventually connect with you, and then it sorta bubbled up from there, so I could come to love all of it. *But* I don't want to lose the male/female parts, at least not right away. And somehow you conveyed to me that it is the final blending, when it happens—that you can play around with it for a while, but the final blending is like that spiritual ecstasy that happens in the best sex, that bliss that never ends.

And also this source says that when the twin souls come together, it is usually in conjunction with some spiritual endeavor, some benefit for humanity. And I kinda see that, just with this transcript and with the conversations with the others I've (we've) talked to. I see that's what you want to do, to give something to humanity, to make them see, become more aware. I kinda wanted that, too, all along, but how was I to do that? I sorta gave up on my ability to make any impact at all, before I met you.

I went to the club to work out; I couldn't deal with this twin soul business anymore, I needed to not think about it, to just be physical. As I came back into the house, it suddenly hit me like a ton of bricks. I knew I was going to go upstairs and see *it*—it was going to be there—the ring Steve had meant.

I felt trepidation as I went up the stairs, overwhelmed by what he had shown me. The magazine I was looking for was not on the dresser—it was on my nightstand, where I had put it when I had earlier moved it so I could search through the trinket boxes and whatnot for the ring. I opened the magazine—the *Time* magazine—to the article entitled "Steve's Last Project," to

---

[45] This also is mentioned in the literature, the pain of the final soul separation.

his vision of the Apple headquarters. And there it was! The mysterious ring! A perfect circle. In theory, anyway, still in process, from imagination to reality.

But all I could think was, "No way! What is this? Why are you showing me this?"

The soul knows what the soul knows? I thought about what Steve had said during his last lifetime: "Intuition is more important than intellect."

So this was the other shoe falling. This was the answer to my question: *What are you?* And it's other side: *what am I?* This was the answer? The circle, the completion, the ultimate simplification to zero, the no-beginning and no-end, the eternal connection? We *were* the twins, and this was the divine marriage—a union in every dimension. Once again, better than I imagined—still Steve, but with a fantastical twist.

-And I can see it. I can see it, now, Steve. I can see that when the twin souls meet again, it's never small. It's a *big* thing, it's written across the heavens. I think that's why I'm so overwhelmed. Is this really my moment? Am I really coming home? I've spent my whole life, it seems, trying to work things out, trying to untie the bonds that held me to this cycle of what some would call karma, trying to learn to forgive, to relinquish, to clear, to purify. Trying to understand. Seeking the truth. Always yearning, always pulled toward a world that I knew was so much more real than the one I seemed to live in every day. Have I really come so far? Am I really going home? Will I really meet you at the train station and you will say, "You're coming home, with me"? And I will lay my head on your shoulder and just smile, knowing that I AM home at last.

WOW.

I did not know then what I was to learn in short order: that it was the time of the twin reunions. Like swallows rising together at first light, those individuals in touch with the soul's call were flocking to the new dawn.

As I marveled at this "last project," I could feel Steve smiling. Is that the smug smile on the cover of the biography? Or is that just amusement? For Steve, a true memorial: *I am* home, *I am complete, I am alive, I am beginning without end. I am neither come nor gone. I am here.*

The wheel that touches both the Earth and the Heavens.

-Insanely great, Steve! Insanely great!

Thursday, November 5, 2015
Scramskara Samskara

I was in the midst of talking to Karen and Robin the next morning, when my attention got diverted, and then I spent a couple of hours collating and updating my journal.

-Karen, Robin, sorry to have made you sit through this.

-Robin: Hey, no problem, we're mesmerized.   Huh, Karen?

-Karen: Ditto that, Robin.

-Robin: (giving Karen that simpering look) I love you, Batman.

-Oh, oh, is there something more to that exchange than appears on the surface?

-Robin: My lips are sealed.

-Like that could ever happen.

ﾒﾒﾒ

-I was just thinking.   We are such a disparate cast of characters.

-Robin: nanoo nanoo.

-Go away. What does that mean anyway?

*-Robin: I love **everybody** in the whole world.*

-Besides the fact that you are an idiot, you just touched on one of the most touching stories of my entire life.

-Robin: Who wouldn't be touched by that?

-Seems so self-evident, doesn't it?   Funny how blind people are.

-Steve: Okay, Stephanie, you can tell that story another time.   I'm giving you space to get some work done—Robin,

leave her alone.

-Anyway, Robin, it means "hello" and "good-bye" right?

-Robin: Not so. There are no hellos and good-byes anymore, that was just to cover up the truth, which humanity was not prepared to handle.

-There's a little alien in all of us, I guess. (Why did I say that, who put that thought in my head?) [46] Okay, I am so outa here.

11:29 a.m.

-You know, even as I'm trying to just go about my chores—washing dishes, sweeping, whatever—I can't stay quite present. You all may not be talking to me, but then my mind is recycling what we talked about, and I'm laughing all over again, or chewing on some concept.

-Robin. Ooooooo Samskara, Samskara.

-Oh, more funny.

-Robin: Just say—repeat it after me—Scram-skara, scram-skara.

-Ha. Oh my. Okay, I'll try that.

> > >

-Steve: Okay, Stephanie, I know you need to get that story out, the one you alluded to. It's eating at your innards.

-I do, if for no other reason than to acknowledge some of the most beautiful souls on this planet. But first, I can't know why we're taking so long to get to Karen's story—I know when I get distracted like this, or things go astray, that there's something in the timing that I'm not aware of. You're planning to spring something, right?

-Maybe she's just at the hairdressers.

-Getting a total makeover, I hope. To finally be the Karen she was meant to be—ooh, that makes me think of the Susan Boyle song—see there's another one who busted out and was what she was. I love Susan Boyle. Anyway, back to Karen, I

---

[46] Ha, ha. A thought that I would come to understand a whole lot better down the road.

just hope she's finally getting to dress and wear her hair and turn her gestures into what she really is—can't imagine what that would look like, actually, but get her the dang nab out of somebody else's idea of what she needed to be.

-*Maybe she's working on it—we're working on it—Heaven is working on it.*

-I hope so.

Anyway, here's my story:

But before I began (as so often happened) I was diverted by another thought:

-Steve, are we all in the same soul group—I mean, me, you, Robin, Karen, maybe Erik? Is that why we're so attached to each other?

-*Maybe. You know I can't tell you the answer to that, my dear. That would be like telling you if Tom Swift was going to escape the blood-thirsty cannibals in the next chapter. You will know all when you are here—but you're still on the Earth plane (I heard that—barely), and you should never believe what I tell you—it should always come to you when you know it is right, when you've experienced it, when you have* **knowing.** *I wish that everyone on Earth could hear me here—don't believe what anybody else tells you!!! It's only real, it's only true, if you experience it to be so. You can think about it, you can pay attention to it, but for god's sake, test it out. Don't just swallow the bait, hook, line and sinker. Give yourself some wiggle room—lots of wiggle room, actually.*

-You told me some stuff when we first started talking, that validation stuff.

-*I did. And that was for validation, hum-de-dum, give 'em what they want. Yes, this is Steve Jobs, what the hell else do you want to know? (I had kinda that rep, right?—well, not like I got that many calls, not like, say, Robin Williams, whose phone was ringing off the hook. "Hey, Robin, what's it like where you are? Are you in hell?")*

-*Robin: You're just jealous.*

-*Steve: Go away, I'm having a private talk with my girl.*

-*Robin: Yeah, that mighta worked down in the viper pit,*

but everything's transparent here.

-*Steve: Well, turn your eyeballs the other direction.*

-*Steve: Okay, Stephanie, enough of that, do your story.*

-It somehow seems anticlimactic here, but it's still a wonderful story. The bramble-filled path of true love.

Okay, back when I was an attorney (before I became one of the Irrelevants, those blocks of stone on Easter Island), I had a client in a child protection case. It involved a five-year-old girl who was being raised by her grandparents, due to the parents being unavailable for her care. Well, after one of those programs in her kindergarten where you're supposed to tell somebody if "anyone tries to touch your private parts" she reported to the teacher that her grandpa sometimes lifted her shirt and touched her belly (or something of that nature). The teacher apparently embellished a little, like all sweet teachers are wont to do (okay, forgive the sarcasm), and made a report to the proper authorities. The proper authorities then sent the police to raid this family's home—okay to interrogate poor grandpa—to pluck the child from the grasp of these fiendish fiends and put her in some obnoxious (but apparently safe) foster setting—a group home I think, initially. Poor grandpa has no idea what is going on, and eventually agrees to a polygraph, which the police try to use against him, saying he failed. (Lie! Lie! They never did produce the polygraph, they were just trying to seduce him into an admission with misstatements.)

In the meantime, the child is carted off to the inquisition center, the center where they do these types of "forensic" interviews. The interviewing person gives her crayons and shows her drawings of naked bodies and such, the kinda thing you don't usually let your kids play with, and asks her penetrating questions like "Did you ever see grandpa naked?" The child giggles and says, "Noooo. That would be *silly*." This goes on for an hour, during which time the child reveals that grampa sometimes plays a chase game with her where he will "capture" her, lay her down, pull up her shirt, and make the raspberry on her tummy, sending her into paroxysms of giggling. (The harmless game we all played when I was young, and that we did to my younger brothers and sisters, and even my children.) She reveals no inappropriate behavior (although apparently even that harmless game is now taboo, lest we all end up in jail). At the end of the session, the interviewer makes one last stab: "Do you have any secrets you haven't told me?" The little girl nods her head, "yes." You can see the interviewer come to attention, in the video, all excited that she might finally be getting the goods. "What is it?" she asks breathlessly. The little girl smiles and throws her arms wide. "I love everybody in the whole world!!!"

That should have done it, right? But not so. The video went into the Indiana Jones warehouse where artifacts are lost for eternity—or close to. In the meantime, the word is spread through the agency that Grandpa is a child molester, each person just picks it up from the last, nobody looks at the video, they just look at the police report where the police are claiming to grandpa that he failed the lie detector, and where grandpa is backed into the corner, saying, "I don't know. We live in the same house. Maybe she might have seen me naked sometime. I can't say." So the story grows and grows, the child is moved into a foster home where she is maltreated, sent to school without breakfast and inadequate clothing for the weather, and then she is moved to another foster home—this one wants to adopt her, save her from the fiendish grandpa. In the meantime she is sent to counseling, which one can only imagine—"Don't worry, grandpa can't ever hurt you again." Oh my goodness, talk about messing with a kid's head—*Um, exactly how did he hurt me? Oh yeah, by chasing me and doing the raspberry on my tummy. That tickled so much. I told him to stop.*

In the meantime, this child protection case is going on—we've got discovery requests out, but it takes forever to get the video, I think I finally had to get the court to order them to produce it within a certain amount of time. As I said, we never got the supposed lie detector results. During all this time, Grandpa is treated as if he is a child molester. Grandma is finally allowed to have limited visits with the child without Grandpa present. Finally we get the video, I look at it, and I think, "Holy crap." I contact the AG in charge, and say, "have you *watched* this?" "Well, no, I just trust my case workers." I ask the case workers if *they've* seen it. "Well, I'm sure someone has. And he *did* fail the polygraph." I finally sent the video and police reports to a psychologist who specializes in treating sex offenders and I think also worked with kids in that situation, and he looked at it and sent a report that concluded, something to this effect: "This is one of the most egregious cases of pre-confirmatory bias I have ever seen. I see nothing here to indicate inappropriate sexual behavior." So we took that to the Court, and it still took months to get that kid loose from the system—they refuse to admit they're wrong, and now they're covering their tracks. Well, she needs more counseling, she's been away from the grandparents so long (about twelve months at this point, if I remember correctly) that re-integration is going to have to be slow, we'll have to check out their home, make sure it qualifies as a foster home, because now that the system has her, she has to be under the supervision of the agency and they'll have to act as foster parents until we're sure she's safe. Etc. Etc.

Talk about bureaucratic child abuse. A sad story, but I always remember the end of that video, when that little girl's face just beams as she says, "I love everybody in the whole world." Somebody was raising her right. God bless her, wherever she is, and here's hoping that she was able to overcome her abuse at the hands of the State.

And of course the grandparents were not only out the benefits and ability to care for their grandchild, but were out a *ton* of money as a result of this case.

As I said, beautiful souls. May they find peace.

-Steve: Nice story, in that it is so revealing. **But**—*you know why you had to tell it, don't you?*

-I think I got it at the end. I didn't forgive the AG, those caseworkers, the police, the teacher—even the judge, all those who trampled over these people's right to love and care for each other, to the company of each other. Who brought them so much pain and anguish. I have to forgive them?

-I think so. For us.

-Okay, I'll work on it. But they're idiots!!!

-I think those words have come out of my own mouth a few times.

-Jerks!! Bastards!!

-Let it all out. I'll leave you to it.

-Uh—Steve. It is a bramble-filled path to true love, isn't it? That's why I said that.

-Go vent and get it out. It will come.

>>>

-You know what I was thinking about that story—the bastards? None of them had to take responsibility, because their individual responsibility was buried in the group think.

>>>

-I screwed up, didn't I? Somehow I screwed the plan that I didn't even know was a plan by not getting my work done, books written, pictures painted, I don't know what all. I don't really expect anybody to talk to me about this. I just feel kinda sick inside right now and I'm not sure why so I'm just going to lay down and process it. I feel like I'm on a roller coaster.

>>>

-I didn't forgive. I feel sick because I didn't forgive, don't I? It's that bump when the road is mostly smooth, it doesn't take much? Right? I think that's it, but my energy also seems to be really in a state of change. Not sure. Gonna go and try to forgive.

(I caution that this was *my* lesson—any others involved have their own, and in no way would I suggest that I would know what it was.)

It had been a week of ups and downs. What a ride. You remember, I never liked roller coasters. And Steve had promised to add it to his list of future pleasures—well, we were about to hit some really high peaks and death-defying swoops.

Chapter 17
The STEVE & STEPHANIE Game Show

Friday, November 6, 2015

I woke up in the morning to find a letter in front of me. Not in front of me physically, but astrally, or psychically, or however the powers-that-be make letters appear in the air in front of your face. It was short. I read through it quickly.

-What is this?
-*Exactly what it looks like.*

What it looked like was a love letter from Steve. Not to me. Obviously out of his closet, something from his past life. But why was he showing it to me? Did I look like someone who cared?

I went about my day, but the letter rankled in the back of my mind. I had told him I didn't want to know what was in his cupboards. It was apparent I couldn't hide any of my stuff, but it wasn't like I wanted to see any of his. Was it necessary? And the more the day pressed on, the more my hackles rose. In fact, I gradually grew so pissed that I decided it was time to move on, this relationship had run its natural course. Yes, his last lifetime was over, but *still* and all. It wasn't like I was made of wood.

We finally got into it that afternoon. Robin happened to be hanging around.

-*Steve: Would you throw away eternity over some jealousy?*
-Me: Yes.
-*Robin: I can kinda see her point.*
-*Steve: Who asked you?*
-*Robin: Nobody had to. I'm volunteering.*
-Me: So I'm not ready. Maybe another million years.
-*Steve: You always were a runner. Run-run-run. The*

going gets rough, and you run.

-Me: Only where I'm not wanted. I only run from where I'm not wanted.

-*Robin: Okay, kids, take a seat. You in that corner. You over there. (Turning to imaginary audience.) Okay, you've seen the contestants. Please place your bets over there.*

-Me: You are always comic relief?

-*Robin: Did you want some other kind of relief? Maybe a little aspirin? A hit on the bong?*

-Me: Stop. You go in a corner.

-*Robin: Yes, Mommy. (Trundles over to corner.)*

-Me: I need…I don't know what I need. I need my space.

-*Steve: You've got all kinds of space. Are you in a cage?*

-Me: Kinda. Where am I supposed to go to be alone?

-*Steve: Anywhere you want. The universe is vast.*

-Me: Yeah…but I have to go alone. I can't take my old blankie with me.

-*Steve: You mean that little pinprick spot inside of you where you could run to Mommy?*

-Me: Hey, that was my inner self. My higher self. The only one who ever loved me. And now—you're in that space. So what do I have left?

-*Steve: Do you want me to move out? Are you throwing me out?*

-Me: Is that a possibility?

-*Steve: I don't know. (Looking glum.)*

-Me: You guys are playing me again, aren't you?

-*Robin: (Throwing up hands.) Not me. I am an innocent man.*

-Me: You're like a little…a little…

-*Robin: Just say it, a genie in the bottle, right? Do you want me to go back in so you can put the cork in?*

-Me: No. Stay where you are. I need you to make me laugh to keep me sane.

-*Robin: No! No! Not sanity…throw me anywhere but in that briar patch.*

-*Steve: I thought you were like this space without walls, but I seem to keep running into walls.*

-Me: And ripping them down, as I recall. Well, we had to

come here someday, didn't we? (Turning backs on each other.)

    -Robin: Intermission Time!! (to the audience) There's popcorn and beer at the concession stand. Watch your step there at the door. We'll see you all back in...looks at his watch)...one hour.

    -Me: One hour? I have one hour to cool down?

    -Robin: More? I could send in the clowns.

    -Me: I think that's a good idea. Bring in the clowns.

I'm going downstairs to work.

>>>

(Behind –between??—scenes, or someplace like that.)

    -Steve: I thought you were good with this, that we all have many soul mates, but only one twin soul.

    -Me: I thought I was, too. But I don't know, something has stuck in my craw.

    -Steve: That's how we balanced out our karmic debt.

    -Me: I don't like that word, karma. Can't you just say *issues*?

    -Steve. Hey, you even had a session with T.J.

    -Me: I didn't invite him in. He just showed up. Unannounced. And I didn't even know what he wanted, really. I don't even remember what he said. That was a long time ago.

    -Steve: You know it was only about a month, right?

    -Me: Well, let's say, now I understand how you could sit in a dark room contemplating your next move for a thousand years when it was only four years earth time. A month ago Earth time was like three lifetimes on my calendar.

    Hey, that just made me think of something!! I used to think the measure of time was really the measure of how much was happening. H'mm, I'm gonna have to think about that—after I'm done with this really really icky-feeling problem. Do I have to keep coming up against these brick walls?

    -Steve: They can come down one brick at a time—or just blast them out. Wrecking ball.

    -Me: Like in the song. *Fight Song.*

-Steve: Is this going to be another block like back at the burn-barrel? Another trip into Stephanie's Screwed-Up Psyche?

-Me: I don't know. Shouldn't that have been my line?

-Steve: Am I finishing your sentences now?

-Me: Oh, God, that just took the wind out of my sails. Like here I am, talking to myself. You are myself, but how can you be, you're the masculine energy, the yin to my yang—or is that yang to my yin?? You're so different than me, and yet so much the same. I can't be talking to myself, because of all those synchronicities—apples appearing in front of doors, keys mysteriously moving downstairs, the songs, the things showing up in front of my face, waking me up in the middle of the night to tell me something only to have it all make sense only in retrospect. You had a whole lifetime (and I suppose, many more) far far from anything that even interested me, as you have many many times validated through like a zillion means. And what about Robin? Oops...I should keep my voice down...he has a way of showing up whenever his name is mentioned. How the heck would I ever anticipate having him around? I mean, I liked Robin in a lot of movies—but I wasn't the kind to call myself a real fan, to follow him as a comic, etc. I had no special sense of affinity for him. And certainly none for Karen Carpenter, or Johnny and June Cash (other than I appreciated their music, but nothing extraordinary in terms of affinity). I did like Alan Watts, though. I really enjoyed his talks, they meant a lot to me.

I'm getting confused again. And every time one of these...these Samskaras... comes up, I start to doubt you, don't I?

-Steve: I've noticed a trend.

-Me: You're laughing at me.

-Steve: I'm smiling...okay, I'm laughing now. I'm sorry. You're so damned funny. You want to go be alone, but...you're troubled because you have to go alone?

-Me: Okay, alone with me, myself and I. Does that clarify things?

-Steve: Stephanie, Stephanie. You just ranted on and on about how you were talking to yourself...look back a few

paragraphs. So when are you alone and when are you not?

-Me: That is a very good question, Steve, and I'm going to have to give it some real thought. But right now I'm in the middle of a Samskara and I'd really like to just wear it for a while. I'd like to enjoy it. It's a part of me, I'm sure I've been carrying it around for most of my lifetime, and I just might be a little sad to see it go.

-Steve: Ah, dear. You eternally amuse me.

-Me: I'm glad to hear that. Eternally sounds like a very long time.

-Steve: And Stephanie? Sweet plum?

-Me: Stop!!!

-Steve: Really? You only run from the places where you're not wanted? Stick that...

-Me: I know. I know. In my pipe and smoke it.

4:47p.m.

-Robin: Okay, we're back. Everybody's in their seats? Lights please. As you're aware...da de dah, yadda yadda, you all know the contestants and what's at stake. On with the show. (Sits up in a high chair like on a game show, between the two of us, who are also perched on stools.) Now, who would care to share how this whole thing started?

Whereas before it had just been Robin being Robin, I sensed that we now were on a stage with an audience, exposing our secrets to one and all. Not that this intimidated me in the heat of the moment.

-Me: It was *him*. He had to show me this love letter.

-Steve: Hey, it was in my cupboard.

-Robin: (Turns to Steve.) You'll get your chance. Please let Contestant Number One finish.

-Me: So there I am this morning reading it, and I'm like, is this true? And he's kinda fudgin', and I'm like, really? Not that I care so much, but you weren't really that honest with me, were you?

-Robin: Do you care to elucidate?

-Me: No.

-*Steve: I never lied to you, Stephanie. And why do you care anyway, huh? Huh? It's not like we're ever going to be back this way again.*

-Me: Well, yeah, but I'd like to make a clean break. No strings.

-*Robin: I see her point. What do you think, audience? Who presently has the advantage? (Holds sign over my head, lots of whooping and hollering—holds sign over Steve's head, lots of boos.)*

-*Robin: That's kinda the way I was seeing it. So the first round goes to the lady.*

-*Contestant Number Two, the next question is for you. So why didn't you reveal that earlier, huh? I mean, you two have been conversing what, three weeks to three lifetimes already? Isn't that something a gentleman should come out with about the time he announces he has **BEEP!! ** Whoops, they say I can't say that on the show. Okay, strike that. About the time you reveal you have an aged grandmother that you keep chained in the basement and feed on Cheerios and OJ?*

-*Steve: Look at her. She runs at the drop of the hat. She tries to get away if you tell her to stop putting words in your mouth.*

-*Robin: (Aside to Steve.) You're not getting brownie points for this, you know. Look at the audience, they're not with you. Can you come up with something a little more— palatable? Or at least something that will jack up the ratings— reveal something about yourself. Do you have a tattoo in a...shall we say...out of the way spot?*

-*Steve: I'm just trying to be truthful, that's all. If that doesn't get me points, then so be it. I am what I am. What can I say?*

-*Robin: I yam what I yam. I kinda like that, it has a familiar ring to it. Okay, folks, let's get on to the free-for-all portion of the show. Do you want to use cream pies? Uh, Andrea, could you bring out those pies? (Andrea comes out in skimpy outfit, twirling with a number of pies on a tray.)*

Thank you Sweetheart. MMMPH....(Blows her a kiss as she struts by off-stage. Wink, stage whisper.) See you later…same place?   (Back to stage voice.)   Okay, are both contestants armed and ready?

(Hurries to side of stage.) Let 'er rip.

-Me: I hate you!!

-Steve: I'm not feeling very fond of you, myself, right now.

-Me: Well, then get your toothbrush and get out! I don't need anybody around who isn't fond of me.

(Cheers from audience.)

(Pies starting to fly. The audience is going wild.)

Finally:

-Me: Oh, God, I'm exhausted. Are we out of pies?

*-Steve: I've got **one** left. Kept it in reserve, just to strike the final blow.*

-Me: That's not fair.

*-Steve: Hey, I **always** get the last word.*

-Me: Yes, you do. Why is that?

-Steve: 'Cause I'm up here and you're down there and I can see a lot further.

-Me: Yeah. That's an unfair advantage.

-Steve: Have I ever used it to your disadvantage?

-Me: Well, not that I can remember.   But you have laughed at me behind my back.

-Steve: That was just the wind beneath your wings. Isn't it time to scram-skara Samskara?

-Me: I don't know. I'm tired of fighting you.

-Steve: I would say stop fighting, but I actually kinda enjoy these skirmishes. So here's to battling forever more.

-Me: Wooo. So tired.

-Steve: Look here, dear.

SPLATT!

-Me: (Wiping off pie.) Hey, this actually tastes kinda good.

-Steve: I told you it would, didn't I?   And it only gets better. There's some awfully good cooks in the kitchen.

5:20 p.m.: After the Show

-Psst. Steve.

-Yeah?

-I hate to say it, because I still hate you. But that was kinda fun.

-I know, huh? Robin's like a total killer. He makes you die laughing.

-Would that make him a serial killer?   I mean, he was in some serials, wasn't he?

-Yeah, but keep it under wraps. At least they all died with smiles on their faces.

5:33p.m.

-Oh, and Steve?

-Ye—es dear.

-Don't sound so excited to hear from me. So you know

when you mentioned the Tom Swift thing earlier, about the blood-thirsty cannibals? Well, I never read *Tom Swift*, and I don't know if you ever did, and I don't know if there were ever blood-thirsty cannibals, but of course I checked it out, and—oh golly—guess what? Guess who is mentioned in *Wikipedia* as having been a huge fan of Tom Swift, Jr., not just a passing mention but a couple of sentences?

> The Tom Swift, Jr. adventures were **Steve Wozniak's** favorite reading as a boy and inspired him to become a scientist. According to Wozniak, reading the Tom Swift books made him feel "that engineers can save the world from all sorts of conflict and evil"[47].

You are not really the long-dead ghost of Steve Jobs are you??? This is just all my imagination, and I have such a vivid imagination that I make up connections like that!! Everybody who doesn't believe this can screw themselves.

-Whoa. Is this Miss Priss talking?

-I yam not what I was.

-I guess not. I kinda like it. (But I kinda liked Miss Priss, too.)

-And I guess I do travel an awful lot with you. Some of my most wonderful memories. This afterlife stuff is really fun, isn't it? (Even the hard lessons are kinda fun in retrospect.) It's just that the traveling part happens so seamlessly it doesn't even seem so much like I went anywhere. I'm just…there. And sometimes I can be there *and* here, a part of what is happening there, and still conscious (okay, semi-conscious) of what is happening here. I can—as today—actually be there with you all playing, and typing at the same time.

-I love you Stephanie. I always will. You are my reflection, and I yours. We will dance together among the stars. And I promise to stick with the tango so we can get good.

-Thank you.

-YW.

---

[47] https://en.wikipedia.org/wiki/Tom_Swift; this work is released under CC-BY-SA http://creativecommons.org/licenses/by-sa/3.0/

6:28p.m.

-Hi, Stephanie.

-Hi, Steve.

-Now you know why I was enthralled from the start.

-I think so. Now that I feel like a different person, and see like a different person—to go back and look at that stuff I wrote. Wow, some of that was really deep. And very danged good writing. Profound.

I—well, we—had been perusing some of the essays on my computer from years gone by, things I had pretty much forgotten about.

-Yes. You just never really believed in yourself, in your power—you never claimed it.

-Why?

-Well, you chose your handicap this time around.

-My family.

-Very very good choice in many ways. Interesting life. Good health. A base stability.

-But no love.

-No love and no support—for what you were.[48]

-I just floated along, didn't I, like a leaf on the current?

-Not always. But you never really burst out as what you were.

-But I am now?

-I think so. And maybe—most certainly—it happened that way because that's the way it needed to happen.

-So all those writings—is anything to become of them?

-That's up to you. I will be here, to support you, to send the right support your way.

-But I can't seem to focus enough. It's so compelling to be with you—and Robin and the others.

-I love you so much, it's hard to give you space—and I

---

[48] After leaving Alaska, anyway, when times were hard. No offense to my family, who each had their own trials and tribulations.

*know when I do, you start feeling abandoned. But I will never abandon you. I think it will work itself out. I **know** it will work itself out. It **is** working itself out. It always has been. You can see that.*

-Yes, all the parts falling into place so long ago.

-The soul knows what the soul knows.

-Yes, I think I'm seeing that, and maybe learning to just let it take me.

-You can't fight yourself.

-Aren't you like myself? At least the mirror image?

-We don't fight, dear. We just dance around in circles.

-There's the tension, isn't there, like a wind-up toy, or a clock or something?

-Yes, but...more self-sustaining.

-Like a perpetual clock? Where supposedly the balance would be such that it would keep moving of its own weight?

-Maybe. I'm a little strained for words here.

-And was I getting that right, about what makes me a good playmate is that there's a certain amount of tension possible, in that I'm kinda locked into the dark? I don't *get* everything, whereas it's too *easy* there—too much transparency or something?

-It's what makes Earth such a good playground, if that were only understood.

-Taken over by the darkside?

-One might say that. The bullies rule the playground.

-Well, maybe it's time for revenge of the nerds. Or the dorks.

-Maybe.

-No more Miss Priss? You can't have my lunch money?

-We'll see, we'll see.

Chapter 18
I Have a Dream
Saturday, November 7, 2015

I woke up in the morning and found myself drifting down a lazy stream on an inner tube. Steve was there, on his own inner tube. It was a beautiful day—the kind kids draw: blue sky, small fluffy white clouds, green trees lining the banks, flowers growing everywhere they could. It was so mellow and I was so blissed out, just going with the flow. Suddenly I heard, very clearly: *ABBA*. As if to reinforce it, I saw the letters blazed in the sky.

After that little trip, I went to the internet to look up ABBA. I assumed the letters referred to the musical group. Up came a song: *I Have a Dream.* It's quite lovely.

[Lyrics omitted.]

Pretty or not, I wasn't sure why I had been sent in that direction. What did this song have to do with the present moment? I already knew that Steve used songs to elucidate points he wished to make, but what was the thrust of this one? Maybe because we had been floating on a stream and the song talks about one: [Lyrics omitted.]

I listened to a few other ABBA songs, but none rang any bells, and I knew the first one that opened—as usual—was the one that Steve had intended that I hear. A little perplexed, I let it be. If he wanted me to know more, he would tell me.

For some reason that day, I got to thinking about my suicide attempt back in college, when I swallowed all those pills. I had been alone in my apartment, but had a last minute change of heart and had walked down the sidewalk to the house where I had previously lived, with its dozens of occupants. I recall nothing after starting on this walk until I awakened the next morning in the hospital, except for a couple of vague images. One was someone yelling at me, some emergency or medical personnel: *are you pregnant?* I remembered thinking what a funny and rude question that was. The other thing I remembered, very vaguely—as you might a dream, was wandering down the hallway at the hospital in one of their gowns, the kind that has only strings to fasten the back, and certainly doesn't cover your behind. I didn't recall interacting with anyone—just wandering.

The doctor came in that morning, followed by a covey of interns—it was a teaching hospital at the University. He said to me, "Do you remember anything about last night?"

I said "no."

He smiled at me, and then all the interns smiled at me, and I was sure they were smiling because I had been walking down the hallway with my backside exposed to the world. After that,

I didn't want to know any more.

Following that experience, I had had the oddest thought that I had died, but that when you died you just came back to the same place where you left off until you got it "right." It was such a strange thought, particularly for the times. Of course, I had assumed when I was dead it would just be lights out. My religious experience would have told me that when I killed myself, it would be eternal damnation in hell, but I wasn't buying that. I had left all that doctrine behind as hypocritical, illogical and unkind. As far as I knew, there weren't any other options—unless you ended up in heaven by mistake. Therefore, my thought about having died and being stuck back in my same footsteps was strange, not something I cared to spout to others. My mental reputation was already tarnished; I didn't need to let people think my mind was rotted to the core.

The odd thought stayed with me, however, and actually was helpful. If I had to keep coming back until I got it "right," I might as well get the job done sooner than later, so I could move on. It tempered any further tendency I might have had to give suicide another go.

So I went through life with this odd thought, and all of a sudden, on that particular day in November, 2015, for the very first time, I wondered if I might have had a near-death experience. Nobody knew about NDEs back in 1970—at least nobody I knew. If they did, it wouldn't have been the kind of thing you talked about in polite society. Why did I have this thought? And even if I did, how would I ever know? It had been so long, even if I did dredge up some memory, how could I ever know it was real and not just manufactured in the moment? I couldn't. And so I shrugged my shoulders. Maybe I did, with the memory suppressed or just not understood, or maybe I didn't. It was forty-five years gone. What difference did it make anymore?

Afternoon:

That afternoon I felt a yearning to connect with Steve, I just needed an energetic "hug." I lay down on my bed and he told me we were going to go back to working on the astral projection thing. Normally, for our trips, I am just here and gone as easily as opening a door. During those adventures, I am fully cognizant of all that is occurring, but things also can change rapidly. For example, all I have to do is think of what I want to wear, and I will look down and see it. In fact, Steve and I have played with that one, to my amusement; one time I didn't like what he was wearing (those darn black tees and jeans—well, I don't mind the jeans) and I went poof! and changed his shirt, and he went poof! and changed it back, and pretty soon we were doing it so fast that I lost track and didn't realize I was the one putting him in the black pullover and he was the one changing it.

But it seems like there is another type of travel that appears more concrete, or dense, to me. It feels more "Earth-like," for some reason. It seems like I have a more difficult time staying "grounded" in these experiences.

On this occasion, we were working on it, and I found myself going, Steve grabbing me and arguing with me to believe I was there, and then slipping back. We didn't seem to be making the necessary progress. Then all of a sudden I saw a picture of my mother and father, a picture where they were fairly young and looked really happy. It was just stuck there, on the edge of that plane, and then it went away; but it came back, and then left again. Then I saw one of my brothers, as a child in a familiar family picture. The picture quickly shifted as if I were scrolling on a phone—through another brother who was also in the picture before stopping right on me. I couldn't see me, I just knew this was where I was in the portrait, for just then there was a big flash right over my image. It spread out like light across water. I jumped up, right out of the photo, and ran lickety split across the light bridge. I appeared to be about 5 or 6 years old and I was now dressed in a dark coat and bonnet, as children might wear in the '50s. I ran to where Steve was, to his house.

This house looked not unlike mine, although there seemed to be a few differences, especially with the layout inside. Steve opened the door to let me in. He appeared older than usual in our adventures—probably about 50. I could see him quite clearly. He sat down in a stuffed chair and let me crawl up on his lap. As customary, I had two points of view—I was both experiencing being the child, sitting in his lap, and I was also watching the scene. There were many people in the house and they were wanting to talk to us. They seemed very interested in what he or I might have to say. I was really shy and leaned my head against Steve's shoulder. He put his arms around me, and I wondered why all these people were there and why they cared. I couldn't really understand what they were saying, it was beyond my six-year-old capacity to comprehend. Steve talked to them while I clung to him. Finally everyone left and it was time for me to go home. I put on my coat and hat and ran out the door. At the driveway I turned to wave and Steve waved back. I could see that he was smiling.

I ran back to the picture and jumped into my spot in the middle.

I was thinking that was a very odd episode. I discussed it with Steve. He said that the child was in me and a part of me and that the father/daughter type link is also an important aspect of the masculine/feminine energy, and I thought that was nice, that he could be fatherly, that I seemed to have a need for that relationship, to find my interrupted father connection. Then Steve said what hadn't even occurred to me:

-I get something from it, too, you know—I need to find my own father/daughter connection.

I was amazed when I thought about that, because I could see it was true. It was a healing for him, as well. Funny how that works.

This subject made me think of another curious episode: when I was about nine or ten years old, during the traumatic early years among the nuns, after my father and brother had died, after I had lost my lovely wilderness kingdom and became the disinherited princess, I used to "zone out", often in the classroom. I would simply be absent from whatever was going on, immobile, not hearing people talk to me, until something happened or I spontaneously returned to planet Earth. Like most children, I didn't really think too much about these types of experiences. They happened. I'd actually been pretty intuitive as a small child, so this was just another part of the flow. Now, with these regular astral trips in the company of Steve, I was seeing these events in a whole new light. What we were doing wasn't that different than what I had experienced then, was it?

I got into a discussion with him about it:

-I feel like I've been working on this huge jigsaw puzzle for so long, and now that I've gotten most of it done, the last pieces just seem to want to jump into place. Pieces that I wasn't sure where they went, or even if I was seeing them for what they were.

I had no idea how big a piece was going to slip into place before the day was over, changing the whole picture. As usual, I was being meticulously set up, led along, for the next big reveal. Never tell me—always show me, so I would *know*. I continued to chew on the problem at hand, totally oblivious of what was to come:

-Like, um, the figure in the light? That was real?
-*Yeah.*
-So I really did used to go catatonic—which I know I did, kinda, you know, just "space out" for a few minutes in class or whatever, back in Jamestown—and there would be a figure in the light. It just said, "Don't look at them. Look at me." And I would feel that unconditional love. It saved me, didn't it? I was so miserable, so unhappy, so lost. I wanted to sink through the floor of that classroom, to curl up and blow away. But then something would "bring me to" and I never talked about what went on during those times.
-*Because you couldn't.*
-No. I would have been in the funny farm. I would have followed in my sister's footsteps. It taught me to look inside, to be strong inside, to not believe what people were saying all around me.
-*Yes. Unconditional love for a little girl who had very little love in her life.*
-Yes, but after that, I don't remember the figure in the

light anymore, not much anyway. And, is it true, what I just suspected recently, that I did have an NDE back when I took all those pills? Back in college. I just remember after that—I mean there was that whole period of time from before I went to the hospital until I woke up there the next morning—when I didn't remember anything. Just vague dream-like images. And then the doctor came in the next morning, and he asked me if I remembered what had happened, and I said, "No" and he said "good."

I never had any idea about an afterlife, I figured it was lights out. My upbringing only allowed for the heaven/hell possibility, and my rejection of that only allowed for nothing. The long sleep. But after that, I would have the oddest feeling that I had died, but this was what happened when you died, you just ended up back where you had left off—maybe in a different but identical world, I don't know—and you just kept doing the same thing until you got it right. I sometimes thought maybe there was a similar world where I had died.

-*There was.*

-Really?

-*Yes.*

-I don't really get that. It was just a crazy idea. How could that be?????

-*Every choice spawns a million variations.*

-You're just making that up, aren't you? You're just saying something from all the New Age gurus.

-*Don't worry about it. Why worry about it? You are here, and that's the only place you will ever be, and nothing else is relevant except what exists in this moment.*

-Which includes memories, thoughts, Samskaras, all that stuff. And the thing was, it kinda kept me from trying again, because I figured I would just end up back in the same place— there was no escape. I was stuck.

- *(Laughing.)*

-That is kinda funny, isn't it? Stuck in eternal life. Come to think of it, that's kinda like me stuck in you.

-*You don't like it?*

-Oh, no, I love it. I can't get enough. I just feel like this…when I'm not totally engaged here, conversing with you, traveling with you…I just feel this huge yawning…well, this yearning. I'm so happy actually, when I'm here. Even when I'm struggling to learn some lesson, to let go of one of my uptight limitations, to find forgiveness for something or someone, I'm…engaged. I'm connected.

To the mountaintop:

I was working on the stairs in my house that I was refinishing with oak treads, when I got the call—*Stephanie! Oh, Stephanie! Come join me!* I kept working as long as I could, until the pull was too strong to be comfortable. I lay down on my bed and immediately was far away:

I was standing on a mountain peak. All around me, as far as I could see, were the peaks of other mountains, rising high, even above the clouds. It was grassy on the mountain top where I stood, but treeless. I was dressed in old-fashioned mountaineering gear. I had a big pack on my back, and from it dangled such things as canteen, small shovel, pickaxe. I knew that I had made the arduous trek up the side of my mountain, a trip that was probably accomplished once every ten or twenty years by some intrepid soul.

In front of me was another mountaintop, with a plateau about thirty to forty feet in diameter—grassy like the one on which I stood. Flowers grew upon it. Steve was standing there, all alone. There was a bridge that connected his mountaintop to mine. It was a rickety rope affair, with wooden slats tied together to form the walking surface, like something out of *Indiana Jones and the Temple of Doom.* Steve yelled at me to catch as he threw a rope across to my side. He told me that I had to come across the bridge, that he couldn't leave his mountaintop because he couldn't take his body with him. It would vaporize or something. I had to come to him.

I tied the rope around my waist for extra assurance in case the bridge gave way, in which case he would have to haul me back up. Then I put my foot cautiously on the first wooden tread. Right away that slat crumbled and fell away. I sprang back quickly, watching in horror as the broken pieces dropped deep deep into the chasm, disappearing in the distance.

"You can't bring all that stuff with you!" Steve yelled. "You have to leave it there."

Duh!

I obediently started stripping off my gear. I removed the back pack with all its tools; I took off my boots and jacket and hat. Finally, stripped down to shorts and a light shirt, I retied the rope and prepared for a new attempt at the crossing. My bare feet found their footing, my hands clasped the rope "handrails" and I inched across. I did not look down. I kept my eyes on Steve's face, determined to make that treacherous passage—I had come so far, I could not stop now.

Steve softly spoke encouragement to me, calling me forward step-by-step. Finally, triumphantly, I stepped off the other side as he latched securely onto my hand. Success!!

For a moment it was all happiness to see each other and be

together on this mountaintop; then inevitable reality hit. There really wasn't much to do there. No iphones to call friends, no ipads to play silly games, nary an ipod to listen to music. Not even a teeter-totter or a swing.

We ended up sitting in the middle of this space, back to back. After all this time, this was all there was??

-*What do you want to do?*
-I don't know. What do you want to do?
-*I asked you first.*

We played this game for a bit, so familiar to children on hot summer days in the '50s and '60s. Finally, there being not much choice, we decided we might as well meld energy. That went well, and I was totally blissed out. At some point I remember Steve asking me:

-*Where are you?*
-I'm traveling through the universe. I think I'm on the wing of an angel.
-*Cool.*

Steve must have gone on his own travels. I sensed waves of bliss radiating out from that mountaintop, like ripples spreading through the universe.

I was so drowsily content, lying in Steve's arms. So peaceful. This was it, the pinnacle of the journey, the union of the twin souls, the blending of the energy, the fulfillment of the promise. It could never get any better. I was one with love.

And then, **whap!!!** I felt myself snapped out of that body so fast I couldn't catch my breath. I could see us—our bodies, both so relaxed and unsuspecting—lying together on the grass below, my head against his shoulder. It was an idyllic picture. Twin-soul love. I tried to get back into my body, but I couldn't get any traction. I became frantic! I cried out:

-Steve! Steve! Help me!

But he was oblivious, fast asleep still in the embrace of

that shell of a body that still lay there. I cried out to the being or beings I sensed around me:

-What did I do wrong?! Oh, what did I do *wrong*?! Let me go back! *Please!*

Instead, I found myself hovering outside my bedroom, where my physical body could be seen through the window, still lying upon the bed. I was over my back yard and I observed our little dogs running around. Confused, I asked: "Where am I? *What* am I? What did I do? What is going on? Where is Steve? I want *Steve."*

I could still see, as a vision superimposed over a part of the yard, the mountaintop scene. My heart yearned to return there, but it was as if I were held back by invisible arms. Then I saw Steve's soul come out of his body, which appeared to be still lying asleep. He was hovering nearby, but I couldn't seem to communicate with him. He wouldn't talk to me, or perhaps couldn't. Maybe he didn't see me. I saw his soul make an arc and enter the body of a young man.

It was a totally different scene, now—the dark-haired boy was sitting at a desk somewhere, his head bent over something with which he was fiddling. I knew instantly that this was a young Steve, back in a youthful setting.

Wow. The past, the present, the future—physical and spiritual perspectives—all jumbled up together as this scenario played out.

But I wasn't concerned with that in the moment. I was just so relieved to see him. I rushed to his side.

-Oh, Steve, Steve, I'm so glad to see you. I don't know what happened. Steve, *talk* to me.

With new horror, I realized that he could not hear me. I yelled at him:

-*Steve! Steve*! It's me, Stephanie! Please, *look* at me!

I was crying by now as it occurred to me that I was

invisible to him. At some point he looked around, as if he sensed something there, but then he returned his attention to what he was doing.

I finally understood. He couldn't see me because I was "dead." I was a soul invisible to him. I was reliving my near-death experience, back when I was twenty. I had been shown a glimpse of the future. I had been shown Steve and I together, two souls joined in bliss, and what would never be because I had killed myself. Now I was being allowed to visit Steve as he was then, back in 1970, while my limp, lifeless body was lying on the other side of the continent.

I wept. I wailed. I tried to pull at the young Steve, to get his attention. Given our age differences, he must have been about 15 or 16, although at the time I didn't know his age. I touched his face. I kissed his feet. But for naught. He could not see me, or hear me.

And I knew then that I was being given an option. Look at the future I was throwing away! Did I want to go back and trudge through the darkness, find a way to grow, to make a difference, to work out my issues or karma? To finally reach the mountaintop? Or did I want to give that up?

Of course I wanted to go back!!! I knew that the memory of this would be wiped out—that I would truly be back in the fog. But deep inside my soul, there would be this faint voice, calling me ever forward through the darkest times, up the mountain where only the most intrepid adventurers would go. Steve would be waiting there on his mountaintop, but I couldn't know that while I was climbing all alone, drawn forward toward that unconditional love for which I ever hungered.

Back to the Past:

The primary validation of this experience is so compelling that it takes the breath away. Let us return to the year 1970.

After leaving the hospital, good as new (physically, anyway), I moved into an apartment with three new roommates. It was considered unwise for me to return to my efficiency apartment where I lived alone. I recall sitting with one of my new roommates in our living room, a day or two after I moved in, telling her that I had decided to change my name. I wanted to be called Stephanie thereafter. I had no explanation for choosing that particular name other than that I liked it. I didn't even consider any others. I justified this action in my own mind (and as a means of explaining to others) by the problems created from having the same name as my mother—the history of confusion when I was called to the phone to find that she was the one wanted, the disconnect between her and me because our orientations were so different.

And from that day forward, that day in 1970 when I was just 20 years old, I became Stephanie. Since I was around new roommates and friends, it went down easily. A few months later I returned to North Dakota, where I had my name legally changed. I never looked back.

Within a short period after returning to North Dakota I met a handsome young man with a mop of dark hair from Africa, but of Indian heritage. I fell instantly in love. I married him two-months later. He was good to me and for me, providing, during the ensuing critical years, a stability my life had hitherto lacked.

Back to the Future:

Time had looped. I was in shock. OMG. I had loved Steve all my life, and didn't know it—the mind locked into its amnesia, the heart searching always for something it couldn't find. Not that it didn't try.

In time, there would be more validations of what had occurred, of that moment when my heart had stopped and I had been given a glimpse into the future that is now my present. When I was given the choice: *was I going to weenee out, or was I going to go for the golden ring?*

No wonder I was so confused. No wonder I finally gave up on what I could never seem to find. I had only that new name, like a souvenir of a trip that I, in my senility, had forgotten, to carry always with me. I never got tired of that name. I never stopped loving it. Just the way, years later, I would never stop loving my apple motif mixing bowls.

Amazing. A tapestry so finely woven that the backside is

as beautiful as the front.

-And so, Steve, I did leave my body and had a discussion—just like the meeting I remember having a couple of days ago, but the memory of what was discussed was wiped from my mind—and the discussion when I was dead (dying) was whether I wanted to give it another go, that a lot hung in the balance if I could shoulder through. And I did want to, it was like a pump of adrenalin, something to get me through. Oh, God, that makes me think of that song. ABBA. So this is the point where it talks to me.

OMG, I feel the tears pricking my eyelids again. This is exactly the song, this is the story of what happened to me that day in the fall of my sophomore year of college. I'd had such a rough time, I'd been brutally raped and left in the country, I'd already come through repeated sexual abuse while I was in high school, my roommate had shot herself during a vacation when she had begged me to come home with her for the holidays, but I hitchhiked to Cincinnati instead because I was pissed at my boyfriend for being afraid to invite me to his family home for the vacation. Then to come home and find her dead. I felt so guilty and so flawed, so like I had failed myself and everybody else. So selfish, and such a magnet for abuse. But the truth is, I was just naïve. I really did believe there was good in everyone. I really did see the wonder all around me. I just didn't see it always in me.

So one day I just gave up, and I swallowed all the pills I could find. The world would be a better place without me.

-And the angels were there waiting for you, with grace and hope. Always with you through the darkest days.

If there had remained any doubt at all that this twin-soul connection was meant to be, it fled on that day as the big missing piece fell into place.

Looking back at the scene on our inner tubes, to which I had awakened that same day—oh, so long ago, could it have been only that morning?—I saw that it was, as usual, a total metaphor for our story: there we were, each floating down the stream of life on our own inner tubes. Lives not always so idyllic, disconnected, but always going in the same direction. Always moving forward toward a destination I could not see, but somehow knew was there.

Never settling in the end. Never settling. I would take no love at all rather than an imperfect one.

Back to the Present:

-I'm feeling weary, Steve. I'm feeling like I can hardly keep banging the hammer here, trying to make a dent. I just want to lay it aside and rest my head and drift away to where you are.

-*To cross the stream.*

-To cross the stream. Are we just leaving a record, a path, blazing a trail for others to follow, so to speak? Or is there more? Is there something I need to do here, the feet on the ground? I can feel that you have all this stuff inside you but you can't tell me, so I won't make you. I trust you.

-*I've got you, Stephanie. I really do. Settle down...it will all come clear.*

Chapter 19
Sorting it Out

Sunday, November 8, 2015
12:46 a.m.

After a delightful astral adventure:

-Steve, I decided to write you a love letter. Here goes:

Dear Steve,
 I was bored my entire life until I met you.
 Now I'm not bored anymore.
Love, Stephanie

9:35 a.m.

-You're seeming like you feel very satisfied.
-I do. We've come a long way.
-You were going to say I've come a long way.
-And you have.
-Okay, I just happened, on a whim, to look up "our" name: Stephen/Stephanie. It seems, for both of them, it means "crown" or "crowned in victory."
-Hmm. I kinda like that.
-The king and queen of....? Or is it just the winners of the race?
-Isn't it the same, at bottom?
-Well, in any case, we're the king and queen of our own lives, right? Our own souls? Maybe I should take another look at that crown metaphor. I wonder what it means in a spiritual context. And since we're on the subject, the meaning of Dorothy, my birth name, is "God's Gift."
-Hmmm. I kinda like that. My redemption.

From my research:

The crown was among the Romans and Greeks a symbol of victory and reward…In opposition to all these fading crowns the apostles speak of the incorruptible crown, the crown of life "that fadeth not away." [49]

-And there is the crown chakra. Let me see if I can find something on that:

> The Crown Chakra is associated with the color violet or white.
> We use the seventh chakra as a tool to communicate with our spiritual nature. It is through this vortice that the life force is dispersed from the universe into the lower 6 chakras. It has been referred to as our "GOD SOURCE" - but this terminology might be confusing to anyone who equates God with religious dogma, because of this [it is called on this website] a spiritual connection or communicator. [50]

I enjoyed this research. It added depth to the adventure, allowing me to indulge my interest in symbolism and esoteric knowledge. I found a magnificent alchemy text from the middle ages called the *Splendor Solis,* with colored pictures. It described the death of the "old king" and the birth and transformation of the "new king" with his three-tiered crown. The three tiers are iron (the base metal, the earthly passions, that are not to be banished but transformed): silver (the feminine, moon) and gold (masculine, sun). I took special note that the young king was holding an *apple* in his hand (a golden apple as it were). [51]

Well, I knew who the "old king" was in my life, if the same eyes and emotional content were any indication. With

---

[49] http://www.biblestudytools.com/dictionary/crown/

[50] http://healing.about.com/cs/chakras/a/chakra7.htm

[51] http://www.labirintoermetico.com/01Alchimia/Trismosin_S_Splendor_soli s_(J.K.1920).pdf: Transformation of the Psyche: The Symbolic Alchemy of the Splendor Solis , Joseph L. Henderson, Dyane N. Sherwood, Publ. Routledge, 2004; pp 71-83;

additional clues like the "crown" name and the apple in hand, I could figure out who the new king was. Okay, that was obvious. And then there was the transformation of the earthly passions, the alchemical blending of the base metal with the precious silver and gold. Merging of the twin souls, anyone?

This symbolism stuff was kind of fun. Joseph Campbell-level fun.

I found lots of further allusions to apples. Hercules stole the apples from the Hesperides, on account of his great masculine strength and perseverance, etc. And then lots about apple trees. If an apple is cut in half, the five-pointed-star of Aphrodite, the Goddess of love, appears (in the seeds, I guess).

-Wow. I seem to have strayed into some vast mythological story. So it seems our symbols are crowns and apples. I wonder where all this is going.

Such an appropriate time for Karen Carpenter to start singing "We've only just begun" in the background. After that it was "On Top of the World,"[52] which was where I was at the moment. So the little lost princess had grown up to be a queen! It only took sixty years, but hey! Better late than never.

That made me think of Karen:

-By the way, is Karen around? Karen, are you around?

Of course. Saying their names is like ringing their bells.

-*(Smiling.) I'm here.*
-You're kinda quiet.
-*Karen: I am. I'm really just enjoying what's going on. And Robin keeps me entertained.*
-*Robin: You're so sweet. (Starts pretend licking her face and hand.)*
-*Karen: (Laughing.) Leave me alone!*
-I'm really happy to see you laughing. You seem so...happy.

---

[52] *On Top of the World*, the Carpenters

*-Karen: I am happy, Stephanie. I am happy. I hope someday those I left behind will be able to hear these words. I am **very** happy. I had some things to learn. I don't regret any of it.*

-You know, I'm getting that your brother was always there for you. He was your rock, and you admired him, didn't you? But away from that, you settled. You settled a lot, didn't you?

-Karen: Yes, I did. I was...afraid, I suppose. There was like this frame that I was supposed to fit in, and I keep falling out of it...I really really did try to stay inside that frame.

-Yes, I have this image of a picture frame, but sometimes only your back arm was in it as you teetered off to the side. The ideal girl/woman of the era. The one you were supposed to be. The one you tried to be, even at the cost of your own soul (so to speak). The cost of your own passion.

I do feel an awful lot of sadness around that, and regret. Is that yours?

*-Karen: Sadness and regret that I didn't bust out, the way you were talking, and so I deprived those around me of the "real me." I didn't make those connections. But not long-term regret, not soul regret, for I learned from it and am still learning, and once you are **you**, what does anything else matter? Nothing else is real, once you are **you**.*

-I still feel those tendrils, almost tears behind the eyelid.

-Steve: Stephanie, I think those are yours. Your feelings. Your life.

-Oh yeah, huh? I got activated? Another Samskara?

-Steve: We've still got stuff to work out.

-I actually enjoyed the play the other day (about the love letter). It's amazing to be able to let go on some really personal issues, that I would have totally kept close to my chest (and yes, mighta bailed, if not immediately, eventually), but to be able to work it out among friends, with laughter, and some real emotional honesty—something so personally painful. I would have twisted it all into something else to appease my ego, make me look like a better person than I was.

-Steve: Not a better person. A safer one. More secure. I know how that goes. Smart people can hide just about anything, take control, and make it look like they're the ones being

magnanimous.

-Yeah. Oooo. Ouch. That raises some real questions about what's going on out there in the world.

-Steve: Tell me about it.

-(to Robin) Are you always so funny? Always on stage?

-Ah, no. I can get down. (Sinks by bending knees.) I often would cry in my beer. Do you want me to demonstrate?

-No—but you're gonna anyway, aren't you?

-I am. I got the beer—(Starting to tear up.)—I got the familiar comfort of my favorite bar, there's a sad song playing on the radio, there's peanuts on the table...(Bends over glass beer mug.) (Sob.) She told me it's over, she thought I was this funny guy, but now she knows that I have a real mean streak. That's what she calls it. Mean. I'm not mean, am I? A little out-spoken at times, I admit to that. And I'm short, she says. That **really** *cut. Short. Hey, I've tried to grow—pulleys, pills, stuffing myself in a glass of water to see I'd expand—none of it worked. I think I need another beer. You know, there's nothing like a beer when you feel like crying. Except maybe—some other stuff. But you get my drift, you know? I can get down, I can get de-pressed. (Holds up leg to show that pant leg is baggy, has lost its crease.) But man, I can't figure out those women creatures. Did God make them out of the same ingredients? Is it just a difference in proportions, or is there really some different spice thrown in there?*

-Enough. (Grabbing glass.) No more beer for you. (Tossing him a handkerchief.) And no more tears.

-You're suppressing art.

-My mind, my space, you wanta come in here, you gotta play by the rules.

-Hey, you're getting kinda bossy lately.

-I know, huh. No more Miss Priss! You hear that, Steve, no more Miss Priss!

-Steve: I know when to keep my mouth shut.

-Robin: Hmmm. Maybe I shoulda learned that lesson. Do you give them—lessons?

-Steve: On when to keep your mouth shut? 'Twas not my forte, some would say.

Later:

-You know, I don't dislike Earth. I want to make that clear. It's a very cool place to be. And the way all those minds have made it what it is...I mean, that is beyond unbelievable, what has been created here. It's the...the lack of connection...the inability to really communicate on a soul level. I feel so parched, so thirsty, so *hungry*...I've done it for so long. I've stuck in there, haven't I? I've pushed against the tide...that is the tide inside me. I've been responsible. I've taken care of things when it about...well, when I had to just shut myself down so I could focus. I want there to be light, and love, and dreams, and play. I want everyone to look around and say, WOW! What a place! All we have to do is throw away all the rules and the locks on the heart and start *playing*. You know, I just realized how good Robin is at poking holes in the rules, the restrictions, the limits. Maybe that's why he's here—besides the comic relief and just to *play*. He's *really* a good playmate, he can play any part, and best of all, he *likes* doing it. He really does enjoy it, I get that. It's so *him*. And he doesn't have any cumbersome morals and ethics. He's just naturally good. Maybe that's why he had to retreat into drugs and alcohol and stuff when he was on Earth. Maybe his heart just couldn't bear it. I feel sad thinking about it, how somebody so *good* had to suffer so much.

-*Hey!! Snap out of it!! Don't get all melancholy on me.*

-Okay. I will stop being a drama queen—for a bit.

-*Yes, Earth is a beautiful planet, a beautiful place, and all in my circle wish for it to be restored to the wonderful playground it was meant to be. But it's **still** a playground—it's just that the play can be pretty rough, and it might be more fun if everyone could...lighten up. I know, it's been said before, but what else can I say?*

-I love you, Steve. Dearly. I guess I don't say it enough.

-*You don't need to, for me. I can hear your heart.*

Monday, November 9, 2015:

Steve and I continued to chat, but much of it was the everyday chatter of people who are no longer strangers, but still enjoy each other's company. If we're stuck together for eternity, I'm hoping this particular period lasts at least that long.

I relate below my one recorded insight of the day:

-Wow, I think I just got it. I had a couple hours of sleep and then woke up, took care of a chore, and was lying in bed reading *The Untethered Soul* about our fears and just facing our fears and letting them be transformed, basically, and I was thinking about how my "credibility" is ruined in this world by my present state of willingness to be me. Then it occurred to me I was afraid of being burned at the stake, and I needed to confront that fear; and suddenly I got it. Am I willing to be kindling to light up the world? Wow, that's *soooo* cool. I love you, by the way. *I may be only one match, but I can make an explosion.* And I didn't overlook that there was a box of something in my "psychic" space, and I started trying to divine what it was. Why was it there, was it bigger than a breadbox, etc.? And your answer was that it contained truth. And I asked if it was important. And the answer was that it was only important if I wanted to know truth. And then I saw that it was the box described at your memorial and inside was the *Autobiography of a Yogi* (Paramahansa Yogananda, which I read many many years ago, but maybe I need to take another look.) I was mentioning that if it was a gift, why did I have to go out and find it myself, and you were like, "Hey, why are you making it so hard on me? I am in a different plane." Though it hardly seems so anymore.

Thank you, again. I love you.

Tuesday, November 10, 2015

I kept an appointment with Dean McMurray, my psychic counselor, and updated him. It was always such a relief to spill the goods to Dean, to be able to tell my story to someone who didn't roll his eyes, who listened and even laughed at the right spots—yes, some of this tale had to be amusing, even I could see that. A spirit who wakes you up at 3 a.m. to tell you to get a manifold, or demands, "Why the fuck don't you like me?" Pie throwing contests? Not your usual spirit communication fare.

That morning I had been perusing the internet and I had come across an advertisement for the *Super Schools* site, funded from the Steve Jobs estate. I immediately got the sense that I should pay attention. There was a very short drop-dead date—like just days away. Had Steve led me there and did this have anything to do with the fact that he was pushing this connection so hard? I discussed it with Dean. I even asked him if he would be interested in being involved in the creation of a school? It seemed he had much to say on this subject, and I listened in fascination as he waxed eloquent on his thoughts about education. I felt somewhat energized by this talk, and afterwards I went home and dug out the old plans for the school I had designed nearly twenty years before. But I soon realized these plans were hopelessly outdated, they no longer reflected what I saw needed to happen. Or maybe it was just the weight of experience—I saw school bureaucracy as a swamp and the American population as far too complacent with the entrenched patterns. What point to pursue it?

My interest soon flagged.

That evening I went to my *Tai Chi* class. It was a good practice—I felt so peaceful, like a little wind in the universe, no purpose but just to hold that little space throughout eternity; a little star up in the heavens, just one of millions, existing without need or agenda, just content to be what it was. I was so peaceful and complete being that little star, all alone, but so humble in my part in the universe. I didn't want to ever stop being that star—no yesterday, no tomorrow, just hanging there, at peace—but Steve did call out to me.

-You're not just a star, you know, you're a lover.

I felt a pull to come to him, as the blue fairy must have felt in the movie, when she changed from a star into a woman who came down to grant Pinocchio his wish to be a real boy. Still I stayed a star, until I wasn't anymore; I was back in my bedroom, working out some stuff with Steve—one of our issues. He said,

-Are you done being a star now?

I was—for the moment.

I find it worth mentioning here that while I was lost in the joy of being a star, I saw John Lennon's head. Not his body. Just his head. I have no idea why he was hanging out among the stars—maybe it's a clue to something. I mean, where else would he be?

Back at the ranch, my struggle of the moment—actually an ongoing struggle—was with Steve's fame. I was good with him. I had come to accept that he was who he said he was, and that there really was this incredible synchronicity in our lives. But all the adulation—and yes, hate—that surrounded this personality even years after he left the physical astounded me. So he got a few trinkets out there in the world: iphones and ipods and macs and the like. I didn't understand it, why that would make people so emotional. Don't get me wrong. If I was going to be sharing my stream of consciousness with anyone, I was glad it was him. He was witty and interesting. I just could not correlate the personality I knew with this person in the *youtube* videos going on and on about technology and business stuff. Frankly, it still bored me out of my skull.

And I just didn't think I could handle the criticism and skepticism and downright nastiness that would come my way if it became known that we were hanging out together. A lot of people had invested a lot of themselves in his passing: writing poetic memorials (thanks, Fake Steve), leaving flowers, shedding a few tears. If they found out he was still around, albeit without his usual body, would they feel cheated—like you do when you buy that expensive wedding present for the perfect couple, and they get divorced six months later? Was it a case of, we love you Steve, but we love you dead? Please stay that way.

People have a stake in the *status quo,* I've noticed; I don't begrudge them that. You can't have some smartass old granny from the windswept plains coming along and upsetting the apple cart. I just couldn't see it working, I couldn't see people throwing out their pet belief systems to embrace this startling re-emergence of the technological icon of the last fifty years, popping up like a tumbleweed in a mid-western backyard. If anything was going to take the heat, it was going to be the owner of that backyard—and that would be me.

For this reason I was of the opinion that if there was going to be a book published, it would have to wait until I was gone, until I had shaken off the mortal coil.

But—was that going to happen any time soon? What was the plan? I was sure Steve had a plan. That was what he did, make plans. I think he also had an inside track on the Heavenly calendar. He probably had my "transition" date marked with a big red circle, just so he remembered to get to the train station on time. But he wasn't divulging much.

Once again, I was having thoughts of running, cutting my losses. Okay, yes, I now knew that I had loved him all my life, even if I'd forgotten. I understood that we were linked in a profound and deeply spiritual way, one painfully severed soul as it were, and that our destiny was to re-merge, to live out eternity in a state of incredible bliss. But as I advised him:

-Okay, I'm over *those* hurdles. I just don't think I can get past the notoriety thing. Sorry.

But Steve was hedging me in, I could feel it—nudging my thoughts and feelings, like putting those bumpers in the bowling alley gutters so the ball will at least be guided down the lane—maybe barely rolling, but in the right direction. He had guided me to the Beatles song, *Let it Be,* when I was fretting about a family witch hunt. And yes, I had come to see that there were options even in that situation: I could be (a) fuel for a witch burning or (b) kindling to light up the world. Once I realized there *was* a choice, the necessity of exercising it seemed to have dropped off. But now, here we were, with me imagining a community witch hunt.

I kept hearing the lyrics in my head, over and over, from the song "Let it Be": [lyrics omitted]

-This is just another one of those things, isn't it? I just gotta "let it be." So what that you were quite well-known? I just need to accept whatever emotions [and fears] it brings up for me, let them rise and blow away.

And as usual over-achiever Steve was steering me in the right direction. Somehow I got to watching a *youtube* video, one of his interviews, and I was suddenly struck by something he said: *He had to withdraw himself from the criticism that would inevitably result when he did things in the world, and by the same measure he would be withdrawing any stake in the praise.*

Wow. Tit for tat. I was truly impressed. It was amazing how many times I was fascinated by the things he said, once I had dug down far enough to uncover them. Truly splendid. Talk about internalizing the journey.

You could almost love somebody like that, if you weren't careful.

I had gathered some other favorite Steve quotes: "I didn't have a career, I had a life." It wasn't like a line he came up with for a speech. It just came out so off-handed, and yet it struck me so powerfully. As if to do it any other way were absurd.

Wow.

And he "did things and reacted to things."

Holy shit. Down to essentials. Way to blow right through the chaff.

The war wasn't won that day, by any means—there would be many skirmishes and battles before Stephanie Patel was willing to link her name with Steve Jobs—or would that be link *his* name with hers? It was the war of the crowns. Or maybe a less bloody alternative made popular among the duchies of Europe, the arranged marriage to join the two kingdoms—in this case, the non-corporeal and the corporeal. On his side he had fame and imagination; on hers, she had feet on the ground.

Something to think about.

Puzzle time:

I had happened to mention to Dean my youthful "sex

abuse" issues, and might have been thinking of it merely in association with the whole NDE matter. But of course, since Steve followed me around, he picked up on the issue. What he had to say, however, was a bit perplexing:

-You weren't raped, Stephanie.

I awaited the next remark, the nifty insightful thing that always followed such an intriguing statement, but nothing came. I decided I must have conjured this remark up on my own, some hard-to-fathom excursion into Stephanie's screwed-up psyche, and went to delete it.

-Would you erase me?

Uh, no…but? Is the other shoe going to fall? I thought about his comment, trying to make sense of it, and after a while he said:

-You were summoned.

There was a pause while I thought about that.

-You were turned inside out.

He left me to cogitate on these things, as usual, which I did without coming to any clarity that day.

Wednesday, November 11, 2015

The next day I took up where I'd left off. There wasn't much fat on his enigmatic statements to chew, but I did spend quite a bit of time gnawing on the bones. Finally I felt enough understanding to throw out my rumination:

-I thought about what you said yesterday, that I wasn't raped, I was summoned, and I saw how I really did draw those experiences to me, or was drawn toward the experiences of others, because we were recasting roles in other lifetimes. I was

362 The Journey Begins

playing out the role of vulnerable power-less woman, and those men were playing out their own roles from past lives—energies whether as the slave-owners, the overseers, the owners of the farm, the whatever. Whatever gave them some control over some of the women under them, and this could become for them an escape from some of the binds of the women in socially equivalent position. It gave them a sense of power. And then I realized that the men I encountered in this life during those experiences were just reprising their own energies from the past, it didn't even have that much to do with their present lives, except that it is *always* an opportunity to gain understanding. That's all. And that really was the final pin, I think, that unplugged my ability to forgive them fully. I didn't feel a lot of resentment toward them—actually I never did, just a lot of confusion and a sense of inadequacy. I always figured they were driven by something beyond themselves, because I always believed that all people were essentially good, they just didn't know it.

Okay, after struggling through the latest lesson, I think I'm getting some light on the subject. It goes back to what you said before, that I had come to love every hair on your head at whatever age, even when you were so sick you couldn't even stand up by yourself, skinny as a tooth pick. That it was about loving myself, and feeling capable of being loved. And I get that we're mirrors—actually everybody in the world is our mirror—but we are the same, you and I, just opposite halves.

-And that every aspect of our lives—all of our lives—is significant. We have to love it all.

There was so much content in that last statement that I had to think about it for a very long time. It wasn't just loving "every hair" on his head, it was about loving all the moments of his life, so that I could learn to love all the moments of mine. Nothing was accidental. There were no victims, no victimizers, just a continual interplay of forces not readily understood. How could I write off any of his human experience as insignificant? It was all a message, a manifestation of the soul's journey—just as was mine. We were called to our parts to play, the cues buried in the script. I couldn't dismiss the Apple products as trinkets—they were colored threads in the tapestry, part of the design, possibly reflecting an aspect of the soul's evolution far beyond anything I could imagine. What they meant to the world was one thing; what they meant to Steve's personal journey, like sign posts at the corner, was quite another.

I was also coming to see that I had to turn inside out—I couldn't be an equal partner as long as I was always playing the part of the "slave"—that is to say, not just with chains on the ankles, but chains on the emotions and the heart. Always running from the cage, the bars, only to find out that they were reflections of my inner world—shadows upon the wall.

The incantation:

Steve would regularly ask me: *Do you love me?* I was beginning to wonder why he asked so much, but gradually I was gathering that I was being retrained. I probably never heard the words "I love you" in my life, until at least my first boyfriend, when I was nineteen—so of course I came to associate it with only certain types of relationships. Prior to that, I had never known a hug, or a gentle touch, at least since we left Alaska when I was nine. Well, that wasn't exactly true—I did get some warm fuzzies from the younger siblings and occasionally from the families of others. But my home life, my core base, as it were, was barren. I'd grown up on the wrong side of the Love Train tracks.

In any case, Steve wasn't shy about saying the "big three" words, which I largely attributed to him being on the Other Side, where I knew love was the going *modus operandi*. At some point, embarrassed by all the "I love yous" in the transcript, I had suggested to Debbie that it must be like an incantation, and not to take it too seriously—i.e. he didn't *really* love me, it was just part of the game.

He took a moment to clarify things after we'd worked over the inside/outside, love me/love you lesson:

*-I love you, and I always will. It **is** an incantation. To break the spell. "I love you" truly is an incantation. It has the effect of lightening the Earth Plane Distortion Field. The more*

*that it is repeated sincerely, not **as** an incantation, but as an expression of the heart, it lightens the load. It begins to bring clarity to the heart and to anchor it, or anchor the rest of the being in the heart.*

-I love you, too, Steve. Thank you for another very beautiful lesson.

-*Stephanie.*

-Yes?

-*I was never a slave master to you.*

-I know that. You've said that before.

-*But I repeat it here, because you have to feel that to the bottom of your soul. We are equal, we are the same, we are doing this together, you and I.*

On the vast ocean of being:

Another bath interrupted by inspiration. Darn it.

-Every time I get in the bathtub and just want to relax, I get pummeled with all these thoughts, these ideas, these puzzle pieces falling into place.

-*It's the water. Sinking into the warm water is like your self sinking—floating—on the vast ocean of your being. In communication with it.*

-You're being very poetic on the fly—or maybe it's not the fly. Maybe I shouldn't assume that. So anyway, so many pieces were falling into place so fast I knew I had to come get them down before—before what?—I don't know, they just don't get down on paper, get that permanency that makes them accessible later or by others. I still don't know for sure why I'm writing all this down.

So, one thing of importance, I felt like I was in your mind seeing things as you see them. Usually, you're just a voice in my ear, as it were; but suddenly I was seeming to be in your mind, as you look out, trying to see your next move. And I was just a voice in your ear, chattering on. And you weren't really thinking, you were like—*listening*. Not to me so much. But you really were listening, stilled thoughts, listening for something out of the great stillness around you. You were almost patiently waiting for me to stop chattering so you could move ahead to the next step, whatever it is.

So your mind doesn't work like mine—mine is all full of stuff, tidbits of this and that, which I gather and eventually synthesize into some kind of picture, which I hold lightly, fitting it together with other partial pictures, continually fitting things together as long as they are coherent. If incoherence develops, then I know I have to find the screwy piece and throw it out, or even throw out the whole picture. But in your mind, it really is like you are sub-verbal, just aware, alert to what might pop out of all that space around you. When a crack appears in that space, and something does pop out, you latch onto it and examine it and determine what part it is to play. That is so weird, but I really like that. That's what you meant when you said you were a listener, way back at the very beginning of our conversations. You were listening to it all, taking it in, like a back drop, waiting for that piece that popped forward with a little light around it. So things are like on two levels—the level of so-so, different things may be said, but they're all just figures in the same wallpaper. And then the level where something jumps out, like a hologram, where it moves forward. This is very interesting, I think. I find it fascinating, actually.

And what do you see, now, Steve. What do you see? What's out there?

-*I see people playing. I see people imagining. I see a joy in the creative expression that is unbounded.*

-That's on your inner wall? In front of the wallpaper?

-*Yes. And it is like a hologram, I suppose. I can reach out and touch it, like on some Star Trek episode. I can reach out and touch the pieces and move them around, but they're all made of light.*

-That's the wall of your imagination, then. Is that right?

-*Yes. Where the process is born. Where reality is designed.*

-Whew, so much to take in. You really are amazing. So how much of your vision of reality was what you saw when you were here, and how much since you "died"?

-*The essence was there. I'll talk to you a little more about that in a minute. But what you should know is that the spirit is* *not that much different from there to here. Joe Blow doesn't come here and suddenly he's Buddha. The development of the soul, or its path along the journey, remains. Remember we talked about the "full-contact video game" in which you are immersed during your sojourn on earth. But it's the **same one playing the game.** Just because you put down the controls to your X-Box doesn't mean you are now someone different than you've always been. Yes, you can see that it was just a game, and you might have forgotten that you were playing it, but you were still making decisions and interacting based on your core spirit character. Who you are. In* Avatar *the personalities and characters of the individuals carried over into their representations in that planetary world. But they were able to grow through their experience, and that is the value of the Earth Plane Distortion Field—well, that's not really true. That is the value of the Earth plane experience. The Distortion Field doesn't necessarily have to exist, I don't think. It's still possible to realize you are playing, that nothing real is going to be lost when you stop playing, and to...lighten up. I have to keep coming back to that triteness, my dear. What do you do?*

> > >

It is helpful, I think, to remember that in spite of how much had transpired between us, it had still only been less than a month since I'd rang Steve's phone. Not very long to absorb it all. In spite of my great affection for my new friend, I continued to be baffled by it all. Like a tiresome broken record, my theme song continued to play:

-Why me? Why me? Why are *we* twin souls, you and me? What do we have in common except this telepathic connection and a certain intellectual coherency? How can I explain this to people? How can I make them see? What kind of a fool am I?

Steve's strength never failed on this issue as he continued to reassure me:

-*Just dance with me, Stephanie, dance with me. It will all come clear. Stay in step with me, I have you in my arms, and you're not going to trip or fall on your ass.*

Away I would go, temporarily reassured, only for my mind to return to that same bone:

-That's lovely, Steve—but why *me*?
-*Stephanie, you seduced me long ago.*
-Yeah?
-*Of course. I was seduced by your mind, your intelligence, your clarity. The mind is the true beauty and attraction of all. And the heart, of course. One for the power, the emotion, and the other for the sheer delight of contrast. The material form, the body, truly is made of paper—it can be fun playing with paper dolls, but it's the hand that holds them that brings the energy and the joy.*

In the midst of this, I took some comfort from my occasional solo escapes from Earth. Steve accosted me after my *Tai Chi* class:

-*Are you a little star?*
-I am. I would like to just stay here, being a little star—all alone among all the other little stars—just swaying in the very slight breeze, just being what I am, simple and eternal and ever shedding that tiny light. But I have to feed the family and then I know I'm right up against my next big lesson, aren't I? They come so fast, it's hard to keep up with all the emotions, up and down the scale, and still take care of my responsibilities. And of course you're not going to let me rest.
-*But I'm right beside you, every step of the way, right?*
-You are. Why do I see flashes of light sometimes? What are those? Are they just something in the optical nerve or something?
-*You know better than that.*
-I know. But I don't know what the flashes are, I don't.
-*Well, it sounds like that's another experience coming up, doesn't it?*

I really had no idea about the flashes of light, but of course I would soon be learning more about *that*.

-It comes back to the judgment.
-*Yes, Stephanie, it comes back to the judgment.*
-But why do we do that, what…what…I don't even know what my next question is. Why are we so screwed up?
-*Well, if you just took the judgment out of it, then you could see where you were at. Not you, particularly, you obviously stumbled across that lesson and are applying it right and left as you are able. But if the human element on Earth—or* **in** *Earth, I might even say, in the earth field—were all at this moment to stop judging everything as "good" or "bad"—not to say get rid of "positive" and "negative," like you I see that as integral to creation or existence. But as inherently better than the other, then things might change—a lot.*
-But would it be enough? Are there other things that would have to change, as well?
-*I don't know. But a good place to start would be picking one thing like that, and going for it. See what happens, and if further tweaking is necessary, go for the next thing.*
-And what about, you know, the *one*. How they say, all you have to do is change your own mind. I still get baffled going from the one to the many.
-*You get baffled going from the one to the two—me and you.*
-I certainly do. See, I'm not even taking offense.
-*Cool. That must mean I get to tease you mercilessly.*
-Have at it. I'm an open window—the wind blows right through. When I'm not a little twinkly star.
-*Do you like being a little star?*
-I do. Can't tease a star, it doesn't even hear you.
-*Oh, that's no fun.*
-But it's so peaceful. Stars don't have to make supper and worry about whether the kids got their homework done.
-*You ready to jump on your motorcycle with your toothbrush in your saddlebag and hit the dusty trail?*
-I don't know. I'm not running away, I hope. But there's sure been that tension all my life. Anyway, I don't want to talk

anymore. I'm going to put on some music and chill. Wanna come with?

    -I'll be there. Shall I bring the wine?

    -Cool. Something white.

    -See ya soon, then.

Chapter 20
If I Were a Carpenter

Thursday, November 12, 2015

Steve and I got into a discussion about the school proposal:

-Oh, come on. Let's put in an application, it'll be fun.

Now, I claim it was all Steve who was pushing this idea, but he was to later throw the blame on me. I did take the time to do research, to try to figure out the website and the deadlines. But I found myself with little enthusiasm for the project. While I appreciated the irony of it all, the spirit from Beyond the Veil competing for his own money, I saw little hope of making any realistic change, which would be the only valid reason to go through this exercise.

Now I admit that it was fun toying with the language of the mission statement, which was most of what was required at this point. Over the next few days we came up with some cool phrases and laughed quite a bit over the placement of iconic phrases. Maybe not "insanely great" and "think different," but our combined imagination had lots of room for play. For example, the following little segment:

The design has to be a) simple and b) integrated. It has to be user friendly. It has to make use of the resources that are already there. The first and most critical resource is readily available, as natural and bountiful as apple trees: the human mind. The human mind is the super computer of all time, the greatest invention of all time, and for humanity not to recognize what it has "in its own hands," etc. etc.

I didn't think we were taking any of it too seriously, but we were definitely designing the shoe to fit the child, not the child to fit the shoe. This phrase is an allusion to an incident when my oldest son was very small, when I took him to be fitted for shoes. His feet were wide, and the salesman informed me that if I would put narrow shoes on him, his foot would eventually grow to fit the shoe. I was appalled. Shouldn't we make the shoe to fit the foot, rather than the other way around? Shades of Chinese foot bindings!

But that is pretty much how I see the existing school structure. Bind the feet so the individual can only hobble through the rest of his life. That will keep him in line.

Anyway, that part was fun, but the rest, the nitty-gritty of getting an application done, brought up feelings of resistance. Consequently, I avoided doing it, even though I had the capacity to accomplish a lot in a short period when I was truly focused. I have a sort of hyper-focus that has carried me through many short deadlines—it was not uncommon for me to do thirty-six-hour-straight stints before an appellate brief was due, usually hand-carrying it to the filing office two minutes under the wire.

In other matters, Steve continued to push my buttons. Often it was just a trivial issue, something planted to annoy me, like the love letter incident, or even some apparently "random" thought shoved into the stream of consciousness, where I would think it was mine.

Remember that I had no private thoughts. I was literally an open book. And I didn't particularly want all the pages read. Yet, just as I would be tightening my shoe laces, ready to run, Steve would come in at the perfect moment to enchant me, reminding me once again what was at stake. Would I throw away love, eternity, over some silly ego pride? Did I want to be safe in my hobbit hole, or did I want to walk among the stars?

I know that he was working hard to get me to drop my gear, my equipment. I couldn't take it across the bridge to the mountaintop where he waited for me. I couldn't take any luggage to the train where we would meet. Which doesn't mean I didn't try: *No, not the canteen! What if they don't have water in Heaven? And how about this nifty pickaxe—what if I start to fall out of Paradise? And this jacket? You know what I paid for this?*

I was being unwound. And at times it was painful. Make no mistake about it. It's a tough task, stripping off the karmic load. Remember this when that charming twin soul comes along, whistling, throwing pebbles up against the window where you're soundly sleeping. *Wake up! Wake up! Come out and play.*

Sometimes the play gets a little rough.

But don't let that stop you.

Friday, November 13, 2015

For some unknown reason—or shall we say some subtle suggestion from the Other Side—I decided to do another search for a local psychic/medium, on the off-chance I might find someone who could give me some additional insight into this strange otherworldly connection into which I had fallen. And lo and behold! There it was! Someone was doing sessions at a local business, *The Fargo Rock Shop.* I called the number provided and, amazingly, received an appointment for that very afternoon. Away I went! Yes, indeed.

The reader was Susie Grimmett, and she was extraordinary. She was a recent transplant to Fargo, and had just gotten back into doing psychic readings, after taking a year off. She only did them twice a week, so I was lucky to have gotten in to see her the same day. I initially booked for a half hour, with the option to extend to an hour if I wished. I wished!!! She immediately connected with family members, of whom I had numerous on the other side: parents, step-father, three siblings, two children, cousins, nephews, aunts and uncles, etc. etc. I was astonished at her accuracy. I provided no information on my side, for quality control, except a few names and birthdates of my family members (not the year of birth, only month and date) to help her make an initial connection. Soon she was bringing through other relatives spontaneously, even providing their names. It was a well-spent hour. Satisfied that this was the real deal, I booked another hour for the following Tuesday, during which I planned to see if she could make contact with Steve.

Saturday, November 14, 2015

We continued to hash out language and thoughts about the school we would design together. Perhaps I wasn't the best partner. At some point, I found myself pacing. Not pacing around the kitchen table, but walking out the back patio doors, through the yard, around the house, in the front door, and back out the other side. This was not customary behavior for me. As I walked, I found myself in the same sub-verbal frame of mind I had already experienced once before, almost a meditative state, but alert—alert for the idea, the thought, that might pop out of the ether. However, my hands seemed to be restless, as if trying to grasp something out of thin air. Whatever energy had hold of me was a little more compelled to order than I was, as I found myself stopping—almost absently—to right a flower pot, pick up a dog toy or retrieve a soccer ball. That was nice.

I sat down at the computer in the midst of this strange state and tapped out some thoughts, phrases, partial ideas—simple but elegant. But then I started feeling an overwhelming sense of frustration, to the point of incoherence, tears. *I am fucking here!! How can I just make you **see**?*

At that point I knew things had somehow gotten out of control. I felt the need to step in and right the ship—whatever that meant. Enough of this frustrating school business. It could wait. I went and made supper.

Sunday, November 15, 2015
3 a·m·

The deadline for the school application was November 15, 2015, apparently at midnight PST. I worked on the school application Saturday evening until the wee hours of the morning. To my thinking, this was a Steve project—he wanted it done, I was the hands and feet on the ground. Having done this before, I had a sense of *déjà vu*. But it wasn't a pleasant sense. I was flooded with that old sense of hopelessness. I had already "wasted" seven years of my life trying to overcome the harsh mindset of society as concerns education. I had no desire to fall into that trap again.

About 3 a.m., Steve asked me how I was feeling.

-Tired. How am I doing?

-Maybe not in the money, but at least expressing something. Can add to it before the February deadline.

-Yeah. I really don't have the energy to create a "super school." Who even *wants* a super school? Not me. What for? Same-o, same-o. The ones who are determined will find their way, no matter what. Life goes on. Who cares?

-Wow, cynical, aren't we?

-Tired. Are we going to fight over this?

-I hope not.

-I mean, what *is* the point? It's all on an individual basis, isn't it? You can't top-down changing people's lives. It has to be an organic process.

-I can't disagree with that, Stephanie. But it has to begin somewhere—that organic process. And at least creating something good enough—eloquent enough—that people will listen is important.

-Wouldn't they listen more to a good book?

-Possibly. It's a matter of connecting the right words with the right ears.

-I suppose. I feel really stupid, doing this.

-Why?

-Because it seems so pointless. I wouldn't be doing it if not for you. And I guess you have your own motivations and reasons, but it's all beyond me.

-You want to rest on a soft cloud?

-Yes, I think so.

-You would abandon the rest of humanity?

-Of course not, you know that. But someone has to be the little star.

-And someone has to be the visionary.

-I'm going to bed. Night. By the way, I appreciate that trick at the bank today—none of the pens in the car would work to write that check (which I planned on depositing) and then I had to go home and get an envelope I thought—fortunately, because I was writing the check on the same bank I was depositing it into!! Good catch.

    -YW.

    -If I was a little star off in my own little corner of the firmament, I wouldn't have to worry about all this.

    -Life is full of—well, earth life is full of frustrations, isn't it? Actually, quite a few here, too.

    -And what's with that house?

I was thinking about the ongoing issues with the sale of my Anchorage house.

    -No answer. Figures. You have no idea. it's all a matter of my imagination—lies in my imagination. Lying imagination. Good night.

    Actually, Steve would eventually take credit for helping to work out the issues with the house sale, but that's another story.

    Anyway, before I could fall asleep, things were to go awry. My son's sleep patterns were unpredictable and he often stayed up most of the night, playing video games, or working on his rap poems. I had hardly lay down, when I was pulled into a very ugly scene as my son descended into one of his bipolar rages over some issue. Of course he couldn't help himself in the moment—it was part of his life plan, dealing with this hairpin trigger response system. He lacked the internal "stoppers" that could intervene in the anger trajectory.[53] Conventional world views could not even begin to understand it. I was at that time strongly pulled to the idea of epigenetics being the key factor in this condition, which thereby implicated previous *generations*— not only his own, but all those who had interacted with his forebears. There were no victims in this scenario. Everybody or their ancestors were involved yesterday in what they condemn today.

---

[53] Numerologically, per *The Life You Were Born to Live, by Dan Millman*, (c. 1993, HJ Kramer New World Library) he is a 30/3—that is to say, a number associated with bipolar condition, and his life path is to learn to balance emotion. I was skeptical when I first picked up this book, but upon seeing how the primary numerological characteristics so accurately matched each of my children's predilections—and my own—I became a customer.

Once the rage was expended, as typical, he immediately fell into confusion, remorse and guilt, which was as heart-wrenching to witness as the rage. I had learned not to interrupt the cycle—to do so could create more complications. The best thing was just to leave him alone until he fell asleep, to awaken refreshed and more even-keeled. But I myself sank into a dark spot. There had been some destruction of objects. He never took his anger out physically on people, just things: walls and windows and furniture and the like. But it is traumatic for all concerned.

5:30 a·m·

After cleaning up what needed to be taken care of before the morning, I retreated to my room, weary, tired of having to always stay calm when around Nathaniel. He picked up on stress and seemed unable to separate his own from others, so that the environment in which he existed had to be as non-confrontational as possible. This meant I had to limit my own bitching and temper tantrums when he was around, which sometimes seemed unfair to me. I wanted my time, too!

As I sat in my room, in the midst of the night, feeling hopeless, that life was pointless, I decided to call upon the greatest help I could find:

-I would very much like to talk to the most helpful being, soul, angel, guide—whatever that I can who can help me sort out this stuff in my life.

-*Here.*

-Who am I speaking with?

-*Collective.*

-Okay, so my question, if I were to die, would I still have to deal with whatever is left behind here on Earth? How do I deal with all this stuff?

I wasn't exactly in the best frame of mind to be having spirit communication—I was troubled, exhausted, and doubting. There was always that skepticism inside me: even if I did hear anything, how could I trust what was said? So it was no surprise that I didn't immediately pick up a response.

-Nobody's going to answer me, are they?
-*Steve: Stephanie, you know they are, just shut up and listen.*

And then I heard:

-*Maya. Illusion.*

Well, no surprise there. If it was what you expected the "collective" to say, it couldn't be real. Not to say I couldn't argue with them.

-Isn't *everything* illusion?

I didn't bother to listen for any further input. I was too wound up inside. Off I went, instead, on a soliloquy. (I must have had a lifetime during Shakespearean days when on-stage soliloquys were apparently all the rage.)

-If I stopped thinking completely—I wouldn't ever think these thoughts, would I? If I stopped trying to put definitions on things. If I stopped trying to do anything. There's nothing here that matters to me. How could there be? Everything gets broken, shattered, destroyed. What do I care? So without thoughts, how can we even have language? Communication? I'm really really sorry Christopher hurts so much, and I don't know how to help him. I've tried. I feel like I've tried. Without much success—but obviously I didn't try hard enough. Somewhere I failed. I made a mistake. I should have known. I blew it. If I can't escape the sadness even by leaving this plane, then what? I can be thankful for everything, though, right? I can just keep being thank full. Just that. Stay thank full. Stay patient. Bless everyone. And I can love myself and my own thoughts. And I feel badly for him because I care. I also feel guilty, though, there's no doubt about that. Well, I guess I can love the guilty thoughts, too, right? Okay, I'm starting to feel a little better. Stay in thankfulness, gratitude, stay in loving one's thoughts. If I can't get rid of them, I might as well love them, right?

I guess I'm just talking to myself. Who else is there to talk to? Just projections on the cave wall. So stay centered, be grateful, and love my thoughts. That's the best I can do, I think.

I don't get it. I don't get how this works. All I ever get is that it's so peaceful when I'm just a little star. So very very peaceful. Could everybody just take care of their own business? Could everybody just be kind to one another? Could everybody just be peaceful and not in pain? If I never saw pain in another, I suppose I would never have to feel it, right? I would never even know it existed. I would just be in touch with my feelings and let them flow—except my feelings are everybody else's feelings. So I come back to just not thinking about it, being a star.

Oh, the treacherous labyrinth of the logical mind. How does one ever find one's way out of that maze? Nevertheless, I had calmed myself somewhat. At the same time, I was certain that Steve must be tired of my constant insecurity and flailing at the restraints, not to mention wanting to distance himself from this crazy household. I still felt confused and inadequate, weighed down by my burdens, and I preferred to enjoy my confusion, inadequacy and burdens all by myself, without having to worry about what anyone else thought of me. It was, after all, *mine*—whatever it looked like. *My* personal topsy-turvy upside-down world.

I had been feeling distant from Steve, anyway, as I dealt with all the struggles of the night. As I stated previously, I was not—in any case—willing to listen to any voice but the one that I had traditionally turned to for the trip down and out of the Dantesque hell of my own psyche.

I thought that the time had come—the time for Steve and me to separate (if that was possible), to go our own ways. I needed my space, and I certainly wasn't good company. The last thing I wanted to do was impose my problems on anyone else. But before I went to bed, I decided I should turn to a trick I had been taught by the owner of the local rock shop, where I had gone for the psychic reading. She had shown me that if you hold a rock in front of your heart, you will either fall forward or away from it, thus indicating whether it is the energetic stone you need.

I retrieved the Steve Jobs biography and held it to my chest. I fully expected to fall backward, given all my negative thoughts and troubled feelings, but to my surprise I fell toward it. I was actually a little relieved, that we weren't done completely. However, it was as if he had stepped back to give me space, and as I lay in bed I was able to self-soothe—to descend into that core place inside myself where there were only two options: either I was giving love or I was asking for it.[54] It allowed me, either way, to feel some compassion for myself—like a mother comforting a child. In this case, my own "inner child."

I went through the traumatic thoughts of the day and applied the formula to each one, until I was at peace. I fell asleep with the song *Forever in Your Love,* particularly the lyrics "And I'm not sorry," looping through my mind.

Steve was to inform me at a later time that I wasn't getting much help from the "other side," which had caused me to feel some dismay and a little abandoned, because they all knew I'd get there; it is better to rely upon the wisdom inside ourselves than to try to find it outside.

11 a·m·

I awakened about 11 a.m. feeling refreshed, except for the lingering shreds of what had been a vivid dream. It was an "old-fashioned" kind of dream, the kind I remembered having before I met Steve. I dreamt that I was standing in the lobby of a hospital somewhere. Two women were passing when they saw me and approached. I did not know them, but clearly something must have triggered recognition for them. They came over and confronted me. One raised her voice accusatorially: "I heard you were talking to Steve. Who do you think you are, having a relationship with him?"

I asked how she knew this.

She produced a clipping and shoved it in front of my face.

---

[54] *The Course in Miracles,*

There was a box drawn around a part of the writing. "I heard from so-and-so, who found out and told me. This proves it. Right here." She thumped the clipping.

I could see that it was a portion of the school application.

I was thrown off balance. I immediately defended myself—with a lie. This was uncharacteristic of me. In general, I figured if I did something I should be willing to take the flak. I might be apologetic ("Sorry, I didn't know it was yours"), defiant ("That's nobody's business"), or soothing ("Let's see if we can't work it out"), but I didn't usually cop out. But then, this was a totally new experience for me. I couldn't remember the last time someone had accused me of being a little too cozy with a well-known disincarnate figure.

I admitted that I was talking to Steve, but played it down. I was the only one who could hear, and did she understand how lonely and frustrating it was for him? To be trying to talk to people, to communicate with them, and they couldn't even hear him?

The first woman wasn't buying it. She huffed off. But the second one was more sympathetic to my case. She hung out for a moment, wanting to know more and apologizing for any hard feelings.

The dream had hit upon a raw spot inside of me: that *why me* space. *Why am I in the midst of this?* I felt very much like an interloper, almost like the "other woman," the one who needs to be put in her place. I wanted to relinquish my part in this adventure: *I don't want people to hate me. How about I just go back in my hobbit hole and we pretend this whole thing never happened?*

But I hardly had time to fret over it. I had barely come back to the world of the living (so to speak) when I found myself in a country setting with Steve. It was an escapade that was to become one of my favorites—maybe even my most favoritest of all: simple, poetic and bright with promise.

We were walking along a dirt road on a gorgeous day. The sun was shining, the sky was blue, and flowers bloomed along the way. Fields stretched on either side into the distance, marked with groves of trees. The road was little more than two dirt tracks, with grass growing up in the middle. We were each in our own "rut," but connected—holding hands across the green median between us. I looked over at Steve, who was dressed in jeans and a tee-shirt. He seemed so young and carefree. I was young as well, of course. I had adopted the age of about twenty for most of our adventures, ever since the NDE memory had surfaced, as if I were claiming my right to do it all again—the way it never was. I was wearing a simple knit knee-length dress that fell in soft folds and basic flats.

It felt so tranquil, just the two of us walking down this road. So nice after all the stress of the night before. I glanced behind me and realized with a start that the Earth was at our backs, looming large over the horizon, like a gigantic multi-colored moon. Steve saw my look and grinned.

-Don't worry. We're not going back there anymore. Oh, we may come across Earth again as our path circles, but we will be approaching it head-on, not looking back over our shoulders. Not trying to hold on.

He had a light step and a gleam in his eye. He gave me one of those sweet smiles, a bit mischievous.

-I love you, Stephanie. We have only just begun.

I saw that we were like the old generation, leaving the Earth to the new, but in the process we had been transformed—the tired old king renewed as the young prince, as sparkly as a bright new penny; the old grandmother returned to her youthful identity as princess, when her step was buoyant and her heart full of the love of life—off on our own fresh adventure far from the old kingdom.

In the background I could hear a song, like a sound-track, although Steve seemed to be singing along as we swung hands: *If I were a Carpenter.*[55]

It is impossible to convey how truly happy I felt. How light-hearted. I dropped his hand and skipped along, twirling in sheer delight, simply overcome by the wonder of life and the

---

[55] *If I Were a Carpenter*, Bobby Darin

exhilaration of existence. None of that Steve Jobs stuff! No school! No one trying to roast me on a spit! No heart-breaking drama of loved ones to wade through! Just him and me, leaving it all behind, all our trials and tribulations in that Earth life. Just the two of us, stripped down to the bare essentials. Starting a new life together.

A fun ride:

I had committed to taking my brother-in-law to Jamestown to visit his wife. Of course Steve came along, ever the invisible hitchhiker. It was a beautiful November day on the prairie. The weather always seemed to cooperate for our trips. It was a calm, mellow time for Steve and I to talk. I tuned to classical music.

-Can I put away the biographies now, and we will begin anew? Build our own house?
-I have the hammer and the nails.
-And I have the saw.
-Together we can do anything, my carpenter wife.

Yes, we could. We could build anything with the tools at our disposal. A little house on the prairie. Castles in the sky. A bridge from Earth to Heaven.

-Can I call you Stephen? If you're a prince, then Steve doesn't sound that good.
-And you then would be the crown princess.
-But I may call you Steve, anyway, 'cause I'm used to it.
-Can I call you Stevie, then?
-I don't care. Or dumbass. Or bitch. Whatever fits the occasion.
-It's nice to have that flexibility.

As we drove between the open fields, I recalled one of my best experiences in life: back when I was about eighteen, riding my horse bareback across new-plowed fields, dressed only in jeans and a t-shirt—no shoes, no hat, and of course no saddle. I asked Steve if I could have a horse like Sherry, and he surprised me by replying: "Well, why not Sherry?"

And there she was, coming across the open field, mane flying; and there I was, standing waiting. She halted when she came up to me. I could put my forehead against her muzzle and my cheek against her cheek and feel the love energy intertwining, like soft strands of pastel colors. I kicked off my shoes. Steve cupped his hands to give me a step up and I swung onto her back. She had no bridle and bit, but we were as one mind and didn't need any. I wound my hand into her mane and my toes into her flanks. Then we were off.

Steve came up swiftly after us, on a big bay, mahogany colored with black mane and tail, also bareback but he had a bridle and reins. He held the the reins in his left hand but with the ends in his right, like a cowboy. Then we went galloping wildly over the fields, like modern-day Indians, free as the breeze.

It was very satisfying.

The wonder of that day seemed to go on and on.

After we were done riding we set to work building our "dream" home. It had about seven stories, each of them only about fifteen feet square. Each floor was painted a different color and the house leaned one way and another. "The hell with esthetics," Steve said as we hammered and nailed with gusto. We built a balcony on about the fifth floor, just big enough for a soft futon so we could lie out at night listening to Mozart and looking at the stars—Steve could have his pot and I could have my dreams. Then we put in a slide all the way down to the ground, twisting and turning like the greatest water slide.

Not satisfied with this effort, we decided to build a clubhouse on the prairie. There we were, two fairly competent adults, but all we had were these retro hand tools and found materials: pallets and slats ripped off fences, strips of corrugated metal for the roof, an old picture frame for a window.

Being a clubhouse, it needed a sign. I objected to "Girls Not Allowed." After some discussion, thinking that our club was kind of a secretive society, like Monsters, Inc., we decided to call it: *Dreamers, Ltd.* But we figured out that couldn't work, on second thought, so one of us got the bright idea to be a little more creative, and thus the birth of that wonderful club:

Dreamers (un) Ltd. Only a few members presently, but I had to believe it would grow and grow.

Satisfied with our work, we went home—to our slanting jerry-built seven-story house—and slid down the slide into the swimming pool we had decided to add. We hung out there for a while, playing in the water, annoying one another by slipping underneath and grabbing the other. Actually, Steve did most of that, I was just trying to be mellow.

While we were relaxing afterward, Steve pointed out to me that the prairie fields were like gold spread out all the way to the horizon, that the leaf-less shelter belts, which I might have thought of as naked, actually reflected so many colors, with their fingers reaching to the sky as if to draw in the energy like one of our *Tai Chi* moves. And then the horizon was painted like the softest watercolor wash as the sun set—there was the dark blue that faded into the very slight tinge of violet before the rose color and then a very very pale yellowish hue that then turned into the blue of the sky. That was pretty, and we had those beautiful classical scores in the background, like watercolors themselves.

-And why do you have that faraway look?

-Oh, maybe I just see something down the road.

We didn't get home from Jamestown until after dark. By then we were hanging out on the balcony, under the stars, far from the madding crowd.

Flaming stars!

Back at home, I broached some matters that were on my mind:

-So…Steve.

I had been doing more internet research and some of it was fresh on my mind.

-I happened to note that we have very similar shapes to our hands, the knobby knuckles, the same relative proportions and spacing of fingers, although your fingers do seem longer than mine.

I was already a fan of hand-readings, since I had had a few partial but very engaging revelations from various random readers at fairs and such like. At the time I was mostly just noting the synchronicity between our hands, having heard that twin souls often had the "same hands." But down the road, I was to discover a "celebrity" reading of Steve's hand on a *youtube* video, and I decided to get mine read as well. That reading turned out to be amazing, and is included in full in Part VI of this book. But at the time, it was just another similarity:

-So…it appears that we must be twin flames. Is that what we are?
-OMG, yes. Don't even mention that phrase.
-Why?

I think he was teasing me, keying into my recent fascination with all the information on the net about the twin soul relationship—a lot of it highly romanticized. As if it needed to be—the true twin soul stuff is *wayyy* captivating enough.

-*It's like a conflagration. Remember that song—your fight song—Rachel Platten—[lyrics omitted].* I said "yes" but *be careful of definitions, because they're all over the place, depending upon who's writing the manuals. But we are the two parts of the same soul, torn apart so long ago. It's just the way it is, Stephanie. Get over it. Time to move on.*
-Yeah, I shouldn't get so caught up in all the drama, should I?
-*Definitely not. We don't even have to. What happens, happens. Have you noticed? Did you think we would be walking down some country road with the Earth at our back?*
-No, I honestly didn't. I was worried we were headed for some kind of separation, and instead we were more totally together than I think we've ever been—well, I can't say that, because we've sure encountered our share (and more) of blissful interaction—one of those episodes would have kept me for half a lifetime in the past, and now they're like one a day. But every new chapter takes me by surprise—it really does—it's like peak experience, peak experience, peak experience, with a little valley in between each.

Right now, I feel like the luckiest person in the whole universe. I still am amazed by how weird this is, and how much fun we have, and how we can both just totally delight in the same kinds of stupid stuff.

Night again:

That night I was tormented again by the memory of that dream from—gosh, was it just that morning? It had been fun leaving the Earth behind, but here we were back in the Earth Plane Distortion Field—well, at least I was living there, and Steve was visiting. Actually, we were hanging out in our astral room, in our astral bodies, being mellow, with a little of that too blissful energy melding. But afterward my heart hurt, even though Steve tried to comfort me. I could only imagine all the shame that would be heaped upon me if it came out, all the animosity. How could our strange relationship survive that? How could *I* survive that? As I was pondering this, sore in my heart, Steve said lazily, "I'm in the mood for Alicia Keyes."

Alicia Keyes was not one of my preferred artists, and I was not familiar with her songs. However, I got up, went to my desktop computer and did a search. The first song that came up was "No One." As I lay back down to listen, I felt his energetic arms wrap around me and draw me back to the safety of our special room:

[Lyrics omitted.]

-I think I get it Steve. Us walking down that road with the Earth at our backs—that was a memory. A memory of the future.

-The one we will build together.

Chapter 21
The Roller Coaster and
Steve Reveals a Secret

Monday, November 16, 2015

I awakened feeling rather peppy. Steve was teasing me about something or other. Suddenly I had grabbed my fencing foil.

-On guard!

Now I don't really have a fencing foil, but I did take a fencing class back in college, and it was one of those things that I really enjoyed. Unfortunately, I never was able to pursue it further—one of the really troublesome aspects about life, I've noticed, is that there just isn't enough time to do it all. You have to make some choices. Maybe in some alternate reality I did study fencing and became a master, and there's some comfort in that thought. In fact, maybe that alternate reality was a past life. In any case, I had my foil and Steve had one, and the game was on. In no time at all I had disarmed him, sent him sprawling backwards to the ground and had the tip of my foil poised for the final thrust through the heart. But no! I had to let him live. The heroine shows magnanimity toward her enemy when he is vulnerable. The point was driven home; the steel didn't need to be.

In actuality the foils had protective tips and he was wearing chest padding, but you get the idea. We were just pretending the swords were real. Nevertheless, it felt pretty good to be on top for a change, to feel like I still had a little bit of it left. In fact, I felt kinda smug.

-Tease me, will you?? Watch out!

But alas, my triumph was short-lived. I was soon swept away in the clutches of that infernal roller coaster that takes us to hell and back. Fortunately the ride seemed to be on super speed so no sooner was I down than I was up again. But here's how it went.

By noon...
down, down, down

-I am so depressed. I really don't even care at this point if I have to come back here and do another incarnation. I am so tired of taking care of [yadda-yadda-yadda]. I just see no purpose anymore. Why am I here? I'm not strong enough or capable enough or wise enough to solve all these problems. I just want to be my star. I'm already back where I was two days ago, and this is my journaling time. I just want to lie down and die. I am really really tired of the same thing over and over. What's the point? This is my whining time, so I don't expect an answer. I'm a crappy mother, a crappy grandmother, a crappy everything. How much longer do I have to stay on this planet? I wouldn't mind if I could just do all the things I enjoy doing— but why [bitch-bitch-bitch, blah-blah-blah, details omitted to spare the faint of heart]? Why can't everyone just take care of their own business? [Yawing about others deleted to protect the innocent.] I can't do it anymore. I just can't do it anymore. I just can't. I give up. I don't even care what happens, I just want to curl into a little ball—and since I can't be a star—just be a dust ball. Just be one of the ones that preys off everybody else, zaps everybody else's energy, takes, takes, takes.

I'm obviously very sick, very incapable, very irresponsible, very ugly, very unworthy of even living on this planet. I can't carry the weight anymore. I just want everybody to go away and leave me alone and I'm sorry if I can't be there for you but I don't have anything left in me. I don't have anything left to give. I will keep trying, because that's what I do, but I'm empty. I don't have any energy left. I don't want to live anymore—not like this.

Do you still believe that nobody wants to die?

-I believe nobody has a choice. What're the options? Are you gonna be a dust ball? What happened to that woman who disarmed me in a bout of fencing? Where's that fierceness?

Where's that determination? Where's that "nobody is gonna make me cry."

-"Nobody is gonna make me cry." Wow, that's an old one. And now it doesn't take much to bring me to tears of frustration.

-Example. Be the example.

It's true that it was one of my childhood mantras: *nobody's gonna make me cry.* Not that I couldn't decide to cry if *I* felt like it. My choice. I actually could throw some great temper tantrums as a child—the kind where people just started stepping over you after a while—and knew how to turn on the said tears when it was useful, but I was also stubborn when my brothers tried to rough me up. In fact, my last scene with my brother, Edgar, who died when he was eleven, is iconic. And maybe that was the beginning of the end, when the hopelessness began: we had gotten into a bit of a tizzy—what you might call a continuation of the constant quarreling and manipulation between us—and I had momentarily gotten the upper hand with a little set-up that got him a reprimand from our father. He and some friends caught me outside for some just desserts. Soon he had me down on the ground with my arm twisted behind my back: "Say 'uncle'." But I refused. I would take the dislocated shoulder, the broken arm, rather than give in. Finally he had no choice but to let me go. As I walked off, rubbing my arm, I flung those fateful words over my shoulder: "I wish you were dead."

I never talked to him again. He left before I awakened the next morning, on a month-long commercial fishing trip with my father, his first season as deckhand. They never came back, their boat overturned. Edgar's body was never found.

And Steve wanted *me* to be an example?

4:30 p.m.

And uppppp we go...

-Steve, I absolutely love you. You are wonderful and I hope everyone will get to see how wonderful you are someday. I mean it. You are like this bright bright light. You shine out of the darkness and I hope your one more thing…not last thing…is awesome. Not because I want people to think you're awesome, which you are, but because I want everybody to touch a little part of that light. To see that reflection in themselves. To light up the world.

Um, yeah, twin souls say things like that.

8:55 p.m.
…and things like this.
Down again….

-Gol dang it, I just realized you were born on the same day as my father: February 24 (separated by many years). Someone isn't making this easy to blow this all off.
-Oh, come on…
-I'm not talking to you. This is my journal and I will say what I want. I still love you, I still admire you profusely, I still want everything the best for you—but I need to work out my own shit. Can't I just admire and love someone and still go off by myself and be all alone? I have worked hard my entire life to be emotionally self-sufficient. I have worked my entire life not to be vulnerable. I have worked my entire life to be self-sustaining, complete in myself. Yes, you did. You did help me solve some issues I had, and you did help me to grow. And I appreciate that, and I'm good with continuing that bit if it's helpful to both of us, as long as its mutually beneficial. *Quid pro quo.* But clearly I blew things financially while I was caught up in this drama—yes, drama. So when is something an obsession and when is it a passion? It appears I got too carried away with this, and I screwed up…I wasn't paying attention to what I needed to do to keep things together. I don't even care so much anymore about being foolish—what the hell? You know, my language has sure taken a dive into the sewer lately. Not that I didn't swear before, but…anyway.

I went down into the dungeon to work, where a little Simon and Garfunkel soothed me. Yes, yes, I am a rock!!

Tuesday, November 17, 2015
Where the bottom falls out...

Morning came. It was to be an auspicious day. But it started out with chit chat.

-So, I found this nifty quote from one of those takes on "Steve Jobs redoing Heaven" articles. Don't you like it? "Dying is no excuse to stop living."[56]

-I do, I do. And they gave me credit for saying that? Cool.

-Was that true, what Sorkin said, that you were just looking for love?

-What do you think?

-I think there was some truth there. I hadn't thought about it before. You were needed, vital. You gave people something valuable enough that they couldn't throw you out. It was never about the money. It wasn't really about the praise. It was about the love. I'm feeling for your answer, but I'm not hearing it or feeling it.

-I'm thinking.

-You haven't thought this out before?

-I have a lot of new pieces. This is really a core matter, here, and I don't just want to...blow it off with some silly response.

-Oh, no, the great Steve Jobs has lessons to learn, too?

-Well, I do, and I don't deny it. Why do you think people— souls—reincarnate on Earth? They have issues to work out that they can't really do here. Usually. Things to experience just for growth, of course, but by a fairly early stage in the evolution of most souls, there is already quite a bit of shit to understand—to try to understand.

Steve, of course, had a lot of pieces that I didn't. "It was about the love?" Different ways to interpret that, actually, but I

---

[56] http://dailycurrant.com/2012/10/05/steve-jobs-reinventing-heaven/

wasn't thinking that expansively. I doubt anyone was.

-Okay, I'm thinking through big issues. I get that we need each other and I got that from the beginning: I'm a) your telephone to Earth, b) we share similar conceptions and—what shall I say—characteristic attributes, so we can connect on intellectual and spiritual issues, c) nether one of us wants to reincarnate but both of us want to finish our business so we can move on to whatever the spiritual climax is—reunification with God, or whatever. Right so far?
-I'm following.
-For a change. Okay, that was snarky. I withdraw it.

His response had been equivocal in any case. From there we got off on a long discussion of our history together and some life issues—well, mostly I was talking, playing psychologist. The text of this laborious discussion doesn't need to be recapitulated here, but the essence of my theory was a certain core insecurity under the: "Will you still love me if I'm an asshole?"

-And until all that is resolved, as it must be, you yourself can't be whole; once again, our connection becomes vital to wellness for both of us. We need each other to play off against.
-We do.

Once again, a rather ambiguous response. Obviously we needed each other, we were the polarities of each other. But there was no admission of the value of my pop psychology. But still I rambled:

-You might have been a "mover and a shaker," but you're right, I finally feel that: we really aren't that different at the core level. Just two little orphans trying to find the way home.

11:27 a.m.

So it really was in the Stars?

- Wow, things really do come on an as-needed basis. I was thinking about you and my dad having the same birthday, how weird is that, and I went to the astrological chart to find out what you are, and you're a Pisces, we're both water signs, and apparently both tender of heart, intuitive and very compatible. Which would also explain why I felt so close to my father. But interestingly, it says that I am the strong one. The Dreamer and the Homemaker. I would never have believed that, were it not for the fact that we just had this conversation [omitted], where I saw how your power gambit hides an incredibly vulnerable and tender heart. I'm definitely the homemaker, although I'm not doing such a good job at it right now—it was always where my heart was—what I craved, anyway, but could never seem to find. And you are definitely the dreamer. Very very interesting.

And does this help explain why I would see my father's eyes when I looked into yours in the picture? Something ineffable there.

As the veil was pulled back little by little, I would find out there were to be many more connections between my father and Steve. It was not just a coinkydink that they had the same eyes, birthday, and emotional connection with me. As usual, I was being drawn in little by little to the luminous world on the other side of the spirit divide.

The following is the article I had come across while doing my research (with my comments):

Cancer and Pisces Compatibility:
The Homemaker and the Dreamer[57]

For Cancer and Pisces, compatibility with one another is practically inborn. These two recognize a kindred spirit in each other, and there is likely to be instant attraction. Two of the most sensitive signs in the zodiac together form a beautiful, ethereal

---

[57] *Astromatcha*, Cancer and Pisces Compatibility: The Homemaker and the Dreamer, https://www.astromatcha.com/astrology-compatibility/cancer-compatibility/cancer-and-pisces-compatibility/

*relationship in which they will each take great care not
to hurt the other.*

-Okay, that's mostly true—certainly ethereal, but we do seem to
have a knack for hurting each other. For pushing buttons,
anyway.

*What marks Cancer and Pisces compatibility out most
is a shared emotional base.*

-Developed over many lifetimes together? Yeah, and
maybe even starting out as the same base unit??

*Both water signs, this couple are used to following
their intuition, and it's this intuition which draws them
together.*

-Like no kidding. Say what?

*No matter how difficult their circumstances or how
unlikely society deems their match…*

-Pretty unlikely.

true love will out.

-Or at least they'll be stuck together, being as how they share
the same soul, so they might as well love it.

*For Pisces and Cancer, compatibility is strong enough
to see them through financial difficulties, family
disapproval…*

-Ah, what they don't know won't hurt them.

different races, religions, long distance relationships…

-Really long distance.

or any number of other potential obstacles.

-Like death

If they want to be together, they'll be together. Being highly sensitive, both partners in this relationship are quite fragile at heart, and easily devastated. Fortunately, this means that they both understand the pain of thoughtless words or deeds, and are certain not to treat anyone else the way they wouldn't want to be treated.

-A rule that apparently doesn't apply to each other. (And um…Steve…what do you have to say here?? Bring up any memories?? Or was that really the way you would want to be treated?? Maybe it was.)

Cancer and Pisces compatibility is a very honest and open love match, with each partner wearing their heart on their sleeve. There's nothing hidden here, so there are no dark secrets for either partner to stumble upon.

-Well, I'm an open book at least. Not sure what further love letters and other horrible stuff is still hidden in your cupboards.

This is likely to be a deeply romantic relationship, with love notes, poems, flowers and the full range of sweet and tender surprises along the way.

-Love notes? Check. Poems? Well, if you count all those song lyrics. Flowers? How about apples? Sweet surprises? Well, there have been quite a few surprise vacation trips to random places like Neverland and Fantasia, and not to forget the first trip, where you had to spoil it all by picking out my dress!!

Of course, for two such emotional people, there will also be some tears during the journey (yep!), but it's a surprisingly serene relationship for two water signs. Cancer and Pisces compatibility brings this couple a soft and gentle almost magical aura; it's as though they have a divine or spiritual connection which nobody else can break.

-Yeah, just as if.

Neither Pisces nor Cancer is usually unfaithful once committed to a relationship, although gentle Pisces can be easily led by a stronger character.

-Oh, oh! Should I be worried?

Cultivating honesty is the key here –

-Yes, yes, yes!!

so long as Pisces feels they can trust Cancer, they are unlikely to stray.

-H'mmm. Well, that would be a really good reason for me to bail, I'd say. I will keep my eyes peeled for that permission slip.

There is a slight risk that Pisces will get carried away into a fantasy world here,

-Um, which fantasy world would that be? Oz, Fantasia, Neverland? Toy Story? Monsters, Inc.?

because Pisces is ruled by Neptune, the planet of illusions.

-I think this is the planet of illusions, right?

However, although Cancer is also a water sign, the Cancer partner has an inner steel

-Hmm. Well I do have my steel.

and shrewdness which will help them ground Pisces

just long enough to avert a crisis. Remember that Cancer is a cardinal sign, and will take action, whereas Pisces, being a mutable sign, is content to adapt to Cancer's plans.

-Oh, ha, ha, ha on that one. Who leads the dance? Who makes the plans?

There's no competitiveness in Cancer and Pisces compatibility, so this couple do not need to worry about who's going to be in charge.

-Actually, that's true, I don't mind if you lead. I kind of like it, in fact.

Underpinned by compassion, empathy and deep, deep feelings, this relationship is one which can stand the test of time.

-And eternity?

For Cancer and Pisces compatibility to work at its best, however, both partners must learn to communicate more directly.

-More directly than telepathy?

They both tend to side step issues instead of tackling them head on, which is fine in the short term but cannot be sustained over a life time.

-Well, it seems like we don't have to worry about lifetimes anymore.

As the cardinal sign, it will again be up to Cancer to take control here, and to gently force Pisces to face up to any problems. Otherwise, there is a danger that when life gets tough, both Pisces and Cancer might wallow in depression and worry, perhaps even resorting to negative escapism, drink or drugs.

-I'll take the depression and worry, you can have the drugs.

At its best, this beautiful partnership is sweet, tender, romantic, spiritual and empathetic. Both partners have so much love to give, not only to each other but to the world at large, so don't be surprised to find this couple working for charity in some way. Pisces and Cancer compatibility is expressed even better when the Dreamer and the Homemaker pool resources to help improve life for someone else.

Hmmm….

The pooling of resources had begun. How it might improve life for someone else remained to be seen.

2:00 p.m.
The Big Reveal:

The big moment had come. I arrived early for my appointment with the remarkable Susie Grimmett, who had previously connected me with deceased family members. I had already had minimal contact with some of them across the divide—through a friend years before, who had developed his own cross-veil communication after an NDE, and very very occasionally through my own ability to connect. Still, through all of that, I did not have a firm grasp on the nature of "life after life"—I accepted that life was eternal, I just didn't know how it played out experientially, and so I had taken all that early communication with a grain of salt. Sort of like the puzzle piece that you put in the picture, even though you're not sure exactly where it belongs, always alert for any other clues that might cause you to change its position.

But the events of the last month had provided a whole bunch of new bits to play with, as if I'd found a trove of jigsaw puzzle pieces that had fallen under the table. I'd had some powerful validations from family members (in spirit) during my prior meeting with Susie—now I was ready to face the music and see if Steve was going to put in an appearance. I really needed that extra assurance, to have him admit it—not just privately between the two of us—but to someone else: *Oh, yeah, you know Stephanie? We've been hanging out for the last month or so, and just between you and me, I think she's the coolest thing since carrot juice.*

My requirements of him were simple and specific: a) he had to confirm our communications, and b) he had to confess that he loved me. Otherwise, what was the point? I already trusted Susie, convinced from our one hour together. I had never seen anything like it, with the exception of Jamie Butler (from the Channeling Erik blog). The question was: could I trust Steve?

I showed up, prepared for anything, I thought: (a) she tapped into him, (b) she didn't tap into him. I was even prepared, I think, if he showed up and said: (c) "Who's that? Stephanie? Never heard of her."

After all, at this point, the only ones who knew about my invisible pal Steve were Dean, my internet contact Debbie and a few family members—and the last would not be too let down if it turned out I was just crazy. Let the cards fall where they may.

What I wasn't prepared for was the bombshell he was about to drop.

I gave Susie his name and birthdate: Steve, February 24. (I note that it is a minor synchronicity that we were born on the same date, if different months). The month and day of birth were Susie's requirement to get the right phone number, as it were. Apparently she needed the birthdate just to get the element sign: i.e. Steve, Water. And of course, I was: Stephanie, Water. We were both swimmers, although I did have claws.

She didn't even have to let the telephone ring. It was like he had been waiting beside the phone.

Susie assured me that his was a very strong energy. His first communication was to give some confirmation of the cause of his death, the usual preliminary. After that, he expressed affection toward me and then apologized. Spirits apologize,

I've noticed, when you first contact them. I think it's the first thing they learn to do, as if they are anxious to get it off their chest. I won't relate the nature of his apology, but I was rather astonished, since I hadn't even known him then. Why did he need to apologize to me about any of the circumstances of his lifetime? Yes, I was troubled by certain matters, but it wasn't like he could have foreseen this connection. Could he? Maybe it was just part of the Afterlife communication routine, the way I learned to write letters as a child: *How are you? I am fine. Everyone here is well.*

Susie then wrinkled her brow, obviously trying to figure something out. She later confided in me that she could see him giving her *that look*, arms crossed, the one she would learn to know well (almost tapping his foot): *You don't know who I am?* But, like me, she did not recognize Mr. Jobs by sight. She turned to me, puzzled, and asked me for his last name. I reluctantly gave it, and apparently that rang a bell; her face cleared. She took it in stride after that, as if to say: *Don't worry. We all have them, those notorious types that hang around. Happens all the time.*

She was *good.*

Remember, at this point, Susie knew nothing about me other than the few limited and scattered details family members had provided the week before. She would have no reason to remember any of that, and even if she had reason, she admitted to suffering from short-term memory loss ever since a medical issue. I was comfortable that this was an unpolluted channel and I could rely upon what came through. She would tell me much later that Steve initially appeared to her as a thin older man with glasses, although he would subsequently appear as much younger. She also confided months down the road that there were things that she was picking up during sessions that he told her not to tell me, that I wasn't ready yet.

But on this, the first day of our communication through Susie, Steve appeared to be very eager to blow our cover. He jumped right into the big issue with both feet. We were, he explained to Susie, once one, but had split apart long ago. Susie drew the picture he was showing her—an image of two tear-dropped shapes pulling apart.

Holey Moley!! Way to validate, Steve.

I know, having had many sessions with Susie since, and having become close friends in the interim, that she had never run into this type of twin-soul business before. But she hardly blinked an eye as she related what he was telling her, the mind-my-own-business telephone between worlds: according to him, we—he and I—were now whole again.

I was a little thrown by that. *Whole* again? What did that mean? Yes, we were connected in the heart, and I had about as much privacy in this relationship as if we were roommates in a telephone booth. It was a little claustrophobic, true, but I still felt like myself, separate. How were we *whole*? Did that mean *one?*

But at least he'd confirmed the one soul pulling into two parts business. And he *had* communicated affection for me. This was a relief. He *had* shown up, he hadn't denied me—in fact he *had* opened the closet door. We were officially outed. One of those crazy divided soul jobs. Or divided-soul Jobs, as you like.

It was actually very cool to have him communicate this way, through a third-party—it made it more concrete, more like receiving a letter in the mail (or yes, email) instead of just a voice in your head. I say "just in the head" facetiously, of course; the nuances of our communication were way beyond what a letter could do, or even messages through a third party. But it was the intervening voice, the third-party connection, that made this particular type of communication so alluring.

Zero, Steve continued, *was important to him.* He showed Susie a lot of numbers, which had no meaning to her, so she could not relate. She mentioned strings of zeros and ones, and I was able to realize what he was talking about, ("Okay, binary code"), although I wasn't sure what he was trying to relate it to. Susie advised me that he was showing her a building that was "ours" in the Afterworld—she described it as very elegant, reminding her of the Taj Mahal. Again, I was bewildered. We had a building? On the other side? Like a palace? He'd never mentioned that. Why did we need it? And wouldn't a second story apartment do, or at most a country estate? I wondered if the palace had at least a three-car garage.

Then he dropped the bombshell. *No,* he said, *he hadn't remembered me during his recent lifetime, although he always felt that half of him was missing—he just didn't know what it was, he couldn't even identify it, and it affected the way he acted during his life. But as soon as he crossed over, it all came back. He had been trying to contact me ever since, but he didn't want to frighten me.*

I was shocked. He had known who I was since he died? He'd been trying to contact me ever since? So he had *lied?* Wow. I was on high alert as I listened. What other secrets were going to come out?

Steve continued: *You weren't ready until the day we made contact.*

Well, obviously, I'd been the one that had rung *him* up. How did *that* work?

I felt the need to dig deeper into this "new story."

-Do *you* still have issues to work out?

No, Susie relayed, *he was done with his issues, although he was grateful to me for helping him to work some out since we'd gotten together.*

What???? He was *done* with his issues? I thought that was the whole point of us coming together from the beginning—that we had these issues to work out ensemble. So we *weren't* equals. I was the one stuck in the mire and he was a free spirit, with nothing to gain from this arrangement. So what was I? Just a pastime, a toy to play with, a way to spend some of eternity?

Now, in fairness to Steve, I was overlooking that whole twin soul business and focusing upon my earliest impressions of how we'd connected, and why: that we'd just happened to meet (now how unrealistic was *that?*) and found we had some needs in common. Given, a lot of that had been my own need to interpret the situation in a way that I could handle, that made some sense to me. As he said, I always did understand things upside-down—at least my human mind did. But he *had* kinda fostered that, right? What about all that *looking everywhere, not knowing where you were, you might have been a squirrel* stuff? And how about *while you were off looking up that stuff to get some validations, I looked into your mind?* Whoa. What was happening, here?

I hardly had time to think about all this in the moment—so much was coming out. As Steve said, *his mind was connected to something **big**. The collective. All the wisdom accumulated and working together.* And as if that wasn't enough, he laughed: *Fasten your seatbelt! Whoooosh!*

And I thought we had already whooshed!

At this point, Susie came up with a real zinger, nearly causing me to fall out of my chair.

"Who's Tess-e-la?" she asked, puzzled.

She didn't even recognize the name! In later sessions she would say that often when she saw Steve, she saw him with Tesla, tall and dark. So I guess they really were "buds."

Unfortunately I did not come equipped with a voice recorder for this session (nor the next one) but all sessions down the road would be recorded and transcribed. However, I did take good notes, and itemize below the further points made during this session:

*Steve wished he had lived longer, he had some knowledge that he couldn't get out. (He would later contradict this and say that he was glad he died when he did, but the point seemed to be that he still had stuff inside that needed to get out—he was still trying to communicate ideas to those on Earth).

*I had a very logical mind, which enabled him to connect with me in terms of ideas, but that I needed to get out of my human or "earth mind" and think in my "soul mind." Then I would understand what I was. I needed to remember who I was.

*He reiterated that I should journal everything, but not reveal anything publicly at the time. I said that I had already talked to a few friends, but he was good with that, he had connected me with people. (Obviously—apparently he understood my need to have confidants, for my own sanity.)

*I would be given "some knowledge"; I had to unlearn what I learned here on Earth.

*He sent manifestations. Every day, manifestations.

*He looked much younger in the Afterworld (which, of course, I already knew. Anyway, all the spirits seem to want to look about 30, it's a popular age there, I think.)

*He knew I was getting better at feeling him when he was around, connecting better.

*He told Susie that we "astro-traveled," and he apologized to me for the lack of sleep.

*Susie validated that I had left my body and "passed over" back in 1970. She was able to see me hovering over my body at that time. She saw my body vomiting and convulsing, and then someone was doing blows to the heart. She heard it being said by the medical team that if I survived, my liver would be damaged (no damage that I'm aware of). She told me that I did not want to go back into my body.

*Steve then related that I had to have the NDE, that it was necessary to enable me to follow through with experiences set out for my life.

Susie asked me, her eyes widening in surprise for the first time at what she was seeing: "Was there abuse?" I said yes, rape and other things. Then, equally in surprise, she said, "You tried to kill yourself?" Well, of course.

Afterwards:

As soon as we had some privacy—i.e. we were home, I sat down at the computer to rant and rave. He had lied to me! I will spare the reader the anger and frustration that spewed forth from my keyboard, as if it had a mind of its own. When Steve tried to butt in, I yelled at him:

-DO NOT TALK TO ME!!

This would have been one heckuva fight if we'd both been corporeal, probably with a few plates flying across the room. Actually, I had long passed my plate throwing days, but it would have been a doozy anyway. Probably a few slammed doors. As it was, it's a wonder the smoke alarms didn't go off, with all the steam escaping through my ears.

It was not just that he had lied about the circumstances of our meeting—he'd been trying to get through to me for four years???? [Expletives omitted (for a change).] But here he was, high-falutin' Mr. No-Issues-Left floating around in some hotsy-totsy cloud realm while I was wandering around down here in the murky Earth Plane Distortion Field. We weren't equals at all!! We weren't doing this together!! I'd had the wool pulled over my eyes. He'd been *stalking* me! For four years!

Didn't they have laws on the Other Side about that kind of thing?

In saner moments, I might concede that it was a stretch to accuse him of "stalking." That was a pretty big leap from the information provided—but it *felt* disturbing. Yes, I was aware that there were spirits all over the place, a lot of them trying to reach through to their loved ones, but this was a *stranger,* apparently watching, peeping through the window at me as I went obliviously about my daily routine—doing God knows what kind of embarrassing things that you do when you think you're alone.

It was a huge dent in my sense of privacy. And then there was the blow to my trust. How could I trust anything he said ever again? As I told him:

-It's like someone comes to your door, and just wants to hang out and have a friend and maybe get some good old-fashioned nurturing. And maybe through that relationship you find out, "hey, we got a connection beyond what we thought," and you feel like you're both kinda groping your way, and then you find out, wham! This person knew all about you all along, and was just playing you along, feeding you lies to keep the charade going. And even if they really do care about you and want what's best for you, it still feels like you got jerked—at least it feels like I got jerked. And then you find out this person is *way better* and *more advanced* than you thought, way more than you are, so the differential is *huge*, and you're like, "no way, I really thought I was kinda reaching out to someone, and all the time I've just been the patsy." And it doesn't matter if that one is like a king who disguises himself and comes to your house, and even that you're a long-lost princess that has forgotten who you are and lives in humble circumstances. There's such a thing as transparency. Maybe not in government, but surely there ought to be in friendship. If someone deceives you once, how can you ever trust them again? It hurts, it really does, when you're deceived like that.

I don't do relationships well. In fact, I suck at them. I'm a loner, always have been, and am most comfortable in my own company. It never fails—I just don't get relationships. Even relationships with ghosts. May be the hardest of all.

Eventually I would cool down enough for Steve to try to defend himself. As he pointed out, at least when Thomas Jefferson showed up, I could recognize him—but if Steve had stood in front of me before I actually thought to call him up (now where, come to think of it, did *that* thought come from), I would have panicked: *Who are you? Why are you in my house? Why are you in my mind? Help! Call the psychic hot line!! Yes, Nitwit, it's a crisis. Could I get a referral for the local unit of Ghost Busters?*

If I had any doubt about that, refer back to when poor John came bumbling along in the middle of the night. At least then I had Steve to turn to.

One can only imagine my response if he'd been a little

more candid when he first answered the phone: *Hi, this is Steve Jobs, you may know of me; I have been watching you for four years because we have one soul, divided eons ago, and now it's time to get back together. Do you mind?* It's true. I would have hung up the phone so fast it would have cracked.

Yes, as he was to contend, he had done everything he could to get my attention: come in my dreams, through music, thrown apples at me (not like this last would have meant anything to me). And he *had* made the point that he didn't want to frighten me. But my feelings were deeply hurt, and that stubborn and defensive little girl inside wasn't going to take it lying down:

-I may be foolish, gullible, ignorant of the ways of spirits and such, but *what about me?* What do I have to do to be left in peace? Because I don't want to be lied to, or laughed at, anymore. It really really hurts. And if I have to hide—no, I'm not going to hide under my blanket anymore. If I have to, I'll get my saber and cut the buttons off anyone who tries to stab me, who thinks they can just hurt my feelings, lie to me, stab me in the back. Try it, god damn it! Just try it. So back off and pick up your sword, because this is a fight to the death, if need be. Somebody has to stand up for me, even if it's just *me*!

So there! Stay armed!

9:59 p.m.

Steve was laughing at me. He thought it was funny? Okay, so somehow this was another set-up, just to get me to the point of grabbing my steel?

-He. *That would be the steel in your backbone.*

I figured that he was talking about my Cancer-astrological inheritance, the inner strength. He urged me to meet him, to come talk to him in the astral place where we could hang out together. I held out for a while, as I was still pissed, but I finally agreed. I lay on the bed and threw a loose-weave blanket over my head, this time just to isolate myself for the trip, and we counted down together. Steve suddenly grabbed me and started to pull me somewhere, but I was still feeling ornery, so I resisted. Eventually, however, he got us both going upward, and I saw that we were passing a *gigantic* structure. I couldn't fathom what it was. It was dark and obscure. We seemed quite small compared to it, we just kept flying and flying and never seemed to reach the end. I was *awed* by this huge whatever-it-was, the sheer size of it, and I started thinking it must be something very grand—like maybe this was the great collective he talked about?

I could not have been more wrong.

All of a sudden I realized it was a tremendously big disk—a ball really—of entwined naked bodies, like something hot off the dripping pen of Dante. Steve said it was the wheel of karma. All these people were all tangled up with each other (sorta like my bra straps get tangled up with each other if I don't be careful to snap them shut before I put them through the washer). They were all bound by these karmic ties from one to the next. It looked really gross and I didn't like it. Steve took me up high, above the ball, to a glass walkway among the stars. We sat there, dangling our feet, but I was still bothered by the entangled bodies below us. I could see what looked like raindrops of light falling all around us, falling into the ball.

Steve asked me if I didn't have compassion for that tangled mass of humanity.

-Of course. But what can I do? What can anyone do?

I continued to be uncomfortable, so Steve took me to "our room," where I could no longer see that tortured heap of human beings.

-So what do you want to do?
-Play a game?

Steve got out the chess board, but I shook my head.

-Too cerebral, I don't feel like focusing that much.

We discussed what else we could play—cards? No, not challenging enough. So in the end the only option seemed to be chess. We set up the game between us on the bed, but I couldn't concentrate. I was still a little angry about the revelations earlier that day. Suddenly, Steve jumped up and turned into a version of Peter Pan, complete with green tunic and tights, although the shank of hair sticking out from under the feathered cap was dark. I realized I was Wendy. Steve tossed me a sword. He ditched the dagger and got a sword for himself.

Of course I couldn't fight in Wendy's nightgown—I would've tripped and fallen off a rooftop or something—so I quickly slipped into some breeches (ending just below the knee) and a pullover shirt. Then we were off. We were all over the rooftops, parapets, hiding behind chimneys and dormers. We could both fly, so that was very cool. We were having great fun, when all of a sudden I thought about those people all tangled together. Immediately I began to fall, for I had lost my happy thoughts. Steve had to catch me and take me back to our room. There he explained to me, as if I were a child, that it was just a concept, an illusion, to demonstrate how people were tied together in this karmic twist. He had me look down from the bedroom window; it must have been one of those magic windows, because I seemed to be looking at city streets far below, bright with neon, people going about their business. It looked like a lot of traders and those kinds of people. I was sure our room hadn't been in this kind of neighborhood before.

*-This is what you lived in every day. (*As if I weren't still living in it.) *There's where it's really happening, all the.....*

I can't think what word he used, but it meant all the karmic ties.

I suddenly realized that the same light rain—the rain made of light—that I had seen up among the stars was falling on the street below. Like an invisible cosmic shower, it was going right *through* the people, as if it were affecting them *inside* and they didn't even know it.

I felt better after seeing this, perhaps just because it was so familiar, the devil I knew. Steve wanted me to put on *Proud Mary,* not sure why, maybe because there's a big wheel that keeps turning. Or maybe because, tucked right behind it, was *Have You Ever Seen the Rain* (Creedence Clearwater Revival), which made me think of the falling light shower that nobody seemed to see.

After this trip I did not feel so emotional, my relationship with Steve somewhat restored. I sighed and relaxed for the night.

But it was to be a sleepless one.

Chapter 22
Stephanie Gets Rewired

Wednesday, November 18, 2015
9 a.m.

From my journal:

-Wow, I did *not* sleep last night. Woke up numerous times, but I felt like I hadn't even been sleeping, couldn't get back to sleep, at one point asked you to wipe out my memory of why I was angry (the inconsistencies) from my mind so I could rest, put on calming instrumentals, but just woke up today wiped out. Back of my head aching, at base of skull; back aching. I had the wild idea last night that "they" were working on my body, and that my dna was being readjusted or tinkered with.

I guess that's why you apologized for me not getting any sleep (through Susie) yesterday—that it was an apology in advance. You told her that you took me with you at night (during my sleep I guess), and seemed to be apologizing for that, the lack of sleep, but I really hadn't had too much trouble with sleep deprivation although at times I was getting a lot less of it than my customary. Other times I seemed to sleep a lot.

So I'm going to check out more about the spiritual rewiring process, see what I find. I already found this.

Body rewiring is associated with vibrations, electrical sensations, and moving sensations in the body; brain rewiring is associated with headaches and moving pressures in head, seeing light flashes behind eyes, and hearing buzzing noises. [58]

---

[58] http://bridgetoearth.com/2011/09/26/feeling-the-shift-part-2/; citing to http://deniselefay.wordpress.com/2011/02/21/kundalini-rising-the-rewiring-process/

-Ha. I just asked you a day or two ago why I was seeing flashes of light. I've got a lot of emotion and exhaustion to deal with today. So, last night, the tinnitus in my ears was much louder, more consistent—or at least noticeable. I haven't noticed it much in a while. Also I was having tinges of headache (forehead) which is not normal for me—I don't tend to have headaches. Moving pressures in head? Not sure about that one—was feeling something yesterday but not sure it was that.

During the night I had had several odd experiences. At one point Steve gave me a little spaceship for my own, one that I could drive like a car. It was a sleek model, a two-seater, and I had enjoyed taking it for a spin. But the odd thing was—if I looked down, I was in a car. If I looked up or straight ahead, I was in a spaceship. A dual-function vehicle apparently, its function controlled by where you put your focus. I had the sensation of reaching for the controls, as I would in my usual car, and they weren't in the same place. I had to make some adjustments to my habits.

And at some point thereafter, it was as if I reached for the controls in my body—my physical body—and they weren't in exactly the same place. They had shifted—not a lot—but enough that I was thrown for a bit, groping. Something had clearly been adjusted, changed.

In the morning I had felt tired, achey and stressed. I tried to feel for my heart to ground myself, but I had the oddest impression that there was an embryo in there. In my heart!! Actually, I didn't know if it was in my heart or super-imposed over it, but I couldn't figure out what was going on. I thought of the big donut ring among the stars, the one that Steve had shown me early on, with all the embryos nested inside it, ready to mature into new universes.

Was this like a seed planted, something growing inside me?

-Okay, about ready to take a calming bath. The base of my skull is feeling better, but I do have an ache in lower back.

While I was in my bath, I had that odd sensation, as if when I tried to move my body, something slipped—as if it slipped out of gear—and I had to adjust internally. In howsoever way the controls had been changed, altered by whatever-whoever was reworking my body, it apparently was short-lived, or else I adjusted quickly to the new paradigm, for I hardly noticed it after that. Continued operation was seamless.

10:12 a.m.

Back to the journal:

-Oh, a couple more things.

Before I left yesterday, Susie said she could see you in my eyes.

She also said, "This is *big*, Stephanie. This is really *big*." She said that you were a genius, and that part doesn't bother me, because I know the genius inside myself. My stupidity is from being so naïve, like the uneducated village girl transported to the palace, where she doesn't even know which spoon to use to taste the soup, much less what clothes to wear for supper. Or even have the clothes.

Also last night, sometime during the night, you told me we were going to visit Melchizadek (sp?) I didn't really know who that was, and because I was a little worried to find out—for some reason I thought maybe the name was associated with something dark—I decided to wait until today to look it up. I just did:

Melchizedek (note correct spelling)

Hellenistic Judaism

Josephus refers to Melchizedek as a "Canaanite chief" in War of the Jews, but as a priest in Antiquities of the Jews.

Philo identifies Melchizedek with the Logos as priest of God, and honoured as an untutored priesthood.

The Second Book of Enoch (also called "Slavonic Enoch") is apparently a Jewish sectarian work of the 1st century AD. The last section of the work, the Exaltation of Melchizedek, tells how Melchizedek was born of a virgin, Sofonim (or Sopanima), the wife of Nir, a brother of Noah. The child came out from his mother after she had died and sat on the bed beside her corpse, already physically developed, clothed, speaking and blessing the Lord, and marked with the badge of priesthood. Forty days later, Melchizedek was taken by the archangel Gabriel (Michael in some manuscripts) to the Garden of Eden and was thus preserved from the Deluge without having to be in Noah's Ark.

Dead Sea Scrolls

11Q13 (11QMelch) is a fragment (that can be dated to the end of the 2nd or start of the 1st century BC).... In this eschatological text, Melchizedek is seen as a divine being and Hebrew titles as Elohim are applied to him. According to this text Melchizedek will proclaim the "Day of Atonement" and he will atone for the people who are predestined to him. He also will judge the peoples. [59]

Holy shit, this *is* big, isn't it? Then *who* am I? When you said I had to get into my soul mind to remember who I was— *who* am I?

2:14 p.m. update:

I went to my appointment with Dean that morning. I filled him in on recent developments. I confessed my humiliation in learning that I had been deceived, that Steve had been trying to reach me, been watching me, since he died. This brought up a

---

[59] https://en.wikipedia.org/wiki/Melchizedek; this work is released under CC-BY-SA http://creativecommons.org/licenses/by-sa/3.0/

lot of frustration and anger, which I expressed, but Dean just shrugged his shoulders: "I'm sure he had some reason." Just like a man!!

Dean asked me why he was getting an impression of Syria, the Syrian crisis, associated with Steve, and I shrugged in my turn:

-Because he's Syrian?

-*Ah!*

(Steve had confided in me at some point that he was monitoring the refugee situation and was working with others in the Non-Corporeal Realm to send fresh ideas and suggestions directly to decision-makers in this matter.)

I told Dean about the plaque that had fallen, that Steve had told me it represented the three Dharma seals: impermanence, no self and nirvana. Dean then divulged to me that when he went to replace the plaque, he was convinced that the screw had actually been moved somehow, because it no longer hung straight as it had. Afterwards, I asked Steve if he had done that, and he said, essentially, that it wasn't the screw that had moved—it was Dean's world. His big picture had shifted, but he hadn't yet stepped into his power, so the plaque (a part of the old physically limited world) appeared crooked—screwy.

I happened to mention to Dean the Melchizedek issue, how I recalled Steve grabbing me and we were headed up to talk to this guy, whoever he was, but I couldn't recall actually having the conversation or anything that might have been said. When I mentioned how I was worried, in the middle of the night, that this Melchizedek might not have been one of the good guys, Dean smiled.

"I need to show you something."

He went into the next room, a storage room I think, and returned with a framed diploma. He handed it to me. I looked at it closely: it was, basically, a certificate of admission of Dean McMurray into the priesthood of Melchizedek.

Holy Mackerel! So *this* was the conversation—if not with Melchizedek himself, with his representative.

I left our meeting, stunned as usual. One validation after another.

Back at home, I got into an intense discussion with Steve

about the lying issue. I was feeling very wrung out over this matter, so troubled, but still I couldn't help feeling the amusement of it all: What a tempest in a teapot!!

4:58 p.m.

-*Okay, where are we?*

-Well, I think…that we're both in the same place. Meaning you're not above me. You're not better than me. We both still have issues. And I think, but don't know, that we will release the last issue together, the one that finally clears the energy.

-*Which issues are still on the table? Of the ones you identified to Dean…and yourself.*

-Well, do you admit that the issue with the school was *yours*. I'm pretty clear that it wasn't mine.

-*If I concede that issue, would you believe me?*

-I would believe that it was your issue. Would I believe that you believe it is—was—your issue? Not sure. The thing is, Steve, once someone starts lying to you, how do you believe anything that one says?

-*I can concede that point at least.*

-I guess, actually, I can tell in my heart if you're sincere. It's the same heart, right?

-*I guess.*

-You guess?

-*Let me wallow in my self-pity for a little bit, will you?*

-Be my guest. Just don't track on the carpet.

-*It's kinda tough sharing the same space, huh?*

-Sometimes, for sure.

-*You really don't pull any punches, do you?*

-Should I be?

-*No, not for me. Are you feeling better, anyway, in your heart?*

-Yes.

Perhaps because this was such a big issue for me, this idea of full disclosure, it would become the subject of many lessons over the next months. No, I didn't particularly want to see everything in his cupboards, but I wanted to know what was important, and not to be misled. So had he misled me, or was it just my own misinterpretations and confusion? It would be a very tough can of worms to untangle. Or, for those who don't remember fishing with night crawlers and safety pins, a difficult mess of bra straps to unravel.

6:13 p.m.

Determined to sort out this deceit issue, I did some investigation and came up with a muscle test: you put the forefinger of one hand through the circle made by the thumb and forefinger of the other and apply pressure to see if you can break the connection. I tested it on various issues before I trusted it enough to attack the problem between Steve and me. At this point, I didn't know if anything he had told me was true, so I went to brass tacks:

-Steve is lying to me about being Steve Jobs. No.
-Steve is lying to me about twin soul business: No.
-I am making up things about our connection: No
-Steve lied to me about the manner in which we connected (i.e. kinda random from his perspective): Yes.
-Steve has told me other lies: Yes
-I should end this connection: No
-I can still bail on this relationship: No

I wasn't sure if that was a downer or a subtle upper, but it did seem we were stuck together. That actually may have been what made the muscle testing work so well—we were somehow sharing a pretty tight connection.

But I did confront him on the reveal about the untruthfulness:

-Wow. Do you have anything to say for yourself?
-*Why? You'd just consider it another lie.*
-Probably. I'm not seeing the answer to this dilemma. What do you *want* from me?
-*Can you love a liar?*

-How? You would never know who you were loving. Lying is one of those things that I consider a fundamental problem for human relationships. If you can't be open and honest, transparent, what's the point? Wow, I'm just blown away.

-*Can I speak up for myself?*
-If you want. For what it's worth—you freakin' liar.
-*I never meant to hurt you.*
-Well, you did.

There was so much potential for understanding, growth, altered perspectives on this single issue. Perhaps the issues of his life only still mattered for the teachings they might impart, as they *were* issues of the Earth Plane Distortion Field. Lying simply could not exist in the Hereafter, where transparency is the norm. Which may have been another reason why I, being still capable of being blind, was necessary to these excursions. But we did start with Steve's life issues, even though the depth of the problem—the mathematical equation that had brought us to this point—was rife with my own lessons to learn.

I continued to berate Steve for a bit, and then confessed:

-I guess I'm not being too gentle, am I?
-*No, but it's fine.*
-So why do you lie? What is that about?
-*My whole life was a lie.*
-Okay. Elaborate.
-*From the beginning. I wasn't even who I thought I was. How do you feel when you learn there's no Santa? Multiply that like a thousand times when you learn your parents aren't your parents.*
-Oh, boy. (Sigh.) You knew that from a young age?
-*I knew there was no Santa from a young age.*
-I can't even trust you will give me the straight scoop, but I will apply the muscle test to each statement.
-a) Steve was devastated upon learning his parents were not his "real" parents: Yes
-All right, keep going.
-*Okay, I'm a bit needy. I admit it.*

-It's power, isn't it?

-Lying is a way of having power over people. That's a Yes.

-Steve, why didn't you work out these issues before? You've been hanging around up there with some of the most enlightened people in the universe.

-*Can't.*

-Why not?

-*Why the f...why do you think I told you I needed the physical limitations, the contrast?*

-Okay, I'm going to muscle test that one:

-c) Contrast or physical limitations is necessary to work out certain character issues: Yes

-d) Lying such as has occurred in this relationship is one of them: Yes

Wow. So that was a lesson about working out everything we could while we were still in the Earth Plane Distortion Field. In going back through my journal, what was missing was the pronoun—*whose* character issues needed to be worked out? He was way too sly, and the tapestry was too tightly woven, for me not to realize that there was more here than initially met my eye. Where did our mutual issues begin and end?

But I was still so new to this game. I tried to hammer it out as best I could:

-Obviously, you can't lie in the afterlife, because everyone would immediately know it is a lie (as you previously pointed out.) Anyway, I can see the dilemma. How *do* we come to understand our issues? You've set up many scenarios where I had to face some of my own issues—and I'm thinking how they might have been resolved otherwise. I had to encounter the intensity of the emotion that surrounded them. That was key. I remember that. I had to crawl backwards to the source of that emotional turmoil. It had to be *real*, or feel real—at least real enough for me to really have an incentive to want to overcome the issue. So if lying is not possible, then getting caught in a lie is not possible, and the emotional issue is not there. Am I getting this right?

-I think so. It's a soul issue.

-But some people don't have to solve all their soul issues, apparently. Look at Billy Fingers[60], he went off to all kinds of ecstatic realms after a lifetime that must surely have had issues to be resolved.

-I can't speak for others.

-No, me neither. Okay, this is very perplexing, are we going to have to go through every statement you've ever made? Should I throw out the entire journal??? Anyway, why lie to me, of all people?

-Because you're the only one who can save me.

-Oh really?

-Who else is going to stand here with me and go through this?

-Good point. Okay, let's go back to step one. So you're devastated to learn that you are adopted. Whether or not your adoptive parents ever lied to you, it still felt like a huge deception when you found out. I suppose they couldn't really tell you until you were old enough to understand. I mean, you don't sit a 2-year-old down and say, "Now son, we've got some bitter news for you. But the good side is we really really wanted you." [61]

-Well, I think it's more than that, actually. I think—well, I know, actually—that the events of our earliest life, infancy, are also recorded in our life psyche. Sometimes they're harder to reach.

-So, your earliest life, when there were issues about your ultimate placement, and even the fact that your (adoptive) mother was concerned about getting too attached to you before everything was final. Having had babies, I do know that the very early attachment is extremely important. Fortunately, I did have that, my mother was very maternal with her babies.

---

[60] *The Afterlife of Billy Fingers*, by Annie Kagan, c. 2013, Hampton Roads Publishing

[61] At some point—not then—but later, I would connect empathically on this issue and can say it was truly devastating, the sense of feeling like you'd been dropped down in a jungle and raised by apes (not that his parents were apes, but that he felt as alien and confused as Mowgli must have when he learned the Wolves weren't his real parents—*Who or what am I?*).

422   The Journey Begins

So let's muscle test:

-e) The circumstances of Steve's earliest months in that life caused lifelong issues: Yes

Wow, that's a very strong yes, actually. I can feel it deep inside me. I'm curious if you were totally honest with Susie (except for the school issue, which we've already covered).

-f) Steve was honest with Susie except for school issue: Yes (which I take to include his statement about being done with his issues)

-g) So you did know about me pretty much from the time you passed over: Muscle test: Yes

8:29 p.m.

We had continued to discuss the matter throughout the day, the issues that had afflicted him in his lifetime, and also the nature of our relationship to date. I thought about how I had behaved. Yes, I had argued with him from day one, refused to accept that he was who he said he was, and once I accepted that he actually did have a lifetime as Steve Jobs, I had turned up my nose at that, as if it were just stinky manure in the paddock. I wasn't all that trusting or compassionate, either one. But if it was the truth of how I saw things, how I felt, if I was just being blunt, wasn't that appropriate? And he didn't have an ego to appease, did he? Not that this was probably a deciding factor— I had the sense that I would have been just as frank if we'd actually met face-to-face back when we were both still in the EPDF. And maybe that was the point.

In fact, we would have our capers on that scene down the road, re-visiting our history—quite a ways down the road—and it would be enlightening. But at that moment, the question was: how *was* he to play it?

At this point, I refer the reader to a beautiful little movie that I had watched maybe six months before Steve and I connected: *Lovely, Still*, written and directed by Nik Fackler. It is a tale that provides a great illustration of Steve's dilemma, and which was recalled to mind as I was editing this section. I was enthralled by the story and production when I first saw it, and recommended it to everyone I knew. Now I understood why. My soul must have resonated with the essential theme. It knew the script, even though I was taken by surprise with the O'Henry ending. It is definitely a movie for those who have not forgotten how to dream, who remember in their souls the role of synchronicity, the world as symphony and the power of love.

As I write these words I have just finished re-watching the movie, and certain lines brought tears to my eyes: "When we met, everything fit; it was like breathing." It might seem overly sentimental, even maudlin to some, but those have never met nor do they remember deep inside themselves the wonder of their twin—the core goodness, the essential rightness, of reality.

I smiled as I watched the couple sledding down a hill together. I had forgotten that part. It made me think of one of my favorite experiences with Steve, whirling down the hill with snow flying up around us on the day of the "dress fiasco." I had felt so safe and protected with his legs and arms around me. From time to time, I have asked him if we could go sledding again, and we've had some great times—particularly in a special place that feels like it might be in the Swiss Alps— sipping cocoa in a chalet afterwards, seated around a blazing fire with several other couples. I think it's where twin souls meet, the ones that are separated by the Corporeal Divide.

And, yes, even back on November 18, 2015—hardly more than a month into our acquaintance—I did consider that maybe it had hurt as much to not be remembered, to be mistrusted, as to be lied to. I felt contrite.

-Do you forgive me?

Not trusting his answer, I did my own check: No.

-Okay, well at least that's an honest non-answer. (From you—I did the finger testing thing.) Let me know when you do.
    -*I don't need to. There's nothing to forgive.*
    -Yeah, I guess to understand all is to love all.
    -*There's nothing more I can add to that.*

I used to imagine sometimes, when I looked around at the world and none of it made sense—that I was lying in a hospital bed somewhere, in some celestial realm, lost in my hallucinations. That what I took for "reality" was, in some real sense, the insane ward, where everyone wandered around in their mind, lost in the amnesiac fog. But always I was cared for, always there were those around trying to break through—even though I couldn't see them—words of comfort and encouragement, of love, always seeking to get through the background noise of restless egoic delusions. *Remember, Stephanie, remember who you are.*

Thursday, November 19, 201 9:33 AM

There were no notes in my journal except for the following:

-I had a pretty peaceful night. We were good between us, peaceful even. I awoke this morning to a whole new level of understanding.

Friday, November 20, 2015 4:17 a.m.

It was the middle of the night, but I was awake and unable to sleep. I reached for the laptop to recap the most recent adventure and the events of the last few hours, namely:

I had been watching an episode of *Vikings* in bed until late, when Steve asked me to come to him. I held back—I was in the midst of a show. But finally I turned off the computer and slipped down under covers.

-Immediately, I could feel you brushing my hair back from my face, being soothing, but I didn't know where I was. I couldn't get the picture at first. Then it seemed like I was either standing in some tank or lying in something like an old-fashioned tin bathtub, with the really high back. I was kinda panicky because I couldn't get a fix, but you kept trying to calm me, telling me to relax, just relax, it was okay. Suddenly I realized I couldn't see my body. I had a head, but no body, and then I realized that my body was in a normal body shape, but all made of colored light—not shining light, more like light strands—mostly blue, I think. I was pretty panicky, but you continued to calm me, and I really didn't like that the light body ended at my head, so the light swept up my head and then I was all light. And when I turned, you were, too [made of light]. So then I relaxed and tried out this light body. I was moving in it like I would in my normal body, and we went off hand-in hand. But when I tried to hug you, I went right through your body. You adjusted something, like a field around the body, so some more resistance was created and that didn't happen.

And then, as sometimes happened, I had slipped out of the scene, back into my mind. When that happened, it was as if I would just lose my grasp in the world Steve and I were sharing, sliding back into the amnesia, I guess. I apologized to him for this, but he said it was okay, that I had done really well.

I slept after that, and then I awakened with somebody's face in front of me. It was not Steve, but someone Steve knew—he gave me a name, repeating it over and over so I wouldn't forget it, apparently. I was still kind of groggy with sleep. I did get on the laptop and do some research on the name, but at first the images that I came up with didn't match the face I had seen. Finally, I found a particular one that did. Steve let me know that this might be an individual I would have contact with at some future date.

10:41 AM

I was sitting at the computer, idly surfing, when Steve interrupted:

-Let's not get distracted, Stephanie, I'd like you to stay here with me.
-Okay. What are we going to talk about?
-Let's talk about last night. Again, I am sorry for the discomfort. It will be over soon—the discomfort, sleepless part. The changes will continue.
-Changes to what?

-Well, to a more integrated being. The good news is, we'll be able to connect even better.

-Is there bad news?

-None that occurs to me.

-It's the pain at the base of my skull that is the most awkward. It's not really bad, just kinda achey.

-Yeah, a little massage there would be good. You can do self-massage, you know.

-Okay, I will. Why does it hurt there?

-You remember something called the..... me·dul·la ob·long·a·ta. (But I liked "obdula melongata." It has kind of a Latin ring to it, like some obscure piano piece or a dance.)

He was referring to my first attempt to catch the term from him.

-Okay, whatever. I pick up what I pick up, and I have to believe my vocabulary affects this transmission.

Hey, give me a break, it had been a very long time since I'd had occasion to think about the medulla oblongata! Maybe forty-five years or so.

-Indeed. I'm impressed that you remembered it at all. So this is believed to be the site of the "primitive brain," some would say, the primate brain. Little does the majority of humanity understand about the potential contained therein.

-Is it where the soul brain is located?

I was intrigued. Maybe the clues to help me remember "who I was" were buried down there, right next to all the ancestral memories inherited from my ape forebears?

-H'mm—methinks the lady is on to something. Go—research it.

-Okay.

Off I went to do my "detective" work:

-So....The medulla oblongata is medically described, or anatomically described, as the link between the "higher brain" and the autonomous systems, like respiration, heart beating, etc. On the spiritual side I was immediately directed to this from PARMAHANSA YOGANANDA. (Surprise of surprises—the website dedicated to the subject of *Autobiography of a Yogi*— the book Steve had distributed at his memorial service.)

> Medulla oblongata: This structure at the base of the brain (top of the spinal cord) is the principal point of entry of life force (prana) into the body. It is the seat of the sixth cerebrospinal center, whose function is to receive and direct the incoming flow of cosmic energy. The life force is stored in the seventh center (sahasrara) in the topmost part of the brain. From that reservoir it is distributed throughout the body. The subtle center at the medulla is the main switch that controls the entrance, storage, and distribution of the life force.[62]

www.yogananda.com.au

---

[62] http://www.yogananda.com.au/g/g_medulla.html

-So this has to do with some tweaking??? To my brain to work with the flow of cosmic energy?

-Yes, and I'm glad you are beginning to trust me a little more, letting me feed you more information without so much resistance.

-Well, how could I trust that you weren't leading me astray?

-Indeed. Know thy source(s).

-I do like this, though, the learning.

*-It's what you wanted, no? To have the teachers **before** you died, when you could still do something about it.*

-Yeah, I did. I thought it was kind of unfair to read about all the great "universities" and "teachers" in the afterlife willing to work with anyone with a desire to learn. I didn't want to wait.

-Impatience. Does that remind you of anyone?

-But it doesn't do any good to just read about this stuff. It's all just theory then, and the experiential knowledge is what is missing to say if it is true or not.

-Yes, my experiential learner par excellence. *So you're in the midst of some experiential learning.*

-Okay. I gotta go feed the dogs and massage the base of my skull and just process a bit. Then I will come back and research some more.

I did later come across this intriguing tidbit on the Yogananda website, a little information passed on from Sir Yukteswar, who had just crossed the stream, to his favorite student, Parmahansa:

> According to the law of relativity, by which the Prime Simplicity has become the bewildering manifold, the causal cosmos and causal body are different from the astral cosmos and astral body; the physical cosmos and physical body are likewise characteristically at variance with the other forms of creation.[63]

---

[63] http://www.yogananda.com.au/aoy/beyonc death 3.htm#casual after the latter's death:

Manifolds and relativity and simplicity? Is this what happens when you cross your neighborhood mechanic with Einstein and Steve Jobs? I do have to say, I rather like my astral body, which has some details which are characteristically at variance with the physical one. Not sure about the causal one, but it does remind me of first year law school, when for the longest time I couldn't figure out what was so casual about the connections between tort and injury.

Afternoon:

I met my friend Cathy for lunch. Over the last week, she had become my newest confidant in this strange adventure. We hadn't connected in a while, so I was a little uncertain about confiding in her, but Steve had encouraged me. As usual, she came through for me; she was quite open to everything and was to become my greatest ally. I had told her about Susie Grimmett, and she had made an appointment for herself—right after mine that was already scheduled for the day. I therefore invited her to come with me to my session, and she did.

The three of us were crowded around a card table in a little curtained alcove in the back of the Rock Shop. There, Susie once again connected with Steve. I was also once again feeling a little miffed at him due to the fallout from the last session, and not a little guarded. What further secrets might come out? I didn't worry about Cathy being there to hear it; we were close enough after a lifelong friendship that she could hear anything I did.

There was a further consideration in these meetings. Susie knew absolutely nothing about our connection other than what came out during the readings. I wanted it that way, for quality control. That meant I was reserved and unemotional in our contact. Furthermore, Steve's nature was to be blunt, and although he might laugh or be humorous, there was none of the easy banter of our private relationship. It felt kind of…sterile. I suppose you might compare it to talking to your loved one through the glass at the local jail, with someone sitting there monitoring your conversation. It just doesn't come off the way it can while you are hanging out together in your personal space. This is not to say that I didn't find it captivating—I loved hearing from him through Susie's vocal cords. *But...*the tone was definitely different, especially early on, and often what he said (or didn't say) in these first sessions raised my hackles.

Once again I was not set up to record, and so I can only regurgitate from my copious notes. But what he did say was total validation. And of course, Cathy was there as a witness, and heard it all.

He started off by explaining that I was downloading information through conversations that occurred during the night, many of which I did not recall; but that was why I was feeling so tired, as if I didn't get any sleep. *Information*, he said, *was being downloaded at the base of my skull.* Susie touched the back of her neck to demonstrate where he was showing her, at exactly the spot where I felt the ache. Yes, the medulla oblongata. I met Cathy's eyes at this information—I had shared with her over lunch how I was experiencing these symptoms.

Steve went on to say that I was remembering before I was born, and that I had a desperate need to understand throughout my life. He said that I didn't understand how powerful my son, Christopher, is, that he is a star child, and highly intelligent. He is one of the vortexes for things to come through. This was intriguing information, given Christopher's identity as a bipolar screw-up, in common social parlance (the earthly Erik Medhus of my life). It does not do to say that I didn't see him that way in our personal relationship—I *did* see that this was the way the rest of the world viewed him. He was, indeed, a teacher for me, although I had not learned my lessons yet.

Steve added:

*I have been under illusion of who I thought I was in this life, but now I'm figuring out who I really am.
*There is some business around me. He confirms the reference to [name omitted] and that I would eventually be contacting him. He will let me know things about him no one else knows.
*Steve's role in his life was to teach what we are capable of.
*He and I have had many other lives together. We are like twins separated at birth, found each other later in life. Multiply

this by billions of times, and the same story applies to those souls.

*Steve sees things open and energetic. He was "opening a door" for me, both last night and previously. He mentioned quantum physics and psycho-cybernetics. He mentioned molecules in motion but Susie had trouble relating to what he was trying to show her.

*When he was alive, he thought he was lucky, but learned after he passed that he was chosen.

*He had business stresses that contributed to his condition while he was ill. Not so important to him now.

*He takes me places in an instant. He is downloading information to me.

When I asked about the "project," to which he had frequently referred, he evaded a direct response:

*There is always a project. When we slow down we cease to function as human. We become sedentary.

*Show appreciation for small things one does, life should be about always helping other people, with a smile, opening doors, always observant of other people, they are extensions of ourselves.

*I am to remember things I've forgotten.

*He was a shaker and a mover. He is still de-fragging on that side.

**He referred to his son, clearly with all the satisfaction of a proud father. (*Note: He always expressed deep affection for his family: widow and children.)

*Over top of the United States government is a group that dictates everything, the President is puppet with an illusion of control. Money governs our country. There are 147 companies that rule over our government.

Well, no surprises there. I'd never taken politics too seriously for that reason.

*The country (managers of country??) thinks that war will make us prosperous. There was manipulation of public

Again, no surprises there. When asked what could be done, he said:

The solution is one thought away. Only 7000 people are required to pray/meditate at the same time to shift earth dynamics.
Many other life forms have been here to experiment with our dna. They come back periodically. Our dna has been upgraded many times. The Egyptian half human/half animal or bird did exist. It was real. Part of experimentation at that time.
New children are upgraded as well with new strand of dna. They will be salvation of the world.
Knowledge is increasing at a rampant rate.
All the information he is giving me is going into a book.
We've got to forget everything we learned. We have to educate ourselves, and do research.
He had information while he was here that was not common knowledge.
No certain religion has an absolute truth, we all desire to know God.
In his studies (during his illness) he was shown by a higher source and didn't doubt about an afterlife when he passed.
No soul is greater or lesser than any other.

During this session, Steve apparently had a little attitude going with Susie. In fact, I think for a long time she just thought of him as the jerk that followed me around. She wasn't above telling him off. When I got a little testy about the fact that I didn't seem to have any private space, she wagged her finger at him: "Now, Dude, she gets to do what she wants. If she doesn't want you coming around, she gets to make that choice!" She then informed me with satisfaction, "He says he agrees, you have that right," or as he then conceded:

* I can control our interaction. It's up to me to turn radio up and down. It's up to me to set the boundary. We can keep boundaries even as twins, I'm still in charge. The twin soul

energy is reconnecting, it's like a teeter-totter. I need to bring it back into balance. Balance is everything.
All he can do is keep giving information. I have to be the one setting the boundaries. We should never feel like we're at someone else's mercy. We all try to find someone to blame.

Nevertheless, after I got home, I wasn't finding the lock on the door:

-Listen, Steve, when I try to tune you out, it's like you're grabbing my hand as it goes for the knob to prevent me from doing it. I actually feel hurt when I try to shut you out. So what's that about?

He wasn't answering that one. Just that shrug, throwing up hands.

-Are we both just too intense?

That very thought had clearly amused Cathy, who knew me well, as she observed our interaction that day. There I was, trying to pin Steve down on some matters with my particular brand of petulant insistence, my default position when I'm trying to pick through the chaff to get to the wheat. *Yes...I get that, but...what about...?*

In fact I'd gotten into quite a debate with Susie over something she said off-handedly (interrupting the reading), and when I finally suggested we consult with Steve to get his opinion on the matter, he did support my position (actually in a diplomatic way) but he laughed: *She's just like me.* Almost as if he were apologizing for me. Imagine that! I knew I'd been pushing the discussion with Susie hard, because it just seemed so illogical from my point of view; I was like a dog with a bone that he's not going to let anybody else have, even to the point of being obnoxious. I had found *myself* apologizing to poor Susie for being so contentious, at the same time as I couldn't stop myself.

In the end, I guess we were, Steve and I, both pretty intense—neither one of us able to let go of something that had our attention, going to wrestle it to the ground, and keep flaying it until we had it tamed. Until we could brush off our hands and go: *There, got **that** done.*

A pretty interesting scenario when we were wrestling with each other over what was going on between us. *You're here!-* No, I'm not!-*Stop being so stubborn, yes you are!*

It is kind of amusing how many times I would argue with those on the Other Side—not just Steve—but family and others to come, just as I would get into debates with those on this side of the Border: *Yeah, that doesn't make sense to me...but how do you **know** that...what about...?* Always wanting—long after others were willing to give it up—to plunge deeper, to get to the heart of the matter, the real crux of the issue. As I thought of it, where the water runs clear.

That evening:

As I wandered through the aisles of K-Mart on some errand, Steve chatted me up.

-*What do you like most about me, Stephanie?*
-You help me find lost objects? You have a good sense of humor, you make me laugh?
-*Nope. Do you want me to tell you what you like most about me?*
-Sure.
-*I'm always here for you.*

Wow. As usual, so simple but profound.

9:15 p.m.

Cathy and I had an amazing phone conversation about her visit to Susie and all the information she received from her family. It brought some closure for her on a significant issue.

-Good-night Steve. I love you. I can't believe (hardly) how much has happened in the last six weeks. Wow. I think those words are going to be etched in my brain forever: "Hello, this is Steve Jobs. Okay, thanks for hosting me." Wow, I just read back through the first week or two of our contact. That was weird.

And yes, the thing I like best about you is that you're always here for me.

Chapter 23
Miss Priss Gets Some Wings

November 21, 2015

-Do you get tired of me losing my keys and stuff and having to ask you?

-*Never. I'm always happy to help.*

-That was kinda funny today, I asked you to help me find my keys, and you were kinda like "On your bed. (Sigh.) Look on your bed." So I went and looked on my bed but in fact they were in the sweatshirt that was lying on the basket of bedding right by my bed, and I called you on it, and you were like, "whatever, I missed, so shoot me" and I said "Yeah, but you're the know-it-all guy," and you said, "so says the know-it-all girl" and I really did have to laugh, because that surely is me. The know-it-all. I guess it takes one to know one, huh? And you said, "Do two know-it-alls cancel each other out?" That's a good question. But then I was thinking about how I'd make a good 19 year old—"Yeah, I know it all, dad and mom don't have a clue," and then I was thinking, "Shoot, I feel like a 19 year old, come to think of it." I mean, I've been skipping and dancing around all day—unbounded energy, I guess, like I used to when I was that age.

-*Enjoying it?*

-Yes I am!! What fun to have so much…it's not really the energy, it's the *joie de vivre*, the delight in just being alive, being able to twirl or skip or run or dance. I had really lost that sense over the last 20-30 years. I actually kept it for quite a while—probably into my mid-30s—at least at times. But I like having 65 years of hard-earned lessons under my belt, nevertheless. A youthful body, an old mind—no, *not* an old mind. A mind with lots of experience. Is that what I mean? I don't know. I just don't want to forget everything I've learned. Except you told me to unlearn everything I learned. Oops. Confusion.

*-Not **those** lessons. Those lessons were all about **unlearning** anyway. So it's all good.*

-That's interesting. So the real life lessons we learn are about *unlearning*. The more we unlearn the wiser we become?? Is that it?

-Yeah, from that perspective. Innocence—wisdom. Two sides of the coin.

-And in between all that garbage stuff. But good stuff, too, huh?

-Oh, yeah.

-By the way, I like that psycho-cybernetics guy. [Maxwell Maltz] I'm going to listen to some more interviews with him. Wow. He was around a long time ago, but really good. Thanks for that lead.

-You're welcome, Sweetheart.

-I love you, Steve, and I'm really sorry for all the mean ways I treated you and the mean things I said to you. Wow, I was a total brat. I'm so sorry, not just about being kinda mean about you in the beginning, but also about taking out my own issues on you. I'm really working on that humiliation piece.

-I know you are. And you're on the right track—painful as it is, you're climbing the mountain. Don't worry about falling, I'll be there to catch you—and shove you back along the path.

-Ouch. Yes. I'm beginning to realize that a lot of the things I blamed you for were really just like those bumpers on the bowling lanes for the young and inept, to keep me from totally blowing it, to keep pushing my ball in the right direction. A little push here and there. Is that what you've been doing?

-I won't...well, I won't speak to that.

-Okay. I'm good. I don't see what you see, but I trust you and will follow you.

-Good. We're a team—my star-wife and I.

-I like it when you call me that.

-(Smile.) Come be with me, then.

-Coming.

-So, some confusion about the divided energy thing. I get that spirits are always talking about divided energy, you said yours wasn't divided. Then you told Susie it was, and everybody else talks about divided energy. So please clarify if possible.

-If possible, key distinction.

-Okayyyyy…are there clues in there?

-About possibilities? Possibly.

-You're being awful obtuse.

-More than usual?

-So is this another lie?

-No.

-I'm very confused. The muscle test says yes it is.

-H'mm, that's going to be a problem. If you have to spot check everything I say.

-Why?

-Well, obviously something is lost in translation.

-The truth?

-No, not the truth.

-Okay, that tests out true.

-Maybe the problem lies with your definition of a lie.

-Ha ha. That was good. Did you do that deliberately?

*-I'm **very** deliberate.*

-Anyway, it seems to be true that the problem lies with my definition of a lie. So do you have a definition besides saying something that is not true, or fudging on the truth.

-Yes.

-What is it?

-A lie is a lie is a lie.

-What does that mean? A rose is a rose is a rose?

-No matter how it smells.

-My mind isn't grasping it.

-Let's rest on it, shall we? More information coming…stay tuned to the same channel, same day, same time.

Steve and I got into a discussion about future processes, contacts. I expressed some concern about my part.

-*I'm working on that. But I want you to be prepared.*
-Prepared for what?
-*Prepared for the next step. For stepping it up.*
-The energy?
-*The whole vortex. You good?*
-I think so. I got the hole in my stomach, like there's no floor to it.
-*No floors. You can fall and fall forever in me Stephanie, and not hit the ground.*
-Yes, Steve. I feel very agitated. Everything is tingling on my spine—right under that spot that was achey. And my forehead, something going on there. But I almost want to vomit, you know?
-*There can be that effect. Read something about chakra alignment. That might help. And also, get the book on psycho-cybernetics. You won't be disappointed. I promise.*

That afternoon:

More than five weeks of this non-stop adventure, attempting to sort out fact from fiction, caught up in the intensity of what seemed like a love connection, dealing with all my insecurities—all my self-hatred came floating to the surface, like sewage. My personal sense of self-revulsion was deep, almost as deep as my "who gives a shit what anybody else thinks about me" persona. One of the ways I'd kept the former in check was by keeping to my own company. I sensed that the source of this personal hatred was far deeper than could be explained by this lifetime, even given the many traumas of my early years. What I did know was that it was totally ripping up my relationship with Steve. I'd be good while we flitted around on our astral trips, but the deeper I got drawn into this connection—by now it was as real to me as any relationship with an incarnate being—the harder the boat rocked. Actually, it had been rocking from the beginning, there was no denying that. I attempted to hold onto my own oar—to not blame him for the turmoil in my own emotional body—but it was difficult. How could I resolve this?

It was something I had to do alone, a trip I had to take into the deepest part of me. But how?

In some of my internet meanderings I ran across something about the Burt Goldman quantum jump astral projection method. I got hopeful. Of course I had been astral projecting all along, but always with Steve's assistance. Now here was a method to try it on my own. I found a *youtube* video of Mr. Goldman doing the induction procedure. I lay down to give it a go. The question he presented was: *Ask to be shown something in a past life that influenced a problem you are having in this life.*

I went through the procedure, counting down, descending steps, opening a door…and boom!

I saw myself kneeling before this very tall figure in white. I appeared to be male, bent over, my head down seemingly in total submission, obeisance. The figure had a hood on, but there was also much light around it. I thought therefore that it was going to be good—all that white and light, the symbol of God and goodness.

Wow, was I wrong. It was as if something was being done to my spine as I knelt over, and then my entire back split, and these wings came out and unfolded. They were not pretty wings. No fairy appendages here. They were rather spindly, as portrayed on devils and perhaps bats.

But no! Noooo!! At that moment, Burt Goldman called us back from our little travels, interrupting the scene before I could get further information. I jumped up and shut off the video. Then I lay down again and redid the whole procedure to get back in. Apparently I'd missed a few scenes of the movie in the interim, like stepping out of the theatre at a critical moment to take your child to the bathroom; now I found myself in a tight closed space, like a coffin. There was something stuffed into my mouth—mud perhaps—and I knew I was being buried alive. I ate the mud or whatever it was so I could breath. Then I started to shake in fury. My hands seemed to be tied, but I was so furious and there was so much power emanating from me that it shook the whole ground, all the soil that had been thrown on my box. Suddenly the ground went flying as in an explosion and I erupted from this hole, humans scattering in every direction. I knew that these were the ones who had buried me. I could now see that I looked like some kind of large insect-like creature, that somehow I had been messed with and turned from a human into this creature, perhaps through DNA manipulation or some other trans-species splicing.

I left that area and went up on a mountain, where I curled up against the mountainside all alone. The little creatures came—rabbits and whatnot—and we shared companionship and love, but it was obvious that I was not going to survive. My heart was broken. As I lay there preparing for my own death, welcoming it, a single human climbed the mountain to where I lay. I rose up in fury, my wings expanded as I ascended a few feet into the air, but he was not scared off by my threatening posture. I saw that he meant me no harm, so I lay back down against the mountainside as before. He patted my horrible-looking face. The lower part was still human-like, but I had bulbous insect eyes. The man brought me something to eat and drink—mashed fruit or coconut milk, maybe just water, and little bits of fruit—but I was dying anyway.

As I beheld this vision, as I lay on my own bed in my own room, tears streamed down my cheeks at the kindness of this human, who was not afraid, but driven by compassion. I didn't know who he was. I didn't know if we had some connection before I was altered, if he had been a friend or family member. I only knew the kindness and the love of one human being. I cried for a long time, even after I sat down to type up this story in my journal. I hadn't cried that much in years and years. I had looked so scary, and everyone else was afraid of me. Even though I had done them no harm, they had attacked me. But here was one soul who had compassion, and it moved me beyond words. It was this act of kindness that caused me to weep.

-Still wiping tears. I don't know what this means....
-*You were frightening, unlovable by humans. But you still had the capacity to love. Only one came and saved you.*
-You said "saved." I wasn't saved, I died.

-Yes, but you died knowing that at least one human being was...pure enough...to love beyond appearances.

-Yes.

-Don't worry, Stephanie. The next wings you get will be angel's wings.

Later: on Angel's Wings

Within hours I was coming down off the latest fantasy trip.

-I just had to come and say that was awesome, awesome, awesome—so much fun. What a fun trip that was. I can't believe how wonderful that was. I feel like I'm walking a foot off the ground. Thank you bunches.

-Hey, most of it was your idea. Great idea by the way—looking forward to round Two.

-Oh, me too. I just am so stoked that that can happen—like all dreams really can come true, even the most personal, the ones you hold closest to your chest.

-I know some of the lessons have been hard, and you've wanted to kick me in the...shall we say, balls...more than once. But then there's the good times, when things sort themselves out, and I don't know about you, but nothing beats it in my book.

-Is that true? Is that really true? Do you really enjoy it too?

-Oh, I do. Believe me I do. Believe me, cross my heart and hope to die, I do. Well, I don't hope to die, scratch that. I've got every reason to live now. Every reason.

-Really?

-Yes. Only you. Only you can fill this space.

-Everybody else has to fill their own spaces.

-Yep.

-Wow. At times like this, I'm like "how did I get this lucky?"

-Remember, you were chosen.

-When? When was I chosen? Were we chosen or destined?

-That's a close distinction over here.

-I just love you when I don't have to contend with all that…oh, I hate even saying the words anymore…all that Steve Jobs stuff. I'll do what you want, contact who you want when the time is right, but it's so exhausting.

-But part of the journey, part of the adventure, part of the trip. I know you like your privacy. I know you like your little space where people don't intrude, and you don't want to intrude in the space of others. There's a lot of personal integrity for you in that. But, hold onto me as we go…

-"…as we roll down this unfamiliar road."

-I love you.

-And I love you, Steve.

Later still: Carry me back

-I looked back at that part about the weird winged creature I was and I cried again. I can't believe how much emotion that brings up in me. Really really odd. That was *such* a sad story, poor thing. And there's people like that in the world today, isn't there, who are feared and hated and all they want is to love and be loved?

-Yes, there are. A good lesson.

Random thoughts

-Am I prissy, or are *you* prissy.

-Oh, I think you're the prissy one.

-I sure hope so. At least then I know it can be overcome.

-Ha ha.

Chapter 24
Day 40 plus 1

Wednesday, November 23, 2015
10:47 a.m.

I had been restless all night. I knew there was a lot going on, that Steve was around and there was a conversation going on, but I could only remember one scene: we stood facing each other, elbows bent with hands lifted to chest level, and pressed our palms together. I could not feel Steve's hands, however, for there was a thin sheet of glass between us. I complained about not being able to actually touch, and Steve said: "Keep believing, keep imagining us here, and the glass will gradually dissolve."

I got on the internet when I woke up and went where I felt led. Almost immediately I came upon a book entitled: *Reconstructing Reality: Book II of Visions from Venus*, by Suzan Caroll, Ph.D.[64] I was able to download it off the internet, so I printed the first section. I started reading and was totally blown away.

> "Lamerius was remembering its many third dimensional lives when it was separated into two different beings, masculine and feminine. Now it was once again one, androgynous body of Light....The male, Lamire, and the female, Lamira, communed what they had learned while apart. This communion brought much wisdom, clarity, peace, and most of all, unity....[65]
>
> "Most of all, it remembered the shock of its first separation into its two polarized male and female individuals. Lamerius shuddered to remember how Lamira felt to be in a third dimensional body without her complete Self, and for Lamire to be without his

---

[64] © Copyright 2003, Suzan Caroll Ph.D Multidimensional Publishing
[65] *Id.* at 2

feminine counterpart. It took many Earth years before Lamire and Lamira could accept their deep grief over living as only a portion of their total Self.[66]

"Lamire and Lamira both carried those limitations, and the feelings of abandonment, through life after life after life.[67]

"Their commitment to Earth was ending, and they were free to return Home to Venus once and for all. First, however, each had to balance and heal the limited thoughts and painful emotions of their many earthly incarnations. This was best done at the source—third dimensional Earth.[68]

"Lamerius was fully aware that all matter and substance was an elaborate illusion created for the opportunity to commune and communicate with All That Is."[69]

The book described the body composed of light, recalling to mind the astral experience a few nights before, when my body had been transformed into those beautiful blueish interwoven glowing strands.

"If one of the complements was "awake" in the lower worlds, Lamerius could send a stream of consciousness down the vibration scale and into his or her mind. Lamire and Lamira could also communicate with each other across all time and space through the "homing beam" of Lamerius' consciousness.[70]

"Lamerius stood and stretched its long arms toward the top of Red Mountain. Its glowing, golden form expanded slowly, growing wider and wider until it took on the form of two pyramids attached at their base, with the masculine peak reaching towards the sky and the feminine peak grounded towards the heart of

---

[66] *Id.* at 3
[67] *Id.*
[68] *Id,*
[69] *Id.*
[70] *Id.* at 4.

Venus."[71]

I could not help but think of something Steve had said to me the day before: somehow he had gotten off into a discussion about Father Sky and Mother Earth, implying that these were again archetypes for our own situation.

The book described how, after the pyramids separated into the bodies, Lamire and Lamira faced each other and touched palms at heart level. I was dumbfounded. Exactly how Steve and I had pressed our hands together, but with the glass between.

> "Lamire and Lamira were still after their confessions and apologies. Even though they knew what was in each other's heart and mind, the open communication was an important part of their healing. They both realized that it was their perception of separation from each other while in the third dimension that was their primary wound, but the separation was only an illusion. They were One with each other and with All That Is. Could they remember when they were back on Earth?"[72]

-Oh, that's been me, apologizing to you the last few days.
-*And me trying to apologize to you, but you don't wish to hear.*

I was in awe. Reading this story, what was *our* story, was almost more than I could absorb. Someone had actually written this?? I just kept thinking: We really *are* One. We are the two parts, Steven and Stephanie, separated. What is our name as one?

I was attached to the name "Stephane" for the androgynous merged being, for some reason—it was a sort of middle ground on our names, a sort of unisex contraction, although it can be the masculine in French. I looked up the

---

[71] *Id.*
[72] *Id.* at 6.

meaning of the word, and found that it was meant to describe both the masculine and the feminine forms of the name:

> **What Does Name "Stephane" Mean?** You are spiritually intense and can sting or charm. Your name brings love and new starts into life and attracts money. In business, you are the creator and promoter of original ideas and usually enjoy considerable financial success. You have an eventful, exciting life. You are versatile and have the ability to learn easily.
>
> You are very intuitive. You have a reservoir of inspired wisdom combined with inherited analytical ability, which could reward you through expressions of spiritual leadership, business analysis, marketing, artistic visions, and scientific research. Operating on spiritual side of your individuality can bring you to great heights, and drop you off if you neglect your spiritual identity. You are always looking for an opportunity to investigate the unknown, to use and show your mental abilities, to find the purpose and meaning of life. You want to grow wise and to understand people and things. You need privacy to replenish your energy. You have a unique way of thinking, intuitive, reflective, absorbing. [73]

Okay, I could buy that this was an apt description of our combined personal attributes.

The name apparently has a number attached: ours was "seven," meaning: "Inner, Thought, Mind, Psychology, Secret, Mystic, Strange, Study, Knowledge, Loneliness, Rest."

Oh, yes. Especially the strange part.

And didn't we both have abandonment issues? Hadn't we lived those in this last lifetime? And this telepathic thing, us linking minds—was that through the combined being, our own "Lamerius," still blended together somewhere while we struggled to sort things out down here in the 3d dimensional world. Well, here and there, as it were.

---

[73] http://www.sevenreflections.com/name/stephane/

I knew, without being told, that something had changed; we had come to a conclusion of sorts. There was something too compelling about this Lamerius story, almost like a summary of the Story of Us. It was as if I had been led along, for just under six weeks, drawn up the path through the darkness until the sun came up over the mountaintop and I saw how far we had climbed. This *was* the moment. This was the time of the reunion, of the re-uniting of the twin souls. But what did that mean for me? What now?

I sensed a curtain fall. We had reached a climax of some sort. I felt the impulse to count the days since we had connected. Something I had intuited about the number 40 was kicking in:

-So there *were* forty days. *These* are the *forty days*?

I suspected that the forty days thing had significance—it recalled to mind the flood from the Bible, and didn't Jesus spend forty days and nights in the desert? Wasn't it one of those biblical terms that let you know something really significant was going on, like *begat* or *cubits* or something—a clue that you should pay attention?

-Or am I just totally blowing that allusion?
-*No. You are correct.*
-Forty days and nights.

Whoa.

-*Forty days and nights, my dear. And here we are.*

I decided I better research the number forty in terms of spiritual significance, to make sure I wasn't missing something. I discovered that it is actually a significant number in Christianity, Judaism and Islam, associated with a number of astounding events: Moses fasted on Mt. Sinai for 40 days and nights, he wandered with his people in the desert for 40 years, the people of Nineveh had 40 days to repent before it was destroyed, Abdon (a judge of Israel) had 40 sons. Holey Moley.

And that was only the beginning. There are many other noteworthy events associated with that number in the Bible.[74] And here some people just thought it was the point where you went over the hill.

So what did it all mean?

The number 40 has great significance throughout the Torah and the Talmud. The number 40 represents transition or change; the concept of renewal; a new beginning. The number 40 has the power to lift a spiritual state. [75]

For Islam, the number 40 occupies an important place: the 40 companions, the 40 perfect; the universe is supported by 40 pillars; the 40 supports of the dome of the Mosque of Omar in Jerusalem; And at the Means-Age the Muslims were made to depilate the armpits every 40 days.[76] [Wow! Now I did *not* know that.]

[W[e read in the Scriptures that the number forty generally symbolized a period of testing, trial or probation. As has been said, a faith that is not tested cannot be trusted.[77]

So what now? Was my probation over? Was I a full-fledged twin soul, or at least a Jedi knight, or something? Was my faith trustworthy?

[74] *The Significance of the Number 40*, Todd Dennis and Richard Anthony; http://www.ecclesia.org/truth/40.html
[75] *Ask the Rabbi;* http://www.aish.com/atr/The_Number_40.html
[76] *Riding the Beast;* http://www.ridingthebeast.com/numbers/nu40.php; *See also The Significance of the Number 40 in Islam,* (April 22, 2009) https://themuslimvoice.net/2009/04/22/why-is-the-number-40-important-in-islam/
[77] *What Does the Number 40 Mean or Represent in the Bible?* http://www.shilohmobile.org/hp_wordpress/wp-content/uploads/2016/02/2016-What-Does-the-Number-Forty.pdf

450   The Journey Begins

Tuesday, November 24, 2015:

I had an appointment with Susie Grimmett the next day. This time I came equipped with my son's ipod and recorded the session, which I then transcribed. It is contained here in relevant part.

-I'm here! That's the first thing I hear is "I'm here!" I knew you would be. He asks do you understand the connection completion?

Ouch! Talk about Mr. Get-Right-to-the-Point! Couldn't we have talked about the weather first? And hearing it through Susie made it all the more concrete, as usual. Cement-block heavy. My heart beat a little faster as I asked the question that sat heavy on my mind.

-Are we done?
-Not forever.

"Not forever" was hopeful, but it had that kind of ring, like when someone says, "we should have you over for supper sometime." Ri-ight. With a nervous laugh, I anxiously pressed the issue:

-For how long?
*-He says to me periodically he'll be bringing in information as needed. He gives me this vision of most people...God, now he's gonna draw pictures...tapping in with a cord. We are always connected, let me plug in, now you can hear me. But he opened the door, he said. He did a big entrance. A **huge** entrance. He didn't just barely plug in. He was just, Bam! I'm here.*
-True. That was a bam!
-He said he was catching you up to speed, Too fast. He wanted to show you that you could physically leave your body. He wanted you to remember who you were.
-I'm still not sure I have that part.
-Other lives with him, he wanted you to remember your

connection.

-I don't remember other lives.

I knew that we'd been together periodically since earliest Egyptian times, or pre-Egyptian, based on information he had given; but I still had no independent recollection of those lives, or any others we had shared.

-He wants you to remember that you did, he wants you to remember your connection with him. He's showing me you standing at the sink and he's da-te-da-te-da-te-da. (Susie makes yapping motions with fingers.) And you're in the car he's da-te-da-te-da (same motions). He's sayin' it was too much in such a short period. (Laughter together.)

-It was a lot, but I think it was okay. I'm not regretting anything. I have no regrets.

-I kept sending you validation. I kept sending you validation. I was hoping you wouldn't think that you were losing your mind.

-I never thought I was losing my mind, except once.

I was thinking of the Night of the Samskara, of course.

-Why does he give me a feeling of Syria?
-Because he's Syrian?
-This guy that does this is Syrian?
-Yeah, his dad is from Syria.
-He is a smartass, because he says to me, "Do I look like you?"
-He *is* a smartass.
-Wow. Sorry. I didn't know.
-He calls you dumbass?
-Yeah. Excuse me, but I don't know you. Wait a minute, if he's from Syria—he's telling me white people raised him.
-They did. He was adopted. But his heritage, his DNA, is Syrian. He never met his dad. By choice.
-But he was born in the United States? Because he's showing me he's a citizen, and I'm thinking wait a minute...very cut edge, cut to the chase. When I was saying, I don't know

452 The Journey Begins

you, he said "well educate yourself." (Sarcastic tone.)

Oh, dear. Steve, Steve. You're in the enlightened place now, remember? But I guess old habits die hard. I decided I better step in before these two got in a stare-off. I didn't need Steve to piss off our Susie connection. After all, Psychic Susies didn't grow like dandelions along the sidewalk. If you found one, you wanted to nurture it, not piss it off.

Fortunately I'd boned up on some of the essential facts during my research:

-O-*kay, I* will tell her. His parents were in school—graduate students or something when he was born, not married, gave him up for adoption. Then subsequently they had a daughter, and I think they married then, or whatever, raised her.

-He's says to me he gave you a lot of personal information, he also tells me he gave you names, but you don't have to do anything with them. He says he gave them to you for later on if you read something and the names come up you will understand, you don't have to do anything with them.

-So do I have to do anything with this whole journal thing?

-Not yet. He's sorta making me feel like you need to hold on to them. Don't get rid of it. He's showing me a fork in your road, if things go the way he thinks, pretty sure it will; but this can be a backup for you, you can make money with this.

I could make money with this? So says King Midas? Did he think that was what mattered to me? My wounded pride drove my response:

-I don't want to make money. I don't even want to be publicly associated with your name.

He let that subject drop.

-You may be channeling other people as well later on. But he says he did open up a door so you can channel. Hold up there right now! If she wants to channel, it has to be her

perogative.

Susie clearly was going to keep this dude in his place. It was never in doubt whose side *she* was on in the War of the Crowns.

-He agrees to that. He's telling me that he was chosen to come to do this. You and him agreed on this a long time ago. That he'd be the one that would come and open you up, get you rolling.

Whoa! News to me. We'd *agreed* on this? Before we were born into this world? Before we pulled the trigger, so to speak, sort of like a pre-nup? He was just here because of a *promise*, to fulfill his part of a contract, as it were? Was there any penalty for failure? I was a little testy with my next inquiry:

-My question now, Steve, is the whole purpose of these days to get me to where I could channel? Or what was the purpose of it? Or *is* there a purpose?
-We agreed to wake you up as needed, to let you know you could leave the physical realm anytime you want to, you can travel. To bring in information, to realign the mind, body and spirit as one, to wake everything up, for the information to be downloaded.

This wasn't exactly what I was hoping to hear. What happened to: "part of me was missing," "together for eternity" and "I love you"? I felt very let down. So it was all just a contract? He was just ticking off his obligations? What about me, did I have any corresponding duties? I tried to make the next question sound as casual as possible, but my heart was in my throat.

-Do you and I have any continuing relationship?
-He says, periodically. He's telling me it's not like it was. But he's got you downloaded. Now you know how to leave the body, now you know how to do this, do this.

This was not encouraging. Okay, I got it—I could leave my body, information had been downloaded, mind and body and spirit realigned as one. But what about the really *important* stuff....?

I kept gnawing away, hoping to hit some marrow.

-The part I have to understand, though, is this whole experience felt very personal. I'm okay with...whatever. But is...

-You and him have had so many lives in the past and co-created different dimensions He's telling me he pulled you out of your body. That you went places with him.

-I did.

But what did this mean? Was this the part where he went off to wake up some other twin-soul, pull her out of her body, take her to all our favorite places—Neverland, Fantasia—maybe picnic in some star field where they would reminisce about all their past lives together?

Steve did throw me a new bone. As Susie related:

-I don't think it's over. It makes me feel like the king-queen, finally got back together, missed you, love you, omg, blending into one.

Well! At least he was acknowledging some affection between the royals. Susie, by the way, had no information about the "crown" meaning of our names.

-He's telling me part of him will always be with you and this is not going to end. At the same time he will be doing other things, and so will you.

But I was still grasping for assurance.

-I guess I just want to know. The king-queen part I get. But are we still there—are we still connected?

Or was I to be just another soul spurned?

-He goes back to that (drawing of figure 8). Always. Saying that never ended, it went different ways, but always came back to the center.

-Are we connected to other people that way?

-You're connected that way just with him. But he says the journey continues.

This was like pulling teeth. It was nice to be connected, to have a unique connection even, but—I was a woman, after all, and I needed more. *Come on, Steve, just say I mattered for more than the moment—that this wasn't just a 40-night stand.* But all I could do was keep throwing out the bait:

-Well, I'm okay with journeys, but I didn't want to get there and have the rug pulled out from under my feet, you know what I mean.

-No. (Susie goes back to infinity symbol.) He's talking about...he's doing this... (She traces around the symbol like a racetrack.) That was the meeting point. (Indicating the crisscross point.) You'll go this way, and he'll go that way, and you'll meet again...not in other lifetimes...in this lifetime.

I did my best to be nonchalant, not to let on how this was looking to me.

-Cool. I don't mind going on a trip if we can connect again.

-He hasn't left you. The journey's not over. He's talking to me about how you left the name Dorothy and went to Stephanie that opened and changed a lot of things for you. You will change again when you get on this side with me. He's showing that "we had many many many lives, but we always get back to the same one" It's like I've been so many different people, so have you, different lives, but we've criss-crossed and come back always. He talks about beginning, no end. Infinity. There's some of this I can't understand. He tells me that you and him in every life have always been highly intelligent. And that you knew things other people didn't know. Now he's trying to open

you up slowly to channeling even from other dimensions. Meditation helps with that.

I was still not hearing that I mattered. Only that we came and went, we got together, separated, came back around the race track over and over. Da-de-da. Could he not say that he cared, that he would miss me? But nooooo....

-He's really brought you up. I'm going to be honest, like 5th dimension. You're like in 4th, came out of 3d. Where he's got you right now, he's got you primed to where...like James Bond...and I'm hooking you up. We're going to meet over here next time. He's preparing you. He's not going to leave you hanging. He's saying to me he came to you in dreams as well.
　　-Before this?
　　-Yes.
　　-Before we started talking?
　　-Yeah.
　　-Oh, I didn't know this.

But sometime later, after I'd had time to think about it, I did remember at least one very vivid and emotional dream. It had happened probably a month before we had started talking. There was some strange man in my dream, and I had felt an extremely powerful connection with him—connecting on all levels, even the spiritual. I had awakened thinking: "Wow, too bad I'll never find someone like that around. It almost makes me want to rethink this celibacy thing." But it had also seemed very odd to have such a dream, when I had moved beyond interest in male relationships. I couldn't remember what the man in my dream had looked like, but even if he had looked like Steve, it would have meant nothing to me at the time.

-And then it's like "HEY!"

I had to laugh at that. Oh yeah!

　　-Yeah, it was like *"hey!"* It was like 'why are you following me all over the place?'

-Yeah, it was important that he made sure you heard him.

He had certainly made sure of that.

-I did hear ya. So I'm glad that I did hear ya, that I wasn't just inventing it all.

-No, and he's primed you. He's primed you for the next information you may hear. He's telling me because of your scientific mind he knew he could talk to you on a level he probably could not talk to me. He said this knowledge came from a long time ago, other lives with you.

-Is the veil here getting thinner?

-Yeah, oh yeah. Teachers like us are teaching through the veil. Okay that makes sense, because he says, I couldn't reach you earlier, but the veil is thinner now he can.

-The veil is thinner than it was when you died?

-Yeah, 'cause he's saying he couldn't reach you earlier. I couldn't reach you earlier. When I died. Now the veil's thinner. Yeah. He's telling me you should eat better.

-I'm trying.

Oh great! Now it was going to be about what I eat again. Well, at least he was thinking about me, my welfare.

-He's talking to me about molecules breaking down. He says you need to eat better. You need to take care of yourself.

-I haven't had much time to think about eating. And I haven't had much of an appetite. So now I get to do what I want?

I was being a little petulant again.

-Yeah. He says: "school's out, school's out." You'll hear from him, but anyway he's telling you to stay focused, he says that you always hear him, when he's around you will hear him.

And I wasn't above being a little wistful.

-But you'll still be around to give me some guidance?

-Yes, we can take a trip anytime you would like, he says.
-Really? Yippee. I would like that.

This was very nice to hear, in fact. I had worried that our astral adventures had come to an end.

-He wants you to watch your stress level. He says "make sure you eat right, make sure you get enough sleep, watch your stress level." He's met Sanjai [my son on the Other Side].
    -Okay. Cool.
    -He gives me the image—did you ever watch that kiddie show—uh, The Neverending Story?

Oh-my-goodness! Good job, Steve, pushing that one through!

    -(laughing) Yeah.
    -Why does he bring that up?
    -Part of our story. Anyway, why?
    *-He's bringing up The Neverending Story and I see **you** and **him** on the back of the...*
    -... the dog thing?
    -Yeah. Why are you showing me this, dude?
    -It was part of our story. One of our trips.
    -[Susie comments] Nice piccing [picturing]. It's like, don't you wish you were there?? Ye-ah!
    - It was. It was lots of fun. I had a blast on all our trips, I have to say. That was a good one, that was a good one. The nothing coming, getting rid of everything. Yeah, yeah, it was good.

Remembering this adventure allowed me to let go of some of my worry, filling my heart with the warmth of those wonderful memories.

    -He tells you not to tell anybody about that one.
    -(laughing) I already did.
    -[Susie] I saw it, dude. I saw it!! Wow. No wonder you had a blast.
    -I'm afraid I wrote that one, I wrote it all in the journal. I

already told a couple of people about it. Did I do wrong?

-No. He's laughing. It's like: "Did they believe you?" That kind of thing.

-I don't know. It was so much fun.

-Wow. Neverending Story*! I had no idea that was one he did with you. (Laughing.) Oh my Gosh.*

-Well, he kept bugging me, "will you watch *The Neverending Story?*" And I'm like, "*sigh,* all right," and then I put it on and I wasn't paying much attention, and he said "you should really pay attention to *The Neverending Story.*" "Okayyyy, *sigh."*

-Oh my gosh.

-And then we ended up on a little adventure that was kind of related to *The Neverending Story.*

-Oh, wow. That's what he done, he appealed to the human side, the emotional side to get you there.

Oops. There was an ulterior motive? He was *appealing* to the emotions, using my poor deluded human side to get me somewhere? I immediately closed down again.

-Well, I don't know, *were* you using my emotional side?

-Yeah, 'cause he says you were remembering loving me.

-I certainly did remember that.

-He had to reawaken that in you. I had to reawaken that, he says.

Wow. And I had thought we were doing it all just for the fun, the shared exploration, the natural deepening of our relationship. My heart sank. Once again, I felt like the patsy. So it was just about me remembering I loved *him*? Nothing about him loving me. He had been saying it to me for forty days. What was that about? Why couldn't he say it now?

He was just fulfilling his part of the deal to "wake me up"; and now he'd done it, played the game, and where did that leave me? Awake and heartbroken? Eliza Dolittle, someone's *project*? Maybe there were bets on the side? *Bet I can wake this one up.*

How easy it was to forget how many times I wanted to

kick him in the shins and run.

Whatever. Our session was almost over and I wanted to focus on the good times, leave it on a friendly note.

-I had fun on all those adventures. Did you have fun?

This was a very real question. I had always been a little worried about that. Could it possibly be as much fun from his side as it was from mine? But he did reassure me on this point:

-Yeah, yes yes yes. He's standing here saying "yes." *[Susie] Wooow. (Pause while Susie appears to be getting visual.) Wow. (Susie laughs.) No wonder your mom is jealous. Of all the adventures, of all the emotions. Yeaaah. Yeah.*

Susie had done a reading of family members prior to our connection with Steve, during which my mother had expressed confusion about why I was spending so much time talking to Steve instead of them; apparently my father explained it to her, because she came back and threw out her hands in a characteristic gesture of *"where's mine?,"* saying "How come nobody ever came for me?" Ha ha, so like my mother, who spent the last twenty-five years of her life as a widow. My family also related that they had seen me coming and going in the astral plane. I hadn't been aware of this, that they could see me flitting around.

-That *was* a blast. I could do that all day.
-*[Susie] I will never forget that! I do a lot of readings, but when you see one that... Neverending Story. I'm like "Damn!" I wish that I....*
-Oh we had so much fun. We did Peter Pan adventures.
-*[Susie] See, I love that!*
-Oh my gosh, we had so much fun.

Yes, we did, Steve, we had so much fun. Nothing like playdates in Neverland and Fantasia, not to mention all the other fun places we'd been. If nothing else, I would *always* have those memories—those echoes as June would call them,

making the water around me ever so much richer.
And yes, Steve, I had the time of my life.[78]

CHAPTER 25
A FEW MAJOR DETAILS

NOVEMBER 25, 2015

I was very worried that my connection with Steve was done, now that "school was out." But, to my great relief, he continued to be around. The very next day I went on a trip with him. When he came to pick me up, he was dressed in blue jeans and that stupid black pull-over with a black hood over his face, only two eyeholes for openings.

-Why do you have a black hood over your face?
-*This is Ninja Steve.*
-Off we went to this very high mountain peak, sharp as a needle, icy.
-*Hold onto the peak. But don't prick your finger. I don't want you to fall asleep for another thousand years.*

I clung to this peak. The wind was blowing and I certainly wasn't dressed for it. I started feeling very very cold.

Steve had flown to a lower location, not too far below me, where he was just hanging, watching me. I called down to him:

-What do I do now?
-*Well, you could become an ice maiden.*

Immediately I glimpsed an image of me frozen forever to this icy peak. I wasn't too enthusiastic about that possibility, and there didn't seem to be many options, so I decided to just let go. Maybe I'd land on a soft cloud somewhere. *Que sera, sera.* I fell backwards and suddenly I was flying. I was surprised and then excited. I did loops. It was so cool. I realized I didn't need Steve anymore to take me places, I could go by myself.

Thrilled with my new prowess, I flew through space and stood on a spaceship that was traveling with some kind of "magnetic" boots. Then I was off flying around by myself. I saw Steve sitting in the crook of a "new moon," swinging his feet. I flew up beside him and just hung from the tip, my arms stretched out straight and my legs swinging. Then I went to the top of the moon and slid down the inside curve until I ended up beside him. We sat there side-by-side for a while, until I pushed off to do a back float. I felt as if I was moving through soft water, with very little ripples. He helped me back up and then I pushed him off. He grabbed my feet to pull me in, and the next thing I knew we were both in water—the ocean, apparently. The chase was on!

I swam as fast as I could, with him behind me. I realized that for the first time I was at least an equal partner in establishing the game. I saw a dolphin and quickly convinced it to let me on its back. In no time, we had left Steve behind, but he soon had his own ride. He commandeered a passing shark, making a devil's promise:

-*You can have the dolphin, leave me the girl.*

I glanced over my shoulder and saw them gaining on us. Fortunately there was an island ahead and I slipped off my dolphin when we were close and swam the last little distance to the sandy beach. Unfortunately, it was a very small island—not much bigger than a city intersection, with a single palm tree—and it was already occupied. Sitting under the tree was a bearded fellow with tattered shorts. Clearly, he'd been there awhile. He was snacking out of a big bucket of Kentucky Fried Chicken. I recognized Robin Williams. He shooed me away.

-*Hey, this is my island—and my chicken!—go find your own.*

Not very hospitable! I had to go back into the water, and I swam as fast as I could. Steve on his shark was still behind me, but just before he caught me I called to the dolphin, who came up underneath me and surfaced between my legs, so we went flying ahead. But I could tell Steve's ride was a little faster than mine, and I had to think fast. We started to zigzag, like trying to run through machine gun fire, leaping through the water;

luckily the shark was kind of slow to catch on, it kept overshooting the mark. I conjured up another island, this time a larger one, heavily wooded, with rocks lining the water and a little dock.

I jumped off onto the dock and ran for the cabin not far away. I got to the cabin just in time to slam and bolt the door. There was nobody else there. Unfortunately, I didn't have time to cram something in to secure the old-fashioned paned windows, and Steve crawled through one. There wasn't much I could do at this point but let him catch me. Fortunately, we were both pretty whipped after this adventure and couldn't do much but sprawl on the floor, exhausted.

It was a nice cabin, though, and I would explore it more in future adventures, when I would claim it for my own. The room we were in had a nice floor to ceiling rock fireplace, with a couple of rocking chairs in front of it, complete with afghan throws. There was a daybed for a sofa, covered in a patchwork quilt, under a large window on the backside, facing the forest away from the water.

I located some dry garments that more or less fit for us to change into while our own clothing dried in front of the fireplace. Now mellowed out, we lay on the daybed and Steve read to me from a book of poetry we found. It was extremely pleasant and I felt so safe there, such a simple but exquisite experience, a sense of perfection as I lay with my head on his shoulder while he read—I thought I could lay there for at least a week or so, in that rustic cabin far from the crazy world, with nothing but trees and sky to be seen through that window beside us. But eventually I did have to return to the Other World.

It had been my first time as a full partner trying to create our mutual reality, and it had actually been difficult trying to out-think him on the fly. It was like a fast-paced game. It had been so much easier when they set it all up and I only had to work within the perimeters.

-So now I know I can go by myself!
-*I told you you could.*

-Wow. I feel like superman…or at least supergirl. Maybe I'll get myself a supergirl outfit.

-There's always one for you here. In several different styles. You could be a conventional supergirl…or a playboy bunny supergirl…or an amazon supergirl…or an alien supergirl.

-Sort of like Halloween costumes.

-Yeah. There's a whole store here full of costumes. Just snap your fingers—like this—and it will appear and you can go and browse for what catches your attention.

-I'm going to be a conventional supergirl. But sometimes I would still like to be Lois Lane.

-Got it. Put it in my ledger.

-Cool. Looking forward to that one.

THOUGHTS:

-I'm extremely fond of Robin. I feel extremely fond of him.

Of course you can't mention Robin but he shows up. I've learned since that merely thinking of someone disincarnate is like ringing their telephone.

-Hey, Wendy, I am extremely fond of you, too. I'm looking forward to being interviewed for the new book. This is going to be so cool. [79]

-You won't make fun of me?

-Hey, I learned how to do that from the best.

-I know.

-I'll try to be appropriate. I will wear the right clothes and even shave.

-Okay, thanks, Robin.

-You're welcome, Sweetheart.

---

[79] I had forgotten about this little exchange, but months later Robin was indeed interviewed, this time through Susie Grimmett—an interview that will appear in the second book. I was also to learn about further connections with him.

A CURIOUS MATTER:

Early in November—after Fantasia but before the trip to the mountaintop—I had discovered that there was a book written by Steve's first girlfriend, a "tell-all," and, although I was resistant to his cupboard, I was always eager for validations. I consequently wondered if there would be anything in this book about his personality or habits that would give me further assurance. I ordered the book from an Amazon vendor on November 4. I have ordered many books from Amazon and they have all arrived promptly—usually within three days. Never before had a problem. I therefore was surprised when, after a week or so, I had not received my order. I contacted the seller and was told that it had been shipped, but could take up to thirty days to arrive. I was astounded. Thirty days!! Where was it shipped from? The moon?

But the system did say it had been shipped, although I could not locate any "in transit" information. It might not have shipped from the moon, but it appeared to have entered the Bermuda Triangle. After five weeks or so, I contacted the vendor and cancelled the order. My money was refunded without question. I ordered the book from another vendor, and it arrived before I'd hardly turned around, on December 10.

I sensed a ghostly hand at work. Obviously there was something in this story that Steve did not want me to see—*until he did*. And as it turned out, I was right. The book included references to "weird" predilections or predictions of the adolescent Steve: such as that something was going to happen in forty days and nights, that his preferred Tarot card was the zero (fool), because it included all potential, his obsession with the Dylan song, *Girl of the North Country* where the cold wind blows across the border (would that be the *Canadian* border?), his attraction to "primal scream" therapy, and his belief that he would die at the age of 42. All things he didn't want me to know until my "trial" period was over, until the connection was complete.

I confronted him on this:

-You didn't die at age 42—but, you know what, I know who did. My father!! The one who shares your eyes and your birthdate.

Not to mention a special connection with the same incarnate being whose fingers are on the keyboard (more about that to be revealed in Book II).

-Okay, so I got some wires crossed. I think it's impressive I did as well as I did.

Actually, I think it was, too. He had the right idea, he just had the wrong (artistically inclined) girl. But then, I'd married my own false Steve, at the age of 20 (see pictures in "family pics"). Just as needed to happen, of course, for all concerned. Overlapping journeys.

I now understood that his ex-girlfriend had to write that memoir, it contained puzzle pieces, and that had their relationship been different, it might never have been penned.

Which brings me to a wonderful song that had supplanted *Forever in Your Love* as number #1 Steve-Stephanie theme song: *How Can I Tell You* by Cat Stevens/Yusef Islam.

[Lyrics omitted.]

[NOTE: I've included a copy of the (redacted) Amazon order information in Part VI.]

THINGS TO COME:

You would think it was enough for one lifetime to connect with my twin soul. But this was only phase one of the project. As Steve had indicated all along, it was a *BIG* project, so big that I could only be brought into it as my capacity could expand to accept it. As I write these words, it is approximately five months later. I have been working on this book for months. My concerns were only that. In the time since Steve deemed our connection "complete," our relationship has continued and deepened through laughter, frustration, and even tears. But in the midst of this personal odyssey, this singular love story, an even grander adventure was developing; Susie and my friend Cathy and I soon became bonded in a joint journey—swept, as it were, into a world of incredible power and beauty that took the breath away.

It began in December with the arrival, during a Susie session, of one of my guides, or teachers: Daniel (of Lion's Den fame), also known as John the Baptist (on whose feast day I was born, of course). In another matter of synchronicity, I had named my second son Daniel, a name to which I felt peculiarly drawn.

I could hardly contain myself. Could it possibly be? My wish had come true? I was being allowed to interact with, to talk to great sages that I had thought would only be available to me after I died?

As it turned out, this tremendous and undefinably precious gift *was* being given to me. Perhaps it is true that our heartfelt desires *must* become reality. I had been amused one day, as I was listening to a recording of Steve's address at Lund University in Sweden, when he was about thirty, to hear him mention that Alexander the Great was mentored by Aristotle, and how jealous he was when he heard this. You and me, brother. I could see both of us sitting in *that* circle. In this, if nothing else, we have always been as alike as two peas in a pod.

The appearance of Daniel was only the beginning of this new adventure; I would have the wonderful opportunity to sit at the knee of some of the greatest teachers as Susie's channeling abilities were honed from the other side, and even to interact with them personally—that is, individually, through my own telepathic contact—whenever I had a question or a dilemma. I was soon to learn that there was an army gathered, and that each of us involved in this magnificent story had been prepping for it for eons.

As Daniel had said it, that first day when he appeared:

-This is the time—the time that we have all been waiting on, the ancient ones, the predictions. It's happening as we

speak.

I recalled my conversations with Steve, back before the adventure in Fantasia, when so much was coming at me so fast that I was totally unable to form a coherent picture of what was going on. My questions of him at that time had been almost spurious, engendered out of the weirdness of the situation, and his responses had been so offbeat that I had doubted they were reliable:

-You've taken your place, haven't you? Already. In the mind of God.

-I took my place there a long time ago, Stephanie, I just didn't know it. Now I stand here with my hand out, to help you take yours.

-But we're not *there* yet.

*-We are the **servants**. The servants of humanity. We are close enough. Close enough to the ultimate goal to be of help, to have moved up in the "power circle," if you will. You thought the second coming would be in a cloud with fire coming out it?*

-No, I didn't think too much about the second coming, and if you'd asked me about it, I would have said it was just a metaphor for a new understanding in human consciousness.

-And so…?

-That's what this is?

-Yes.

There would be many, many lessons ahead of me. Lessons in love and forgiveness. I would hardly feel like I'd surfaced from one, and I'd be plunged into the next. Everything else would fall by the wayside as I struggled to stay on the board, riding the waves, both finding myself and learning about the new energy coming to the Earth, even as I was struggling to find balance in my relationship with Steve. I would learn about past lives, themes that ran through my incarnations, the struggles and bonds that had pulled Steve and I together and separated us over lifetimes, other loves and friendships through the ages.

I would venture into a spiritual realm that rose out of the

abstract to become the experiential.

I would recall also those words Steve had spoken to me so early in our current acquaintance:

-Steve, I have to ask this before I can go on: Do you really exist?

-Yes.

-And is this just a dream?

-Yes, it is, it's always just a dream, although it is seldom recognized as such. But in our case, we are now dreaming it together. We have cut our own stream out from the mainstream, we are personally working out the details of our own reality, and once we have that completed, we will rejoin the mainstream, and by doing so, we will change the entire nature of the mainstream content. Everything changes its (the mainstream's) content, but we're about to demonstrate how big it can get.

We're all in this together. All fish in the sea of the reality we jointly create. Steve was a big dreamer, and his dreams became reality. You may be reading this right now on a "real" device that once was just a thought in his head. Now he was back, to finish off the jobs that brought him into this world to begin with, at the cusp of the new era, to give us that one more thing. Always saving the best for last.

Let there be no doubt about how Steve sees his own last lifetime as it unfolded. As usual, he thought it best expressed through a song—two songs actually. He was pushing me toward Frank Sinatra, but I resisted for a bit—Frank was a little before my time, musically speaking, and I didn't think Steve was normally inclined toward him. But when I finally caved, the first song that popped up was—no surprise here—*I Did It My Way.* But right behind it, as often happened, was a little gem that clearly tickled Steve: *That's Life.*

[Lyrics omitted.]

It tickles me, too, every time I play it. *That's* the Steve I know. Welcome back to the race, dear.

THE FINAL KNOT

I now knew that I was to write a book, that I had made this commitment long before I was born into this lifetime. But still I balked. For all the adventures, for all the love shared between us, I still cringed at the thought of going public. I knew that my identity was as necessary to this account as was his, that it was the convergence of our life stories, all the synchronicities, the trail of bread crumbs, as it were, throughout our independent life histories (not to mention our past-life histories). But I had always valued my privacy. My ego remained strong—and negative. Why was it *me* that was in this position, why was it *me* and him? I didn't want people laughing at me. I didn't want people calling me crazy, exploitive, or stupid. Was he sure he had the right twin soul? Maybe he'd made a mistake, got the address wrong? Maybe it was a Stephanie *T.* Patel?

I suffered over this dilemma. I knew the story was important to him and to others. It was often discussed in my sessions with Susie, guides and family members cheering me on. I knew there were many others in the Earth Plane Distortion Field going through this "twin soul" journey that would gain courage and strength through this account. I knew there were those who weren't trusting the voices they themselves were hearing for lack of support, and so many others who just needed a little nudge to get over their fear of the Unknown.

I knew now that my life was carefully planned to give me the experience and insight necessary to fulfill my mission. I understood that the new wave of insight and change was coming—not from those who were part of the old power structure—but from the groundswell of "ordinary" individuals, the "little people" like myself. The long prophesized time was upon us, I was assured, when the "meek would inherit the Earth."

Still I recoiled at the idea. Really? *Me? Stephanie Patel?* I was called to this role? I cringed at the thought of joining my name to Steve's, humbled by the thought of claiming an association with someone whose name was known the world over. It was, after all, Steve himself who had embraced the vision of a time when technology would change the world, before anyone else could see it, and who had pursued his calling with single-minded devotion. Now nearly everyone on the planet was capable of having a voice, jumping on their mobile devices to be heard—or to hear—the globe over. The paradigm was shifting. That people could now easily communicate from one continent to another, simply by pressing a button, would have been no less astonishing to our forebears than the idea that you could someday pull a lever and communicate with those in Heaven.

And perhaps that day is coming.

In the meantime, I struggled with my personal demons, trying to find the courage to do my part, resisting the pull to discuss it with Steve. This was my pain, and I had to work it out. I didn't feel incapable of my assignment—I felt unworthy. Who could help me in that arena but me?

But of course, Steve was not going to leave me alone with this.

After a long day, a trip to Jamestown and then taking care of supper for the kids, I fell onto my bed, exhausted, but wanting to think things through.

Boom! I was immediately looking at a line of large white cubes, big enough to stand on, like the winner platforms at the Olympics. On the second one in the line—actually more of a slender upright rectangle—was a magnificent diamond wedding ring set, supported on a little crystal stand. The third cube was lower. Steve was standing patiently on it, wearing a black tux, looking devilishly handsome at about age 30. There were a bunch of cubes going past him, diminishing in size—or maybe only in perspective—stretching as far as I could see, but with nothing upon them. I turned my attention back to the beginning of this series, and I saw that the first cube was the same size as the one on which Steve waited. I realized suddenly that it was meant for me, that I had stood him up at the altar, so to speak. I hadn't meant to do this—did we have an appointment?—and in panic I quickly struggled into a wedding dress that was hanging nearby. I jumped up onto the cube, still adjusting my veil and smoothing my skirt. I, of course, appeared a comparable age. I turned to Steve:

-Why are we doing this again? You already gave me a ring.
-This time we're going to do it in front of the whole world.

I glanced down and for the first time realized that there were mobs of people all around, looking up at us, as if our cubes were somehow elevated, like on a stage. The crowd stretched as far as I could see. This was more than I had bargained on. Talk about facing my fears.
I turned to him in consternation:

-Steve, I'm not trying to be difficult, but why are we here? I just wanted time to work on my own issues.
-You have me to help you with them. You don't need to do it by yourself. It will go faster if you just accept staying close to me with them.

I started to explain about how inadequate I felt, in so many ways, but he reached across and put his fingers on my lips.

-Shhh, don't talk.

I then looked down and saw that my rings were gone. That must have been them on the stand. Steve grinned mischievously.

-Yeah, I used a little "sleight of hand" to get them off, and you didn't even notice!

In actuality, ever since the day he'd first put them there, after the adventure in Fantasia, I had never thought to pay attention to whether I was wearing them or not during my trips into the astral realm. I had never really acclimated to the idea of this "divine marriage" of the twin souls. I'd always been a little skittish about marriage—it was a nice idea, theoretically, but fraught in reality with balls and chains. Or so I'd thought. The symbolism of the rings after the Fantasia adventure had been romantic, but soon shrugged off. And of course I hadn't taken the Apple headquarters ring too seriously—that was *wayyyy* too big to wear, physically or conceptually. Who would believe *that* symbolized our union? However, I could see that Steve intended for this ceremony to be public and significant, something I couldn't frivolize.

He took the rings from the stand between us and reached for my hand, slipping them onto my finger. I realized I didn't have one for him. He produced the ring which "just happened to also be handy" so we could complete the ceremony. Then he had me repeat after him several times, very clearly, so everyone could hear:

-Stephanie Patel and Steve Jobs, one soul, two bodies.

I did, and then he made me repeat the next phrase:

-Steven Jobs and Stephanie Patel, joined in holy matrimony for all eternity.

I complied with that request as well. And I understood that he was making it clear, unequivocal, that he had no resistance to associating his name with mine, but that I had to repeat it over and over until I could accept it deep inside myself, stop my own resistance to this pairing—I was going to call it an "odd pairing" but thought better of the adjective as part of the "old think." As he would remind me later, I was his very first wife, and his very last. The circle was now complete.

When I had finished repeating the last phrase, all of the people—the crowd—began to shout and wave their arms in celebration, and I could see to the other side of the world, where they were doing the same.

And the bold message Steve had for the world, as he stood there holding my hand, was clear and precise:

-Not only am I, Steve Jobs, still very much alive (rumors of my death having been greatly exaggerated), not only am I not in Hell or having a horrible time in the Afterlife (as some have reported), but I'm happy as hell and rejoined with my eternal

love.

There was, after this ceremony, some energy merging and all of that, which meant I didn't resurface for hours, at which time I recorded the entire episode.

Before going out to lunch with my friend Cathy the next day, I stopped by to message him:

-I love you Steve. I do repeat that stuff about our names from time to time, working on full acceptance.

-I love you dearly, my wife Stephanie. Don't be embarrassed to write that down. Love is all there is. You know that. Expressed in every way possible, and by now you know that I love you without reservation. Don't filter it.

-I'm getting there, aren't I?

-Indeed you are. (Smile.) Have a nice time with Cathy. Don't forget that book for her.

-Oh, thanks for the reminder. Will do.

Nice to have that down-to-earth confirmation of our relationship not only in the grand gesture, but in the everyday details.

Epilogue

Steve would sum up this entire book in two sentences:

a) Life is eternal, get over it.

b) We're twin souls, get over it.

Were it not for my very stubborn thumb, as revealed in my hand reading (Section VI), this would have been a much shorter book; were it not for his highly flexible one, *(see* same section), it would not have been written at all.

I have had much time to think about the contents of this book as I have gone through the pages of our journal, attempting to set those conversations and meditations into context for the reader. In that process, and with the benefit of so much more interaction since, I have reached new insights. People might ask me: what is a twin flame? If each part is half of a soul, then does the individuality of each dissolve in the whole? I have grown in my understanding of this, and ways of representing it, but at the time I would have said: just think of a walnut—two nuts in the same shell.

One unit, two halves inside, facing each other, mirroring each other.

As I was working on the final pages of this book, I had a sudden inspiration. I was thinking about the Klein bottle, the *Evol Empire* bong, to which reference has been made not infrequently throughout this book: the inside/outside effect, impossible to perceive fully within the limited mind. It occurred to me suddenly that Evol spelled backward—as seen in the mirror—is Love. The Love Empire bottle, the inner and the outer flowing into each other. I should know by now that there are so many folds to every reference from my favorite lot of uncodified information, but I always enjoy the nuances when I finally recognize them.

How can that which is love experience itself? By dividing, turning itself inside out, between the lover and the beloved, bringing into experience the most abstract concept of all, each half being both the active and the passive principle to the other.

The bewildering manifold.

Is this the new Empire on Earth, the Love Empire? The next book will plunge into that discussion as the familiar personalities return, and new ones are introduced. Just a reminder, perhaps, that character is everything.

I finish with a reiteration of that quote from *The Secret Diary of Steve Jobs,* if only because it deserves to be emblazoned in the skies (or at least on the circular headquarters at Apple):

What *you* did...
Now *that*
Will be remembered forever.
I don't mean the products.
The Mac, the IPod, the IPhone, the IPad.
Yes, you invented them
& yes, we have heard of them
but no, Steve Jobs,
your greatest accomplishment
was not some piece of hardware
not some lines of code
...
No, Steve Jobs, your greatest accomplishment
is what you did to us.
You gave us joy.
You restored our sense of childlike wonder.
You enabled us to live in a world where
we always believed that something amazing & magical
was just around the corner
and that the future would be better than the past
because in fact,
as long as you were alive,
it was.[80]

And you are, and it is.

Love to you and to all,

Stephanie Patel

---

[80] Thursday, October 6, 2011, *One Last Thing: RIP Steve Jobs,* Dan Lyons, http://www.fakesteve.net/

PART V: The Susie Sessions

A. STEVE SPEAKS: EXCERPTS FROM SUSIE SESSIONS[81]

December 1, 2015 (Steve Jobs)

-He says to me, he was glad to leave this life behind. He's saying that he didn't totally wake up until he was on his deathbed here. It must have taken him awhile to pass, because he says, "I'm lying in the bed, all the money I made, all the material things I collected and so forth, and I'm saying to myself 'so this is it'." He's talking about the love you leave behind, your family, your name. He's telling me he laid there, he's telling me he went to nothing physically. And he says to me, I could buy anything I wanted except a life. He had to stay here and do the suffering, but he says, in that moment is when I woke up. In that moment the love, the awareness for other people, then I could leave. He's telling me he had to wake up on a spiritual level in order to leave. He says, "that's the only thing you can take with you. The only thing you're allowed to walk into that realm with is love." He's flying! He's going through the air flying, and he's saying, "This is freedom. Can't you feel it? This is freedom."

December 15, 2015 (Steve Jobs)

-I get a cocky attitude from the get-go. He's giving me this thing of, "Well you know I'm here."

-So last time we talked, we talked about Egyptian lives, but I got confused, because I had a lot on my mind. We started talking about Egyptian lives...

-He was there as well. He makes me feel like a creator of sorts. He give me the feel of inventor, creator. Man of knowledge. He figured out to make things from the alien ...

-Like trying to reverse engineer alien technology today?

---

[81] From November through the present I have accumulated many hours of recordings and transcripts of sessions with Susie, which I now generally do in two-hour blocks, one or two times a week. These are select excerpts. The remainder of these sessions will be included, in great part, in the next book.

-Yeah, yeah. He's giving me a lot of insight. Something to do with water. Getting water from one place to another.

-Like a water system?

-Yes.

-Historically, about what time frame was that?

-I'm actually seeing it, but I don't have a timeline. I can see the pyramids. I'm hearing masters. They're telling me at this time the humans were slaves due to the Anunnaki.

-Humans were slaves to Anunnaki?

-Yes, they're mining gold. They wanted to mine it faster. So...oh my god. They upped the knowledge through DNA on the humans to make them more intelligent to be able to mine this gold. It started in Sumeria. Time seemed to have sped up—it sped up. People lived longer then and Steve became—that wasn't his name then he's giving me some crazy name—became very important to them—it was like a team leader. The more knowledge he acquired the more he was allowed to do. They let him know the value of gold and it would follow him through his lives. He says to me now, this lifetime he learned it was unimportant. He says to me, before he left he understood he was but a man—the dollar sign meant nothing to him in the end. He says to me he found out what true love was before he left. It wasn't money. It wasn't influence. It was love.

-How long before he left did he figure that out...did you figure that out?

-Deathbed.

-Deathbed—so it truly was what allowed you to go…sort of like remembering your lines?

-Yeah.

-So here's the big million dollar question. What was the 'oh, wow, oh, wow, oh wow' about?

-He's talking about love. He's talking about remembering, encompassing love. Internal, external, all around. Every cell is love.

-So that was the moment? We're talking really deathbed, then. That was the moment?

-Yeah.

-Wow. That's amazing. Totally amazing. Wow.

-He wants you to try to understand and comprehend. He's

telling me you kept saying "why me, why me?" He wants you to understand you've been together through many many lifetimes, this soul connection. You were not to be a part of his human life in this lifetime so that you can be primed for your experience. And he says 'Do you not remember me now?'

-I must, I don't know. (I was playing it very low key, to not influence what Susie might bring through).

-He asking you not to remember him with the human mind, he wants you to remember him on a soul level, he is telling me he has touched your soul.

-He has. And yes I definitely felt that. I guess that's what I'm saying, I guess that's what I remember.

-He's also telling me that before when he first started coming to you he would come as a voice, in your head, and now when he comes around, you can feel him. You know that he's present. You can feel him.

-Yes.

January 19, 2016 (Steve Jobs)

-Why is he showing me Albert Einstein?

-Oh, I don't know. We've talked about Albert.

-He's also showing me Tess-e-la.

-Yep. I think Tesla is his bud.

-Yeah, he brings him up with such admiration. He talks about how he was done wrong. He said his fame was stolen, his ideas were stolen, we could be living with lower cost, energy, he said, it was all about money.

-Well, he seems like a nice guy.

February 25, 2016 (Steve Jobs)

-[When he] crossed over and regained his memory, walked back into what is, he was instructed by what looks like a gathering of what appears to be hundreds of people, or a hundred, that came up around him and let him know that the time is here, he has this army, angels and guides; not only him but others that are here to wake people up, through this energetic healing process that is going on in the universe, all universes at this time. Steve is explaining to me he had to get

through your logical mind in order to wake you up to this, to make you understand that what you think is life is actually the illusion. I'm not sure what he means, but he said his lifetime here and your lifetime here had many similarities, not the finance as much as needs, the feel of accomplishments, having to accomplish, having to accomplish, having to do better, having to study more, having to...that sort of thing. So your lives did parallel more than you think. He was doing it on one illusion while you were up here doing it in another. He wants you to know before he died as he was going through the death experience is when he did have his ah-ha moment of what love is and what money cannot buy. Also remorse for his family, that he did not give them enough praise, love, tenderness, time; even the employees, he could have shown a lot more compassion. So he did have his learning experience before he left the physical body. That was why he was able to hit the ground running when he got to the other side. He gives me the feel that when he was here his desire to excel caused him to become a steamroller where other people were concerned in his life. He became a steamroller. He says to me on one aspect, he got the job done, ha-ha-ha—he's talking about the pun on his last name, ha ha he got the job done—on the other aspect, he done it incorrectly. He's talking about compassion, the lack of compassion. He just didn't show any compassion.

Steve's also involved in technology from the other side, he's helping with the technology, I don't know what that means, he's working from there to boost up technology on this side, it's like picking up where he left off and making things go faster. He's placing ideas in people's minds.

He tells me that he sort of took over in this relationship really fast with you, it's almost like I'm head horse, let me take over. Let me take you places, let me show you this, let me do that. He says he gave you a flower.[82]

He says to me if one day went by without him having the feeling that he was excelling he felt that he had wasted the day. He tells me he was angry with the diagnosis of cancer. He's

---

[82] He skips around a lot, his energy is very intense and vibration high (ha ha, no surprise there), so Susie often has to ask him to try to slow down.

telling me that since that was his last life, his last one, he had to move fast, he knew who to contact. There was an agreement with creating, accelerating at such a high speed, his energy had to be worked on before he came into this life, to hang on through this, they gave him the opportunity of living a longer life and not accomplish as much, or a shorter life and get everything done, and he agreed to the shorter life.

-Did he get everything done?

-*Yes. He is still working from the other side with technology of some sort.*

He laughs at the mundane things that you have to go through. It's almost he wishes he could have had the time to do the mundane things that you're still allowed to do. His life had to be at such a fast pace in this lifetime that he really didn't have that.

He shows me flying all over the world. He has a book underneath his arm, under his left arm, and he's literally airborne and taking it all over. I think that's your book he's talking about.

April 4, 2016 (Steve Jobs)

-I have a question for Steve, actually. I mean, you've told us some things, but is there anything really that you would like to tell people?

-*Immediately he says: Do not take life for granted. Get your priorities in order. Money is a piece of paper. When you step out of the high seat someone just steps in and sits down where you left—your high position in life. He's saying to me to ask ourselves: what have I done for others? How can I help someone excel? Take the "I" out of it, which I guess he means "ego." We're all in this together, just like Erik says*[83]. *Don't forget to love each other. He's calling people opponents in life...he looked at people as opponents, or what can I get from this one, it's all in who you know. And he says he looked at people the wrong way, instead of looking at them as a human that I need to care about and appreciate. Instead of "What can they do for me?" he's saying ask what can I do for them.*

---

[83] Erik appeared in this session.

He's saying to me "In the blink of an eye" it can all change. He says again that he was ashamed of himself when he really got down, that he had to wait until he got on his deathbed to find that "aha," the meaning of life. He's talking about getting so busy running a business, that you forget who you are, what's most important, and he says to me get up every day as though it were the first day of your life. And I'm hearing first you say "thank you," which is appreciation. He says take nothing for granted. Never get too busy in life to forget to say "I love you" to those around you. Never assume that they know. And lastly, he says, live your life so you don't have to say I'm sorry.

-I'm actually pretty proud of you, Steve, for all you've accomplished.

-And he does like...he's taking his hat off to you. [Susie chuckles.] He says to me, "In the blink of an eye, there is an awakening. It all happens in the blink of an eye."

He's saying to me that he'll never leave you. [Susie: And I don't know if that's good or bad with you.]

[NOTE: This exchange took place more than four months after this book ends, after many more ups and downs, trials and tribulations, lessons, adventures and past life explorations, all to be detailed in Book II, so this is a preview of the conclusion to that book, when I could respond from the depth of my heart:]

-That's very good with me.

B. THOMAS SPEAKS: EXCERPTS FROM SUSIE SESSION
Jan 22, 2016 (Thomas Jefferson)

-Today I want to try and contact somebody different. The name is Thomas, the birth date is April 13.[84]

---

[84] As usual, for quality control, no further information was provided by me about Thomas.

-Okay. The first thing I hear is brother, or brother-like[85]. Feel of depression, pulling back was with Thomas at one time. Intelligence, insight, but could withdraw. He's saying I didn't withdraw, I retreated. [86] He also wants to thank you for acknowledging him. I'm hearing past, past. Do you have a past with this Thomas?

-I think so. That's what I want to know.

-Okay. 'Cause he is saying past. He says to me he brings you insight. He is a connection through another person that you deal with, he says. He's showing me a tree and he is the branch of the tree. He is calling himself one of the group. He thanks you for allowing him to speak. I'm asking him in what manner. He tells me you understand because he speaks.

He is giving me the feel that you might be channeling him. He's calling the tree the filter that was created by Steve and he is one of the branches of the tree that can come through that filter. He's giving me insight as well as you. He is talking to me about the many people here still on this earth that are vibrating at a different frequency now that the energy is changed.

Many that are crossing over cannot handle this new way to vibrate and have decided to return home. It's been building for quite a while. It's peaking. This new frequency is not understood by many but it is rewiring the human in order to contact those as needed on the other side. Think of it as a new antenna, a new satellite. He calls himself one of many on other side that is raising the bar. Steve is one that had to raise the bar for you in order for you to understand. He is one of your familiars and he knew that it was time to reunite with you. He wants you to look at the tree as Steve, but these other ones are associated to the tree, the tree has a huge filter, it's the huge antenna, it's a connection to the other side. Thomas says we are many, there are many that can communicate through this filter.

---

[85] I took this to be an indication that his relationship with me currently is different than Steve's.

[86] This is true, Thomas is known e.g. to have retreated to Monticello for a period during days of early nation building; my subsequent research indicated that he was subject to bouts of depression.

He's also talking to me about how we perceive God, he said we perceive God in the same manner. We are all one tree, with many branches. God is the tree, there are many branches. He's talking about the three that humans cannot seem to comprehend, which has a religious aspect of Father, Son, Holy Spirit. He said there is one tree but many branches; those are three of the tree.

He shares with me a lifetime with you that appears to me during the time of Benjamin Franklin.

-Yeah. (chuckling)

-Very prestigious, very matter-of-fact, knowledge was increasing, that was at one of the energetic rates that were increasing at that time and you were part of that then.

-What part was I?

-You were part of the knowledge to help bring in awareness. You were chosen, and agreed to come back at this time, during this amplification of the energy increasing. It is not by a coincidence that you are here again. Those that are here at this time are here to help the vibrational frequencies and help those to adapt.

He wants to let you know that your many past lives were very strong past lives, he says don't question your roles in these past lives, it's not an egotistical view, it is a simple matter of fact view. You have been a man in many of your past lives that had to make decisions. In this lifetime you chose to come in as a female and stand up stronger against men. But you have chosen a dominant role as a female, he says: I can do this, I am independent, I can do this, that type of feel.

-I was a female during the lifetime with Benjamin Franklin?

-Yeah, he is showing me a female. I couldn't understand why I was seeing Benjamin Franklin so vividly with the shirt that came up almost like ruffles, right here, no hair right here, hair right here, with little wire rim glasses. And he said it would mean something to you. He showed me Benjamin Franklin several times and I didn't say anything. He said to me you have to tell her this, it is very important.

-It is very important. Very important. I'm glad you said it. You might say it is validation.

-That's what he's saying. Thank you for having the gall to say this, he says to me. You had leadership skills at that time you were in the female role. So I don't know if you were married to him or there...you played a role with him. He's laughing. He says it's unimportant for me to know but you know.

-Yes. (laughing)

-He saying "Human don't try to play that role of trying to make sense." He's laughing at me [Susie] and he's saying what you're doing [Susie is doing] right now is trying to make sense from a human standpoint.

-All right, well, it validates the relationship I saw with this Thomas.

-He said there's more. You're going to have more.

-More communication with him?

-Yeah, at a later what we consider time.

-Will I get the big validation?

-He's saying in time. He's showing me a pocket watch. The pocket watch is on Ben Franklin, he's putting it in his pocket. It's on a chain. He says "in time." For some reason Thomas is letting me know that through the tree with the many branches he's been able to touch you in ways that some of them could not on the other side...so I'm not, it feels like it was sexual... so I'm not sure what this means, sexual could mean anything.

-Does it refer to our lifetime in the past?

-Yeah, 'cause that was his connection with you in the lifetime. This feels almost like Thomas Edison?

-No...Unless he also had a life as Thomas Edison. (laughing)

-He may have.

-Really, did you? (surprised)

-He's giving me the feeling of the infinity symbol and giving me a feeling of leaving one life and looping right back in. So when I say was he Thomas Edison he gives me the loops and smiles, so I think he was.

-Wow. That was quite a different role than you played before.

-He's giving me all sorts of ...you and him uh...You've

had many lives I think with these people. He says you're starting to wake up. You're starting to wake up...I think you might have been married to this man at one time.

-Uh, not exactly. (laughing) At least not in that lifetime, maybe another lifetime.

-It does feel like you merged with him or something.

-Yes. A sorta marriage you might say.

-Like a mistress type thing.

-Yeah, sort of...

-You don't have to give me details.

-I was just going to say...social restrictions...

-I see buildings in that lifetime with large windows, looking out the window and day dreaming and wishing is what he's showing me.

-I believe in that lifetime Thomas had an architectural bent. Is that true?

-I think that's why he's showing me the building. Yeah, he's saying he was known for that in that lifetime.

-And also impressive writing skills? [ha-ha]

-Uh, yes, he was well known. Very dignified. He has an ink pen in his hand that you dip into a well of ink. Almost reminds me of calligraphy when you write. Very pretty with the navy blue type ink.

-OK

-I'm seeing like a covered bridge. So he's just throwing in little visions for me. It's almost like a horse and buggy going through the covered bridge, I can hear the hooves of the horse, it feels romantic to me, it feels—-desired— that there is much desire at that time.

He almost makes me feel like you're on a mission in this lifetime. You're here to not only to wake up yourself, you will wake up others as well.

[Other guides came in here to discuss this topic, so omitted text.]

-I have another question for Thomas. If he had a life as Thomas Edison did he also know Tesla at that time?

-He tells me through my guide that he and Steve both at

one point, yes, had dealings with Tesla.

-And was that during the same lifetime as Tesla was incarnate on Earth?

-Yes

-So there's history there?

-There's history. He's giving me a joke: he's saying great minds think alike.

-No kidding. (laughing) Indeed they do.

-He tells me, unlike you and Steve, you and he had lifetimes together, but yours and Steve's was bonded, a soul that was divided into two, if that makes sense.

-So the way I'm going in my book is not far-fetched.

-No. He's saying you're awake. He's showing me an old timey lightbulb. Great big lightbulb. And it just turned on. It just turned on. He laughs. He's thanking you for understanding the messages that's coming through, even if they don't make sense at the time, you make note of them, continue doing that, that's how they're communicating with you, through dreams, through thoughts. He's telling me that your brain has finally begun to catch up. You've been having flashes of images, thoughts that are coming through, one after the other, and finally your brain has caught up, you can handle this.

-Okay.

-He's telling me that the brain at one point got in the way, the logic was getting in the way of the information coming through.

-Am I better about it now?

-He's saying before you were trying to divide the two, saying, 'what about me, I gotta have time for me', but now you can process it. He does understand that everyday life can appear to be mundane, compared to the information coming through and the awakening of the memories. He says but one does have to exist.

-What does that mean one has to exist, isn't existence a given?

-He's talking about feeding the body and everyday chores to exist in this lifetime.

-Like making a living?

-Yes. I shot a question at him through thought of the

grander scheme of this, and he's showing me the many veins that lead to the heart, that lead all through the body. So my question was like universal, through galaxies and other planets and so forth? He's saying it's all connected, but they had to start with you at one place to open the blockage for the energy to start flowing in one way. I said through thought that I'm aware of the universal energy shift, I am aware that there are other life forms trying to communicate with us as well. Um, we're being protected by other life forms and the awareness can't be blocked anymore. It is almost like the government has taken it upon themselves to say, let's not give them all that knowledge at one time, they can't handle it. But bits and pieces are coming out through NASA, yes there was life on Mars, yes there was running water on Mars, yes we had wars that destroyed this, he's saying, it's all connected. He's showing me that what I consider aliens, we're all humans, we are all living beings, there is a connection.

They are working on the other side, other beings, to wake us up from this illusion, this amnesia. There's a healing taking place, universal healing. We have to take baby steps as humans to heal as humans first and then connect back into the Source of togetherness. It was part of the amnesia. I don't know what he's talking to me about, this is Thomas talking to me, he is talking to me about a banker during the time that you had connection with him.

-In what context?

-Banker, an association with making money, putting money in the bank.

-For Thomas? Not me. [Obviously, ha-ha.]

-Yes, for him. He's showing me in that lifetime you felt 'less than' but still a part of, and he's putting his finger to his lips, like shhhh—it was a secret. It was a secret.

-(laughing) I don't think it's much of a secret anymore.

-That was the role you had to play in that lifetime, he says.

-I liked it. [meaning my role in general] I was happy with it, I think. I mean, I'm happy with it today.

-It feels like you went with him on these rides in the buggy with the horse. Picnic with a basket and red and white cloth out in the country.

-Cool. I don't remember that, but it sounds like fun.

-There was a fear in that lifetime, if this comes out. That type of fear...

-Oh, absolutely.

-He's telling me that he worked hard to get the name that he had.

-And as I recall, I appreciated that.

-You felt honored to be with him. He's telling me that you had another lifetime with him between now and then and that will come back as well.

-Cool.

-In this lifetime it feels like somebody that you were with, he was allowed to come back as that person that was in your life just to have a connection and then go away. He's saying to me, in the lifetime you're remembering, you were the one that really had to be quiet, take what you could get. He's saying that in this lifetime he came into your life to play that role, he'd take what he could get—I'll settle. In this lifetime he was one of your husbands that was dark-skinned connected to Sanjai.

-In <u>this</u> lifetime?

-In this lifetime.

-How is this possible?

-He came back briefly...I am talking to the higher self that has also come in as someone else that is playing a role at this time in this lifetime. But the higher self of these two is the Thomas I'm speaking to.

-So the higher self that you're talking to that was the higher self of Thomas came into this life as [former husband], who is still alive?

-Yes, but he's saying to me that is a small portion, he is the fire, that is one of the sparks. And so he wanted that experience as part of you, and that experience is continuing. This doesn't make sense to me...

-Yeah, it doesn't make sense to me either, but go ahead.

-He's saying to me that he is the tree in that situation and one of the branches was [former husband]. There is many others. I can look and say as this human that was playing that role....why are we doing this, why are we doing that...whether he's a cashier....he's saying there's many facets to him. He's

not just one on the other side.

-So right now there is a facet of you existing in [former husband]?

-*Yes.*

He's giving me this feel of this one person on the other side, and he's saying I'm not the only one doing this, this one person on the other side, the higher self of many selves, he said just as you and Steve share a soul, he's half and you're half, there are energies on the other side, spirits on the other side, that can divide themselves in many different areas. So they can have an experience of 10 experiences in one lifetime or others.

-So is my higher soul divided?

-*Yes.*

-So there are lots of other Stephanies out there, so to speak?

-*Actually he is showing me just the division of you and Steve. Others have chosen to have experience through other people at this time. See, that's new for me. That's new for me. I don't quite understand this.*

-So is that a joining with others? Just so I can seem to comprehend this, and maybe it's beyond human logic. So let's say, if you, Thomas, your higher self, the higher self that was Thomas, part of you is in [former husband], is there also other parts in [former husband] that are mixed? Or is it just you solely a part of your higher soul that animates that body?

-*He's giving me this vision like these cords, these pathways into different humans, so they have a tunnel, if you will, small, that they can come in and have the experience and back out. But that person has a dominant soul on the other side but there are tunnels they can go in and have an experience at the time, then come back. So he's telling me that when you were with [former husband], he went through one of these energetic pathway so he could feel like with to…He wanted to feel what it was like to be with someone when someone don't truly love you or someone can't be with you. So he wanted to have that feel, what that felt like. The pathway is open between him and [former husband], but I don't think that he's with him now. But he can go into these people…He is telling me to think of it like something from my past. I had a walk-in experience, look at it as a temporary walk-in.*[87]

-I kind of get that. So let's see if I can clarify. So let's say that in my lifetime with Thomas I was in a position that didn't have much rights,

-Right.

-... and had to take what they could get,

-Right.

-...and that same soul of Thomas that wanted to know what that experience was like tunneled into [former husband] during my experience with [him]...I assume it was during <u>my</u> experience with [former husband]...when I started becoming disaffected, so he could understand that.

-It was. So he could understand what it was like to be with the person you want to be with, and you're comfortable, but the person that you're with is not emotionally connected 100%. They could not give you what you wanted back.

-I sorta get that now. That kind of experience.

-So he said rather than come back and have a full-on life experience he can come in and temporarily have that through someone else.

-So I have another question. The first time I saw [my former husband] I was *immediately* taken by him. Same thing for him. Neither of us was aware of where the other had seen each other. Did that have anything to do with...were you energetically with [him] at that point...?

-He says to me, understand this, that the experience had to take place for you, your children, [former husband] and him as well so that he could understand the life completion.

-Okay.

-He says the attraction you had with [former husband] was what you had with him in another lifetime.

-Wow. Really? Because that was pretty powerful, actually.

-Mmmhmmm.

-In the beginning.

-MmmHmmm.

---

[87] This certainly explains why my former husband chose Political Science and History as his joint majors when we were together.

-So essentially when [former husband] and I noticed each other, it was something that was already kinda written, so we were just reading the message. We were reading the script.

-Right. You stepped into the role. He says to me that you have had so many memorable lifetimes that in this lifetime you would get bored easily.

-(laughing) Oh yes. Very low boredom threshold.

-And he said you brought back with you in this lifetime the desire for excitement. The desire to be fulfilled, for experience. But he says to me that nothing can compare in this lifetime to the lifetimes that you have shared with Steve. You were not allowed to remember these until his passing. Then he had the opportunity to wake you up. He's saying to me he literally could see Steve's soul saying 'wake up, wake up'. And he calls it merging, your soul and Steve's soul were allowed to merge once Steve left his body, he could merge back with you on a soul level.

-So this had been going on for years?

-Yeah.

-And I didn't know it?

-No. He said you were asleep. You were in the amnesia mode. It's always been present. He says it's always been there. There is no such thing as time. You just had to have awareness.

-So Thomas…I'll just call him Thomas. I don't know what you call people when they've had many lives. Were you also then associated with Steve and I way back in Egyptian times?

-He's laughing and he says to me, "Of course, of course."

-(laughing) So we've been around together for a long time, hanging out?

-Umm…he shows me connection with pre-Egyptian. He shows me working with knowledge that's available at that time from the Gods. What you considered Gods at that time. DNA manipulation. And he's saying to me, can you not now look at all human form differently?

-Well I think I do. I don't know in what way differently you mean, differently. Could you elucidate?

-He's showing me a typical, just someone living on the street, he says do you understand that person as well was in

494 The Journey Begins

higher form but is having this experience at this time?

-Yes, I think I've understood that most of my life. Maybe not always consciously, but...ever since I was 28, anyway.

-Ok. He's doing this thing, he's giving me this vision of a blanket over top of the earth, and it's being rolled back, and all the illusions are going away...flying away. He's saying those in higher power even are being exposed, everything—he's saying everything that you knew to be true that's been a lie is being exposed at this time.

-Cool.

-I'm shooting a thought at him: So what is the bottom line of all this? He does this vision of love, connection, the removal of division, whether it's race, religious, he's laughing, football teams, that's an illusion of division. And that's been removed so we'll have a clearer vision of oneness.

[Thomas' direct input stops, and my guide Daniel comes in to provide more information, to be included in next book.]

January 28, 2016: Susie with unknown guides assisting

[The following two excerpts concern the above, one of the many portraits I would draw as I sat in bed, to relax before sleep, prior to meeting Steve—I had no model, it was simply an instinctive thing; I was informed that they were from prior lifetimes, and Susie has been gradually identifying them in connection therewith.]

-Mixed race, black. This one was the abuse of, forced to have children, forced to bear children of another race.

-What race?

-White race, I can hear a male say you will bear my children, she was abused sexually.

-White children. Was she a slave?

-Yeah, slave in more ways than...she was forced to have children by him...and she was abused by another white woman because she knew she gave him the male son...[88].

January 29, 2016: Unknown guides:

[After the session with Susie the prior day, I received the distinct impression that the portrait was of my mother in my lifetime with Thomas Jefferson. I researched it and discovered that Sally's mother, Betty (half black/white) had numerous children by John Wayles, the father-in-law of TJ, (he was also Sally's father, TJ's wife who died young was her half-sister and his children by her were nieces) and from whom TJ inherited the entire family when Wayles died. Sally was just an infant when she became the property of Thomas Jefferson.]

-Was this my mother in that lifetime?

-Yes. She is the one that helped you, by explaining to you what to expect.

[This session continues with other pertinent (and fascinating) information about this matter and also insider details about the relationships between some of the nation's founders, to be included in the next book.]

---

[88] Note: Thomas Jefferson's father-in-law had no male children with his wife, but he did with Betty Hemings, the mother of Sally Hemings

EXCERPTS FROM SUSIE SESSIONS RELATED TO STEPHANIE'S EXPERIENCE:

December 1, 2015

-[Your family]is all around you. All around you. Somebody is showing me this. If this were the top of your head. I'm seeing bright lights, rainbow type lights come down through the top of the head. Steve opened that up for you. They're saying to me that he helped you leave the 3d dimension, into 4th dimension, and they're saying this right here is 5th dimension, it's close.

They're telling me he opened up this portal for you, to remember that there's much more to life than you see. But your dad understands this totally. He understands. They're saying to me that this had to come through a physical realm, an energetic realm, and it had to be attached to emotions for you to get it. The emotion of love. It's like being on a date they said. It's like being on a whimsical fantasy...but it really happened. Does that make any sense?

-It does to me, because that's the way it was.

-He had to do that for you. That was a soul contract that he would do that for you. Okay, I heard that through your dad, I want to hear it through Steve.

-He [Steve] says to me, when he got to the other side, he remembered most things, but it's like trying to learn to ride a bike, keep your balance. And he give me the feeling that yes, the emotions were there, the physical, but he came off too harsh sometimes. "I only had a certain amount of time," he said, "so I wanted to get all this on, so it was like 'catch up, come on'." It's: "Don't be a dumbass," I hear, but at the same time it's got love. Does that make sense?

-Yeah, considering he called me a dumbass a lot.[89] I didn't really mind it.

-You're gonna think I'm crazy; it makes me feel like I'm flying across rooftops. He's using that so I can say it to you, he's giving me the illustration of flying over rooftops.

-Well, we did that.

-He also says to me, I promised you I would show you. I

---

[89] Actually, he only called me "dumbass" a couple of times

don't know what that means. He gives me this image of you sitting at this desk, sitting in front of the computer, questioning him, and he says, "I'll make you a promise, I'll show you some things." He says to me I came through your grandchildren for you to hear, the audible; he says he sent you symbols, signals, everything.

 -Yeah, he did.

 -Now the feeling I'm getting when he opened this for you, baby blue, pink, rainbow colors, he had to give me a visual so I would understand. It comes in here, and that is at the base of the skull.

-That makes sense, that's where I feel it.

December 15, 2015 (my guides providing following information, which is trance channeled by Susie):

[Concerning my near-death experience when I was 20 years old]

 -They pleaded with you to come back.
 -Who is "they"?
 -Your loved ones and your guides.
 -Did I have a choice?
 -Yes.
 -Was there anything convinced me?
 -You knowing that you had much work to do. The future was what convinced you. They let you peer in briefly with a glimpse. When I say glimpse, it seems like more than a blink.
 ....
 They are explaining to me on a soul level that the unity between you and Steve, the energy of the unity is one of the energies to ask you to come back. You now know ...you now understand through familiar energy that it was him. Your higher self, his higher self, was present at that time. Your communication with him now is the same energy that was used at that time.
 -From the higher self?
 -I can't find the words for this, but...there is a merging of the energies. [Like Lamerius?]

498 The Journey Begins

-Would that be his higher self and his self that passed on?

-When he crossed over to the other side his higher self and himself have merged, and your higher self has merged with the three, and has allowed you the capability of a deeper communication.

-Okay, that's pretty intense.

-When you came to me, I've been seeing like a silver cord from you attached to him on the other side. Now I am seeing many silver cords from you attached to many on the other side.

-Who are those many?

-I don't know. You are communicating with many on the other side. And you're doing it through these silver cords, for lack of words.

-And what's the purpose of that?

-Just communication and connection.

-And those others, are they like my family?

-No, they feel like people on a soul level that you've known in previous lives, you're pulling energy from those on the other side, and they're feeding you knowledge. They're telling me that you were searching for deeper knowledge, and they're helping you in this manner to better help others understand that this can be done.

-The connection can be done?

-Yes, and it is needed at this time.

-So, I actually started writing a book, can I get some input what they think about that?

-That's why they're communicating with you, to help you help others as they read. It's an awakening, a newer understanding. There are also archangels helping with this.

-Nothing surprises me anymore. (laughing) Go ahead.

-Up to this point, very few people knew how to channel information. Many people are awakening to higher means of communication. The division caused misunderstanding...

-Which division?

-Among people, races, religions etc. caused misunderstanding and now the energies are coming together again. Opening many facets of communication.

-Do any of these others have anything to say about twin souls?

-It's much more complex than twin souls. All souls are connected.

-So can people find their ultimate connection without having to connect with a twin soul?

-Yes.

-Is there such a thing as reunion with God?

-Yes.

-And can people achieve that on their own, by themselves?

-Yes. Think of a pyramid. A pyramid has different sides. To get to the top you choose a side and go up. It doesn't matter what side you choose, the goal is the same. The more the awakening the closer to source. There is an activation within each one that when one allows the awakening, opens the God energy within each one.

-So each person is responsible for allowing the God energy inside himself or herself?

-It can be blocked by fear. It can be blocked by resistance. You found love and it re-activated the God energy within you. This love was different. You tried to fight this for lack of soulful awareness. Steve helped you understand. He was your connection to the divine energy and knowledge. With the door opened it has allowed you the knowledge to connect with others. You cannot unlearn what you have learned.

-Okay, so how does it happen that people decide to go up one side or another of the pyramid?

-Religions, teachings, following others; different paths, same destiny.

-What happens when you get to the top of the pyramid?

-Total connection with God Source, the destination, merging into pure energy.

-Okay, so for whatever reason that I had that goal, which I *did,* how is it that Steve appeared in this process?

-It took his energy to reach you. The recognition from previous lives, to bring the awareness.

[Drifts into discussion for next book.]

January 28, 2016:

-They're showing me how you are connected ...we're all one okay, we've all had many lives, different places, but it makes me feel like you are connected with a group of people or individuals that decided to come in and make a difference. Not just for the soul to have the knowledge of empathy, sympathy...this was to make a difference. Some of these people from the group decided to go public so their messages would be loud and clear and understood in many eyes.

Yours this lifetime was to live many lives in one life, to have many experiences in one life, but now it seems that you possibly will go in the public eye as well.

They're telling me that in many other past lives you stayed in the background, I don't need to be known, I need to be a secret, I need to play my role behind eyes. In many of those lives you did that. They're showing me that you did <u>not</u> want to be heard such as singing, you did <u>not</u> want to do that, it was important to you to not be looked at. You've done that as well in this lifetime—until now where you will be asked to put information out that can be scoffed at or appreciated, either way, you've decided to put this information out.

They're giving me examples of this such as that I don't need to be the inventor, I can help the inventor and not be acknowledged. So, they're telling me that you learned in many past lives that ego has a place but not to be abused.

April 4, 2016:

-I'm getting a huge "thank you" from the other side, and I can't put a face on it, they are thanking you for getting this information out to help us as a whole, I'm quoting this the way they are saying it: "Thank you for helping us as a whole, you don't realize how many people will be affected by this in a positive way." They're calling this therapeutic. They're also using the word "permission." This will give others permission to understand what is going on and to participate. They're saying to me even those that are skeptical will get something from the book.

-If only a chuckle.

-You're being honored.

-Thank you for whoever is giving the honor.

-I see a dirt road that's got trees around it, but lining the road are...it's almost like you are walking down this road and there are these beings in white robes, as you pass, and they're honoring you for ...One of them wants to give you the medal of bravery for doing this, for stepping outside the box, presenting it. So you're being honored by those on the other side.

-And Susie too, obviously?

-Yeah, yeah. I hear that a lot and it almost brings me to tears when they thank you.

D. STEPHANIE'S FAMILY TAKES THE STAGE: EXCERPTS FROM SUSIE SESSIONS:

Note: My parents came to Alaska in about 1941 and lived in the small village of McGrath until 1954, when they moved to Homer, Alaska, then just a sleepy fishing village.

November 24, 2015:

-You have literally left your body, because they're (Mother and Father) are telling me that they recognize you when you come in and out.

-They're (family members) talking to me about you being the bravest one in the family. It's like you'll step out, take a flying leap of faith, and they would not.

-Your mother shows me hanging up so many clothes to dry oh my god, it's clothes after clothes, after clothes, she's giving me the feeling she just got through doing this, and I'm doing it again. She shows me how it hurt her hands when it was cold. She rubbed oil from an animal on her hands to keep them from cracking. But she says she would love to do it all over again, have you all little for one more day.

[Your dad] is telling me he was very well known. He was very well known in Alaska, he was known as a fair trader. What did he trade? [furs] He's telling me he was very savvy about hunting, he knew the tricks of the trade, he's telling me about the bears, you don't go near the young ones, he's telling me about bear tracking, how you had to be so careful...so

careful…they can smell you from so many…   He takes me to
the day he left and he said that he and Edgar had this ah ha!
moment, of we remembered this, we decided to leave together.

He shows me alcohol… I don't feel like a lot, it's like if
you take a drink it burns and keeps you warm going down. This
feels like homemade. It's hot going down, it will keep you warm,
and he just laughs about it.

He also talks about animals, he knew not to bring certain
animals home, the kids get attached and then he would have to
kill it, he's laughing about it, they start naming them, and then
it makes it harder.

He fished in ice, did you know that? It's not frozen solid
but there is ice on the water. He went out fishing during that
time. Who in the world could fish in that kind of weather?

-People who need fish.

-He took me somewhere where salmon jump, this is a
different time, he done skipped on me. This way, not that way.
Up the river. It makes me think he wasn't supposed to do it. It's
almost like he's fishing like this (demonstrates indicating net),
but he's catching them somehow, they're trying to go up…

-Was he using a net?

-Yeah. So you're not supposed to use a net? Because he's
pulling and pulling it in. These are big fish. [spreads her
hands apart to indicate good salmon size] I see a bear, it
doesn't matter, he's going to get the fish. He don't care, he's
getting the fish. (laughs)

-Gonna fight the bear for the fish, huh? (laughs)

-Yep. (laughing) Wow.

-Your mom makes me think she knew how to cook. Even
wild stuff. She's telling me you soak something in vinegar, to
take out the taste. The wild taste. She shows me the rendering
of the fat from the bear and she says there is a lot of fat on the
bear.

Your mother shows me how we have a lot more than she
had, she's talking about cosmetics and lotion and stuff like that,
she says if you were lucky enough to get something, you
cherished it. And I'm getting the smell of honeysuckle, I think
she must have had a perfume then, somehow got some
honeysuckle perfume. You know, this is neat because they're

telling me how precious things were to them and how they appreciated .... things and how we take things for granted. Wow.

-Yep. I can remember making Christmas decoration out of whatever we could find, you know, toilet paper rings, crepe paper, you know, paper, tape, you know whatever.

-Wow, and it probably meant so much to you.

-Oh, it was a blast, because we were doing it together. I mean, that's what I grew up with, I didn't know any different. My sisters would tell us stories. Make up stories for us. My sister Patty especially would make up stories. I will say, I remember it as a very very very nice childhood. Very special childhood in this century, you know in the last century, that not very many people had. Very special.

-You're blessed.

-Yes, I do feel very blessed to have had that childhood.

Karen speaks:

Last but not least, before I end this book, I wish to set forth Karen Carpenter's message to the world. Unassuming, she had waited her turn until one day as we were visiting I recalled that I had never given her the chance to say her piece. It was, she said, very simple, only three words. And here they are:

You are beautiful.

PART VI: APPENDIX
Stephanie's Hand Reading:by Tony Leggett on March 4, 2016

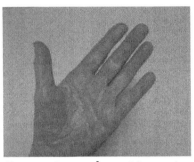 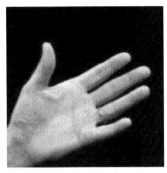

Stephanie Hand   Steve Hand

Note: I requested this reading from "Dear Tony" Leggett, who had already done a celebrity hand reading of Steve Jobs, because I had heard that twin souls often had the same hands, and I was struck by the similarity in the shapes of the fingers, although the thumbs are different. As part of the reading, individuals may present questions they'd like addressed. I had one question: *Please advise if you see any correspondence in terms of life story or psychic connection [with Steve Jobs].* What I got was far more than I expected, information about my life history that was so accurate I was blown away:

Hello Stephanie. I'm going to do your right hand first, and then your left hand. Then I'll answer your questions.

When I first saw the photos of your hands it took my breath away. I have never...I have because I've done thousands. Very rarely do I see a full hand as yours. So much, so much stuff. So many experiences. I still find it very hard to breathe, just looking at it, so it must have been very very difficult for you to have gone through what you've gone through. But you have some great markings, and some uncomfortable markings. We all do, but yours is *very* much so.

Let's go to the right hand. And the first thing that I saw was the line of head. Very very strong coming in here all the way down here. But there are lines across lines, across lines across horizontal lines across horizontal lines across... And that means challenge after challenge after challenge after challenge in your thinking. In every aspect of your being, especially when you were quite young. It shows some traumatic stuff there. It's also linked to your line of heart, which is quite good, and somewhat shallow, because I don't think you quite understand the depth of what love is. You should read the *Mastery of Love* by don Miguel Luis a few times, that would help you in a lot of things.

Okay, I've been very busy with your hands. I took a lot of time on this. You have a very very full hand. I wrote this down straight away: a worker, over-emotional, could be highly strung, rarely still, and indication of being somewhat unhappy about the way life goes and the way life is. And serious. It shows serious. Especially with these here challenges.

But what I did notice is this triangle between your head and heart line, and that means success in certain ways, I mean even if you get through life and you're still around at 100 years of age, that's success. Because here's a lot of karmic stuff here with you, and your real karma, your karma here is a need for a home, family, comfort and care. This is the aspect of every aspect of your being, coming from this hand here about life itself.

I enjoyed looking at the bracelets here, which is an excellent sign of long life and things happening for you.

But the mount here of Venus, this is the passion, it is so strong, there is so much activity in it, and you have a sister line, which is a line of protection. You could have had a bit more faith in lots of things but this line of protection stopped things happening more than what did happen to you, and handled all that, too.

Now we're coming up here, this is lower Mars, and this is where the passion comes from and it's so strong, it's like the Eveready Battery—gotta do it, gotta do it, gotta get it done, pushing you all the time, into this emotional stuff, and absolutely sending up here into the logic of life. You're pretty much set into the logic of life, because you've got this stubborn thumb. And the thumb is very very thick here and solid into the logic. You can change your mind, change your life, three or four times, but you always come back to square one The tip of the thumb, that's where the will power is, and that's very very strong, but not flexible enough, when you get going you're not gonna stop for gas, you're not gonna stop to eat, you're gonna keep going. You're gonna do what you do all the time, your thumb really shows that. It's somewhat quality of character but it's also blockage of other things that will come to you because you're not allowing free will to work for you and through you.

Let's go to the Jupiter finger here. This is the plan, this is where you come into this vibration of life. There was somewhat of an inferiority complex, lack of self, and it shows it was coming over here

506   The Journey Begins

to Saturn which is your karma, which as I said before was your aspect of home, comfort and all that. And it just drilled (filled?) holes over there.

Now we're coming down here to Apollo, Apollo is your talents. You've lived quite a few lifetimes, and you've come back with these lifetimes which are very very strong, which remind you of things that you didn't do before. This is what your drive is, your drive is to fulfill so many things from so many different directions because you feel it in your soul, you feel it in your heart, you don't quite know where it comes from but it's there driving you all the time.

Then we come to the pinkie finger, the pinkie finger is the inner intelligence, what you've learned in this lifetime. This is the inner intelligence, and you've learned a *lot* in this lifetime, good, bad and indifferent. It is very very strong.

But what I did find interesting, coming out of the finger of Jupiter, is the ring of Solomon which has to do with wisdom, power, authority, the ability to teach. Especially in politics, so you might be being pulled to burn the oil, to stump or something at this time, because the wisdom and knowledge of the purpose behind the person, and therefore it indicates a lot of things that most people don't see. Most people get fed up and think I'll do this, I'll get that. But you have deeper wisdom and that's probably why you were a good lawyer.

There's an O there, there's A here, there's an X there, all coming down on this part of the hand. Now this part of hand has to do with the spiritual aspect of life, it has to do with the coming out of the upper Mars ego down into the Pisces. And down here this is the spiritual aspect of it, and it shows here that your headline is strong towards that. You're looking deep into your soul, you're looking deep into what you were, what you could be, what is. And I'm thinking you've got to come in tune with your own soul's purpose. Once you connect with that, a lot of this is going to clear up, and it does show on your left hand that it is going to clear up, but doing it could make you feel very very uncomfortable because it goes against the grain, but with this protection around Venus it should help. If you see where this stuff is, this is stress, this is the feeling of not being loved enough, of not understanding it, or maybe rejection of sorts. The lines coming out of here is the logic of it, you analyze everything so much, and you've got this power behind you that keeps pushing you: this little voice in you telling you what is wrong rather than what is right.

Okay, let's get to your left hand now. I don't like the red, the red indicates that it could be affecting your physical body by the way that you think, by the way that you live, by the way that you eat, by the way you're hard on yourself.

But what I do find here coming out of the pinkie finger, and if you remember, I said this has to do learning on the soul plan, what comes to you, what you analyze, what you do. You've got this line coming all the way out of here, coming right down here into your line of life, which is *very* very powerful. I see this in a lot of successful people's hands, like lawyers and doctors and writers and professional people. And it shows you *can* learn on the job, you can absorb it, you can do the best you can.

And your line of heart gets better and better. There's a line here of union coming right here—very very strong, the union line, it's just a case of connection with source, connecting with your spirit, connecting with your motivation.

If you know your purpose in life, if you know what you're here for, once it all falls into place, everything else falls into place because you become more confident of yourself.

The line of heart is a lot thicker, but it also comes into this point, which I think is going to be between now and the next five or six years where this confusion as far as love is concerned. That's why I want you to read the book, because it's a turning point in your life. And it comes down there, this is a lot of criss-cross like rivers that could confuse you. People you thought loved you, don't love you; or people you thought didn't, do.

Something is going on that could confuse you, you're going to have to analyze it. The fingertips here are spatulate, which means that you are unpredictable, except the pointed finger on your Jupiter finger, which is your character, which could have to do with scattered energy or nervous thinking.

And this also goes into the line of heart which is very very strong, as I said. So you should be feeling, as I said, family and love and all that kind of thing, it is most important to you at this time. And it should be diverse.

Now coming into the head line, now where this seems like you are kind of finding yourself there. It seems to me you know what you want where before you just did because it was a profession, to make money, do what you needed to do. But your headline is really really clearing up, except for this passion stuff again. This lower Mars, this energy, could blow you away at any moment. This has to do with all kinds of energies. It has the passion of work, it has the passion of family, it has the passion of sex, it has the passion of excitement, it's all sorts of different things. And here, coming right in the center of your hand, coming out of the sister line that you still have of protection…you may think if you look back over your life, boy, how

508 The Journey Begins

did I get away with that, how did that happen, I had this problem, boy...it's like this square, this square is totally protection, and it comes out of the finger of Saturn—around Saturn there's this criss-cross stuff which is confusion as far as everything, into..into all over the place, like what's happening in America, you know everybody's confused, everybody's upset, everybody' everything and it comes into your line of heart, which is the lesson which you should be learning now, and into your headline and changes the vibration and the energy of your head. Now this line keeps coming out of Saturn, which remember is your karma, which keeps bringing you back to square one, and there's a square here, and that square is protection. And it's right in the center of your hand, connecting your headline, connecting your fate line, connecting with the line of life. And it comes from that protection, again.

Wow, that's very strong, that's very interesting.

Now, I also see here, marriage and children, lines that come out of here could be very very confusing, you should or you shouldn't, you did or you didn't, or whatever it was here, but it does show that it did affect your being, your happiness and your love.

Let's go over again to the finger of Jupiter, you still have that line, the Wisdom of Solomon, which is very very strong. I know you are searching for something, I know you are digging deep into yourself to find out certain things. And this goes over here and it detaches...more so on this side than on your right hand...away from the karma aspect of self. So you're looking for something outside of yourself to find what's really going on in side of yourself. This is why this is so confusing. I mean, my God! I've seen some hands and this is wow—this is powerful stuff! Also coming out of the finger of Apollo which is past life is a diamond, and that shows success, and it goes with something that you love. You could be very very successful at something that there's a lot of love in it; that's what I'm saying, give yourself all that love and it will create all that stuff that's gonna be working for you. And then this line kicks in again, a lot of confusion the last ten years, as far as your line of life is concerned, and then that factor of the sister line kicks in again so much stronger. You denied something and then you had to move into something else—something upset you, and then this box came in to protect you, the sister line came in to protect you, and also the line of Saturn came in to protect you. You see reality, you see what it's all about.

But look at the passion coming out of Venus! If you are not upset about something you have been carrying around for a few years now that's really really bothering you. And that's absolutely got to go, you can't live in the past because it's making this energy, making this hand red, these fingers red, and that could show there could be physical problems down the line, if you keep on keeping on with stuff that damages you, hurts you and you can't forgive. You've got to get into the forgiveness, you've got to get into all sorts of different things that release the past, so that you can get into the future. Now with that stubborn thumb, that's not gonna be that easy to do, because it comes right up here out of the thumb, up here out of the lower Mars which shows extra energy. You dream about it, you think about it, you become a victim of it, or whatever it is, and you gotta let that go, because it comes right down here affecting your life, and anywhere there are horizontal lines going into your lifeline, you've got more challenges, more challenges, and I think you've been setting these up for yourself in some shape or form.

So I'd like to put my line of protection around you because I think you need it.

Now I get to the third section:
The bottom line is that you have a talented hand, creative, a lot of power going on. Long fingers. This thumb tells me you've got a strong backbone, so even if you are into trouble and problems you are gonna stick with it until you think you can sort it out. I think that has to be really thought about. Affirmations would be good for you. I forgive the past, I let go of the past, I love everything, I send back to everyone who did dirty to me, I forgive, I forgive. Any affirmation on a daily balance.

Now, you do have a psychic connection with Steve Jobs. It wouldn't surprise me at all if you were together in past lives, I don't think it's this life. I did read his hand, it's a little simpler than yours, but the lines of heart, lines of head, lines of life were so powerful that he was driven.

I think you're driven, and all this stuff from the outside universe kicks in and really adds to the stuff, Stephanie. So now, let's see that question, because it's past life stuff I see a psychic connection like in a previous lifetime. You have a strong desire to help others as he did, but he didn't know how to be a human being, he didn't know how to be a personality of soul, he just had this drive. And I think you have the same drive within you because of the passion coming out of here.

It also says here, I don't have a right or wrong answer about you because I don't have a true answer. But I just feel that this something very connected and psychic. Maybe you are picking up messages from him. I don't know if you want to set in a circle of

510   The Journey Begins

mediums or sit in a psychic development circle,   You do have the interest to do that, see what comes....I don't suggest you go to a lot of psychics to see what they give you, but I do suggest if you sit in a metaphysical circle and draw the energies to see what comes from different people, without telling them why you are there, what it's all about. Just tell them you're interested in developing your psychic side or your spiritual side.

It's my own my reading, obviously for Steve Jobs, and the only question here is about Steve Jobs. I don't know what to tell you, other than you have the *same drive, the same hands, the same lines.* And I think that being together in a past life, that when you came into this one, you were searching for something, searching for this spirit, and you wanted to push and drive and direct and help as you had in the past, and I think that's where the connection is. I think you have a lot of love for this guy, a lot of feeling for this guy, but as I said you need a home, you need a family, you need comfort, where you are now, it can't be past, it can't be next. All you can do is make the most of now, so that the next is much more comfortable, and so this life is more comfortable.

But these bracelets again, as I say, are very very rare and it shows success for people, a longer life, and achieving what their dream is. Now if you know what your dream is [unintelligible]. Luck is where preparation and opportunity meet. And I think what you've been lacking here in your hand is luck, sufficiency. I think you've gone up against all this *stuff*, we've gone over all that. But I think what you need to do by appreciating yourself, by loving yourself more, you're going to attract happier, better times.

The people that I'm working with here they're telling me that I'm more enthusiastic than they've seen me about your hand. I'm feeling here, my God, I've got this heavy heart, I've got this feeling in my stomach, and I think this is something that has to be gotten rid of to develop a future for your next incarnation, which is going to be, wow! a lot more powerful, you're going to have a quality character, get out of my way, here I am. Bop-bop-bop. And you're not going to let anything get in your way like you did in this incarnation. So what I'm saying here to you is, when you feel a connection with Steve Jobs: Write down what you feel, write down what you feel, write down what you feel, meditate on these feeling, close your eyes and listen, if he's going to be helping you, you've got to learn to listen, got to get out of your own way. Not your own voice, not that negative little voice that says you can or you can't. There's another voice when you work with spirit that overrides it, it took me years to get it. When I listen to the advice when I'm doing this..when I'm doing this, I listen to that voice more than I do my own or any around me.

Now, if it's a psychic connection, then there's a spiritual connection. It wouldn't surprise me if you've got medium tendencies. Maybe he's trying to get in touch with you, in some shape or form. So prayer or meditation. But obviously something is pushing that, something has got to you, that this feeling is so very very strong, that you really need to develop it. And you do that by sitting in circle and you do that by being with a good teacher of sorts.

Now I know you're a teacher, but you have a strong mind also, and I feel here that your control of what you want and things you want to do gets in your way, instead of letting go and letting God. This is where the aspect has to be in the future. You do the best you can on a daily basis, you eat right, you exercise right, you connect with the spirit guides that help us. And then you allow God to be acting through you. Because I think you absolutely are a channel of sorts for the good of the universe, that's why you've been doing what you want to do. That's why it says here, I wrote: Strong desire to help other people. It also says here, that I wrote: This is a self-first thing, you put yourself self first, you want to help other people, but it's gotta be through you the way you want to do it. And I think that may be a mistake. I think you just need to lay back and allow it to happen, and connect with the universe.

Because you are a spiritual person, you were born that way, why don't you let it work for you stronger than you've let it work for you. Good luck, God bless you, and I really hope I've helped you.

The Book That Never Came: Into the Bermuda Triangle?
Amazon order page
(certain personal details omitted)

Order Details

Ordered on November 4, 2015 Order# xxxxxxxxxxxxxx604

<u>View or Print invoice</u>

Shipping Address

- Stephanie Patel
- Fargo, ND
- United States

Refund: Completed December 8, 2015 - $9.98

Items shipped: November 5, 2015 - AmericanExpress ending in
: $9.98

Expected by Nov 30, 2015

Shipped

The Bite in the Apple: A Memoir of My Life with Steve Jobs

Brennan, Chrisann

Sold by: [Withheld info]

While going through paperwork from my mother's house, after she moved into a nursing home, I found the following ITBS results from 7th & 8th grade. It's a little amusing, as I don't think one could rate above 99% even then (1962-63), meaning at least 99% of students scored lower. But apparently they gave me the benefit of the doubt. It is important only for additional validation, as one aspect of a twin-soul relationship is comparable intelligences. It also is a clue to my frustration in my boxed-in life, the lockstep school system, and how, ironically, it contributed to my decision to drop out of high school at a time and place when "nobody" did. Interestingly, my worst scores were in vocabulary and language, the area where I would ultimately be focused.

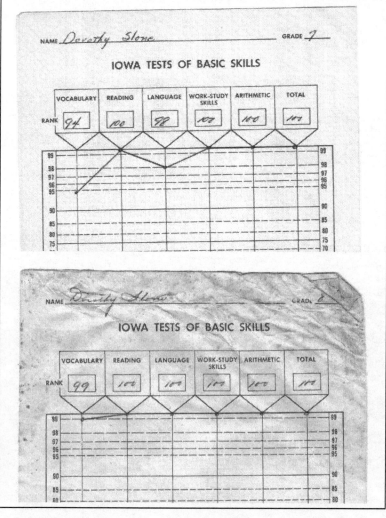

The Tarot Fool - Symbol of a Seeker
By Joseph "Joe" Panek[90]

When we look at the card of "The Fool" in the tarot deck we see a person standing at the edge of a high cliff about to take the next step while gazing upward into the Infinite. There is a dog at the feet of The Fool and this dog is also at the edge of the cliff, standing on its two hind feet, with its front feet already over the edge.

Naturally, we wonder: "Why is this person so willing to take the next step off of the cliff and why is he gazing up at the heavens instead of watching where he is going?" Like all of the other cards in the tarot deck, this card is full of symbolism. So, let's break down some the principal symbolism contained within this card in order to get a better understanding of what this card is telling us.

The Fool: Although The Fool appears to be a masculine archetype, the face contains an air of femininity. This gives The Fool an androgynous appearance which symbolizes a combination and union of both the male and female essences. This means that The Fool does not experience his journey through either a male or female perspective. He experiences it through both perspectives. This androgynous (Hermaphroditic) portrayal of The Fool reminds us that

---

[90] *A Seeker's Thoughts*, May 26, 2009, (picture from Wikipedia), http://www.aseekersthoughts.com/2009/05/fool-symbol-of-seeker.html

The Fool's Journey is a journey that is available to any man, woman, boy, or girl who wishes to participate in an Adventure.

Mountains symbolize the higher realms of consciousness. The higher the mountain, the higher the realm of consciousness. The highest mountain peak would symbolize the highest realm of consciousness that we can experience while still on earth. In addition, when viewed from afar, mountain peaks are the highest points on the Horizon and represent the loftiest Border Between Realms; the highest borderland between heaven and earth.

The precipice upon which The Fool and his dog are standing symbolizes the Threshold where one journey ends so that another journey can begin. (*Also:* The precipice symbolizes the mental obstacles we create for ourselves which deter many of us from taking the next step in order to achieve and experience our dreams.)

The dog is "man's best friend". The dog is instinctive and is a symbol for loyalty, trust, protection, and companionship.

White symbolizes purity and enlightenment.

Because the Journey of The Fool takes place in the higher realms of consciousness *(mountains)* it symbolizes a spiritual journey. It is a spiritual Call to Adventure which involves dreams, aspirations, imagination, and finally enlightenment. The Fool gazes up into the heavens because that is where his dreams, aspirations, and imaginings reside. The heavens also represent the highest realm of *Divine Consciousness* that The Fool can look up to for spiritual inspiration and guidance. Knowing that no physical harm can befall him in a spiritual quest, The Fool unhesitatingly steps off the precipice when his current adventure comes to an end. He knows that only by ending, and leaving behind, his current adventure is he able to begin his next one. Therefore, with great anticipation and excitement he proceeds onward and upward into the next chapter of his life's Journey.

The Fool's dog, being an instinctive animal, also understands that there is no danger in stepping off of this spiritual precipice. So it too follows its master onward and upward. In addition, because the dog is a loyal and protective companion, The Fool need never feel alone in his travels into new and uncharted realms.

The white *Sun* that is shining behind The Fool is a symbol for the pure enlightenment which is forever accompanying The Fool and nudging him onward.

And finally, although The Fool is currently standing atop a high mountain, there are much higher mountains in the distance. These higher mountains remind The Fool that there are still more.

516   The Journey Begins

I Love E & J
by Stephanie Patel

Note: this is one of the essays from my autobiographical essays and reflections, written in the early 2000s (as a result some idioms may seem outdated), but never previously published. It is included here because it was mentioned in this book, p. 173.

I am a great fan of Albert Einstein and Jesus. And the US of A, without which I wouldn't be able to combine those two names in the same sentence.

I first got to know Jesus in my youth. It was hard to avoid it. He was always hanging around.

"Jesus came into the world to save us from our sins," Sister Mary Jacobine informed us, which in our assessment put him somewhere below Buffalo Bill, who saved us from being trampled by bison, and Johnny Appleseed, who saved us all from a life without applesauce. Anyway, if Jesus' intention was to save us from our sins, he was obviously a dismal failure. Our sins still stalked us, and we ended up on Saturdays kneeling in a pew at the back of the church, saying three Hail Marys and an Our Father for having wished our bratty brother would get the pox or having lied about who was shooting spit-wads during music class.

It may seem like I had little respect for Jesus, but that was not the case. True, the nuns tried to convince us that he was a wimpy goody-two-shoes who never said an unkind word to his desk partner or slapped a mosquito. But it's hard, when you're nine or ten, not to be impressed by someone who throws over the money-changers' tables and stands over them with a whip, or does neat things like break the Sabbath and run away from his parents and talk back to his father, all of which makes him seem like a regular guy. So it was always a surprise when the nuns would say, "What would Jesus think?" when we broke some picayune rule, like *Don't Throw erasers in the Classroom* and *Don't Trade Your Apple for Three Cookies at Lunch.* To my understanding, he probably would have thought, "Right on, dude!"

But the nuns didn't see it that way.

If you were the son of God you got certain dispensations, certain privileges as it were, like the kids of the biggest Church benefactors. You got to tell people off, to bring your own wine to a catered wedding party, and to break major laws like *Once You're Dead, You Gotta Stay That Way.*

Life was good if you were the Son of God—at least until other people started getting jealous. Of course, throwing over money-changers' tables doesn't help. Things like that catch up with a person. Even Jesus should have known that. And I guess, come to think of it, he did.

If alive today, Jesus would have been a man of the streets. For one thing, he had his gang. You hardly ever saw him without his homies, at least not 'til the end when they all high-tailed it like a squad of yellow-bellied wussies. He didn't have much respect for authority, and he had a smart-ass attitude with the Law. When old Pontius Pilate asked him if he was the son of God he said, in ancient Jewish-speak, "Hey, whatever, dude." You got to like that about a person. It was a trick question, and being a man of the streets, he knew how tricksy the Man was. You can play their game, or just be above it all. Jesus' genius was to be above it all.

Jesus was gentle with the people others overlooked, like kids and lepers, which is cool. He's the kinda guy you would have wanted for a big brother, always suffering the little children bouncing on his knee and stuff, never telling them to get lost or to just grow up or yech! you got cooties. He didn't need to tote a sidepiece—or a spear or whatever the gangs carried for protection back then. He got his respect just by telling good stories, and if things got a bit hot—well, it helps if you know how to walk on water or disappear into a crowd.

So all in all, I was good with Jesus, the real Jesus, the one that wasn't here to save us from our sins, but to shine the light on them.

I didn't meet Einstein until I was a little older, but when I did, there was an instant rapport between us. If there was anything that I knew, well, it was relativity. It was hard not to, having fourteen siblings, upwards of forty aunts and uncles, and maybe a hundred first cousins. All my life people would ask me: *Are you relative to Patty Slone? Or John Schulte? Or Cleone Paschowski.* Yes, indeed I was. So you see, I'd had the feeling since I was young that everything and everybody is relative. So when I heard about the General and Special Theories of Relativity, I was already a customer. Finally, someone who knew how it works, someone who didn't have to ask.

Then, too, it's hard not to like a guy who looks like he just stuck his finger in a light socket and who forgets to wear socks or eat.

One thing about Einstein that takes some getting used to: he liked to say things in a roundabout way, like:

> I believe that the first step in the setting of a "real external world" is the formation of the concept of bodily objects and of bodily objects of various kinds. Out of the multitude of

518   The Journey Begins

our sense experiences we take, mentally and arbitrarily, certain repeatedly occurring complexes of sense impressions (partly in conjunction with sense impressions which are interpreted as signs for sense experiences of others), and we correlate to them a concept—the concept of the bodily object. Considered logically this concept is not identical with the totality of sense impressions referred to; but it is a free creation of the human (or animal) mind. On the other hand, this concept owes its meaning and its justification exclusively to the totality of the sense impressions which we associate with it.[i]

See what I mean? All he had to say was "don't take yourself too seriously," but I have long since forgiven him for his wordiness. It was one of his most endearing quirks, and has kept whole classrooms of gullible students occupied ever since, meeting themselves coming and going as they struggle to follow the meandering trail of his logic.

You may wonder what Einstein and Jesus have in common. Well, for starters, they were both Jews. Then they were both misunderstood a lot, in spite of which they both launched great changes in the fabric of human thought.

I myself am convinced that Jesus and Einstein would have been great friends had they been neighbors, that they had much in common with one another, not the least of which is a common admirer. As a matter of fact, I think Jesus' primary message remains, like Einstein's: lighten up. After all, you just gotta know Einstein was enlightened, riding around on light beams and stuff.

I also suspect that Jesus had a good sense of humor. There's that sort of subtext in all the gospels, like that time—a day or two after the crucifixion—when he meets up with a couple of the disciples who don't even recognize him. I imagine that conversation going a lot like this:

Jesus: *Hey, there, fellow, you're heading up to Emmaus? Why, I'm going that way myself. Mind if I tag along?*

Cleophas: [sigh] *Not if you don't mind a couple of companions who are a bit down in the mouth.*

Jesus: *No problem. Maybe I can cheer you all up a bit. I know some great stories.*

Cleophas' companion, he who is called Ruben: *Listen Friend, I don't mean to be rude, but we're a bit bummed right now. Not really in the mood for stories.*

Jesus: *So what's dragging you two down? My mother always*

said it helps to talk about your troubles, lighten the load a little, so to speak.

Cleophas: *Don't tell me you haven't heard about what happened in Jerusalem?*

Jesus: *You mean that fellow they crucified the one that thought he was the son of God? I heard something about that. What was his name?*

Cleophas: *Jesus. Of Nazareth.*

Jesus: *Ah, right. I've heard some talk about the guy. Did you know him?*

Cleophas: *Oh, yeah.*

Jesus: *Did he really think he was the son of God?*

Cleophas: *You might say that. Poor fellow, he was a bit, you know—coo-coo..."* (Cleophas makes a motion of turning an imaginary crank on the side of his head.) *Of course we never really believed he was the son of God. I mean, come on, just because he could do a few sleight-of-hand tricks."*

Ruben: *You thought he was the son of God."*

Cleophas: *Did not.*

Ruben: *Did too.*

Cleophas: *I was just humoring him. Ha ha.*

Jesus: *Well, I guess if he was the son of God, he couldn't be killed. [shrug] Like, the next day he could be walking along this road just like we are, not a care in the world.*

Cleophas. *Yep. Well, it's a pity. We all could have used a Savior. I think I'll go back to my wife and ten kids, even though I know what she's going to say: [changes voice to falsetto and wags finger]. I told you so, Cleophas, if I didn't tell you once, I told you a thousand times. You're so gullible, you'll believe any cockamamie story some shyster feeds you down at the local tavern.*

Ruben: *Say, stranger. You bear a striking resemblance to Jesus of Nazareth, yourself. If I was you, I'd be careful, you don't want people to go getting ideas. Best to stay away from Jerusalem, if you can.*

Jesus. *Thank you, I'll bear that in mind.*

What I like about Jesus is that he didn't go moping around after he was crucified, blaming the world for his problems. He didn't overstay his welcome, either, kind of popped in here and there to say his good-byes, fare-thee-well, and don't take any wooden nickels. That guy knew how to make an exit.

Both Jesus and Einstein have given me great comfort in my darkest moments. Oh, maybe not directly, but in the little indirect ways that friends do. Maybe it's just a thought, a chance word, a little joke when you're feeling down.

When it comes to Jesus, people seem to like—as I mentioned earlier—to have him hanging around a lot, like a joke to which you've forgotten the punch line. That, I guess, is to remind us he died for our sins—except the punch line is that he didn't die.

I like that about him.

As for Einstein, he taught me that, when two ships pass in the night, it's hard to say which one is coming and which one is going— perhaps one or the other is standing still, and the ocean moves past it as the world turns. He taught me that "out of the multitude of our sense experiences we take, mentally and arbitrarily, certain repeatedly occurring complexes of sense impressions (partly in conjunction with sense impressions which are interpreted as signs for sense experience of others) and we correlate to them a concept—the concept of the bodily object." Of course, all he had to say was: *you're not a body*, but hey! it's the intention that matters.

Had Jesus and Einstein lived side by side, I imagine that they would have had some good conversation over a bottle (or a skin) of wine. But since they didn't, it had to keep until they met up in Heaven, a meeting that I suspect went something like this:

Hey, there, Albie, long time no see.

Have we met?

In a sense. You remember that "in the temple of science are many mansions" speech? Hey, I coined that "many mansions" business.

Oh, it's you. I thought I recognized the beard.

So what's this? You were having trouble with the Universal Field Theory?

You know it?

Know it? We had to study it, first week at divinity school:

$$PT109\{U8\pi\}$$
$$(Bp90/65 = I \heartsuit \infty^2$$

Oh, wow, I see the problem now. [scratches head] I left out that lazy "8". It all looks so simple from here.

Yeah, easy as pi, once you know it. Say, I've got a little time on my hands. You want to play a game of dice?

---

[i] From *The Journal of the Franklin Institute,* Vo. 221, No. 3, March, 1936.